# TALES FROM THE DEVELOPMENT FRONTIER

# TALES FROM THE DEVELOPMENT FRONTIER

## How China and Other Countries Harness Light Manufacturing to Create Jobs and Prosperity

Hinh T. Dinh, Thomas G. Rawski, Ali Zafar,
Lihong Wang, and Eleonora Mavroeidi
with Xin Tong and Pengfei Li

**THE WORLD BANK**
Washington, D.C.

# Contents

v

## Boxes

## Figures

## Maps

# Tables

# Foreword

It used to be common wisdom that labor-intensive manufacturing is the key to the take-off of developing countries. And indeed there have been some exemplary cases of nations achieving rapid development by this route, the most notable being that of China. Yet, there are many instances of developing countries that have had no success with this, and also cases of some developing economies seemingly bypassing this stage. *Tales from the Development Frontier* is an important publication that presents analytical reviews and case studies that show how selected developing countries have developed light manufacturing to create jobs and foster prosperity. China's emergence as a powerhouse in light manufacturing is a major focus of this volume, but other countries in Africa and Asia are also included. Mindful of the adage that there is as much to learn from success as failure, the case studies examined in this book cover both triumphs and disappointments, eliciting from them lessons on the development of light manufacturing and how this sector can be leveraged to accelerate growth in poor countries where the initial conditions may not be quite ideal.

The book offers important insights into China's rapid rise. It argues that the focus on domestic competition and international openness as key drivers of growth highlights the contribution of often underappreciated policy tools such as industrial parks, industrial clusters, and trading companies and emphasizes the role of cooperation between public and private sectors. Light industry can create jobs and lead countries out of poverty through a widening process of learning-by-doing. The studies show that the government's role is to provide a conducive business ethos, which varies with the business life cycle of firms, and they emphasize that the government's role is to encourage and back winners rather than pick and prod winners. The book brings out the role of focused, targeted initiatives that can help break the poverty trap and ignite growth that begins small but can eventually lift broader segments of the economy.

Each successful enterprise or industry described in this book began as a family workshop, a microenterprise, or a group of small entrepreneurs meeting a limited demand in a small area. Although these fledgling ventures confronted market, institutional, and regulatory environments loaded with daunting obstacles, they managed to find room for organic growth, supported by focused government policy interventions to ease the binding constraints. At some point, though not necessarily at first, cooperation and even partnership with government policy makers helped to power a gradual transformation that turned small informal firms into modern corporations capable of establishing national and, eventually, international distribution networks. The book argues that this sequence of ground-level entry and gradual organic growth to a larger scale represents a common element in the growth of light manufacturing in the United Kingdom and other early developers, as well as the recent successes such as China.

*Tales from the Development Frontier* is an engaging and comprehensive book that tries to advance our understanding of industrialization and development by analyzing actual experiences on the development frontier: the poor economies. With its rich array of material, the book will motivate and support new research in this field. And, more important, it is hoped that this study will embolden policy makers, entrepreneurs, and even worker groups in low-income countries to think creatively to capture the opportunities of the manufacturing sector and to design better policy and, ultimately, to spur economic growth that is sustainable and inclusive.

*Kaushik Basu*
Senior Vice President and Chief Economist
The World Bank

# Preface

How did China emerge from decades of poverty and isolation to become the world's second-largest economy? While many readers will recognize the contribution that education, hard work, or giant state-owned firms made to China's recent achievements, this impressive book highlights a central, but less widely understood feature of China's recent development: the rise of world-class manufacturing complexes that originated in the efforts of individual entrepreneurs and family businesses in industries such as garments, shoes, and furniture and in many cases with the active investment promotion and facilitation by local governments via industrial parks and zones to overcome infrastructure bottlenecks and poor business environment.

The book delivers a clear message: light manufacturing, with its low capital requirements, limited scale economies, readily available technology, and sales potential in domestic and international markets, retains potential as a springboard and the best hope for poor countries to expand output, employment, productivity, and exports. Just as China's nascent producers used low labor costs to pry open markets formerly dominated by firms based in Hong Kong SAR, China and in Taiwan, China, producers in Bangladesh, Cambodia, Ethiopia and other low-income nations can seize new opportunities arising from steeply rising wages and costs in China's coastal export hubs to inject fresh momentum into their own economies.

In the past, development economics often focused on what developing countries did not have and could not accomplish. One example of this was the attempt to prop up heavy industries using an import-substitution strategy based on what I call the old structuralism. This was followed by a focus on governance issues as epitomized by the Washington Consensus. The results of such strategies were generally disappointing. The analyses in this book highlight a change in mindset: as the leader of a low-income country, Deng Xiaoping understood that it was necessary to stop dwelling on what was wrong and what needed fixing and instead work to turn available strengths and resources into competitive outcomes in both domestic and international markets.

At its heart, development economics should promote the efforts of low-income country governments to set up effective policy frameworks and design interventions that allow the private sector to develop competitive industries and tap into latecomer advantages. It is time for a new phase of development thinking focused on structural change, driven by changes in endowment structure and comparative advantage. This approach, which was adopted by many successful East Asian countries, highlights markets as the fundamental institutions for resource allocation, with the state contributing a proactive facilitating role in the process. This book, initiated while I served as the World Bank Senior Vice President and Chief Economist (2008–12), documents China's success in implementing this approach in a practical and highly readable manner that highlights the Chinese path to shared prosperity.

The book demonstrates the shortcomings of policies that tilt excessively toward either the Washington Consensus or the earlier interventionist approach. The authors combine analytical reviews, case studies, and the testimony of individual entrepreneurs, including material from numerous African and Asian economies, to distill policy lessons that can illuminate the prospects for rapid industrialization in today's developing countries. They view public-private collaboration as a critical underpinning of successful industrialization and provide specific illustrations of success and failure from Chinese and international experience.

I welcome the book's detailed account of how the initiatives of private entrepreneurs, together with the subsequent support of local and national governments, contributed greatly to China's explosive growth. The book offers concrete and specific guidance that will inform the efforts of policy makers and entrepreneurs to initiate a new round of catch-up industrialization in today's poor nations. Its multiple contributions make the book a source of knowledge and inspiration for historians of China, policy makers, economists, and readers throughout the world who are interested in development issues.

*Justin Yifu Lin*
Honorary Dean and Professor,
National School of Development, Peking University;
Former Senior Vice President and Chief Economist,
The World Bank

# Acknowledgments

This book has been prepared by a team composed of Hinh T. Dinh (Lead Economist and Team Leader), Thomas G. Rawski, Ali Zafar, Lihong Wang, Eleonora Mavroeidi, Xin Tong, and Pengfei Li. Other members of the 2010 and 2012 missions to China made important contributions: Vandana Chandra, Frances Cossar, Kathleen Fitzgerald, Tugba Gurcanlar, Anders Isaksson, Claire Margraf, Vincent Palmade, and Anqing Shi. Gabriela Calderon Motta is the Team's Assistant. The work has been carried out with the support and guidance of the following World Bank senior managers: Kaushik Basu (Senior Vice President and Chief Economist), Justin Yifu Lin (former Senior Vice President and Chief Economist), Maktar Diop (Vice President, Africa Region), Shanta Devarajan (former Chief Economist, Africa Region), Zia Qureshi (Director, Operations and Strategy Department), Gaiv Tata (Director, Africa Finance and Private Sector Development), and Marilou Uy (Senior Advisor, Special Envoy Office and Former Director, Africa Finance and Private Sector Development). We thank Augusto Luis Alcorta and Anders Isaksson (United Nations Industrial Development Organization) for their valuable input and support. We are grateful for the valuable comments of Dwight H. Perkins (Professor, Harvard University), John Sutton (Professor, the London School of Economics), Xiaobo Zhang (Professor, Peking University, and Senior Research Fellow, International Food Policy Research Institute), and John Page (Senior Fellow, Brookings Institution). We thank Klaus Rohland (China Country Director), Ardo Hansson (former China Lead Economist), Chorching Goh (current China Lead Economist), Min Zhao (Senior Economist), and other Bank staff in the World Bank Beijing office—Jieli Bai, Yezi Bu, Xiaoting Li, Yuan Mi, and Vanessa Yan Wang—for their valuable advice and support. We thank the following Bank staff and colleagues in Washington for their valuable input and support: Pierre-Richard Agénor,

Hy T. Dinh, Doerte Doemeland, Kathryn Ann Funk, Diana Gibson, Arianna Lego-vini, Célestin Monga, David Rosenblatt, Van-Can Thai, Volker Treichel, Pham Van Thuyet, Dipankar Megh Bhanot, Aban Daruwala, Saida Doumbia Gall, Nancy Lim, and Melanie Brah Marie Melindji.

The team would like to thank the many people who have advised, guided, and supported the work throughout the preparation of this book. In particular, we are grateful to those people who generously gave their time to discuss with and to be interviewed by us. It is impossible to list all of them here, but their affiliations are mentioned in the introduction.

We owe special thanks to the following:

Bangladesh: Rokeya Quader (Chairman, Desh Group of Industries) and Aneeka Rahman (World Bank Country Office, Dacca).

Canada: Loren Brandt (University of Toronto) and Ralph W. Huenemann (University of Victoria).

China: Bai Lin (Guangdong GOSUNCN Telecommunications Co. Ltd.); Bai Shengwen (Little Giant Machine Tool Co. Ltd., Yinchuan); Chan, Jacky (Regina Miracle International [Group] Ltd.); Chen Haofeng (Yiwu Danxi Brewage Co. Ltd.); Chen Yongpin (Administrative Committee, Guangzhou Economic and Technological Development Zone, Guangzhou Hi-Tech Industrial Development Zone); Cheng Guo (Administrative Committee, Chengdu Economic Development Zone); Cheung, Emily (Chung Tai Garment Factory Ltd.); Chiu, Frank (Regina Miracle International [China] Ltd.); Chou, Kingsley (Karandonis [Foshan Nanhai] Shoes Ltd.); Dong Wenzhu (Small and Medium Enterprises Bureau, Jiangxi Province); Fan Zhongfei (Administrative Committee, Zhejiang Haining Warp Knitting Industrial Zone); Gao Fu (Ministry of Industry and Information Technology); Gu Yuhui (Management Committee, Haimen Industrial Zone; Management Committee, Dieshiqiao Market, Jiangsu Province); Guan Rong (China Association of Development Zones); Guo Xiaolu (Chengdu Aimiqi Shoes Industry Co. Ltd.); Huang Fuhao (Sichuan Wuhou International Shoe Center); Huang Longrong (Pengzhou Municipal Government, Sichuan Province); Huang Xubin (Wenzhou Joywest Clothes Co. Ltd.); Jiang Guanglin (Administrative Committee, Yinchuan Economic and Technological Development Zone, Yinchuan Hi-Tech Industrial Development Zone); Jiang Yanhong (Shenzhen Everich Industrial Development Co. Ltd.); Kao Ming Zheng (Foshan Gang Auto Mold Parts Co. Ltd.); Lai Zengnong (Qinye Industrial Co. Ltd.); Lan, Bruce (INOX Bin Products Ltd.); Lau, Jimmy (Chung Tai Garment Factory

Ltd.); Li, Cindy (Shenzhen Eternal Asia Supply Chain Management Ltd.); Li Qiang (Ministry of Industry and Information Technology); Li Wenbin (Administrative Committee, Xinhui District Economic Development Zone, Jiangmen, Guangdong Province); Li Ying (Sichuan Aiminer Leather Products Co. Ltd.); Liang Hui (Management Committee, Haimen Industrial Zone; Management Committee, Dieshiqiao Market, Jiangsu Province); Lin Panwu (Fudebao Furniture Co. Ltd.); Lin Yao Huan (Bonanza Metalware Ltd., Xinhui District, Jiangmen, Guangdong Province); Liu Huaidong (Administrative Committee, Xinhui District Economic Development Zone, Jiangmen, Guangdong Province); Liu Pei (Jinan University, Guangzhou); Liu Peiqiang (China Association of Development Zones); Liu Ying (Chengdu Cameido Shoes Investment Co. Ltd.); Liu Zhaofeng (Guicheng [Foshan Nanhai] Shiken Jiaye Steel Pipe Co.); Lou Zhangneng (Yiwu Foreign Trade and Economic Cooperation Bureau); Luo Xinghao (Zhejiang Wanyu Knitting Co. Ltd.); Ma, Samuel (Jiangmen Qipai Import and Export Co. Ltd.); Mao Weihua (Zhejiang Wanfang New Materials Co. Ltd.); Mao Zengyu (Administrative Committee, Pengzhou Industrial Development Zone, Sichuan Province); Ni Teng (Science and Technology and Informatization Bureau, Guangdong Province); Pan Kefa (Wenzhou Jundeli Leather Co. Ltd.); Pan Pingping (Wenzhou Bureau of Commerce); Pan Wenquan (Sichuan Development and Reform Commission); Pi Dayun (Administrative Committee, Chengdu Economic Development Zone); Pu Xinda (Administrative Committee, Zhejiang Haining Warp Knitting Industrial Zone); Qin Peng (Jiangsu Meiluo Home Textile Co. Ltd.); Qiu Zhihai (Foshan Nanhai Shengfeng Shoes Co.); Qu Jian (China Development Institute, Shenzhen, Guangdong Province); Ren Huan (China Association of Development Zones); Shen Min (Halead New Material Co. Ltd.); Shi Rongyao (China Association of Development Zones); Song Dongshan (Department of Commerce, Zhejiang Province); Tan Huanxin (Guangdong GOSUNCN Telecommunications Co. Ltd.); Tao Jianwei (Zhejiang Baojie Digital Knitting Share Co. Ltd.); Wan Junming (Small and Medium Enterprises Bureau, Jiangxi Province); Wang Jici (College of Urban and Environmental Sciences, Peking University); Wang Li (Chengdu Wuhou District Government); Wang P. (Weihai Zipper, Yiwu); Wang Shijian (Nanchang Peiweimeng Knitwear Co. Ltd.); Wang Yu (Zhejiang Weihai Zipper Co. Ltd.); Wang Zixian (Special Commissioner's Office, Shenzhen, Ministry of Commerce); Wu Yangyue (Chengdu Deqin Furniture Co. Ltd.); Wu Youjia (Jiangxi Youjia Food Manufacturing Co. Ltd.); Xia Jingbin (Enterprise Service

Bureau, Enterprises Construction Bureau, Guangzhou Economic and Technological Development Zone); Xie Ruihong (Jiangxi Julong High-Tech Co. Ltd.); Xie Yanxian (Guangdong Fortress Chemical Co. Ltd.); Xiong Qi (Sichuan Development Zones Association); Yang Chuanjin (Yiwu Zongnan Leather Products Co. Ltd.); Ye Huajun (Pengzhou Development and Reform Bureau); Ye Zhibin (Investment Promotion Division, Guangdong Finance and High-Tech Service Zone, Subzone 3, Nanhai District, Foshan); Yip, Joe (EH Supply Chain Management Co. Ltd.); Yu Minghong (Administrative Committee, Zhejiang Haining Warp Knitting Industrial Zone); Zhang Hanping (Aihao Writing Instruments Co. Ltd.); Zhang Hengchun (Shenzhen Guangming New District); Zhang, Jack (Nanchang Huaxing Knitting Industrial Co. Ltd.); Zhang Jianwei (Administrative Committee, Xinhui District Economic Development Zone, Jiangmen, Guangdong Province); Zhang Yingtong (Administrative Committee, Guangdong Financial Hi-Tech Zone); Zheng Houze (Bureau of Foreign Trade And Economic Cooperation, Yiwu); Zhou Huirong (Economic Services Bureau, Guangming New Area Hi-Tech Park Management Office, Shenzhen, Guangdong Province); Zhou Qiang (Administrative Committee, Pengzhou Industrial Development Zone); Zhou Sheng (Foshan Nanhai Shiken Huaqiang Petrochemical Equipment Co.); Zhou Shunping (Jiangmen Qipai Motorcycle Co. Ltd.) ; Zhu Jianyong (Huatong Group Co. Ltd.); Zhu Lanqin (Yiwu Danxi Brewage Co. Ltd.).

Ghana: Kwabena Bonsu (Managing Director) and Akua Wirekowaa (Chief Legal Counsel) of Bonsu Furniture, Accra.

Mauritius: Ahmad Parkar (Chief Executive Director, Star Knitwear Group).

Pakistan: Aamir Rasheed Butt (Sialkot Chamber of Commerce).

United States: Nicholas Lardy (Peterson Institute for International Economics, Washington, DC), Kenneth Lieberthal (Brookings Institution, Washington, DC), Scott R. Pearson (Stanford University), Yingjun Su (University of Pittsburgh), Wenfang Tang (University of Iowa), Haihui Zhang (University of Pittsburgh), and Xiuying Zou (University of Pittsburgh).

Vietnam: Pham Thi Thu Hang, Secretary General, Vietnam Chamber of Commerce and her staff; officials of the Vietnam Furniture Association in Ho Chi Minh City; Mr. Quy Nguyen, owner of Ho Nai Furniture Company, and owners/managers of many other furniture companies throughout the country.

The book has been edited by a team headed by Robert Zimmermann. Earlier drafts were edited by Bruce Ross-Larson and Meta deCoquereaumont. The maps in the book have been cleared and redrawn by the World Bank's Cartography Department, and we thank Jeffrey N. Lecksel for his valuable help. The World Bank's Publishing and Knowledge Division handled the production of the final printed and electronic books under the guidance of Stephen McGroarty, Paola Scalabrin, and Janice Tuten. The financial support of the Bank–Netherlands Partnership Program (BNPP TF 09717), the Japan Policy and Human Resources Development Fund (PHRD TF 096317), and the United Nations Industrial Development Organization is gratefully acknowledged.

# About the Authors and Contributors

## Authors

**Hinh T. Dinh** is Lead Economist in the Office of the Senior Vice President and Chief Economist of the World Bank. Previously, he served in the Africa Region (1998–2008), where he advised management and staff on strategy, economic policy, and related operational issues for Central, Southern, and West Africa. Prior to that assignment, he served in the Finance Complex at the Bank (1991–98), working on risk issues of large countries in East and South Asia and Latin America, and he also served in the Middle East and North Africa Region of the World Bank (1979–91). His research focuses on public finance, international finance, industrialization, and economic development. His latest books include *Light Manufacturing in Africa* (2012), *Performance of Manufacturing Firms in Africa* (2012), and *Light Manufacturing in Zambia* (2013).

**Eleonora Mavroeidi** is a Junior Professional Associate in the Office of the Senior Vice President and Chief Economist of the World Bank. Previously, she worked as a consultant at the Brookings Institution's Global Economy and Development Program and at the Johns Hopkins University School of Advanced International Studies and as a trainee at the Directorate General for Research of the European Commission.

**Thomas G. Rawski** is Professor of Economics and History at the University of Pittsburgh. His research focuses on the development and modern history of China's economy, including studies of China's reform mechanism and achievements, as well as analyses focused on productivity, investment, industry, trade, labor markets, the environment, and economic measurement. His publications include *Economic Growth and Employment in*

*China, China's Transition to Industrialism, Economic Growth in Prewar China*, and, as editor, *Chinese History in Economic Perspective, Economics and the Historian, China's Rise and the Balance of Influence in Asia*, and *China's Great Economic Transformation*.

**Lihong Wang** is Consultant with the World Bank Group. She has worked with various departments there including the East Asia Region, Development Economics, Financial and Private Sector Development, and the International Finance Corporation. She worked as Investment Officer with the International Finance Corporation, based in Chengdu and Beijing, China (2006–09) and as the Private Sector Specialist and a core team member in the Doing Business Project (2002–06).

**Ali Zafar** is Senior Economist in the Africa Region at the World Bank. Previously, he served as a consultant with the Middle East Region, the East Asia Region, and Development Economics at the World Bank (2008–11), in the Africa Region at the Bank (1999–2006), and as Adviser at the United Nations Development Programme (2007). He has advisory and operational experience in more than 15 countries. His research focuses on macroeconomic policy in low-income countries, public finance, and international trade.

# Contributors

**Pengfei Li** is a Banting Postdoctoral Fellow at the Department of Political Science, University of Toronto. He taught at East China Normal University, Shanghai, from 2011 to 2013. His research focuses on industrial clusters, social and business networks, regional economic development, and transnational knowledge flows, with a regional interest in Asia.

**Xin Tong** is Associate Professor at the College of Urban and Environmental Sciences, Peking University. She has been teaching and conducting research at Peking University since 2003. She is an economic geographer with interests in industrial geography, especially from the perspective of sustainability.

# Abbreviations

| | |
|---|---|
| AGOA | African Growth and Opportunity Act (United States) |
| EU | European Union |
| FDI | foreign direct investment |
| FTC | foreign trade company |
| GDP | gross domestic product |
| GDS | Grands Domaines du Sénégal (Senegal) |
| OEM | original equipment manufacturer |
| R&D | research and development |
| SAR | special administrative region (China) |
| SME | small and medium enterprise |
| TVE | township and village enterprise |
| WTO | World Trade Organization |

All dollar amounts are U.S. dollars ($) unless otherwise indicated. Where other currencies are used, the conversion to U.S. dollars relies on the average exchange rate for the year concerned (line rh in International Financial Statistics [database], International Monetary Fund, Washington, DC, http://elibrary-data.imf.org/FindDataReports.aspx?d=33061&e=169393).

Note on Chinese Names: In China and many other Asian countries, the family name is typically written before the given name in most everyday contexts. We have adopted this practice here for our Chinese interviewees and authors who are living or active mainly in China and who are not otherwise known by a Westernized name. These individuals are shown in the reference lists without the standard comma between the family name and the first name (thus, *Wan Juning*, family name first; no comma). Individuals who have followed the Westernized name order and who are known in this way are presented as such in the text (thus, *Lihong Wang* with *Wang* as family name). Their names are shown in reference lists with the standard comma included (thus, *Wang, Lihong*).

# Introduction

This is a companion volume to *Light Manufacturing in Africa* (Dinh and others 2012), which lays out a strategy for injecting new industrial growth nodes into low-income economies without waiting for solutions to economy-wide development problems in infrastructure, governance, human capital, and institutional arrangements.

Despite widespread agreement among economists that labor-intensive manufacturing has contributed mightily to rapid development in China and other rapidly growing economies, most developing countries have had little success in raising the share of manufacturing in production, employment, or exports (Clarke 2012; Collier 2007). *Light Manufacturing in Africa* systematically explores potential growth opportunities in a carefully selected group of industries: agribusiness, apparel, leather goods, woodworking, and metal products. It specifies the constraints that need to be addressed before local and international entrepreneurs can take advantage of the latent comparative advantage available to many low-income economies in the target industries and proposes policies that can ease these constraints and thereby open the door to rapid increases in industrial output, employment, productivity, and exports.

The present volume recounts efforts to establish light manufacturing enterprises and clusters in several African and Asian countries, especially China. The outcomes include both inspiring success and miserable failure. Our case studies reveal how some industrial development initiatives in poor countries—where, by definition, underlying conditions present seemingly insurmountable obstacles—manage to accelerate growth and show why others produce no lasting impact.

Light industries, such as textiles and clothing, agricultural processing, meat and fish preservation and packaging, leather goods, and woodworking, have represented the leading edge in early industrialization both historically and today. Why? There are many reasons, including the ready availability of raw materials and labor, the universal demand for food and clothing, the simplicity and widespread diffusion of the relevant technologies, the limited capital and skill requirements, and the absence of scale economies. These circumstances allow small start-ups to produce light manufactures without deep technical knowledge, large-scale financing, or complex equipment.

Among the early industrializers, organic growth powered a gradual transition whereby capable (and lucky) entrepreneurs managed to outpace small-scale rivals and build their firms into large, well-capitalized, sophisticated operations that established national and, eventually, international distribution networks.

This sequence of easy entry, natural growth, and the gradual emergence of large, sophisticated producers pushed light manufacturing to the fore early in the development of today's rich countries. The United Kingdom pioneered this long-term process of modern economic growth, as Simon Kuznets (1971) characterized it. Subsequent work by Moshe Syrquin and Hollis Chenery (1989, 82) confirms that "the main features of transformation, identified by Kuznets as the core of modern economic growth on the basis of long-term experience in advanced countries, can clearly be identified in the shorter time-series of a large number of developing countries." (See also Chenery and Syrquin 1975.)

Table I.1 documents the initial dominance of textiles and food processing in manufacturing and, hence, in overall growth among the early industrializers.

The combined impacts of the Great Depression, World War II, and the Soviet Union's rapid industrial growth under policies of

**Table I.1  Contributions of Light Manufacturing in Food Processing, Textiles, and Garments to Industrialization, 1839–1981**

*percent*

| Country | Year | Share of industrial output, % |
|---|---|---|
| *Early industrializers* | | |
| United Kingdom | 1907 | 47.6 |
| France | 1896 | 62.2 |
| Germany | 1875 | 58.6 |
| Italy | 1861–70 | 84.3[a] |
| United States | 1839 | 32.9 |
| Japan | 1900 | 72.7 |
| *20th-century followers* | | |
| Argentina | 1900–04 | 53.8 |
| | 1963 | 46.1 |
| China | 1933 | 66.2[b] |
| | 1952 | 31.4[b] |
| Taiwan, China | 1940 | 63.5[c] |
| | 1981 | 27.6[c] |
| Brazil | 1963 | 45.6 |
| India | 1963 | 56.0 |
| Indonesia | 1963 | 46.0 |
| Korea, Rep. | 1963 | 40.2 |

*Sources:* Amsden 2001; Kuznets 1971; on Japan: Ohkawa and Shinohara 1979; on China: Liu and Yeh 1965; on Taiwan, China, in 1940: Odaka and others 2008; in 1981: Macro Database, National Statistics, Directorate General of Budget, Accounting, and Statistics, Taipei, Taiwan, China (accessed August 30, 2012), http://ebas1.ebas.gov.tw/pxweb/Dialog/statfile1L.asp.
a. Includes wood processing.
b. Includes factory output only.
c. Includes leather and fur products.

near autarchy convinced many economists and policy makers that low-income countries could not compete effectively with the West in producing manufactured products. The implication that poor countries could industrialize only by relying on domestic demand encouraged inward-looking import-substitution policies in these countries.

Such thinking turned out to be wrong. Led by Taiwan, China, a succession of low-income economies, mostly in East and Southeast

Asia, showed how exports, particularly of light manufactures, could rapidly advance the economy-wide growth of production, income, employment, productivity, and exports more generally. Between 1965 and 1990, the combined share of Hong Kong SAR, China; the Republic of Korea; Singapore; and Taiwan, China, in global exports jumped from 3 percent to 9 percent, and their share in the exports of developing economies rose from 12 percent to 46 percent (World Bank 1993).

Paradoxically, both the advance of globalization, which has steeply reduced international transaction costs, and Asian successes in penetrating rich-country markets for garments, toys, and other light manufactures have raised the bar for prospective newcomers in the fiercely competitive world of light manufacturing. Although the reduction in trade barriers and transport costs has sparked an unprecedented expansion of global trade and opened new opportunities to tap overseas markets, the profusion of established competitors can stifle opportunities for start-up firms to compete effectively in local markets or break into the export trade. As the Ghana furniture case study shows (chapter 7), Ghana imports almost 80 percent of its furniture despite the country's large timber resources. The *Financial Times* notes that "cheap Chinese wares have forced local factories to close and acted as a disincentive to anyone thinking of local production" in African countries, with specific reference to Kenya, Nigeria, and South Africa (Rice 2012, 3).

As such examples show, the ubiquity of cheap and serviceable imports from China and other Asian manufacturing powerhouses has steeply curtailed the prospects for the organic evolution of domestic production in low-income economies from the informal beginnings to modern factories that can withstand head-on competition with domestic and overseas rivals in garments, shoes, and other light manufacturing products. Many African countries are also facing the consequences of an unfortunate sequencing of trade liberalization in the 1980s, having liberalized trade in finished products ahead of inputs, which allowed the imports to wipe out domestic manufactures. Further difficulty arises from the generally low levels of human capital—meaning not only formal education, commercial knowledge, and business experience on the part of would-be entrepreneurs, but also government capability and effectiveness at the local and national levels—in today's low-income economies compared with Asian countries such as China.

While placing fresh obstacles in the path of would-be industrial latecomers, the accelerating pace of globalization also offers opportunities. In the same way as rising costs in Taiwan, China, as well as in Hong Kong SAR, China, opened the door to China's emergence as a major exporter of light manufactures beginning in the 1980s, rapid cost increases in China's leading centers of labor-intensive industry, particularly the costs of unskilled labor, are now creating openings for new entrants to become established in global markets for low-end manufactures. Existing flows of imports provide would-be entrants with precise details on the product characteristics and retail prices needed to challenge incumbent suppliers. An additional benefit of globalization is the proliferation of footloose entrepreneurs and procurement companies that possess the knowledge and capital resources to support new exporters, as occurred in China several decades ago.

As we write in early 2013, the coastal regions that powered China's export boom are rapidly losing traction as low-cost exporters of textiles, garments, toys, footwear, and other labor-intensive products. The erosion of competitiveness is concentrated at the low end of the price-quality spectrum, precisely the spot at which producers in low-income countries may find opportunities to break into international markets. China's fading dominance in these markets is visible in the multiple cost pressures surrounding low-end producers and in policies aimed at replacing labor-intensive production with skill- and technology-intensive operations that will shift the structure of production toward higher–value added goods and services. Chapter 1 examines the relevant issues in detail.

These changes do not mean that China will cease to export light manufactures. Indeed, China's highly developed infrastructure, deep supply chain resources, and economies of scope and scale arising from the agglomeration of textile, clothing, and other light industries along the coast will enable well-positioned producers to prosper and even expand beyond the point at which the previous Asian export leaders were forced to shut down or transfer production to lower-cost venues. Thus, China's exports of textiles and garments rose 3 percent in 2012 relative to the previous year's achievement despite the negative impact of domestic cost increases and slack overseas demand (Zhang 2012).

Furthermore, China's immense size, large regional variations in income levels (which generally decrease moving inland from the coast), and extensive network of expressways and telecommunications create the potential for maintaining an international cost advantage in labor-intensive manufacturing by shifting operations to the interior. This is certainly the ambition of local governments in central and western China, which are competing tooth and nail to attract corporate refugees from high-cost coastal locations in the hope of following coastal leaders in using foreign investment and manufactured exports as building blocks of local prosperity. Chengdu, Sichuan Province, is one of many inland cities that have created industrial parks and implemented preferential policies in an effort to transform "the city into an inland hub for the electronic information, biopharmaceutical, machinery, and food-processing industries," along with garments, footwear, and furniture (Li 2012, 16) (for example, see chapter 5).

Even so, China's retreat from the production and exportation of labor-intensive, low–value added goods must continue because official plans envision an annual growth in minimum wages of no less than 13 percent (bringing them to 40 percent of local average wages), along with an increase in fringe benefits and social safety nets.

The gradual withdrawal of China-based firms from this production space is creating new opportunities for the expansion of light manufactures in low-income economies. China's success in using these products as a springboard to accelerate national growth shows the enormous potential of this new opening.

Entrepreneurs and procurement specialists working for large retail outlets are seeking new production venues for labor-intensive goods currently being produced by firms along China's coast that have reached or will soon reach the end of the line. China's interior will attract some firms, but this path has drawbacks—higher transport costs, reduced local supply chain capacity, and, possibly, less-effective government cooperation—and, at best, offers only a temporary respite from a nationwide trend of rising labor costs.

How can low-income countries respond to this combination of opportunities and obstacles to promote domestic industrialization?

It is widely agreed that developing economies enhance their prospects for expanding productive activity, including light manufacturing, by promoting macroeconomic stability; expanding utility grids, transport and communication networks, literacy, and public health; and removing the obstacles to business start-ups and crossborder flows of commodities and capital. Indeed, the recent performance in these areas is encouraging, particularly in Africa, where widespread improvements are occurring in price stability, fiscal balance, infant mortality, and other important macroeconomic indicators (Arbache, Go, and Page 2008).

As argued in the companion volume, *Light Manufacturing in Africa*, economy-wide policies of this sort are unlikely to overcome the inertia of extreme poverty that impedes progress in low-income countries. Decades of development experience going back as far as the 1950s demonstrate that such measures, however fruitful in improving long-term prospects, are unlikely to ignite a self-supporting process of expansion and upgrading. What these countries need is a focused initiative to inject new elements of prosperity and growth even as large segments of the economy remain unaffected. Without such a breakthrough, poor countries are unlikely to avoid the stalemate between poverty and limited growth.

For China, small-scale agricultural reforms initiated in the late 1970s that revealed unsuspected latent potential to raise yields and productivity were the catalyst that jolted the economy onto a dynamic new growth path, rapidly enlarging the incomes and life chances of hundreds of millions of villagers formerly mired in absolute poverty. Ethiopia's recently established rose industry (chapter 6) stands out as an African initiative that began in one corner of the national economy and subsequently generated benefits that have extended to a much wider orbit.

Today's opportunities in light manufacturing offer an inexpensive and practical pathway to improve the circumstances of millions of people in many low-income economies. The targeted development of light manufacturing—specifically, consumer goods manufactured with modest inputs of fixed capital and technology and the extensive application of unskilled or semiskilled labor—is a promising entry point for accelerating industrialization and prosperity in low-income countries. Light manufacturing is a tested and proven path for industrialization in low-income countries (Chenery 1979; Chenery and Syrquin 1975).

The companion volume emphasizes six key binding constraints to competitiveness that nascent light manufacturing clusters and enterprises in Africa must overcome (Dinh and others 2012):

- The availability, cost, and quality of inputs
- Access to industrial land
- Access to finance
- Trade logistics
- Entrepreneurial capabilities, both technical and managerial
- Worker skills

The business environment frequently receives the blame for Africa's consistently weak manufacturing performance (Bigsten and Söderbom 2005; Collier and Gunning 1999). While bilateral and multilateral donors often urge African countries to improve the investment climate as a matter of priority, we know that other developing economies have expanded the production and exports of light manufactures before resolving such issues. A member of our study team who visited Chinese factories in 1975 and 1982 encountered numerous instances of low product quality (sewing machines that leaked oil onto the fabric, electric motors that failed in hot, humid weather), passive management (a manager at a large plant insisted that he did not know the unit cost of his product), administrative confusion (would-be investors abandoned the newly established Xiamen special economic zone after managers refused to specify prices for land, electricity, and water), delays in moving merchandise through customs and port facilities, and indifference toward customers. Documentary research summarized in chapter 1 reveals other examples of major shortcomings in China's business environment during the years that the country was storming onto the global markets for light manufactures.

Emerging light manufacturers in developing countries must, of course, compete with today's Chinese firms, not with the much weaker firms of the 1980s. But powerful market forces have begun to undermine the competitive advantage of China's well-established coastal centers of labor-intensive, low-end manufacturing (see above). As the profits of these producers of apparel, leather products, and other labor-intensive manufactures continue to be squeezed, the firms will either shift to other lines of business or move to the interior, to other Asian countries, or, as suggested in this report, to African countries such as Ethiopia, Tanzania, and Zambia.

In this environment, prompt action can deliver quick results. During an August 2011 tour of the Pearl River Delta, China's leading export region for light manufactures, the late Meles Zenawi, prime minister of Ethiopia, "was keen to encourage Chinese manufacturers" to invest in his home country. His offer produced a quick response: "within weeks of his visit an official Chinese delegation visited the country, and one Guangdong manufacturer, Huajian, has now set up a shoe manufacturing facility" (Moody and Zhong 2012, 12). Huajian began production in January 2012, employing Ethiopian workers to manufacture and export, initially, 20,000 pairs of shoes a month (Dinh 2012). The factory now has three production lines and employs 1,600. The value of its exports accounts for 57 percent of Ethiopian exports of leather shoes. If the company realizes its initial promise, Ethiopia will surely benefit from additional investment in leatherworking and other labor-intensive industries.

Ramping up investments in light manufacturing in low-income countries requires more than inviting foreign visitors to investigate local opportunities. The key for policy makers is to create conditions that encourage domestic and international entrepreneurs alike to tap the potential for transforming domestic labor and materials into substantial volumes of production, employment, and exports.

Our two-stage study of light manufacturing advances the understanding of what it takes to establish light manufacturing by laying out specific actions built on successful experience in low-income countries. It accomplishes the following:

- Identifies specific sectors as potential candidates for start-up
- Pinpoints constraints that have obstructed manufacturing in these sectors
- Highlights concrete reforms that can create opportunities for private domestic or foreign entrepreneurs to initiate light manufacturing operations in specially established industrial parks or districts

This approach builds on the work of Chenery (1979) and Hausmann, Rodrik, and Velasco (2005) who visualize development as a continuous process of specifying the binding constraints that limit growth, formulating and implementing policies to relax these constraints, securing modest improvements in performance, and then extending and renewing growth by identifying and pushing against the factors limiting expansion in the new environment. We consider this prescription for limited, sharply focused policy measures more effective because limited financial and human resources or rent-seeking activities often prevent full implementation of national-level reforms. Our approach is also consistent with the new structural economics, which views economic development as a process that requires the continuous injection of improved technologies and upgrading of skills (Lin 2012).

Following Chenery, our approach emphasizes that development begins somewhere, but not everywhere. In Africa, as in China, applying limited resources in funds and high-quality administrative personnel to implement sharply focused reforms holds the promise of initiating new clusters of production, employment, and, eventually, exports without first resolving economy-wide problems of land acquisition, utility services, skill shortages, administrative shortcomings, and the like.

But why China? Because of its size and historical development, China is unique. Its development of light manufactures is of great interest for this reason alone. In today's globalized world, any country introducing light manufactures must face competition from Chinese producers. As the newest example of industrialization through the development of light manufacturing, China is as much a beacon as a rival. Other Asian economies, including Japan; Korea; Malaysia; Singapore; and Taiwan, China, have taken the same path, but at a much earlier time. China's recent success magnifies the importance of its experience for current development efforts. China also illustrates a successful transition from low- to middle-income status: another reason its recent history is relevant to today's low-income countries.

In the past, policy recommendations aimed at low-income countries have drifted toward extremes: first, they devalued the potential of the private sector and exaggerated the contribution of state action, and, then, more recently, they have sided with the Washington Consensus, which takes the opposite perspective by suggesting that government functions be limited to the (still important) task of establishing suitable conditions for private sector dynamism.

However, our case studies show that manufacturing firms in developing countries face tremendous risks. Even if the potential rewards are correspondingly high, recent developing-country experience provides numerous examples of private sector initiatives withering for lack of public sector support. In contrast, the recent history of China and other East Asian countries shows that public-private partnerships can contribute mightily to the development of bottom-up light manufacturing clusters. This leads us to suggest that the best path for low-income economies to realize opportunities to accelerate growth through light manufacturing involves harnessing the joint efforts of the public and private actors.

This book consists of three parts.

Part I documents China's experience in the development of light manufacturing since the 1970s, including an examination of how China resolved the six binding constraints on growth in this sector. It also discusses the policy tools that China has used to turn the country into a powerhouse of light manufacturing within such a short period of time. The analysis is rounded out by selected case studies on light manufacturing initiatives in China.

Part II offers case studies and analysis to highlight the experience of light manufacturing elsewhere in Africa and Asia with a view to examining additional instances of success and failure in addressing the six binding constraints that can block the emergence of light manufacturing clusters.

Part III discusses the policy implications of the Chinese experience and the extent to which policy lessons may be drawn from this experience and from our other case studies for application in developing countries.

Our study team conducted field visits to enterprises in China and in a number of other countries. (The interview questionnaire is provided in the appendix.) In China, the team conducted missions in 2010 and 2012. In October 2010, the team visited Ganzhou, Ji'an, Nanchang, and Nankang in Jiangxi Province; Hangzhou, Shaoxing, Wenzhou, and Yiwu in Zhejiang Province; and Beijing. In July 2012, the team visited Foshan, Guangzhou, Jiangmen, Nanhai, and Shenzhen in Guangdong Province; Chengdu and Pengzhou in Sichuan Province; and Haining in Zhejiang Province. The cities and provinces have been chosen by the study team based on (1) the large size of the simple light manufacturing clusters in these places and, particularly, in the five sectors that are the focus of our study and (2) the large number of small and medium private sector enterprises in these areas. Guangdong, Jiangsu, and Zhejiang are among the coastal provinces that have spearheaded China's economic growth, led by dynamic private sector business. Jiangxi and Sichuan, located in the central region and the western region, lag behind the coastal provinces, but have witnessed remarkable development in the past decade. Furthermore, compared with the coastal regions, which have gradually moved up to more sophisticated industries, the central and western provinces may shed more light on how other low-income developing countries might embark on the industrialization process.

In addition, the case studies on China highlight Zhengzhou in Henan Province, Haimen and Yangzhou in Jiangsu Province, Ganzhou and Nankang in Jiangxi Province, Yinchuan in Ningxia Province, Chengdu in Sichuan Province, Yongkang in Zhejiang Province, and Beijing.

One of the authors has conducted research on Chinese enterprises over the last 40 years and has interviewed enterprise personnel at various times during this period. Other authors have visited enterprises in Bangladesh (Dacca), Ethiopia (Addis Ababa), Ghana (Accra), Mauritius, Pakistan (Sialkot), and Vietnam (Hanoi, Ho Chi Minh City, and Hue).

The provinces, enterprises, government offices, and individuals visited in China by the team are identified in table I.2 and map I.1.

**Table I.2  Offices and Enterprises Visited by the Study Team, China, 2010 and 2012**

| Location | Entity |
|---|---|
| *Mission, September 2010* | |
| Jiangxi Province (23 enterprises) | Dahai Fashion Clothes Co. Ltd., Ganzhou Julong Hi-tech Industrial Co. Ltd., Hong Kong Guoding International Furniture Co. Ltd., Huaxing Knitting Industrial Co. Ltd., Jiangxi Bentian Food Technology Co. Ltd., Jiangxi Hengsheng Garment Manufacturing Co. Ltd., Jiangxi Youjia Food Manufacturing Co. Ltd., Jinggangshan Food Co. Ltd., Ji'an Wahaha Beverage Co. Ltd., Jinze Garments Manufacturing Co. Ltd., Jishui County Shunjie Shoe Plant, Jishui County Silver Fox Leather Products Co. Ltd., Jishui County Xingyu Gloves Materials Co. Ltd., Longnan County Rice and Flour Processing Co. Ltd., Nanchang Chenggong Garments Manufacturing Co. Ltd., Nanchang Peiweimeng Knitting Co. Ltd., Nankang Furniture Industrial Base, Pusaike (Jiangxi) Bio-technological Co. Ltd., Qianqiu Food Co. Ltd., Qinye (Longnan) Industrial Co. Ltd., Xinjingtai Industrial Co. Ltd., Yifeng Knitting Co. Ltd., Yuanjian Shoes Co. Ltd. |
| Zhejiang Province (15 enterprises) | Shaoxing Bolan Home Textile Co. Ltd., Shaoxing Dafa Cloth Co. Ltd., Shaoxing Jinnuo Garments and Accessories Co. Ltd., Shaoxing Jincheng Textile and Garments Manufacturing Co. Ltd., Wenzhou Aihao Writing Instruments Co. Ltd., Wenzhou Jundeli Leather Co. Ltd., Wenzhou Lixin Shoes Co. Ltd., Wenzhou Zhuangwei Garments Co. Ltd., Yiwu Danxi Brewage Co. Ltd., Yiwu Huatong Meat Products Co. Ltd., Yiwu Zongnan Leather Products Co. Ltd., Zhejiang Bangjie Garments Co. Ltd., Zhejiang Fudebao Furniture Co. Ltd., Zhejiang Wanyu Knitting Co. Ltd., Zhengjiang Weihai Zipper Co. Ltd.. |
| *Mission, July 2012* | |
| Zhejiang Province | |
| Government | Administrative Committee, Zhejiang Haining Warp Knitting Industrial Zone; Maqiao Subdistrict Committee, Haining Municipal Communist Party of China |
| Enterprises (2) | Zhejiang Wanfang New Materials Co. Ltd., Halead New Material Co. Ltd. |
| Guangdong Province | |
| Government | Administrative Committee, Xinhui District Economic Development Zone, Jiangmen City; Guangzhou Economic and Technological Development Zone; Science and Technology and Informatization Bureau; China Development Institute, Shenzhen; Investment Promotion Division, Guangdong Finance and High-Tech Service Zone, Subzone 3, Nanhai District, Foshan; Economic Services Bureau, Guangming New Area, Shenzhen |
| Enterprises (15) | Guangdong GOSUNCN Telecommunications Co. Ltd.; Baoguang Shoes Co. Ltd.; Regina Miracle International Ltd.; Chung Tai Garment Factory Ltd.; Karandonis [Foshan Nanhai] Shoes Ltd.; Shenzhen Everich Industrial Development Co. Ltd.; Foshan Gang Auto Mold Parts Co. Ltd.; INOX Bin Products Ltd.; Bonanza Metalware Ltd.; Xinhui District, Jiangmen; Guicheng [Foshan Nanhai] Shiken Jiaye Steel Pipe Co.; Jiangmen Qipai Import and Export Co. Ltd.; Foshan Nanhai Shengfeng Shoes Co.; Guangdong Fortress Chemical Co. Ltd.; Foshan Nanhai Shiken Huaqiang Petrochemical Equipment Co.; Jiangmen Qipai Motorcycle Co. Ltd. |

*(continued next page)*

**Table I.2  (continued)**

| Location | Entity |
|---|---|
| Sichuan Province | |
| Government | Pengzhou Municipal Government; Administrative Committee, Pengzhou Industrial Development Zone; Sichuan Development and Reform Commission; Foreign Economic and Trade Division, Chengdu Wuhou District Government; Sichuan Development Zones Association; Pengzhou Development and Reform Bureau; Administrative Committee, Pengzhou Industrial Development Zone |
| Enterprises (12) | Chengdu Hongyou Furniture Manufacturing Co. Ltd., Chengdu Longyang Real Estate Co. Ltd., Chengdu Sunhoo Industry Co. Ltd., Chengdu Xuyao Shoes Industry Co. Ltd., Chengxin Leather Garments Co. Ltd., Chengdu Aimiqi Shoes Industry Co. Ltd., Huamao Jinye Construction Investment Co. Ltd., Sichuan Wuhou International Shoe Center, Sichuan Aiminer Leather Products Co. Ltd., Chengdu Cameido Shoes Investment Co. Ltd., Poyicon Home Products Co. Ltd., Chengdu Deqin Furniture Co. Ltd. |

## Map I.1  Cities Visited by the Study Team, China, 2010 and 2012

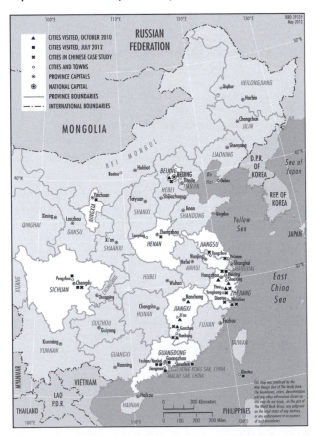

# References

Arbache, Jorge, Delfin S. Go, and John Page. 2008. "Is Africa's Economy at a Turning Point?" Policy Research Working Paper 4519, World Bank, Washington, DC.

Amsden, Alice H. 2001. *The Rise of "The Rest."* Oxford, U.K.: Oxford University Press.

Bigsten, Arne, and Måns M. Söderbom. 2005. "What Have We Learned from a Decade of Manufacturing Enterprise Surveys in Africa?" Policy Research Working Paper 3798, World Bank, Washington, DC.

Chenery, Hollis B. 1979. *Structural Change and Development Policy.* Oxford, U.K.: Oxford University Press.

Chenery, Hollis B., and Moshe Syrquin. 1975. *Patterns of Development, 1950–1970.* Oxford, U.K.: Oxford University Press.

Clarke, George. 2012. "Manufacturing Firms in Africa." In *Performance of Manufacturing Firms in Africa: An Empirical Analysis,* edited by Hinh T. Dinh and George Clarke, 47–83. Washington, DC: World Bank.

Collier, Paul. 2007. *The Bottom Billion.* Oxford, U.K.: Oxford University Press.

Collier, Paul, and Jan W. Gunning. 1999. "Explaining Africa's Economic Performance." *Journal of Economic Literature* 37: 64–111.

Dinh, Hinh T. 2012. "Opinion: Could Africa Be World's Next Manufacturing Hub?" *CNN Opinion,* June 20. http://www.cnn.com/2012/06/15/opinion/africa-manufacturing-hub/index.html.

Dinh, Hinh T., Vincent Palmade, Vandana Chandra, and Frances Cossar. 2012. *Light Manufacturing in Africa: Targeted Policies to Enhance Private Investment and Create Jobs.* Washington, DC: World Bank. http://go.worldbank.org/ASG0J44350.

Hausmann, Ricardo, Dani Rodrik, and Andrés Velasco. 2005. "Growth Diagnostics." Cambridge, MA: John F. Kennedy School of Government, Harvard University. http://www.hks.harvard.edu/fs/rhausma/new/growthdiag.pdf.

Kuznets, Simon. 1971. *Economic Growth of Nations.* Cambridge, MA: Harvard University Press.

Li, Jiabao. 2012. "Westward Ho! For China's Processing Trade." *China Daily,* U.S. edition, June 26.

Lin, Justin Yifu. 2012. *New Structural Economics: A Framework for Rethinking Development and Policy.* Washington, DC: World Bank.

Liu, Ta-chung, and Kung-chia Yeh. 1965. *The Economy of the Chinese Mainland.* Princeton, NJ: Princeton University Press.

Moody, Andrew, and Zhong Nan. 2012. "China 'Picking Up the Pieces' in Africa." *China Daily,* April 27. http://www.chinadaily.com.cn/cndy/2012-04/27/content_15155495.htm.

Odaka, Kōnosuke, Osamu Saitō, Kyōji Fukao, and Toshiyuki Mizoguchi. 2008. *Ajia chōki keizai tōkei 1, Taiwan* [Asian historical statistics 1, Taiwan]. [In Japanese.] Tokyo: Tōyō Keizai Shinpōsha.

Ohkawa, Kazushi, and Miyohei Shinohara. 1979. *Patterns of Japanese Economic Growth*. New Haven, CT: Yale University Press.

Rice, Xan. 2012. "African Manufacturers Demand Help to Compete with Chinese." *Financial Times*, July 21–22.

Syrquin, Moshe, and Hollis B. Chenery. 1989. "Patterns of Development, 1950 to 1983." World Bank Discussion Paper 41, World Bank, Washington, DC.

World Bank. 1993. *The East Asian Miracle: Economic Growth and Public Policy*. World Bank Policy Research Report. Washington, DC: World Bank; New York: Oxford University Press.

Zhang, Yuwei. 2012. "Textile Sector Frayed, but Resilient." *China Daily, USA Business Weekly*, August 3–9.

Part I
# Tales of China

# The Development of Light Manufacturing

## Introduction

From today's vantage point, it is clear that China's reforms beginning in the late 1970s succeeded beyond their architects' wildest dreams. At the outset, success was not guaranteed. Well-informed outsiders doubted that, with economics teaching, research, and policy advice locked into what one Chinese commentator described as "a state of ossification or semi-ossification of thinking" (FBIS 1981, K2), moderate reforms could shift China's economy onto a new, productivity-led path toward growth. Ambitions were modest: reformers aspired to ameliorate long-standing difficulties in feeding China's immense populace and improve outcomes across all segments of the centrally planned economy. There was no thought, at least in public discussion, of seeking a market outcome or creating a "socialist market economy with Chinese characteristics," in Deng Xiaoping's resonant phrase: all this came more than a decade later. The prevailing theory, articulated by long-time economic specialist Chen Yun, likened China's economy to a caged bird.[1] Chen and other reform advocates proposed boosting the economy's capacity to take flight by modestly expanding the role of markets, prices, and choice: enlarging the cage, not setting the bird free.

## Light Manufacturing before the Reforms in the 1970s

China has a long history of handicraft production of cotton, silk, and woolen fabrics. Modern factory production, which began in the late 19th century, expanded following the 1895 Treaty of Shimonoseki, which allowed foreign nationals to build and operate factories in open or treaty ports. Decades of foreign pressure dating from the 1839–42 Opium War had obliged China's Qing rulers (1644–1911) to allow foreigners to reside and conduct a growing array of commercial, educational, and religious activities outside the control of the Chinese authorities. Once foreigners gained the right to establish factories, domestic opposition to the operation of Chinese-owned manufacturing facilities faded, giving a double boost to China's nascent industrial sector.

### The Early 20th Century[2]

Factory production developed rapidly between 1895 and the outbreak of World War II. In manufacturing growth among Asian countries, China ranked second only to Korea over 1890–1913 and third behind Korea and Japan over 1920–38 (Bénétrix, O'Rourke, and Williamson 2012). Factory growth occurred under conditions of free trade forced on China by a succession of international agreements dating from the Opium War, which allowed unrestricted competition from imported goods and, after 1895, from foreign-owned domestic firms, most operated by British or Japanese nationals. Except in Manchuria, China's northeast region, where entities controlled by the Japanese government began to invest around 1915, factory ownership rested almost exclusively in private hands.

Growth surged. Mining and manufacturing expanded at an average annual rate of 9.4 percent during 1912–36, well ahead of growth in Japan and the Soviet Union. Factories expanded at an annual rate of 8.1 percent, closely behind Japan's 8.8 percent (Rawski 1989).

Despite the advantages enjoyed by foreigners, Chinese entrepreneurs stood up to unrestricted competition from an array of foreign rivals that included powerful multinational enterprises. In 1933, the year for which the data are most complete, Chinese-owned firms produced 74 percent of factory output in Shanghai and neighboring Jiangsu Province, a region that generated nearly half the country's factory output that year. Nationwide in 1933, Chinese-owned firms accounted for 73 percent of factory output; only in Manchuria, where Japanese involvement pushed the share of foreign-owned production to 59 percent, did domestic ownership occupy a subordinate position.

Chinese entrepreneurs were particularly successful in the light manufacturing sectors that dominated prewar industrial output. Rawski (1989) notes that, in 1933, 78 percent of factory output came from textiles, clothing, and footwear (40 percent); food, beverages, and tobacco (34 percent); and wood, leather, and rubber products (4 percent).

Cotton textiles, prewar China's largest manufacturing sector, acquired a "well-deserved reputation as a battleground between products from overseas factories, domestic plants operated by Chinese and foreign businesses, and Chinese handicraft producers" (Rawski 1989, 92). The factory sector, dominated by Chinese entrepreneurs (65 percent of production in 1933, with labor productivity at 95 percent of that of foreign-owned firms), performed well in this fiercely competitive environment, gaining market share at the expense of imports and domestic craft products. By the early 1930s, factories located in China, including some owned by British and Japanese firms, produced about 8 percent of the world's cotton yarn, trailing only the United States, Japan, the United Kingdom, and India, and 2.8 percent of the global output of cotton piece goods, ranking behind the same leaders and also the Soviet Union, Germany, France, and Italy (ILO 1937). "China's factory yarn industry grew faster to higher levels of production than any ... in the world" before World War II (Kraus 1980, 152).

After eight years of war had disrupted transport and marketing links and sharply curtailed production, Shanghai's textile magnates celebrated Japan's 1945 defeat by ordering large quantities of machinery from overseas. When Communist insurgents overwhelmed the incumbent Nationalist (Guomindang) regime, many of these operators fled from Shanghai to Hong Kong SAR, China, diverting shipments of machinery to the British colony and resuming operations in their new home. The ensuing dynamism of the colony's textile industry illustrates the entrepreneurial legacies that have contributed massively to China's recent economic boom.

Flour milling and matches provided additional tales of growth. By the early 1930s, Chinese millers had annual processing capacity of more than 3 million tons. In 1933, the output of 1.7 million tons was 58 percent higher than the Japanese production that year. Domestic entrepreneurs also dominated the prewar market for matches, fending off competition from imports, which peaked in 1912, and from China-based Japanese and Swedish firms, at least one of which was bought out by Chinese rivals.

During the early 20th century, light manufacturing, while contributing only modestly to a national economy still dominated by agriculture, grew substantially, stimulating the formation and expansion of new suppliers who furnished a variety of inputs. The growth of cotton textile production sparked backward links to chemicals (which also served the food processing industry) and machinery. Shanghai's Dalong (formerly Ta-lung) Machinery Works, established in 1902 and still operating more than a century later, is a case in point. Beginning with equipment repair, the firm progressed to producing parts and eventually to manufacturing textile equipment. Finding that prospective clients doubted the quality of these machines, the firm purchased several textile plants and stocked them with its own equipment. The profitability of the plants provided excellent advertising for the firm's wares. While the outbreak of war curtailed the firm's expansion, the distribution of price lists printed in English and Chinese signaled the firm's intention to compete overseas as well as in domestic markets for textile machinery (Rawski 1980).

## The Central Planning Era, 1949–78

Following the 1949 establishment of China under the leadership of Mao Zedong and the Communist Party, the country moved to restore economic and monetary stability and then to create a planned economy loosely modeled on that of the Soviet Union.

Under China's central planning system, the state monopolized domestic and foreign trade, set the prices of key commodities, determined output targets for major enterprises and branches, allocated energy resources, set wage levels and employment targets, operated the wholesale and retail networks, and steered financial policy and the banking system. In rural areas beginning in the mid-1950s, the government dictated cropping patterns, set price levels, fixed output targets for all major crops, and enforced a unified system for the purchase and sale of crops.

As in the Soviet Union, planners in China concentrated resources on what they viewed as priority industries, with the objective of accelerating the economy's capacity to expand industrial capital formation and strengthen China's military, while limiting the reliance on imports. Although shifts in China's industrial reporting system make tabulation of the long-term trends in sectoral shares in manufacturing output difficult, it is clear from state sector employment trends during 1952–78 that China's planning system directed resources to priority sectors such as machinery, metallurgy, and chemicals rather than textiles and food processing (table 1.1).

China's planned economy offered little scope for private business, which was largely eliminated under the socialist transformation policies of the mid-1950s. As the plan system took shape, resource flows increasingly reflected government instructions rather than market transactions. The rationing of grain, cloth, and other important household items extended nonmarket allocation into the consumer sector. The placement of workers, the selection of investment projects, and links between suppliers and customers were often based on administrative decisions that took little account of price. Prices, frozen for long periods, became unmoored from relative costs or scarcities (Perkins 1966).

**Table 1.1  State Sector Employment Growth in Major Industries, China, 1952–78**

| Sector | Workers, millions | | Index, 1978 (1952 = 100) |
|---|---|---|---|
| | 1952 | 1978 | |
| All industry | 12.5 | 50.1 | 400.8 |
| *Light manufacturing* | | | |
| Textiles | 1.0 | 2.7 | 270.0 |
| Food processing | 0.5 | 2.0 | 400.0 |
| *Priority sectors* | | | |
| Machinery | 0.9 | 9.4 | 1,011.8 |
| Metallurgy | 0.3 | 3.1 | 908.8 |
| Chemicals | 0.2 | 2.9 | 1,588.9 |

*Source:* NBS 2000a.

The late 1950s brought a further weakening of market forces. The Great Leap Forward of 1958–60 replaced household cultivation with collective agriculture and severely curtailed the market system in rural areas, where more than 80 percent of China's people lived (Yang 1996). At the same time, the rapid unraveling of the Sino-Soviet alliance and U.S. efforts to organize an international boycott of trade with China reduced China's access to global markets, a change reinforced by the aggressive pursuit of self-reliance at the local, regional, and national levels within China.

While the plan system and rural collectivization dramatically curbed the role of market forces in the daily operation of China's economy, the political system sought to suppress ideas on profit seeking that had permeated Chinese society for centuries. The following passage from a collection of Chinese newspaper articles compiled by the Xinhua News Agency (1975, 164–65) illustrates the torrent of antimarket, antibusiness propaganda that portrayed commerce, markets, and profit seeking as inimical to socialist ideals:

> In the years 1959–61 … Liu Shao-chi [Liu Shaoqi, chairman of the Communist Party before his 1968 ouster], renegade, hidden traitor, and scab, pushed a revisionist line in the countryside. He advocated … the extension of plots for private use and free markets, the increase of small enterprises with sole responsibility for their own profits or losses, and the fixing of output quotas based on the household [rather than collective farming] … and … freedom to practice usury, hire labor, buy and sell land, and engage in private enterprises. … [T]he people of Tachai [Dazhai, a model agricultural collective that reported remarkable economic gains] persisted along the socialist orientation and repulsed [market alternatives].

The pressure from advocates of antieconomic thinking was intense. Hou (1999, 181–85) reports "large-scale wage reductions for high-level intellectual workers" in 1957, 1959, and 1961 and notes that "intellectual workers … were mostly excluded" from wage increases in 1959, 1961, 1963, and 1971. He describes 1976–90 as an era of "no payoff to education." Apparently referring to the late 1980s, a decade after the reforms began, Hou notes that the average monthly pay in universities was Y 57 (about \$15 at the prevailing exchange rate), which was less than the average monthly pay in the food and drink sector.

Despite the generally antieconomic character of policies, institutional structures, and political discourse during the two decades following the 1958 launch of the Great Leap Forward, vestiges of market-oriented behavior remained, ready to bloom again if given any space to do so.

Local officials frequently complained of deviant individual behavior, particularly among rural villagers engaged in traditional profit-seeking activities of the sort that the people's communes sought to suppress. Although the famine brought on by the Great Leap Forward abated after 1961, dietary inadequacies persisted in most rural areas.

"By the fall of 1959 hunger suddenly emerged without warning," a local official in Fujian Province explained. "For the next 20 years the problem of hunger was part of our lives" (Huang 1989, 61).

Retrospective accounts confirm that underfed villagers pursued opportunities to supplement their incomes by raising poultry and selling handicrafts, vegetables, and pig fodder, and they also show that grassroots authorities often suppressed these efforts in the name of protecting socialism (Friedman, Pickowicz, and Selden 1991; He 2003; Thaxton 2008). The commune system, which set out to extinguish China's tradition of small-scale rural capitalism, seems to have sharpened the entrepreneurial instincts of Chinese villagers and fueled the explosive response to the modest rural initiatives that signaled the start of China's reform era.

In addition to collectivizing farms, the agenda of the Great Leap Forward included a nationwide effort to expand steel production rapidly by developing small rural factories ("backyard furnaces"). This campaign diverted vast numbers of people from farming, thus contributing to China's 1959–61 famine, and encouraged deforestation on an immense scale, leading to widespread erosion and increasing the risk of droughts and floods. Despite the terrible cost, this initiative opened the door to the decentralized pursuit of local industry, which, decades later, blossomed into the township and village enterprises (TVEs) that helped lead China's march out of poverty. These firms were a breeding ground for entrepreneurs. For rural workers, a factory assignment, even if it meant no increase in income, represented a step up from "the least-desired position as a full-time agricultural labor[er]" (Parish and Whyte 1978, 110–11). For rural leaders, the TVEs provided opportunities to turn political networks to commercial advantage.

The Great Leap Forward's final institutional legacy was to establish firmly the responsibility of local officials to lead in upgrading and transforming the regional economy under their control, along with the traditional task of maintaining economic stability. For two decades, antieconomic policies implemented in the name of socialism made this initiative look like a huge mistake. Once reforms aligned official objectives with the desire of ordinary citizens to improve their material well-being, however, the power of official incentives to foster local economic growth quickly emerged as a major contributor to China's enduring economic boom (see chapter 10).

## The Reform Experience, 1978–Present

When the reforms began in the late 1970s, China was an improbable candidate for the achievement of huge economic gains. The majority of Chinese were underfed. There were no private companies, and there was little in the way of legitimate private marketing. Political preferences curtailed both regional and foreign trade. One analyst described China's domestic system as a cellular economy made up of isolated local systems (Donnithorne 1972). China's foreign trade in 1970 amounted to a mere $5.53 per person (NBS 2000b, 2011). Visitors were astounded at the widespread ignorance about the outside world, even among well-educated and seemingly cosmopolitan elites.

### The China Difference: Why Modest Reforms Produced Explosive Growth

China's early reforms were hardly revolutionary (see box 1.1 for a chronology of key reforms). In the countryside, the management of cultivation was transferred from collectives back to households. The state raised its purchase prices for both quota (compulsory) and above-quota (noncompulsory) grain procurement and expanded the scope of market allocation for agricultural inputs and nonstaple farm products. China ventured farther into foreign trade and established special economic zones in the southern provinces of Fujian and Guangdong to encourage foreign investment, an arrangement "reminiscent of the foreign concessions" in the former treaty port system (Chu 1985, 36). In the urban sector, reform emphasized enlivening state enterprises by allowing them

**Box 1.1  Milestones of China's Economic Reforms**

1978: Economic reform begins; the household responsibility system sparks the reversion of farming from collectives to household management.

1979: Four special economic zones are created; international trade and incoming foreign direct investment (FDI) begin to expand; initial efforts to enliven state enterprises improve incentives and expand markets.

1984: New reform push begins: dual price system begins; enterprises are recognized as key economic agents; the State Council approves additional national-level economic zones.

1989: Challenges to reform arise following the suppression of urban protests in Beijing and elsewhere.

1992: Deng Xiaoping's southern tour accelerates the momentum of reform; the Communist Party decides to aim for a "socialist market economy with Chinese characteristics."

1993: State-owned enterprises begin to shed excess labor.

1994: Fiscal reforms codify central-provincial revenue sharing, deepening pro-growth incentives at all levels.

2000: The central government initiates the Great Western Development Strategy (the Go West policy), which is aimed at reducing regional economic disparities.

2001: China joins the World Trade Organization (WTO).

to sell any output over plan requirements on expanded markets, to keep a portion of their profits (formerly remitted in full to the state), and to allocate retained earnings to technical upgrading and to bonus payments, housing, and other employee benefits.

These modest reforms produced an explosive response. Grain output rose 37 percent between 1978 and 1984–86 despite an 8.1 percent decline in sown acreage, implying that average grain yields rose some 45 percent during those years (NBS 1990). Although not shown in official data, farm labor declined sharply, as millions of villagers took up nonagricultural work. China's rural revival reflected much more than an increase in work effort as incentives for individual effort were restored. The reforms unleashed a torrent of entrepreneurship, the sort of behavior that the political system had discouraged and often punished during the preceding two decades (Chan, Madsen, and Unger 1992; Lyons and Nee 1994; Oi 1999).

Why the big response? Household farming and the market allocation of farm inputs and outputs are common in poor countries, as are improvements in the terms of trade of farm households. If these circumstances were sufficient to trigger big growth spurts, the development problems of low-income countries would have vanished decades ago.

There are several reasons why modest agricultural initiatives and renewed engagement in international trade produced unexpectedly large benefits. Closing large gaps between private thinking and public discourse—what Kuran (1995) describes as preference falsification—can unleash rapid economic change once people lose their fear of punishment for expressing private views (a preference for household farming, for example) rather than conforming to orthodoxy (support for collective farming despite its widely understood failings). Other factors were also influential.

**Switching the focus from politics to business.** When asked what changes the reforms brought, a veteran industrial manager replied: "We switched from politics to business" (July 2012 interview). The biggest impact came in the countryside. The restoration of individual incentives meant that farmers worked hard on all fields, rather than reserving their best efforts for the tiny private plots allowed under the commune system (Mead 2000). Regions that historically specialized in crops such as sugar or tobacco, but that had been required to grow grain under the commune system, reinstated traditional specializations, thereby, doubling or tripling average incomes in some cases. Rural factories, formerly restricted to selling products within their home county, could expand the production of their best products and serve wider markets (Perkins 1977). The partial deregulation of commerce spurred the expansion of local specialization. The button village in Qiaotou, in Zhejiang Province, thrived once it became possible to establish button sales outlets in department stores nationwide (chapter 5).

**Leveraging beneficial legacies from the planned economy.** Retrospective accounts emphasize the heavy costs of the quantity-oriented, target-centered planning practiced in China before the reforms (for example, Naughton 1995). This is true enough, but China's plan system also created beneficial legacies. These included large stocks of industrial equipment and the expertise needed to operate and maintain them. It included a vast array of government-run technical schools, universities, research institutes, and professional associations, many oriented toward fields such as textiles and machinery. And it included a publishing industry that printed and distributed large runs of accessible and inexpensive books and journals "to popularize technology for workers, peasants, and educated youth" (Perkins 1977, 246).

**Making up lost ground in international markets.** China's neglect of international trade opportunities during the 1960s and early 1970s coincided with a period of steep export growth in the sort of labor-intensive, low–value added goods in which Chinese producers could be extremely competitive. U.S. President Richard Nixon's 1972 visit to China and the restoration of diplomatic relations between China and the rich industrial economies of Japan, North America, and Western Europe removed long-standing barriers to trade. Furthermore, China's renewed interest in capturing trade opportunities coincided with the erosion of cost advantages in Hong Kong SAR, China, and in Taiwan, China, the leading exporters of labor-intensive manufactures. Large numbers of ethnic Chinese factory owners in these economies were searching for ways to continue their profitable export operations. They were eager to pursue opportunities to initiate production in China at the moment when China began to open its doors to foreign trade and investment. The resulting combination of the commercial skills and technical knowledge of these entrepreneurs with China's immense resources of low-wage labor sparked a massive export boom.

**Building on a rich base of human capital.** China's greatest advantage over other developing countries resides in its human capital. Alongside the enduring struggle to maintain adequate nutrition in rural areas were efforts to expand school attendance, popularize simple hygiene, combat infectious disease, and extend basic medical services. These efforts paid big dividends not so much at the initial stage of development when imitation activities were more prevalent, but, later on, when China started to shift to the production of higher–value added goods and services.

The levels of literacy and numeracy in 19th- and 20th-century China were among the highest in the preindustrial world (Baten and others 2010; Rawski 1979). Modern China built on this base: the 1982 census, conducted shortly after the start of reform, reported a literacy rate of almost 89 percent among young people 15–24 years of age, reflecting near-universal school attendance.[3]

China's stock of human capital also includes an unusually wide array of business skills, which has formed the underpinning for historical and contemporary economic achievements at home and abroad.

The extensive use of bookkeeping and accounting in households, lineage trusts, and guilds, as well as in businesses, confirms the widespread commercial orientation and numeracy during the Qing era (1644–1911) and the Republican era (1912–49) (Gardella 1994; Yuan and Ma 2010). Writing about the early decades of the 20th century, Wright (1984, 325) refers to China's "abundance of small-time entrepreneurs."

These observations reflect the long-standing realities of Chinese life and thought. Anticipating the *Wealth of Nations* by nearly 2,000 years, Han Fei-tzu (1959, 44) used language that matches Adam Smith's description of individual behavior:

> In the case of workmen selling their services in sowing seeds and tilling farms, the master would … give them delicious food and by appropriating cash and cloth make payments for their services. Not that they love the hired workmen, but that … by so doing they can make the workmen till the land deeper and pick the weed more carefully. The hired workmen … speedily pick the weed and till the land. … Not that they love their master, but that … by their so doing the soup will be delicious and both cash and cloth will be paid to them. Thus, the master's provisions and the workmen's services supplement each other as if between them there were the compassion of father and son. However, their minds are well disposed to act for each other because they cherish self-seeking motives.

China's enduring tradition of commercial activity and market participation by elites and villagers alike counters Polanyi's contention (1944, 43–44) that, before the English enclosure movement, "the alleged propensity of man to barter, truck, and exchange is almost entirely apocryphal. … [And that] no economy prior to our own [was] even approximately controlled and regulated by markets."

Thus, despite 20 years of official efforts to denigrate entrepreneurship and profit seeking, "when China stopped suppressing such activities … the response was immediate. Shops, restaurants, and many other service units popped up everywhere … [because the] Chinese … had not forgotten how to trade or run a small business" (Perkins 1995, 231). Wenzhou District, Zhejiang Province saw a revival of traditional credit associations (*hui*) and "old-style private banks (*qianzhuang*)" (Dong 1990, 95; Tsai 2002). The "1980s witnessed … a massive expansion of economic contracts, so that by the mid-1980s a single *xian* [county; China has more than 2,000] could have up to half a million

**Table 1.2  Growth of Township and Village Enterprises, China, 1978–90**
*number, millions*

| Year | Firms | | Workers | |
|------|-------|---------|-------|---------|
|      | Total | Industry | Total | Industry |
| 1978 | 1.52  | 0.79    | 28.26 | 17.34   |
| 1985 | 12.22 | 4.93    | 69.79 | 41.37   |
| 1990 | 18.50 | 7.22    | 92.65 | 55.72   |

*Source:* Editorial Committee 1993.

legally binding contracts" (Nolan 1990, 9, citing a Chinese publication). Lyons and Nee (1994) give examples of local contracts and the resulting conflicts.

The wide distribution of entrepreneurial, commercial, and organizational skills is a key factor explaining the economic trajectory of ordinary overseas Chinese. It is also a central component of the economic boom following the onset of reform initiatives in the late 1970s. The rapid expansion of TVEs reflects the activation of latent reserves of entrepreneurial, managerial, and accounting capabilities in China's countryside (table 1.2). These firms were typically controlled and operated by village authorities. Some were private, but concealed their true ownership behind a nominally collective organization. "Operat[ing] entirely outside the state plan" (Sachs and Woo 1997, 33), TVEs tended to respond quickly to market pressures. Industry (a category dominated by activities outside long-standing patterns of rural activity) shows a net gain of more than 4 million firms over 1978–85, followed by 2 million more in the next five years. Employment at industrial TVEs expanded by 24 million during 1978–85, with another 14 million workers added over 1985–90.

The initial burst of activity following the reforms was limited to the domestic economy. When these activities linked up with FDI and the knowledge network of overseas Chinese, especially in Hong Kong SAR, China, and in Taiwan, China, the result was extraordinary growth in production and exports (chapters 4 and 5). Many TVEs, which often started as primitive workshops, evolved into substantial operations and began to penetrate markets abroad. The value of TVE exports jumped from Y 9 billion in 1986 to Y 27 billion in 1988, Y 49 billion in 1990, and Y 119 billion in 1992. By 1992, TVEs accounted for 42 percent of goods exports and supplied 53 percent of China's manufactured exports (Editorial Committee 1989, 1993). These factories contributed heavily to China's march toward recognition as the world's workshop.

## Obstacles Constraining China's Development Capacity

While these advantages eased China's path to reform, the legacy of central planning included both constraints and growth accelerators.

**Unbalanced factor proportions.** China's vast population and high population density were straining the country's limited resource base long before the establishment of the new government in 1949. Historians have traced the gradual decline in cultivated area per person; the steady encroachment of farming into wetlands, grasslands, and forests; and the gradual removal of plant cover as rising numbers of people searched for fuel, fodder, and fertilizer (Elvin 2010; Elvin and Liu 1998; Perdue 1987). While population per square kilometer is not particularly high on a national level, the density of human habitation in the eastern and southern regions is far above the national average (map 1.1).

These pressures intensified during the post-1949 decades of socialist planning. The combined impact of population growth, industrial expansion, conversion of fragile grasslands to cultivated farmland, massive tree felling in support of the backyard steel campaign of the 1950s, and the construction of numerous (and often poorly designed) dams— what one author has termed Mao's war on nature (Shapiro 2001)— intensified the strains on environmental resources already stretched thin by centuries of dense human habitation. The pursuit of this pollute first, clean up later development path led to more severe environmental consequences for China than for Japan, North America, and Western Europe.

**The investment system bias toward capital-intensive production.** China's plan system eliminated the market for capital. Officially approved investment projects received state funds at zero cost. At the same time, the *hukou* system of residential permits excluded rural workers from competing for urban jobs in the state sector entities that implemented most investments. As the policy bias favoring urban residents opened a growing gap between urban and (much lower) rural incomes, investors

**Map 1.1  China: Regional Variation in Population Density**

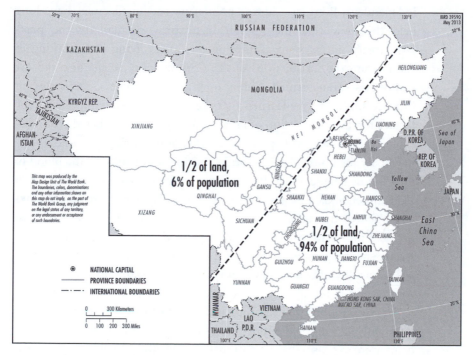

*Source:* World Bank, adapted from Naughton 2007.
*Note:* Based on population data for 1935.

perceived a high wage-rental ratio, the exact opposite of the scarcity relations dictated by overall factor proportions. The resulting bias toward capital-intensive investments with limited employment potential continued into the reform era (Rawski 2006a).

**The antibusiness legacy.** Multiple strands of antibusiness thinking are evident in China. Traditional Confucian thinkers posited a social hierarchy topped by scholars and followed by farmers and artisans, while merchants and soldiers were relegated to the lowest rungs. This cultural degradation of commerce did not prevent merchants from achieving social and economic prominence, but the tradition of demeaning commerce survives in China to this day.

Throughout the 19th and 20th centuries, as foreigners gained control of some territories formerly controlled by the Qing (1644–1911) and Republican (1912–49) governments, China remained nominally independent. Even so, Chinese politicians and intellectuals have long held the view that the foreign incursions—particularly the post-1842 treaty port system exempting foreigners living and working in China from the jurisdictions of the Chinese legal, regulatory, and tax authorities—transformed China into a semicolony. Generations of Chinese students have learned that the treaty port system, followed by Japan's forcible occupation of large swaths of China, inflicted economic exploitation along with political humiliation. During the mid-1980s, university textbooks accused foreign businesses of sucking the blood of the Chinese people under the treaty port regime. In the wake of the 1989 Tian'anmen Square protests, the Communist Party rewrote schoolbooks and opened museums "with the explicit purpose of showcasing past national humiliations" (Rachman 2012, 6; Z. Wang 2012). Despite the recent encouragement of foreign investment, public attitudes retain a latent hostility to business that can quickly rise to the surface, especially with respect to foreign-owned and, particularly, Japanese entities.

The Communist policies implemented during the prereform decades systematically curtailed opportunities for private business. Large private firms were expropriated or nationalized shortly after the new government took control in 1949. A few years later, socialist transformation shifted smaller private firms to the public sector. Once the people's communes were established in 1958, legitimate private business in the countryside was restricted to tiny private plots occupying only some 5 percent of the cultivated area. In essence, private businesses were "deemed as illegal" (Wang 2008, 28).

Retroactive enforcement of sanctions against private business was commonplace during the late 1960s, as shown by examples in the northern coastal city of Tianjin (Brown 2012, 155–58):

> In 1968 Hao Baohua, a man "of poor peasant background … was approved for removal [from Tianjin, his ancestral home] … along with his wife and seven children [after being classified] as a 'reactionary capitalist' … because he had run a tofu shop in Tianjin for 20 years … before nationalization."

> Liu Ende, classified as a "capitalist … because he had run a wonton (*hundun*) stand before nationalization," poisoned himself a day before his scheduled 1968 deportation to the countryside.

Remnants of these attitudes persisted even after the restrictions on business formation were relaxed. In the early reform years, individuals with high incomes were sometimes suspected of criminal connections. Expropriation and persecution of former entrepreneurs surely discouraged potential business entrants, particularly in the absence of legal protections for private businesses (see below).

## Major Structural Changes Accompanying the Reforms

Unlike the Russian Federation and some of its formerly socialist neighbors, China eschewed rapid marketization in favor of gradual reform, aptly described by Naughton (1995) as "growing out of the plan." Except for the reinstatement of household farming, the first 15 years of reform focused on marginal changes, leaving largely intact the plan system's main elements, including state enterprises, the planned allocation of materials at fixed prices, and state trading companies, but allowing the entry of new firms and an expanded role for product markets in which prices increasingly reflected the interplay of demand and supply. Following the decision in 1992 to pursue a socialist market economy with Chinese characteristics, reform initiatives expanded to include stocks, as well as flows: privatization of TVEs and state-owned firms, elimination of planned allocations of materials, and furloughing and eventually dismissing tens of millions of state sector employees.

Three key changes opened the door to massive expansion in light manufacturing.

**China rejoins the international economy.** China entered the reform era in economic isolation. Its share of global trade in 1970, 1975, and 1980 was less than half that in 1913 and 1960 (table 1.3). China's 1970 trade ratio—the sum of exports and imports as a share of gross domestic product (GDP)—was only 5 percent.

The trade picture changed rapidly. The first step was the creation of four special economic zones along the south China coast, allowing duty-free imports of equipment and materials for export production, permitting foreign investment, and dispensing with much of the domestic regulatory machinery. Such experimentation is characteristic of Chinese policy making (Heilmann and Perry 2011). The small scale of the special economic zones partly reflected domestic opposition to

**Table 1.3 Long-Term Trends in International Merchandise Trade and FDI, China, 1913–2012**

| Year | Merchandise trade | | Trade ratio,[a] (exports + imports)/GDP | FDI, $, billions | |
| | Exports + imports, $, billions | Share of world trade, % | | Incoming | Outbound |
| --- | --- | --- | --- | --- | --- |
| 1913 | 0.8 | 1.9 | — | — | — |
| 1952 | 1.9 | 1.1 | 9.5 | .. | .. |
| 1960 | 5.2 | 2.0 | 8.8 | .. | .. |
| 1970 | 4.6 | 0.7 | 5.0 | .. | .. |
| 1975 | 15.6 | 0.9 | 12.6 | .. | .. |
| 1980 | 38.0 | 0.9 | 12.5 | 0.1 | .. |
| 1985 | 69.6 | 1.8 | 22.9 | 2.0 | 0.6 |
| 1990 | 115.4 | 1.6 | 29.8 | 3.5 | 0.8 |
| 1995 | 280.9 | 2.7 | 38.7 | 37.5 | 2.0 |
| 2000 | 474.3 | 3.6 | 39.6 | 40.7 | 0.9 |
| 2005 | 1,421.9 | 6.7 | 63.2 | 72.4 | 12.3 |
| 2010 | 2,972.9 | 9.7 | 50.3 | 114.7 | 68.8 |
| 2011 | 3,641.9 | 9.9 | — | 124.0 | 65.1 |
| 2012 | 3,866.5 | 10.3 | 45.2 | 111.7 | 77.2 |

*Sources:* Data for 1913: Brandt, Rawski, and Zhu 2008; total trade and share in world trade: WTO data; trade ratio for 1952–75: NBS 2005; data for 1980–2011: NBS 2011; FDI: UNCTADStat (database), United Nations Conference on Trade and Development, Geneva (accessed September 30, 2012), http://unctadstat.unctad .org; data for 2012: NBS 2013b.

*Note:* World Trade Organization (WTO) data show that world trade grew by 2.0 percent in 2012. — = not available; .. = negligible; FDI = foreign direct investment; GDP = gross domestic product.
a. Based on trade and GDP in domestic currency at current prices.

rapid opening of the economy. Chen Yun, a leading economic specialist, reportedly opposed plans to establish special zones around Shanghai because of its "concentration of opportunists [capitalist entrepreneurs] who would, with their consummate skills, emerge from their cages if given the slightest chance" (Zhao and others 2009, 102).

The rapid expansion of exports from the zones, buoyed by the arrival of ethnic Chinese entrepreneurs seeking a new home for the labor-intensive export production pushed out of nearby regions by rising labor costs, effectively broke the foreign exchange bottleneck that had long constrained economic growth. Together with the comparable impact of the agricultural reforms on long-standing food shortages, these initial trade reforms reshaped China's economy.

The unexpected success of the four special economic zones spawned, first, a trickle and, eventually, a flood of imitators. Local and provincial governments, eager to accelerate growth and attract overseas investors, scrambled to obtain approval for new zones. As the scale of activity increased, the varieties of merchandise trade, foreign investment, and special zones multiplied: processing and compensation trade (see below), joint and cooperative foreign investment projects, and economic, technical, and high-technology zones. The central government approved 14 new zones over 1984–88 and another 18 during 1992–93. Provincial governments joined in: by 2006, there were 1,346 province-level zones (Li 2009). Zone operations scaled up quickly. In 1994, for example, technology development zones housed 11,748 enterprises with nearly 800,000 workers and $1.3 billion in exports; by 2010, there were more than 50,000 enterprises, 8.6 million workers, and exports worth $247.6 billion (NBS 1996, 2011).

Operating under streamlined rules, many producers, especially in the southern coastal regions, adopted new organizational forms to advance beyond the limits of the slowly evolving domestic economic system. Processing trade, for example, enabled firms to sidestep the domestic procurement system by importing, processing, and then reexporting fabrics, metals, machine components, and other key inputs. Compensation trade allows the foreign investor to receive a share of finished goods in return for providing equipment, technology, parts, and components. Foreign firms obtained privileges that foreshadowed subsequent domestic reforms. During the late 1980s, for instance, PPG, a U.S. firm, received permission to recruit workers for its new glass factory through newspaper advertisements at a time when most firms were obliged to accept workers assigned by local labor bureaus. In this way, China's open-door policy served as a partial substitute for accelerated economic liberalization. While domestic reform advanced at a more deliberate pace, reflecting complex consensus-building efforts (Naughton 2008), special zones and other novel institutional arrangements injected new flexibility that allowed the economy to grow more rapidly.

China's experience richly illustrates Romer's insistence (1993) that the domestic impact of international trade and investment resides in flows of ideas as much as in shipments of commodities and capital. The open-door policy stimulated knowledge flows through multiple channels. Overseas Chinese were the most fertile source of new knowledge, particularly during the early reform years. The location of the first four special zones reflected this reality: Shantou and Xiamen (ancestral homes to large numbers of outmigrants), Shenzhen (bordering Hong Kong SAR, China), and Zhuhai (adjacent to Macao SAR, China) all have deep links with emigrant communities known for their economic prowess (Wang and Bradbury 1986).

The economic opportunities linked to the reform initiatives encouraged hundreds of thousands of ethnic Chinese entrepreneurs, managers, engineers, teachers, and traders to return to China. Their capital, business knowledge, technical skills, and networks gave a huge boost to China's economy and to the reform process, particularly in the early years. Linguistic and cultural affinity simplified the information transfer.

The new regime allowed opportunities for rising numbers of Chinese nationals to work, travel, and study abroad. The resulting flood of firsthand information about the outside world was eagerly received by a society long deprived of such contacts.

The growing array of economic zones allowed the Chinese people to tap into new knowledge flows without leaving China. Reform leader Deng Xiaoping—who clearly understood the role of the zones as laboratories for testing reforms, schools for learning free-market mechanisms, and bridges for introducing foreign capital and advanced technology—remarked that China's zones "are a show-window, a window of technology, management, knowledge, as well as [China's] foreign policy. By running the [special zones, we] can introduce technology, acquire knowledge, and learn management know-how."[4] China's state enterprises joined foreign firms as investors in the new zones, precisely to capitalize on these opportunities.

Although inflows of FDI soared, the large scale and swift expansion of aggregate capital formation reduced the foreign share of capital formation (see table 1.3). The share of FDI in aggregate fixed capital formation peaked at slightly more than 16 percent in 1994 and then declined steadily to slightly more than 5 percent in 2000–01, with further declines thereafter as the growth of investment inflows slowed, while overall capital formation continued to grow (Jiang 2006).

These modest shares belie the massive impact of foreign investment. The arrival of foreign firms reverberated deeply into China's economy and society. A first wave of investment from Hong Kong SAR, China, and from Taiwan, China, was followed by a second wave of Western FDI. Foreign-invested firms exposed millions of Chinese to new ideas, products, organizational structures, production processes, management methods, quality requirements, and much more. Consider these examples:

> When China's First Auto Works (FAW) entered into a joint venture arrangement with Volkswagen, the German firm provided FAW with a manual describing its paint standards. FAW, which had never developed formal paint standards, translated the manual and asked its suppliers to conform to the VW paint specifications. (1996 interview)

> In the vehicle industry alone the arrival of global assembly firms, accompanied by hundreds of first-tier suppliers, has led to the creation of intricate supply chains involving thousands of Chinese producers of automotive components; thousands of firms supplying metal, plastic, glass, rubber, fasteners, and equipment to the component producers; and millions of workers, all exposed to the operational patterns of international firms like Toyota, General Motors, and BMW. (2005 interview)

The knowledge and skills acquired by participating in supply chains organized to satisfy foreign firms are easily transferable to other uses. New Chinese firms can tap into established supply chains to acquire high-quality components and hire executives, managers, engineers, designers, and skilled workers who have benefited from direct or indirect involvement with foreign firms. In this way, information and skills originating in foreign firms readily spread across China and throughout sectoral economic structures.

**The restoration of domestic economic competition.** China's plan system eliminated market competition by nationalizing or collectivizing farming, industry, handicrafts, and commerce; forbidding private start-ups; matching suppliers with customers; shrinking the number of retail outlets; and confining rural manufacturers to local markets. However, Chinese planning, unlike its Soviet precursor, conferred substantial control over investment budgets to provincial governments. As a result, China's planned economy harbored latent competitive potential, as most provinces installed new capacity to manufacture textiles, steel, machine tools, farm equipment, and many other products.[5] Once market entry was permitted, market competition expanded rapidly, especially in light manufacturing, where rural TVEs quickly challenged once-dominant state enterprises in a growing range of product lines. Steeply declining profits marked the path of competition (Naughton 1995).

Because government revenue at all levels depended heavily on industrial profits, local and provincial governments intervened regularly to protect local firms by, for example, reserving local supplies of underpriced materials for local processing or preventing inflows of manufactured products that competed with local goods. Such local protectionism was common during the early stages of reform. To respond to difficulties associated with regional trade blockades, the National People's Congress passed the Law on Unjust Competition in 1993, and, in 2001, the State Council issued order 303, Stipulation of the State Council to Forbid Regional Blockade in Market Activities (World Bank 2005; Zhang and Tan 2007). These measures, along with the erosion of price anomalies and the expansion of domestic road networks, led to a gradual decline in local protectionism. The steep increase in the number of trucks (from 1.3 million in 1980 to 4.0 million in 1990 and 16.0 million in 2010), many operated by individuals or small private firms, was particularly effective in eliminating local protectionism as a major force in China's economy (NBS 2011).

The relaxation of plan-era business entry restrictions is evident in the growing numbers of industrial firms (mining and utilities, as well as manufacturing). In 1978, there were 1.1 million industrial firms, 70 percent of them in rural communes (NBS 2000a; TVES 1986). By 1995, the number had risen to 7.3 million (OTNIC 1997).

As the number of firms rose, competition intensified in most sectors. Although state policy reserved some sectors (such as banking, insurance, rail and air transport, and petroleum) for centrally controlled state enterprises and conferred advantages on state firms through controls over access to bank lending and stock and bond issuance, fierce competition emerged, especially in sectors such as light manufacturing that did not rank near the top of official priority lists.

As a result, competition is a prominent feature of Chinese economic life: competition among domestic firms, between foreign-invested firms and domestic rivals, between imported and domestic products, between urban and rural firms, between state and private companies, among localities competing for investment funds, and between industrial clusters and industrial parks competing for preferential treatment by policy makers.

**Private business comes back.** When China embarked on economic reform, it had no clear laws and regulations on private business. Decades of suppressing individual entrepreneurs had thrown a pall of suspicion over private ventures and created high levels of uncertainty. Anyone starting a business with personal savings and, often, the savings of relatives and associates faced risks beyond those of market shifts, technical failure, or management errors. Entrepreneurs could become political targets accused of being capitalists or exploiters and exposed to the danger of arbitrary fines or the confiscation of goods by unaccountable bureaucracies.

The political, legal, and regulatory climate for private business has improved substantially since the start of reform. Brandt and Rawski (2008, 19) outline major changes, as follows:

> At the start of reform, private business operated in a legal limbo. Some entrepreneurs disguised their firms as collectives; ... others purchased informal protection from powerful individuals or agencies. A succession of amendments to China's 1982 constitution slowly expanded recognition of the nonpublic economy, first as a "complement" to the state sector (1988), then as an "important component" (1999) of the "socialist market economy." ... The Law on Solely Funded Enterprises, which took effect in 2000, guarantees state protection for the "legitimate property" of such firms, but without using the term "private" or specifying any agency or process to implement this guarantee.

> Further constitutional amendments adopted in 2004 breached the former taboo on the term "private" by stating that "citizens' lawful private property is inviolable." The long march toward official recognition of private business came to an end only in 2007 when, following five years of fierce debate, China's legislature enacted a landmark Law on Property Rights which, for the first time, explicitly places privately held assets on an equal footing with state and collective property.

These changes and others—especially the Communist Party's decision to welcome entrepreneurs into its ranks—have improved the standing of private businesses and reduced their noneconomic risk.

Despite the limited protections of China's legal environment, the private business sector has delivered remarkable gains. From a near-zero base in the late 1970s, dramatic expansion pushed the count of private industrial firms (employing eight or more workers) and individual

**Table 1.4  Contribution of Private and Individual Business Firms to the Economy, China, 2006–08**

| Contribution | 2006 | 2007 | 2008 |
|---|---|---|---|
| Urban fixed investment, % | 15.6 | 18.3 | 19.2 |
| Share of total exports,[a] % | 13.8 | 16.0 | 17.0 |
| Share of tax payments, % | 14.0 | 12.7 | 13.6 |
| Share of short-term bank loans, % | 2.71 | 3.06 | 3.37 |
| Annual increase in employment, millions | 10.2 | 10.0 | 9.3 |

Source: Minying 2009.
Note: Private firms employ eight people or more; individual firms employ seven or fewer.
a. Private firms only.

firms (seven workers or fewer) to 5.7 million by 1995 (OTNIC 1997). Although largely neglected by China's banks, which extended only 3 percent of short-term loans to private business, China's private sector contributed 13–19 percent of aggregate investment, exports, and fiscal revenue during 2006–08; these data exclude contributions from firms partially or fully owned by non-Chinese investors, including investors from Hong Kong SAR, China, and from Taiwan, China (table 1.4). Firms partially or fully owned by foreign investors have come to play a key role in China's vastly expanded foreign trade, accounting for more than 55–58 percent of total exports during 2006–08 (NBS 2013a); note that foreign–invested firms include private, partially private, and partially state–owned firms.

Job creation is the greatest achievement of China's private sector. Private businesses added 30.3 million workers over 2006–08. During the decade ending in 2010, domestic private and individual firms added 89.4 million workers, far more than aggregate job growth of 40.2 million (NBS 2011). Without private sector job growth, aggregate formal employment would have been substantially lower in 2010 than in 2000 or 1990.

Comparisons with other transition economies highlight China's extraordinary wealth of entrepreneurial resources. The ex-socialist countries of the former Soviet Union and Eastern Europe "have lower rates of entrepreneurship than are observed in most developed and developing market economies" (Estrin and Mickiewicz 2010, 26) (figure 1.1).

Rawski (2011) assembles comparable data for China and finds an annual average of 61.6 enterprises per 1,000 people during 2000–05. Even though these data appear to contain substantial underestimates

**Figure 1.1  Micro, Small, and Medium Enterprises Per 1,000 People, Selected Transition Economies, 2000–05**

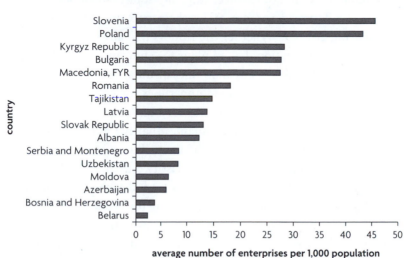

average number of enterprises per 1,000 population

Source: Estrin and Mickiewicz 2010.

Note: The figure omits countries with high numbers of enterprises (Czech Republic, at about 87 per 1,000, and Hungary, at about 55 per 1,000, in 2003; León 2007) and countries with low numbers of enterprises (Armenia, Croatia, Estonia, Georgia, Lithuania, Russia, and Ukraine, all reporting no more than 0.05 per 1,000 in 2005). See "Economy Statistics: Micro, Small, and Medium Enterprises," NationMaster .com, Rapid Intelligence, Sydney (accessed September 13, 2010), http://www.nationmaster.com/graph/eco_mic_sma_and_med_ent_num_percap-medium-enterprises-number-per-capita.

and show an improbable downward trend after 1999, this result surpasses the figures for all former Soviet bloc economies except the Czech Republic, at 87 enterprises per 1,000 people.

Despite the impressive accomplishments of China's private sector, major issues remain, even after more than three decades of reform.

*China Daily* editorializes that "despite the policies and regulations [favorable to private business] being in place, private investors often encounter difficulties in getting them fully exercised."[6]

Government officials and administrative systems are "now more friendly to businesses" than in the past, says a Shanghai financial analyst, "but they still tend to pay most attention to large companies and State firms" (Zhou 2011). The *China Daily* editorial cited above calls for "measures to ensure that the private sector gets the same treatment as its State and foreign counterparts. ... Private businesses do not need preferential terms; what they need is simply fair treatment."

In August 2012, large numbers of private businesses in Shenyang, the capital of Liaoning Province, suddenly shut their doors. The reason was "widespread rumors of harsh inspections and large fines" (Wu and Liu 2012, 5). Whether the rumors had any basis in fact (the municipal administration denied plans for abnormal inspections and invited citizens "to report any high fines or unlawful inspections" to a government hotline), this episode underlines the continuing absence of robust mechanisms to limit arbitrary and ruinous government actions against individuals or companies that the authorities choose to punish. However, the presence of the millions of light manufacturing firms that have emerged in the last two decades highlights the growing support of local governments and the changing attitudes toward business. Nonetheless, the remaining uncertainty obliges businesses of all sizes to seek informal alliances with powerful leaders who can shelter them from arbitrary official interventions. Such relationships, of course, depend on the continued access to power of the patrons.

The success of private operators provides eloquent testimony to the determination, resourcefulness, and flexibility of Chinese entrepreneurs.

## Reform Outcomes in Light Manufacturing

China's plan system channeled resources into sectors that contributed to the growth of producer goods and national defense. Planners viewed the production of light manufacturing and other consumption items as costs rather than benefits. They recognized the essential contribution of goods such as food and clothing, but sought to limit the scale of such activities to concentrate resources on industrial equipment, military hardware, and other high-priority categories.

This strategy succeeded in attaining the key objectives of the plan system. However, it came at a heavy price (Lin 2012a): an unbalanced economic structure, slow urbanization, inefficient use of capital, and low efficiency in industrial production. Personal consumption languished. Although there was no repetition of the famine that ravaged China's countryside during 1959–61, food availability remained below the minimum standards calculated by World Bank researchers (Rawski 2006b). Retrospective studies indicate that per

**Table 1.5 Output Growth in Major Light Manufacturing Products, China, 1970–2010**

| Year | Yarn, million tons | Cloth, billion meters | Garments, billion pieces | Shoes, million pairs | | Beer, million kiloliters |
|------|------|------|------|------|------|------|
| | | | | Cloth | Leather | |
| 1970 | 2.0 | 9.2 | 0.4 | 121 | 47 | 0.2 |
| 1980 | 2.9 | 13.5 | 0.9 | 203 | 157 | 0.7 |
| 1990 | 4.6 | 18.9 | 3.2 | 750 | 438 | 6.9 |
| 2000 | 6.6 | 27.7 | 20.9 | 517 | 1,468 | 22.3 |
| 2010 | 27.2 | 80.0 | 28.5 | — | 4,190 | 44.9 |

Sources: NBS 2000a, 2011; NBS-ITD 2001; for 2010 garments: chinairr.org (accessed August 12, 2012), http://www .chinairr.org/data/D13/201103/10-70396.html [in Chinese]; for 2010 leather shoes: ResearchinChina 2012. Note: — = not available.

capita consumption in the 1970s had changed little relative to the 1950s or even the 1930s (Bramall 1989; Lardy 1984). Lin (2012a) notes that, between 1952 and 1978, while national income grew by over 400 percent, consumption grew only 77 percent. Output data on major light manufactures support this finding (table 1.5). In 1970, for example, China produced 168 million pairs of cloth and leather shoes, or only one pair for every 5 of the country's 830 million people (NBS 2011).

**Reform Drives Rapid Expansion of Light Manufacturing**

As reform policies took hold, the demand for light manufacturing products surged. This initial burst of demand came from two sources: first, rising incomes, especially in the farm sector, that reflected the immediate success of rural reform initiatives and, second, pent-up demand for consumer goods, especially among urban residents whose incomes substantially exceeded rural levels. An additional impetus for expansion came from the gradual realization that, with the cooperation of (mostly Chinese) overseas business operators, China was in an ideal position to export light manufactures. Later, the success of the reform program powered economy-wide increases in productivity and incomes, transforming China into a huge market for garments, shoes, and other light manufacturing products. The output growth in major light manufactures illustrates the massive increase in scale that accompanied China's reforms (see table 1.5). While exports also grew rapidly, a large and expanding share of light manufactures was directed toward domestic sales that were fed by rising incomes.

**The emergence of competitive sectors.** Newly established economic zones, with Shenzhen in the lead, contributed to the expansion of light manufactures (figure 1.2). The prominence of overseas investment and sales ensured that new facilities were geared to China's domestic factor proportions, thereby increasing the pace of employment growth at a time when China's farm economy was disgorging millions of workers who had been underemployed in the prereform commune system.

Light manufacturing spread far beyond China's new economic zones. The low priority accorded most light manufacturing industries under the plan system meant that there were few incumbent producers whose interests or markets Chinese officials felt obliged to protect. Chinese policy makers began to call these light industries competitive sectors, where a variety of entrants, including private firms, were allowed to compete for market share.

**Figure 1.2 Manufacturing Output, Shenzhen Special Economic Zone, China, 1982–89**

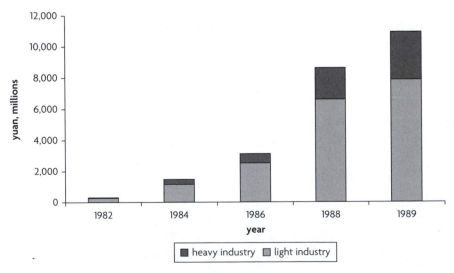

*Source:* CADZ 1989.
*Note:* The values for each year are in current prices. In 1989, $1.00 was roughly equal to Y 3.80.

The result was something approaching a competitive outcome, with many types of firms struggling to meet the requirements of domestic and overseas consumers, while each group retained a considerable market share. Firms included state-owned enterprises such as the large cotton textile factories that dotted the landscape of north and central China; foreign-linked firms, many guided by entrepreneurs based in Hong Kong SAR, China, or in Taiwan, China; and large numbers of domestic private firms, ranging from home workshops to large, well-financed corporate groups.

Small- and large-scale entrepreneurs alike responded enthusiastically to the opportunities made possible by the gradual relaxation of the prereform constraints. The light manufacturing firms ranged from small workshops managed by individual proprietors whose main assets seemed to be pluck and determination to sophisticated factories equipped with advanced machinery and run by phalanxes of highly qualified managers and engineers.

Linking the two extremes were industrial clusters that had originated in home workshops and sometimes developed into giant complexes that could move global markets in specific product niches (chapter 3).

The coastal provinces of Guangdong and Zhejiang emerged as leaders in the growth of private business, demonstrating the potential of industrialization that originates with individual proprietorships and can spur the creation of large multinational business structures. In both Guangdong's FDI-driven development and Zhejiang's spontaneous domestic model driven by small and medium enterprises (SMEs), entrepreneurs responded immediately to the initial relaxation of stringent limitations on private business.

Starting in the late 1970s, political and legal changes gradually expanded the scope of permissible private activity. Despite periodic retreats on policy reforms, favorable policy changes gradually accumulated, lessening the risks of starting a business and motivating growing numbers of people to take the plunge.

Han and Pannell (1999) document the winding path from intolerance to growing enthusiasm for private enterprise. At first, private business was seen as complementary to the dominant public sector. Later, measures such as compensating victims of past expropriations, allowing private firms to apply for loans, and simplifying business licensing signaled a gradual legitimation of private entrepreneurship.

Setbacks periodically slowed this gradual expansion of the operating space for private entrepreneurs. In 1983, the government described its policy toward enterprises with more than five workers as "not to encourage, not to publicize, and not to diminish": hardly enthusiastic support (Han and Pannell 1999, 277–79). The retrenchment that followed the violent suppression of urban protests in May–June 1989 led to a short-lived rollback of private sector expansion. But then came Deng Xiaoping's 1992 tour of southern China, with its ringing endorsement of reform and growth, followed by the Communist Party's announcement of the long-term goal of building a "socialist market economy with Chinese characteristics." These steps firmly established the private sector on the path of growing influence that continues to this day (figures 1.3 and 1.4).

Because of data shortcomings, neither the scale nor the timing of the sudden rise in the number and output of private firms can be

**Figure 1.3 Light Manufacturing Enterprises by Ownership Structure, China, 1999–2010**

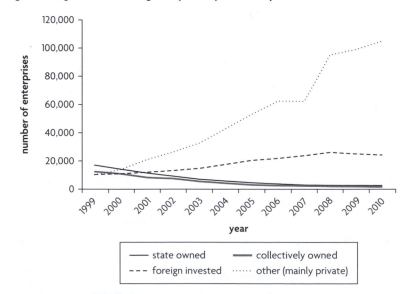

Source: China Light Industry Federation 2010.
Note: "Other" includes privately owned firms with and without foreign investment.

**Figure 1.4  Output Value of Light Manufacturing by Ownership Structure, China, 1999–2010**

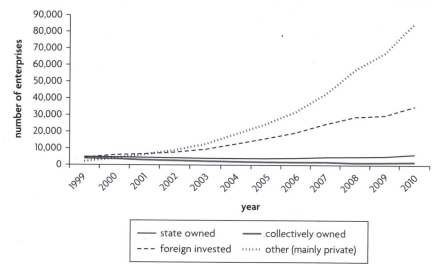

Source: China Light Industry Federation 2010.
Note: "Other" includes privately owned firms with and without foreign investment.

considered more than indicative.[7] The overall picture of the steeply increasing number of private firms and the rapidly expanding output of the private sector is, however, certainly correct.

One of the most important reforms was to reduce the scale of the public sector. Experiments with privatization developed gradually during the 1990s, leading to a steady decrease in the number of state-owned and collective-owned enterprises. By 1995, private enterprises had grown to account for more than 90 percent of China's light manufacturing firms. Large-scale privatization of state-owned and collective-owned enterprises began in the late 1990s.

**The growth of clusters.** Start-ups in individual light manufacturing trades—for example, shoes, buttons, aluminum extrusion, or cigarette lighters—often cluster in the same locality, imitating successful pioneers by subcontracting or producing components or engaging in transport, packaging, and other ancillary activities. Many of these clusters generate substantial output, employment, and export earnings (see chapters 3 and 5 for more detail).

**Figure 1.5  Labor Productivity of Light Manufacturing Firms, by Ownership Structure, China, 1999–2007**

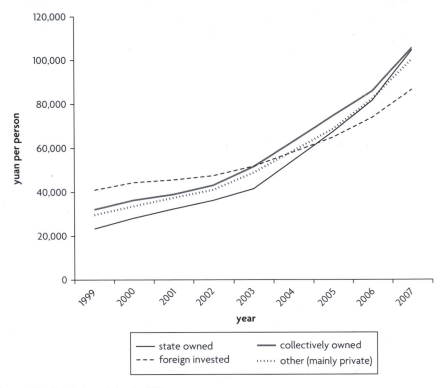

Source: China Light Industry Federation 2010.
Note: "Other" includes privately owned firms with and without foreign investment.

Market competition and the reform of state-owned enterprises led to a convergence in productivity among firms with different owner-ship structures (figure 1.5). In the 1980s and 1990s, labor productivity was some three times higher in firms with foreign investment than in domestic firms. Foreign companies had advantages in technology, management skills, and export channels to affluent markets; they also received preferential treatment in taxes and services. Massive privatiza-tion of state-owned and collective-owned enterprises reduced the pro-ductivity gap in the late 1990s. Average profits per worker in domestic and foreign-invested companies had become quite close by 2009 (China Light Industry Federation 2010).

## China Becomes a Light Manufacturing Export Powerhouse

As China's reforms took hold, the output of light manufactures rose, and sales moved into international markets, boosting China's trade ratio and its share of global trade (see table 1.3). This was made possible by the knowledge, finance, and networking effects of overseas Chinese (see above). China gradually assumed a leading position among trading countries. Its trade ratio, which rose from 29.8 percent in 1990 to 39.6 percent in 2000 and 50.3 percent in 2010, surpassed that of all other countries with populations greater than 100 million, including Japan and the United States. Trade was concentrated along the eastern seaboard, where trade ratios were even higher: 105.9 percent in Zhejiang Province and 122.9 percent in Guangdong Province in 2010 (NBS 2011).

Light manufactures were a large component of China's export surge. The country's share of global garment exports more than doubled over 1995–2008, accounting for a third of global flows in 2008 (table 1.6). Its share of global exports in the broader category of textiles and apparel rose from an average 5 percent during 1980–85 to 15 percent over 2000–05 and then doubled by 2010, reaching a third of global exports.

Comparing China's top 10 export categories in 2000 with those in 2010 shows both a large increase in exports of light manufactures and the category's relative decline in China's overall export mix (table 1.7). Over the period, export values nearly quadrupled

**Table 1.6  Share of Global Exports of Textiles and Apparel, China, 1980–2010**
*percent*

| Year | Textiles and apparel | Apparel |
|------|:---:|---:|
| 1980 | 4.6 | — |
| 1985 | 5.1 | — |
| 1990 | 6.3 | — |
| 1995 | 12.3 | 15.2 |
| 2000 | 14.6 | 18.2 |
| 2005 | 15.6 | 26.8 |
| 2008 | — | 33.2 |
| 2010 | 32.7 | — |

*Sources:* Textiles and apparel: Qiu 2005; "Sharply-Slowing Textile Exports Worry Industry," *China Daily*, June 1, 2012, http://www.chinadaily.com.cn/bizchina/2012-06/01/content_15443709.htm; apparel only: Gereffi and Frederick 2010.
*Note:* — = not available.

**Table 1.7  Top 10 Export Sectors, China, 2000 and 2010**
*$, billions*

| 2000 rank | Value | 2010 rank | Value |
|---|---|---|---|
| Electrical machinery and equipment | 46.0 | Electrical machinery and equipment | 388.8 |
| *Apparel* | 32.6 | Power generation equipment | 309.8 |
| Power generation equipment | 26.8 | *Apparel* | 121.1 |
| *Footwear and components* | 9.8 | Iron and steel | 68.1 |
| *Toys and games* | 9.2 | Optics and medical equipment | 52.1 |
| Iron and steel | 9.1 | *Furniture and bedding* | 50.6 |
| Mineral fuel and oil | 7.8 | Inorganic and organic chemicals | 43.2 |
| *Furniture and bedding* | 7.0 | Ships and boats | 40.3 |
| Inorganic and organic chemicals | 6.8 | Vehicles, excluding rail | 38.4 |
| *Leather and travel goods, handbags* | 6.6 | *Footwear and parts there of* | 35.6 |
| Value of light manufacturing exports in top 10 | 65.2 | Value of light manufacturing exports in top 10 | 207.3 |
| Total value of top 10 exports | 161.7 | Total value of top 10 exports | 1,148.0 |
| Light manufacturing share in top 10 exports, % | 40.3 | Light manufacturing share in top 10 exports, % | 18.1 |
| Light manufacturing share in total exports, % | 26.2 | Light manufacturing share in total exports, % | 13.1 |

*Sources:* Calculated by the United States–China Business Council from China Customs Statistics, https://www.uschina.org/; overall annual exports: NBS 2011.
*Note:* Light manufacturing exports are displayed in italics.

in apparel, more than tripled in footwear, and increased sevenfold in furniture. Despite these steep increases, light manufacturing fell from 5 categories among the top 10 export sectors to only 3; toys and leather goods dropped out of the list in 2010. Moreover, the share in overall exports of light manufacturing exports in the top 10 sectors fell by half, reflecting steep increases in the export sales of electrical machinery, power generation equipment, iron and steel, and optics and medical equipment.

While both the overall output value and the export value in six major segments of light manufacturing rose between 2001 and 2010, their share in overall industrial output fell slightly, from nearly 17 to 14 percent, while their share in industrial export value plunged from 28 percent to 16 percent, reflecting the extraordinary growth of new generations of export products (table 1.8).

**Table 1.8  Share of Major Light Manufacturing Sectors in Industrial Output, China, 2001–10**

| Sector, year | Gross output value, yuan, billions | Export value Yuan, billions | Export value As a share of gross output value, % |
|---|---|---|---|
| Light manufacturing industry total, 2001 | 9,544.9 | 1,624.5 | 17.0 |
| Food processing from farm products | 409.8 | 45.0 | 11.0 |
| Food manufacture | 162.8 | 14.3 | 8.8 |
| Textiles | 562.1 | 158.9 | 28.3 |
| Garments, footwear, hats | 259.6 | 135.5 | 52.2 |
| Leather and fur products | 157.3 | 89.0 | 56.6 |
| Furniture | 43.5 | 15.9 | 36.6 |
| Subtotal | 1,595.1 | 458.6 | 28.8 |
| Share in industry total, % | 16.7 | 28.2 | n.a. |
| Light manufacturing industry total, 2010 | 69,859.0 | 8,991.0 | 12.9 |
| Food processing from farm products | 3,492.8 | 198.2 | 5.7 |
| Food manufacture | 1,135.1 | 74.4 | 6.6 |
| Textiles | 2,850.8 | 462.0 | 16.2 |
| Garments, footwear, hats | 1,233.1 | 334.5 | 27.1 |
| Leather and fur products | 789.8 | 231.2 | 29.3 |
| Furniture | 441.5 | 120.3 | 27.2 |
| Subtotal | 9,943.1 | 1,420.6 | 14.3 |
| Share in industry total, % | 14.2 | 15.8 | n.a. |

*Sources:* For 2001: NBS-ITD 2002; for 2010: NBS-ITD 2011.

*Note:* Data are for above-scale enterprises (*guimo yishang*), an aggregate that includes all state sector firms and all other firms with annual sales above Y 5 million. n.a. = not applicable.

## What's Happening Now in Light Manufacturing?

Several factors have contributed to a reduction in the competitiveness of light manufacturing in Chinese coastal areas in recent years.

### Labor and Land Costs Are Rising

Labor costs have risen steeply in China's coastal regions (Heerink and others 2011) (table 1.9). Hefty increases in legal minimum wages reflect escalating difficulties in recruiting and retaining entry-level workers as well as official efforts to rein in income inequality. Nonetheless, average money wages have generally outpaced the rising statutory minimum: over 2000–08,

**Table 1.9  Wages in Selected Coastal Locations, China, 2000–12**

| Measure | 2000 | 2004 | 2008 | 2010 | 2012 |
|---|---|---|---|---|---|
| *Legal monthly minimum wage, yuan* | | | | | |
| Shandong | 320 | 410 | 610 | 920 | 1,240 |
| Shanghai | 445 | 635 | 960 | 1,120 | 1,450 |
| Jiangsu | 390 | 620 | 850 | 960 | 1,140 |
| Zhejiang | 410 | 620 | 960 | 1,100 | 1,310 |
| Fujian | 420 | 400 | 750 | 900 | 1,100 |
| Guangdong | 450 | 510 | 860 | 1,030 | 1,300 |
| Shenzhen | 547 | 610 | 1,000 | 1,100 | 1,500 |
| *Average annual wage* | | | | | |
| Shenzhen, yuan | 23,039 | 31,928 | 43,454 | 50,460 | 65,431[a] |
| Urban household consumer price index | 100 | 104 | 118 | 121 | — |
| Exchange rate, yuan to U.S. dollar | 8.28 | 8.28 | 6.94 | 6.77 | 6.36[b] |

*Sources:* Wage data for 2000–08: Wang 2011, except for Shenzhen, which is "2000–2010 nian Shenzhen pingjun gongzi biaozhun diaochengbiao" [Adjustment table for Shenzhen average wage standards, 2000–10] [in Chinese] (accessed August 17, 2012), http://www.jmxfw.com/job/201012/283916_1.html; wage data for Shenzhen, 2010–11: "Shenzhen 2009-nian yilai linian zhigong pingzhun gongzi he zuidi gongzi" [Average annual wages and minimum wages for Shenzhen since 2009] [in Chinese] (accessed August 17, 2012), http://blog.sina.com.cn/s/blog_6a4df4140100zars.html; other wage data for 2010: ODM Group 2010; other wage data for 2012: World Bank; consumer price index and exchange rate: NBS 2011.

*Note:* Numbers in italics indicate that the wage standard is at the upper end of a range of figures.
— = not available.
a. Data are for 2011.
b. Data as of August 18, 2012.

the ratio of average minimum wages to average money wages dropped all along China's coast: from 37 percent to 23 percent in Shandong, from 37 percent to 27 percent in Jiangsu, and from 34 percent to 29 percent in Zhejiang (Wang 2011). In Shenzhen, the statutory wage minimum rose 143 percent over 2000–11, while average money wages jumped 174 percent.

Under pressure from market forces and official regulations, nonwage labor costs have risen as well. New requirements oblige employers to contribute to safety net programs for pensions, unemployment benefits, and health care. Enforcement of workplace regulations on wages, hours, contracts, safety, and the environment has gradually intensified. To recruit and retain blue-collar workers and limit employee turnover (companies visited in July 2012 reported monthly labor turnover of up to 30 percent), companies have ramped up the provision of food, housing, entertainment, air conditioning, and other amenities.

**Table 1.10  Cost of Industrial Land in Dongguan, Guangzhou, and Shenzhen, China, 2001–08**
*yuan per square meter*

| Year | Dongguan | Guangzhou | Shenzhen Municipality Inside special zone | Shenzhen Municipality Outside special zone |
|------|----------|-----------|-------------------|--------------------|
| 2001 | 180 | — | 1,679 | 324 |
| 2002 | 200 | — | 2,647 | 329 |
| 2003 | 220 | — | 1,803 | 472 |
| 2004 | 240 | — | — | 376 |
| 2005 | 265 | — | 3,270 | 709 |
| 2006 | 301 | — | — | 1,158 |
| 2007 | 375 | 183[a] | — | 606,[a] 668 |
| 2008 | 606[a] | 444[a] | — | 624[a] |
| *Average of available data* | | | | |
| 2001–04 | 210 | — | 2,043 | 375 |
| 2005–08 | 387 | 314 | 3,270 | 782 |
| 2005–08 index, 2000–04 = 100 | 184 | — | 160 | 208 |

*Source:* Fan and Wu 2009.
*Note:* Data appear to represent the purchase price for 50-year utilization rights. — = not available.
a. Huang and others 2009.

Land costs have also risen steeply. All land in China is owned by the state. Industrial enterprises can acquire use rights, typically for a 50-year term, either directly from the state or from other users already granted rights. Transaction prices for industrial land in three cities in Guangdong Province, China's leading center for garments, toys, and other light manufacturing exports, show the rising trend (table 1.10). In Dongguan, China's top supplier of low-wage, labor-intensive export goods, average prices for industrial land were 84 percent higher in 2005–08 than in 2000–04. In Shenzhen, near Hong Kong SAR, China, land prices rose over the same period by 60 percent in the special economic zone and 108 percent in districts outside the special zone. In Guangzhou, land prices rose steeply in 2007/08.

## From Labor-Intensive to High-Technology Manufacturing and Services

Current Chinese policy is aimed at restructuring the economies of coastal export strongholds by replacing labor-intensive and environ-mentally damaging production with high-technology manufacturing and services. A major policy address by Wang Yang (2012), a Central Committee member and party secretary of Guangdong Province, emphasized the importance of "accelerating the transformation and upgrading of the economy." His plan for low-end manufacturing is clear:

> Only by changing the economic structure with an excessive share of low value added industries can we continue to raise workers' incomes, effectively increase domestic demand, and promote continued development of the economy.... [W]e must heavily emphasize the transformation and upgrading of traditional manufacturing industries and develop labor-intensive sectors with substantial technical and knowledge components. Strengthen brands, standards, patents.

Secretary Wang offered an explicit roster of desirable manufacturing sectors (automotive, shipbuilding, equipment for rail and air transportation, petrochemicals, steel, large-scale equipment) and services (finance, invention, research, design, logistics, and network services).

In an article describing economic policy statements by Guangdong Governor Zhu Xiaodan, *China Daily* quoted a local economist's suggestion that the province "should retain some low-end but not heavily polluting industries ... and promote innovative products" (W. Li 2012, 13).

Similar priorities are evident at the local level. Administrators of economic development zones in Jiangmen, in the Pearl River Delta, explain how to upgrade stronger firms and accelerate the closure of weaker ones using preferential electricity allocations:

> Power supply has not increased as rapidly as the demand. ... In peak seasons, power is in shortage. In that case, we prefer to serve enterprises with the best social and economic returns or higher productivity. If an enterprise is making losses or is of low productivity, we may advise it to stop production and distribute less power to it. (July 2012 interview)

This policy environment is reminiscent of Singapore's risky, but successful effort to transform its industrial structure during the 1980s (Leggett 2005). Government officials there took steps to drive up manufacturing wages, anticipating that rising labor costs would hasten the exit of low-end industries and that the high quality of Singapore's workforce, infrastructure, and governance would attract a new generation of more sophisticated, high–value added manufacturers regardless of the rise in labor costs.

## The Migration of Light Manufacturing to the Interior and to Low-Income Nations

As the share of the six main light manufacturing sectors—food processing from farm products; food manufacture; textiles; garments, footwear, hats; leather and fur products; and furniture—declined in domestic industrial output from 17 percent in 2001 to 14 percent in 2010 and their share in export sales tumbled from 28 percent to 16 percent, manufacturing operations migrated inland from the coastal regions (see table 1.8). *China Daily* (J. Li 2012a, 13) reported as follows:

> Costs, including those of labor and land, are now the main causes of Chinese processing-trade companies' decisions to move inland. ... [N]eighboring countries, including Vietnam, India, and the Philippines, have managed to attract overseas investments from China by offering lower costs and preferential policies.

Information about specific sectors confirms this view.

> [In textiles], the increasing cost of labor has spurred the transfer of low-level processing jobs to other Asian countries such as Bangladesh and Vietnam. ... Chinese textile producers will have to become more innovative to survive. (Zhang 2012, 16)

> Previously a huge advantage for the Chinese toy industry was the ... lower cost of labor and material, but [the manager of a Ningbo toy producer says that he] ... is now considering switching production to high-tech products such as electronics instead ... [and may have to] give up with this industry and target higher-profit goods. (Yu 2012, 15)

According to a Chengdu shoe executive, "rising costs ... have taken their toll on China's footwear manufacturers, who have done little to improve their core competitiveness ... as increasing costs drove orders for low-end footwear to emerging markets" (J. Li 2012b, 16).

An entrepreneur in a stainless steel product company in Jiangmen, Guangdong Province offered a similar account of how rising costs create pressures to relocate production:

> We made a rough calculation. Compared with that of five years ago, labor cost has increased by 50 percent. This has a huge effect on our business. Export to western countries is also greatly influenced by bad economic

situations. So we are exploring markets in developing countries. I have thought to move the manufacturing activities to Southeast Asia, but not to Africa yet. (July 2012 interview)

Cost pressures are influencing the China-based operations of foreign companies as well. Thus, the "German sportswear company Adidas … plans to shut down its only self-owned apparel factory in China, a move analysts said is in response to increasing costs in the country," while "rising wages in China led Coach to start looking for alternate places to make its wallets and handbags [with the intent of reducing] … China's share of its production to about 50 percent from almost 80 percent today."[8]

The government's Go Outward policy encourages direct overseas investment, which has grown explosively (table 1.11). From $2.7 billion in 2003, annual flows of nonfinancial overseas direct investment surged to $52.2 billion in 2008, $60.1 billion in 2011, and $77.2 billion in 2012.

"China will guide all sorts of companies to make orderly" investments abroad, Premier Wen Jiabao announced, and, while Wen focused on "energy, raw materials, agriculture, service, and infrastructure industries," policy changes aimed at facilitating these objectives also opened the door to the rapid expansion of offshore investments in labor-intensive light manufacturing (Ding 2012).

**Table 1.11  Outbound Nonfinancial FDI, China, 2003–12**
*$, billions*

| Year | Amount |
|------|--------|
| 2003 | 2.7 |
| 2004 | 2.9 |
| 2005 | 5.5 |
| 2006 | 12.3 |
| 2007 | 21.2 |
| 2008 | 52.2 |
| 2009 | 56.5 |
| 2010 | 68.8 |
| 2011 | 60.1 |
| 2012 | 77.2 |

*Sources:* For 2003–08: Ding 2009; for 2009–10: NBS 2011; for 2011: Ding 2012; for 2012: NBS 2013b.
*Note:* FDI = foreign direct investment.

The new policies explicitly encourage overseas investments by private businesses. Commerce Minister Chen Deming said in 2011 that the government would "launch more measures to aid companies investing overseas" because "China's outbound investment has created huge benefits for both China and other countries" (Ding 2011).

In August 2012, "China's top economic planner ... announced plans to make it easier for private companies to look for opportunities overseas" (Lan 2012). To this end, "the National Development and Reform Commission" has stipulated that official approval "will no longer be required ... for overseas resource development projects with an investment worth less than ... $10 million" that do not involve natural resources and that "nonresource projects with an investment of up to $100 million could be approved by provincial- and municipal-level authorities and not the central government" (Lan 2012).

## What China's Early Years of Development Tell Us

At the onset of the reforms, most Chinese did not have enough to eat. Private business occupied only a tiny fraction of the economy. At best, entrepreneurs were tolerated as a semilegal fringe of the planned economy. Rural markets, retail shops, street vendors, peddlers, private traders—key sources of business start-ups in most economies— languished under the prevailing ideology of extreme opposition to capitalism.

China's economy suffered from many of the same problems that beset today's poor countries, including weak infrastructure, a financial system that bypassed small business, endemic corruption, and high transaction costs.

Despite these obstacles, following the implementation of effective policies based on the endowment structure of the country, China's development during the early reform years shows that rapid growth can emerge from unlikely beginnings, that the right kind of government support can foster a turnaround, and that development can accelerate in the face of long odds (Lin 2012b).

# Notes

1. See "Chen Yun: XinZhongguo jingjizhanxian dianjiren" [Chen Yun: founder of new China's economy] [in Chinese], SINA, August 24, 2009, http://finance.sina.com.cn/roll/20090824/17036657167.shtml.
2. Most of this section and the data therein are taken from Rawski (1989).
3. "China: Literacy Rate," Index Mundi (accessed August 22, 2012), http://www.indexmundi.com/facts/china/literacy-rate.
4. "Make a Success of Special Economic Zones and Open More Cities to the Outside World," *People's Daily*, February 24, 1984.
5. The literature on the Chinese economy highlights interregional competition as one of the key drivers of Chinese economic growth. One major reason local governments have such a strong interest in fostering local economic development is the embedded interregional competition mechanism. See Qian and Weingast (1997); see also Cheung (2008); Xu (2011).
6. "For a Stronger Private Sector," Editorial, *China Daily*, U.S. edition, August 1, 2012, http://www.chinadaily.com.cn/opinion/2012-08/01/content_15636687.htm.
7. Private firms are included under the category referred to as "other" ownership in the figures and the data in Chinese sources, that is, other than the state or collectives, to avoid the still-discomfiting term private. The light industry category within China's industrial nomenclature covers most sectors discussed in this book under the heading of light manufacturing with the exception of textiles and garments. The Chinese concept of light industry also includes additional products, such as paper, bicycles, sewing machines, watches, and ceramics. The data coverage is both incomplete (some firms avoided identifying themselves to local offices of the Administration of Industry and Commerce) and distorted (some firms concealed private ownership behind false declarations of collective affiliation and showed ownership by local governments or some local public sector entity). In addition, private enterprises were underrepresented before 1999 because of the limited coverage of official data. Beginning in 1999, coverage was limited to enterprises with annual sales exceeding Y 5 million. Beginning in 2005, the ownership classification followed the affiliation of each firm's dominant investors. Data on 2004 are not available.
8. See Yang, Chen, "Adidas to Shut Down Factory in China," *Global Times*, July 19, 2012; "Gone to China: Not Coming Back," *Bloomberg Businessweek*, July 9–15, 2012: 27.

# References

Baten, Joerg, Debin Ma, Stephen Morgan, and Qing Wang. 2010. "Evolution of Living Standards and Human Capital in China in the 18–20th Centuries." *Explorations in Economic History* 47 (3): 347–59.

Bénétrix, Augustín S., Kevin H. O'Rourke and Jeffrey G. Williamson. 2012. "The Spread of Manufacturing to the Periphery 1870–2007: Eight Stylized Facts." University of Oxford Department of Economics Discussion Paper 617 (July). http://www.economics.ox.ac.uk/Research/wp/pdf/paper617.pdf.

Bramall, Chris. 1989. *Living Standards in Sichuan, 1931–1978*. London: Contemporary China Institute.

Brandt, Loren, and Thomas G. Rawski. 2008. "China's Great Economic Transformation." In *China's Great Economic Transformation*, edited by Loren Brandt and Thomas G. Rawski, 1–26. New York: Cambridge University Press.

Brandt, Loren, Thomas G. Rawski, and Xiaodong Zhu. 2008. "International Dimensions of China's Long Boom: Trends, Prospects and Implications." In *China's Rise and the Balance of Influence in Asia*, edited by William W. Keller and Thomas G. Rawski, 14–46. Pittsburgh: University of Pittsburgh Press.

Brown, Jeremy. 2012. *City Versus Countryside in Mao's China*. Cambridge, U.K.: Cambridge University Press.

CADZ (China Association of Development Zones). 1989. *Zhongguo kaifaqu nianjian 1989* [China development zones yearbook 1989]. [In Chinese.] Beijing: China Financial and Economic Publishing House.

Chan, Anita, Richard Madsen, and Jonathan Unger. 1992. *Chen Village under Mao and Deng*. 2nd ed. Berkeley, CA: University of California Press.

Cheung, Steven N. S. 2008. *The Economic System of China*. Hong Kong SAR, China: Arcadia Press.

China Light Industry Federation. 2010. *Zhongguo qinggongye nianjian 2010* [China light industry yearbook 2010]. [In Chinese.] Beijing: China Light Industry Yearbook Press.

Chu, David K. Y. 1985. "The Politico-economic Background to the Development of Special Economic Zones." In *Modernization in China: The Case of the Shenzhen Special Economic Zone*, edited by Kwan-Yiu Wong and David K. Y. Chu, 24–39. Hong Kong SAR, China: Oxford University Press.

Ding, Qingfen. 2009. "Outbound Investment Unlikely to Outstrip FDI." *China Daily*, July 2. http://www.chinadaily.com.cn/china/2009-07/02/content_8344945.htm.

———. 2011. "China to Help Firms Investing Abroad." *China Daily*, September 9. http://www.chinadaily.com.cn/usa/business/2011-09/09/content_13655892.htm.

———. 2012. "Wen Vows to Boost ODI, Foreign Trade." *China Daily*, March 6. http://www.chinadaily.com.cn/bizchina/2012-03/06/content_14768495.htm.

Dong, Fureng. 1990. "The Wenzhou Model for Developing the Rural Commodity Economy." In *Market Forces in China, Competition and Small Business: The Wenzhou Debate*, edited by Peter Nolan and Fureng Dong, 77–96. London: Zed Books.

Donnithorne, Audrey. 1972. "China's Cellular Economy: Some Economic Trends since the Cultural Revolution." *China Quarterly* 52: 605–19.

Editorial Committee. 1989. *Zhongguo xiangzhen qiye nianjian* [China township and village enterprise yearbook 1989]. [In Chinese.] Beijing: Nongye chubanshe.

———. 1993. *Zhongguo xiangzhen qiye nianjian* [China township and village enterprise yearbook 1993]. [In Chinese.] Beijing: Nongye chubanshe.

Elvin, Mark. 2010. "The Environmental Impasse in Late Imperial China." In *China's Rise in Historical Perspective*, edited by Brantley Womack, 152–69. Lanham, MD: Rowman & Littlefield.

Elvin, Mark, and Ts'ui-jung Liu, eds. 1998. *Sediments of Time: Environment and Society in Chinese History*. New York: Cambridge University Press.

Estrin, Saul, and Tomasz Mickiewicz. 2010. "Entrepreneurship in Transition Economies: The Role of Institutions and Generational Change." IZA Discussion Paper 4805, Institute for the Study of Labor, Bonn.

Fan Gang and Wu Liangcheng. 2009. *Chengshihua: yi xilie gonggong zhengce de jihe* [Urbanization: assembling a series of public policies]. [In Chinese.] Beijing: Zhongguo jingji chubanshe.

FBIS (Foreign Broadcast Information Service). 1981. "Daily Report: China." October 27. U.S. Department of Commerce, Washington, DC.

Friedman, Edward, Paul G. Pickowicz, and Mark Selden. 1991. *Chinese Village, Socialist State*. New Haven, CT: Yale University Press.

Gardella, Robert. 1994. *Harvesting Mountains: Fujian and the China Tea Trade, 1757–1937*. Berkeley, CA: University of California Press.

Gereffi, Gary, and Stacey Frederick. 2010. "The Global Apparel Value Chain: Challenges and Opportunities for Developing Countries." Policy Research Working Paper 5281, World Bank, Washington, DC.

Han Fei-tzu. 1959. *The Complete Works of Han Fei-tzu: A Classic of Chinese Political Science*. Vol. 2. Translated by W. K. Liao. London: Arthur Probsthain. http://xtf.lib.virginia.edu/xtf/view?docId=2003_Q4/uvaGenText/tei/z000000042.xml.

Han, Sun Sheng, and Clifton W. Pannell. 1999. "The Geography of Privatization in China, 1978–1996." *Economic Geography* 75 (3): 272–96.

He, Liyi. 2003. *Mr. China's Son: A Villager's Life*. Boulder, CO: Westview Press.

Heerink, N., F. Qu, X. Shi, B. M. Fleisher, R. Fearn, Z. Ye, and M.-F. Renard, eds. 2011. "Sustainable Natural Resource Use in Rural China: Has China Passed the Lewis Turning Point?" *China Economic Review* 22 (4): 441–692.

Heilmann, Sebastian, and Elizabeth J. Perry, eds. 2011. *Mao's Invisible Hand: The Political Foundations of Adaptive Governance in China*. Harvard Contemporary China Studies 17. Cambridge, MA: Harvard University Press.

Hou, Fengyun. 1999. *Zhongguo renliziben xingcheng ji xianzhuang* [Formation and present circumstances of human capital in China]. [In Chinese.] Beijing: Jingji kexue chubanshe. http://house.qingdaonews.com/content/2012-04/28/content_9213986.htm.

Huang Qing, Sun Weidong, Yang Zhongguang, and Lu Jing. 2009. *Guanyu jianshe yongdi gongying he kaifa liyong qingquang de diaocha baogao* [Survey report on conditions of supply, development, and use of land for construction]. [In Chinese.] Guangzhou, China: Land Utilization Department, Guangdong Land Office. http://www.landchina.com.

Huang Shu-ming. 1989. *The Spiral Road: Change in a Chinese Village through the Eyes of a Communist Party Leader*. Boulder, CO: Westview Press.

ILO (International Labour Organization). 1937. *The World Textile Industry: Economic and Social Problems*. 2 vols. Geneva: International Labour Office.

Jiang Xiaojuan. 2006. "New Stage of China's Opening Up." [In Chinese.] *Jingji yanjiu* [Economic research] 3: 4–14.

Kraus, Richard A. 1980. *Cotton and Cotton Goods in China, 1918–1936*. New York: Garland Publishing.

Kuran, Timur. 1995. *Private Truths, Public Lies*. Cambridge, MA: Harvard University Press.

Lan Lan. 2012. "Economic Planners Ease Conditions for Overseas Bidding." *China Daily*, August 10. http://www.chinadaily.com.cn/business/2012-08/10/content_15657766.htm.

Lardy, Nicholas R. 1984. "Consumption and Living Standards in China, 1978–83." *China Quarterly* 100: 849–65.

Leggett, C. 2005. "The Fourth Transformation of Singapore's Industrial Relations." "Proceedings of the 19th Annual Conference of the Association of Industrial Relations Academics of Australia and New Zealand, Sydney, February 9–11," 347–56.

León, Lorena Rivera. 2007. "Understanding the Potential Macroeconomic Impact of the Implementation of Technologies for Digital Business Ecosystems in Europe." PowerPoint presentation, Directorate General for Communications Networks, Content, and Technology, European Commission, Brussels. http://www.digital-ecosystems.org/events/2007.01/macroeconomic-impact.pdf.

Li Guowu. 2009. "Spatial Distribution, Growth Process, and Leading Industries of Province-Level Development Zones in China." [In Chinese.] *Chengshi fazhan yanjiu* [Urban studies] 16 (5): 1–6.

Li, Jiabao. 2012a. "Westward Ho! For China's Processing Trade." *China Daily*, U.S. edition, June 26.

———. 2012b. "Nation's Shoemakers Search for Survival Strategies." *China Daily*, U.S. edition, June 26.

Li, Wenfang. 2012. "Guangdong Governor Pledges to Prioritize Local Consumption." *China Daily*, U.S. edition, July 13.

Lin, Justin Yifu. 2012a. *Demystifying the Chinese Economy*. Cambridge, U.K.: Cambridge University Press.

———. 2012b. *New Structural Economics: A Framework for Rethinking Development and Policy*. Washington, DC: World Bank.

Lyons, Thomas P., and Victor Nee. 1994. *The Economic Transformation of South China: Reform and Development in the Post-Mao Era*. Cornell East Asia Series 70. Ithaca, NY: East Asia Program, Cornell University.

Mead, Robert W. 2000. "An Examination of China's Agricultural Reforms: The Importance of Private Plots." *China Economic Review* 11 (1): 54–78.

Minying. 2009. "2008-nian Zhongguo minying jingji fazhan xingshi fenxi" [Analyzing the situation of China's private sector development in 2008]. [In Chinese.] *Xinwen zhongxin Zhongguo wang.* http://www.china.com.cn/news/zhuanti/09myjjlps/2009-09/25/content_18603550_4.htm.

Naughton, Barry. 1995. *Growing Out of the Plan.* New York: Cambridge University Press.

———. 2007. *The Chinese Economy: Transitions and Growth.* Cambridge, MA: MIT Press.

———. 2008. "A Political Economy of China's Economic Transition." In *China's Great Economic Transformation,* edited by Loren Brandt and Thomas G. Rawski, 91–135. New York: Cambridge University Press.

NBS (National Bureau of Statistics of China). 1990. *Quanguo gesheng zizhiqu zhixiashi lishi tongji ziliao huibian* [Compilation of statistical materials for China and for its provinces, autonomous regions, and municipalities]. [In Chinese.] Beijing: China Statistics Press.

———. 1996. *Gaige kaifang shiqinian de Zhongguo diqu jingji* [China regional economy: a profile of 17 years of reform and opening-up]. [In Chinese.] Beijing: China Statistics Press.

———. 2000a. *Zhongguo gongye jiaotong nengyuan 50-nian tongji ziliao huibian 1949–1999* [Fifty-year collected statistics on China's industry, transport, and energy, 1949–1999]. [In Chinese.] Beijing: China Statistics Press.

———. 2000b. *China Statistical Yearbook.* Beijing: China Statistics Press.

———. 2005. *Xin Zhongguo wushiwunian tongji ziliao huibian 1949–2004* [China: 55-year compendium of statistics 1949–2004]. [In Chinese.] Beijing: China Statistics Press.

———. 2011. *China Statistical Yearbook.* Beijing: China Statistics Press.

———. 2013a. China Statistical Database. National Bureau of Statistics of China, Beijing. http://219.235.129.58/welcome.do#.

———. 2013b. "2012 nian guomin jingji fazhan wenzhong youjin" [Stable progress for the national economy in 2012.] [In Chinese.] January 18. NBS, Beijing. http://www.stats.gov.cn/tjfx/jdfx/t20130118_402867146.htm.

NBS-ITD (Industry and Transportation Department, National Bureau of Statistics of China). 2001. *Zhongguo gongye jingji tongji nianjian 2001* [China industrial economy statistics yearbook 2001]. [In Chinese.] Beijing: China Statistics Press.

———. 2002. *Zhongguo gongye jingji tongji nianjian 2002* [China industrial economy statistics yearbook 2002]. [In Chinese.] Beijing: China Statistics Press.

———. 2011. *Zhongguo gongye jingji tongji nianjian 2011* [China industrial economy statistics yearbook 2011]. [In Chinese.] Beijing: China Statistics Press.

Nolan, Peter. 1990. "Petty Commodity Production in a Socialist Economy: Chinese Rural Development Post-Mao." In *Market Forces in China, Competition and*

*Small Business: The Wenzhou Debate*, edited by Peter Nolan and Fureng Dong, 7–42. London: Zed Books.

ODM Group. 2010. "Minimum Wage by Province in China, 2010." ODM Group, Hong Kong SAR, China. http://www.theodmgroup.com/2010/08/26/minimum-wage-by-province-in-china-2010/.

Oi, Jean C. 1999. *Rural China Takes Off: The Institutional Foundations of Economic Reform*. Berkeley, CA: University of California Press.

OTNIC (Office of the Third National Industrial Census). 1997. *Zhonghua renmin gongheguo 1995-nian disanci quanguo gongye pucha ziliao zhaiyao* [Abstract of materials from the PRC third industrial census of 1995]. [In Chinese.] Beijing: China Statistics Press.

Parish, William L., and Martin King Whyte. 1978. *Village and Family in Contemporary China*. Chicago: University of Chicago Press.

Perdue, Peter C. 1987. *Exhausting the Earth: State and Peasant in Hunan, 1500–1850*. Cambridge, MA: Harvard University Press.

Perkins, Dwight H. 1966. *Market Control and Planning in Communist China*. Cambridge, MA: Harvard University Press.

———, ed. 1977. *Rural Small-Scale Industry in the People's Republic of China*. Berkeley, CA: University of California Press.

———. 1995. "The Transition from Central Planning: East Asia's Experience." In *Social Capability and Long-Term Economic Growth*, edited by Bon Ho Koo and Dwight H. Perkins, 221–41. New York: St. Martin's Press.

Polanyi, Karl. 1944. *The Great Transformation: The Political and Economic Origins of Our Time*. New York: Farrar and Rinehart.

Qian, Yingyi, and Barry R. Weingast. 1997. "Federalism as a Commitment to Preserving Market Incentives." *Journal of Economic Perspective* 11 (4): 83–92.

Qiu, Larry D. 2005. "China's Textile and Clothing Industry." School of Business and Management, Department of Economics, Hong Kong University of Science and Technology, Kowlon, Hong Kong SAR, China. http://s3.amazonaws.com/zanran_storage/www.bm.ust.hk/ContentPages/18112599.pdf.

Rachman, Gideon. 2012. "Book Review: China's Official History of Foreign Repression." *Financial Times*, August 27: 6.

Rawski, Evelyn S. 1979. *Education and Popular Literacy in Ch'ing China*. Ann Arbor, MI: University of Michigan Press.

Rawski, Thomas G. 1980. *China's Transition to Industrialism*. Ann Arbor, MI: University of Michigan Press.

———. 1989. *Economic Growth in Prewar China*. Berkeley, CA: University of California Press.

———. 2006a. "Recent Developments in China's Labor Economy." In *Restructuring China*, edited by Katsuji Nakagane and Tomoyuki Kojima, 18–47. Tokyo: Toyo Bunko.

————. 2006b. "Social Capabilities and Chinese Economic Growth." In *Social Change in Contemporary China*, edited by Wenfang Tang and Burkart Holzner, 89–103. Pittsburgh, PA: University of Pittsburgh Press.

————. 2011. "Human Resources and China's Long Economic Boom." *Asia Policy* 12 (July): 33–78.

ResearchinChina. 2012. "China Leather Shoes Industry Report, 2012." Report YSJ055 (September), ResearchinChina, Beijing. http://www.researchinchina .com/htmls/report/2012/6530.html.

Romer, Paul. 1993. "Idea Gaps and Object Gaps in Economic Development." *Journal of Monetary Economics* 32 (3): 543–73.

Sachs, Jeffrey D., and Wing Thye Woo. 1997. "Understanding China's Economic Performance." NBER Working Paper 5935, National Bureau of Economic Research, Cambridge, MA.

Shapiro, Judith. 2001. *Mao's War against Nature: Politics and the Environment in Revolutionary China*. New York: Cambridge University Press.

Thaxton, Ralph A. Jr. 2008. *Catastrophe and Contention in Rural China*. New York: Cambridge University Press.

Tsai, Kellee S. 2002. *Back-Alley Banking: Private Entrepreneurs in China*. Ithaca, NY: Cornell University Press.

TVES (Township and Village Enterprise Services, Ministry of Agriculture). 1986. *Xiangzhen qiye tongji zhaiyao* [Abstract of statistical materials on township and village enterprises (1978–85)]. [In Chinese.] Beijing: Nongmuyuyebu xiangzhenqiyeju.

Wang, Jici, and John H. Bradbury. 1986. "Changing Industrial Geography of Chinese Special Economic Zones." *Economic Geography* 62: 307–20.

Wang Mei. 2011. *Zuidi gongzi yu Zhongguo laodongli shichang* [Effects of minimum wages on China's labor market]. [In Chinese.] Beijing: Zhongguo jingji chubanshe.

Wang Yang 2012. "Zhichi shehuizhuyi shichang jingji de gaige fangxiang jiakuai zhuanxing shengji jianshe xingfu Guangdong" [Support the reform path of the socialist market economy, accelerate transformation and upgrading to build a prosperous Guangdong]. [In Chinese.] *Nanfang ribao* [Southern Daily], May 16: A01–A03.

Wang, Zheng. 2012. *Never Forget National Humiliation: Historical Memory in Chinese Politics and Foreign Relations*. New York: Columbia University Press.

Wang, Zhikai. 2008. *The Private Sector and China's Market Development*. Chandos Asian Studies. Oxford: Chandos Publishing.

World Bank. 2005. *China: Integration of National Product and Factor Markets; Economic Benefits and Policy Recommendations*. Report 31973-CHA (June 13). Washington, DC: Poverty Reduction and Economic Management Unit, East Asia and Pacific Region, World Bank. https://openknowledge.worldbank.org/ handle/10986/8690.

Wright, Tim. 1984. *Coal Mining in China's Economy and Society, 1895–1937*. New York: Cambridge University Press.

Wu Yong and Liu Ce. 2012. "Shenyang Stores Close Amid Inspection Rumors." *China Daily*, U.S. edition, August 8.

Xinhua News Agency. 1975. *New China's First Quarter-Century*. Beijing: Foreign Languages Press.

Xu, Chenggang. 2011. "The Fundamental Institutions of China's Reforms and Development." *Journal of Economic Literature* 49 (4): 1076–1151.

Yang, Dali. 1996. *Calamity and Reform in China: State, Rural Society, and Institutional Change since the Great Leap Famine*. Stanford, CA: Stanford University Press.

Yu, Ran. 2012. "SME Manufacturers Hammered by European Economic Slump." *China Daily*, U.S. edition, August 16.

Yuan Weiping and Debin Ma. 2010. "Merchant Account Books and Economic History Research, the Case of Tongtai Sheng Business Accounts." [In Chinese.] *Zhongguo jingjishi yanjiu* [Research on Chinese economic history] 2.

Zhang, Xiaobo, and Kong-Yam Tan. 2007. "Incremental Reform and Distortions in China's Product and Factor Markets." *World Bank Economic Review* 21 (2): 279–99. https://openknowledge.worldbank.org/handle/10986/4458.

Zhang, Yuwei. 2012. "Textile Sector Frayed, but Resilient." *China Daily, USA Business Weekly*, August 3–9.

Zhao Ziyang, Pu Bao, Renee Chiang, Adi Ignatius, and Roderick MacFarquhar. 2009. *Prisoner of the State: The Secret Journal of Zhao Ziyang*. New York: Simon & Schuster.

Zhou, Feng. 2011. "Give SMEs a Fighting Chance." *China Daily*, U.S. edition, August 4.

# Resolving the Binding Constraints

## Introduction

The companion volume, *Light Manufacturing in Africa*, lays out a comprehensive rationale for focusing on basic light manufacturing in low-income economies and emphasizes the feasibility of entering domestic and global markets despite limited capital, knowledge, skills, infrastructure, and market-supporting institutions (Dinh and others 2012). This chapter addresses two simple, direct questions: Did the constraints highlighted in the companion study affect the efforts to create light manufacturing clusters in China beginning in the late 1970s? And, if so, how did Chinese entrepreneurs and governments deal with these constraints? The answers, which show how energy, persistence, and cooperation can overcome substantial obstacles, demonstrate the potential for breakthroughs elsewhere despite initial handicaps.

# Six Binding Constraints on the Growth of Light Manufacturing

*Light Manufacturing in Africa* identifies six binding constraints on African competitiveness in light manufacturing:

- The availability, cost, and quality of inputs
- Access to industrial land
- Access to finance
- Trade logistics
- Entrepreneurial capabilities, both technical and managerial
- Worker skills

We now examine the challenges represented by these constraints.

### Input Availability, Cost, and Quality: Inability to Deliver Inputs on Time

Because inputs typically account for more than 70 percent of the cost of light manufacturing products, a small variation in the price of inputs can wipe out any labor cost advantage that might be available. Beyond price competitiveness, countries increasingly compete on their capacity for the timely delivery of large quantities of products of consistently high quality. Success depends on access to diversified, reliable, and plentiful sources of good inputs. Even simple products require many inputs; a padlock, for example, has at least 12 parts.

Examples of major policy issues involved in input sourcing include import tariffs (all sectors), weak or incomplete local supply chains (for instance, the provision of fabrics, buttons, zippers, ribbons, and other inputs needed by garment makers), price controls and export bans on agricultural products, barriers to the importation and distribution of high-yield seeds, and disease control in the livestock sector.

### Access to Industrial Land: Deficits in Industry-Ready Land

The inability to buy or lease industrial land can cripple efforts by both small and large firms to take advantage of market opportunities and reach competitive operational scale. Small firms need land to set up and expand; larger firms need land to add to their factories and warehouses; and both can benefit from using land as collateral for loans.

## Access to Finance: Inadequate

While most entrepreneurs rely on personal savings and the savings of family and friends to start up a business, expansion requires access to finance. All growing firms, especially small and medium ones, need additional resources to purchase new equipment, upgrade technology, improve buildings, and buy land. Small firms often lack good access to formal finance. Even if finance is available, inadequate collateral and lack of a credit rating may block access to loans.

## Trade Logistics: Too Many Delays and Gaps

Poor trade logistics—slow and inefficient transport, border delays, and inadequate communications—penalize firms that rely on imported inputs and hit exporters coming and going. In addition to raising costs, poor trade logistics cause production and shipping delays that often disqualify producers from competing for contracts with global buyers, especially in the time-sensitive apparel industry.

## Entrepreneurial Capabilities, Both Technical and Managerial: In Short Supply

Entrepreneurial capabilities encompass the managerial, technical, and commercial skills of firm owners and managers, often the same person in small enterprises. Managerial skills ensure that production is efficient and reliable and that the business is profitable, well known, and respected. Technical skills include the expertise and ability to develop new products and improve the quality or change the features of existing products in response to shifts in market demand. Commercial skills include the ability to spot opportunities; avoid market and regulatory risks; deal with customers, workers, suppliers, business rivals, and government officials; and respond quickly and effectively to unexpected opportunities and risks to business ventures of any size. Shortcomings in the production process attributable to weak entrepreneurial and technical skills, such as production waste and unreliable delivery, can lead to a drop-off in competitiveness.

## Worker Skills: Still Lacking

Worker capabilities reflect formal education (literacy and numeracy), work experience, and attitudes, including the enthusiasm of workers for learning new skills and routines, their willingness to cooperate with unfamiliar partners, and their desire to trade leisure for higher incomes.

## Neutralizing the Six Constraints in China

Chinese producers have achieved success in creating and expanding light manufacturing industries and clusters despite formidable obstacles.

### Input Availability, Cost, and Quality: Gradually Expanding Clusters and Markets

Before China's reforms began, inputs, final goods, labor, and capital were allocated by the state. Although planning was considerably more decentralized in China than in the Soviet Union, with provincial and even local governments assuming considerable responsibility for the allocation of inputs, lack of access to inputs was a major obstacle to the early growth of light manufacturing clusters.

**Self-reliance and antimarket ideology.** Material balance planning and the antibusiness ideology of the 1950s to the late 1970s severely truncated marketing arrangements. Widespread closure of retail and wholesale markets during the Great Leap Forward of the late 1950s was followed in the late 1960s and early 1970s by the disruptions of commerce associated with the Cultural Revolution. For example, the number of retail outlets in Guangzhou, the capital of Guangdong Province, shrank from 3.8 per 100 population to 0.3 between 1957 and 1978 (Vogel 1989).

The market organizations that did survive were swaddled in red tape. Factory managers faced tight limits on cash transactions. Outside traders seeking to attend rural markets were required to obtain "letters of introduction furnished by industrial or commercial departments, at or above the level of the *hsien* [county] in the areas from which they came" and also had to "seek the approval of local market control organs" (Donnithorne 1967, 297–98). Even individual peddlers needed licenses to attend local markets. They could move goods in search of higher prices, but not "if the two places concerned are far apart." Although flagrantly irrational arrangements led to calls for "economically appropriate methods" (Donnithorne 1967, 308), politically inspired disruptions of large and small commercial links were common. A 1992 analysis focused on Fujian Province, but, reflecting circumstances that appeared typical of other coastal provinces, concluded that "when they seek to obtain current inputs, farmers and small businessmen face a byzantine and unreliable supply system" (Lyons 1994, 151).

Local protectionism, a legacy of the emphasis on local self-reliance begun during the Great Leap Forward of the late 1950s, erected another barrier to domestic commerce. Provinces and even counties sought to limit their (domestic) imports and exports of products such as grain, cotton, wool, and tobacco. This restrictive behavior partly reflected the lingering fear of food shortages, but price distortions also contributed. The systematic underpricing of farm products inflated the financial rewards to processors of farm goods, thereby leading governments to steer local produce to processing plants under their control rather than to more efficient factories in external jurisdictions (Findlay 1991; Watson, Findlay, and Du 1989).

In some sectors, the combined impact of self-reliance and antimarket ideology undermined the supply of materials for light manufacturing.

> During 10 years of "Cultural Revolution" [1966–76], many traditional products of the leather industry were labeled as feudal, capitalist, or revisionist items; leather shoes were banned from entering the market. ... Toward the end of the Cultural Revolution period, the Ministry of Light Industry faced a serious shortage of hides, the material for making leather shoes. (China Light Industry Federation 2010, 607)

The planning system's well-documented tendency to focus on quantity at the expense of quality, innovation, precision, timing, packaging, customer service, and other vital dimensions of supplier behavior left a powerful imprint on China's industrial economy. Producers routinely churned out goods with small defects. For example, Shanghai's garment exporters used imported equipment because Shanghai-made sewing machines, China's best at the time, leaked oil onto the fabric being sewn.

Fearing that unreliable suppliers would disrupt efforts to meet annual plan targets (essential to the career prospects of managers), firms pursued vertical integration and shunned arrangements that increased dependence on outsiders. A 1965 report illustrates this tendency:

> When at first Tsinan [Jinan] Automobile works planned to give the job of casting iron parts to other plants ... cadres ... feared that factories in cooperation would not be able to deliver the goods in time [to meet plan targets]. After three major debates ... some cadres still insisted on having a part of the products manufactured in their own plant. Later, the Party

committee … decided to have three months of stock ready before resolutely cooperating with other plants. (Rawski 1980, 129)

As a result, China's prereform industrial structures tilted away from the specialization and division of labor that are the lifeblood of industrial clustering. Widespread suspicion of interdependence limited opportunities for start-up firms to build experience, reputation, and assets by producing parts and components for established producers.

**Cluster formation and expanding markets.** Light manufacturing clusters originated in activities on the fringes of the planned economy. While the plan system focused on transactions mediated by government agencies and instructed suppliers to deliver specific quantities of particular goods at official prices, the new clusters operated entirely outside the plan system. Firms worked with information garnered through semilegal peddling, with materials that were discarded by larger firms or assembled through a variety of unauthorized channels, and with equipment that was self-made or scavenged from state enterprises.

Although the planned economy aimed for full control of important materials, limited capacity to assemble information (no computers or faxes, limited telephone networks), process data (no computers, few desktop calculators), and distribute instructions (no photocopiers, computers, or fax machines, limited telephone networks) meant that plan provisions often clashed with actual requirements even when firms and local governments provided planners with accurate information rather than seeking advantage by submitting false reports. Managers resorted to barter to fill the inevitable gaps, allowing large leaks of materials, equipment, and products from plan channels. To obtain urgently needed supplies and equipment, Chinese firms deployed agents known as *caigouyuan* to get around the ineffective system of planning and allocation. Chinese regulations even allowed "certain provinces and cities … to establish purchasing offices at industrial centers" (Donnithorne 1967, 291).

These informal procedures, though frowned on by plan authorities, sometimes developed into widely recognized institutions. A 1958 report related the following:

A Shanghai teahouse, which, in the old days, had been a center for rice dealers and certain other traders … now was an acknowledged mart for metals and machinery, with patrons coming from all parts of China. For example, a man from Inner Mongolia, charged with buying a generator, had failed to get a suitable one ... through the usual channels ... but succeeded when visiting this teahouse. ... Shanghai ... [served as] a nationwide market where goods unprocurable elsewhere could be obtained ... partly because of the activities of "a group of people acting as intermediaries for disposing or getting hold of many of the privately held items not obtainable on the market." (Donnithorne 1967, 290)

Scattered evidence confirms the survival of spontaneous capitalism throughout the period of socialist planning and rural collectivization (Donnithorne 1967). These informal operations, often straddling vaguely defined boundaries between legitimate and extralegal activities, facilitated the emergence of the small light manufacturing start-ups that formed the basis for large and successful light manufacturing clusters (see chapter 3 for more details).

National reforms that began in the late 1970s, though focused on large-scale operations, state enterprises, and urban manufacturing, had beneficial side effects on private operators. Initiatives that allowed state-owned firms to retain a small share of their earnings provided enough incentive for managers to consider profitability. In turn, this increased the willingness to try cost-reducing subcontracting arrangements with small firms.

While reforms did not eliminate the state allocation of materials, which continued into the 1990s, the reforms did move above-quota production into market or semimarket channels, which expanded as the economy grew. The dual price system introduced in 1984, which allowed for some unplanned and unallocated production of most commodities, enlarged the scope for the market-based distribution of industrial inputs, intermediate goods, equipment, and building materials. While designed to complement the expanding rights of state-owned firms to deploy retained earnings and to sell above-quota output, the reforms provided new opportunities for rural firms and start-ups to acquire materials, expertise, and sales outlets. The growth of retail business both within and beyond the dominant network of state-owned retail outlets was hugely important to the emergence of light manufacturing clusters.

Although detailed information is lacking for the early reform years, we do possess data that illuminate the gradual expansion in market opportunities. The farm sector, which provides key inputs for textiles, food processing, and leatherworking, remained under tight control during the early reform years. Government-mandated prices applied to more than 90 percent of all agricultural goods in 1978 and close to 80 percent as late as 1983 before dropping to about 75 percent in 1984 and 40 percent in 1985 (EAAU 1997).

The 1985 industrial census showed that enterprise self-sales accounted for 68 percent of heavy manufactures and 61 percent of light industrial goods, but only 33 percent of industrial materials and 24 percent of mining products (Naughton 1995). The shift toward market-determined prices for production materials lagged behind comparable changes affecting retail goods and agricultural products (table 2.1). As late as 1990, only 36 percent of production materials changed hands at market-determined prices. The decisive turn came in 1992, when the share of production materials transacted at market prices jumped to 74 percent. This reform sequence meant that emerging light manufacturing clusters could find opportunities to sell their products, but might still have trouble obtaining inputs.

**How the state contributed inputs.** While accounts of cluster formation in Zhejiang Province emphasize the central role of thousands of household firms, government cooperation and support were essential to local economic development (chapter 3). In the early stages of cluster development in Zhejiang, the government contributed especially by easing supply constraints and establishing and upgrading markets in two ways.

*Freeing up materials for market allocation.* Official efforts to ease supply constraints on local manufacturers are evident from the provincial shares of market-determined prices for retail sales, agricultural commodities, and production materials (table 2.2). Though these data are for 1994, more than 15 years after the start of reform, they show clearly the unusual circumstances in Guangdong and Zhejiang provinces. China's two leaders in private sector manufacturing allowed more than 90 percent of production materials to flow through market channels. No other provinces reached this level.

**Table 2.1 Price Determination in Commodity Markets, by State or Market, China, 1990–96**

*percent*

| Market and year | State order | State guidance | Market forces |
| --- | --- | --- | --- |
| *Retail commodities* | | | |
| 1990 | 29.8 | 17.2 | 53.0 |
| 1991 | 20.9 | 10.3 | 68.8 |
| 1992 | 5.9 | 1.1 | 93.0 |
| 1993 | 4.8 | 1.4 | 93.8 |
| 1994 | 7.2 | 2.4 | 90.4 |
| 1995 | 8.8 | 2.4 | 88.8 |
| 1996 | 6.3 | 1.2 | 92.5 |
| *Agricultural products* | | | |
| 1990 | 25.0 | 23.4 | 51.6 |
| 1991 | 22.2 | 20.0 | 57.8 |
| 1992 | 12.5 | 5.7 | 81.8 |
| 1993 | 10.4 | 2.1 | 87.5 |
| 1994 | 16.6 | 4.1 | 79.3 |
| 1995 | 17.0 | 4.4 | 78.6 |
| 1996 | 16.9 | 4.1 | 79.0 |
| *Production materials* | | | |
| 1990 | 44.6 | 19.0 | 36.4 |
| 1991 | 36.0 | 18.3 | 45.7 |
| 1992 | 18.7 | 7.5 | 73.8 |
| 1993 | 13.8 | 5.1 | 81.1 |
| 1994 | 14.7 | 5.3 | 80.0 |
| 1995 | 15.6 | 6.5 | 77.9 |
| 1996 | 14.0 | 4.9 | 81.1 |

*Sources:* Guo 1995; EBCPY 1996, 1997.

***Establishing and upgrading markets.*** Zhang (1990, 97–101) writes of Wenzhou, in Zhejiang Province, that

> the basic precondition for the successful development of Wenzhou's rural commodity economy is the establishment of an open market network. [During the 1980s] about 415 commodity markets of different sizes emerged in Wenzhou's villages. … Most of Wenzhou's rural commodity markets are located on the sites of traditional country fairs. … *[M]ost*

**Table 2.2  Share of Prices Determined by Market Forces, by Commodity Type and Province, China, 1994**

*percent*

| Province | Retail sales | Agricultural commodities | Production materials |
|---|---|---|---|
| *National average* | *90.4* | *79.3* | — |
| Anhui | 91.9 | 81.7 | 85.5 |
| Beijing | 79.0 | 94.2 | 68.8 |
| Fujian | 91.9 | 91.0 | 87.1 |
| Gansu | 87.8 | 85.0 | 77.9 |
| Guangdong | 92.6 | 98.8 | 93.0 |
| Guangxi | 90.2 | 81.2 | 88.9 |
| Hainan | — | — | 87.2 |
| Hebei | 88.8 | 88.8 | 81.3 |
| Heilongjiang | 87.8 | 81.2 | 51.9 |
| Henan | 87.2 | 60.0 | 68.0 |
| Hubei | 90.2 | 72.7 | 71.1 |
| Hunan | 85.2 | 79.3 | 86.5 |
| Jiangsu | 92.8 | 77.4 | 77.8 |
| Jiangxi | 84.6 | 74.7 | 74.9 |
| Jilin | 91.8 | 85.9 | 84.4 |
| Liaoning | 96.4 | 90.4 | 82.5 |
| Ningxia | 80.6 | 81.5 | 72.0 |
| Qinghai | 70.7 | 77.5 | 77.7 |
| Shaanxi | 84.3 | 77.2 | 87.3 |
| Shandong | 89.0 | 73.5 | 73.3 |
| Shanghai | 94.9 | 91.7 | 78.3 |
| Shanxi | 97.4 | 80.9 | 71.6 |
| Sichuan | 89.2 | 80.6 | 78.1 |
| Tianjin | 89.0 | — | 72.4 |
| Xinjiang | 92.1 | 74.2 | 60.1 |
| Yunnan | 93.6 | 67.3 | 81.7 |
| Zhejiang | 92.8 | 76.5 | 90.6 |

*Source:* Guo 1995.

*Note:* The source provides no data for Guizhou, Inner Mongolia, or Tibet. — = not available.

*of the commodities traded there are … small-scale final and intermediate industrial products made by local family industries. … Only a small* amount of the goods traded are sold locally; most are sold to neighboring provinces and *xian* [counties]. … Wenzhou's rural markets have become the collection and distribution centers for certain commodities, with the markets' scope extending into every province in China, and even including international trade. … *A distinctive feature … is the formation of specialized markets …* [such as] the button market in Yongjia xian's Qiaotou. (Italics in original)

While the reopening of rural markets on the sites of traditional country fairs may have occurred spontaneously, the rapid expansion of the scale of market activity, the shift toward industrial rather than farm products, and the emergence of market sites as national and even international centers for the exchange of specific categories of merchandise could not have occurred without the energetic cooperation of local governments.

### Industrial Land and Infrastructure: Supplying Serviced Land Parcels for Industrial Use

**Industrial land.** All land in China belongs to the state. The government assigns or sells land use rights, which may then become transferable through market transactions.

In the initial stage of cluster formation, production is typically conducted in households. Once clusters begin to grow, however, access to land—for factories, warehouses, and worker housing—becomes vital for continued development.

As clusters grow, industrial parks can resolve multiple issues by providing serviced land (with connections to electricity, water, and other utilities) and even prebuilt structures (plug-and-play facilities) for manufacturing, storage, and housing. Industrial parks can also reduce conflicts between manufacturers and residents over effluents, traffic congestion, and noise. When asked about the government's role in supporting their businesses, the majority of our interviewees at firms in 2010 and 2012 mentioned the provision of land for industrial construction at discounted prices.

Beginning with the establishment of four special economic zones in the late 1970s, government agencies at the local, provincial, and national levels have provided ample supplies of serviced land parcels for industrial use. In 2009, China's national-level development zones occupied 2,831 square kilometers, employed 13 million workers, and generated $1.2 trillion in export sales (CADZ 2010). There were 1,346 province-level zones in 2005.

To achieve this, there has been much land appropriation. Complaints about arbitrary and corrupt practices in converting farmland to industrial use, often well founded, are a continuing challenge to local administrators. From an economy-wide perspective, it is clear that China's modern industrialization has been based on the ability of governments at all levels to seize land for the expansion of light manufacturing and other industries. Comparisons with other countries highlight the success of Chinese government efforts to overcome the barriers to economic growth arising from limited access to land suitable for industrial development.

**Infrastructure: Continuing challenges amid successful development.** When China embarked on reform, its physical infrastructure was inadequate to meet the needs of industry. Despite massive investments in infrastructure, the rapid growth of private enterprise often outran infrastructure capacity, leading to periodic congestion, delays, and shortages. Once development gathered momentum, economic expansion powered ahead despite the frustrations and costs associated with lagging infrastructure.

*Electricity.* The report of a World Bank mission to China in 1980 gives a good overview of China's infrastructure situation in the early days of reform. On electricity, the report noted that "despite considerable growth in generating capacity, the supply capability has lagged behind demand, and shortages exist, particularly in the northeast, north, and east grids. … Demand management and rationing are apparently well organized" (World Bank 1983a, 238).

Electricity shortages have been an intermittent feature of China's economy since the onset of reform. Visitors to a Beijing manufacturer of cashmere and angora garments in 1982 were informed that unscheduled power outages had disrupted production for 64 hours over the previous month, obliging the company to discard valuable raw material that had become stranded in dyeing vats (1982 interview). Visitors invited to tour a joint venture machine tool plant in Beijing's suburbs

25 years later were told to arrive between 11 p.m. and 7 a.m., the only hours that electricity was available (2007 interview). A factory visit planned for the 2010 World Bank mission was postponed because of a power outage (chapter 1). Manufacturers in the Pearl River Delta region often equip plants with backup generators. Industrial park administrators discuss dealing with electricity rationing as a routine management task (July 2012 interviews).

*Telecommunications.* The 1980 World Bank mission report (1983b) did not mention telecommunications, apparently because there was so little to mention. In 1975, visitors wishing to place international telephone calls from Beijing had to go to the international post office. Facilities remained primitive throughout the first decade of reform. In the mid-1980s, researchers at the Chinese Academy of Social Sciences sometimes found it more convenient to dispatch bicycle messengers to arrange meetings rather than to use the capital's problematic telephone system (interviews).

After expanding slowly during the first two decades of reform, the pace of development in telecommunications accelerated sharply beginning in the late 1990s as first landlines, then mobile phones, and finally Internet access spread rapidly. By 2011, most citizens and all but the most remote villages were linked to national and global telecommunication networks: telephone connections reached 94.81 per 100 persons (including 73.55 mobile links); in the same year, 84.0 percent of administrative villages and 38.3 percent of households enjoyed Internet access (NBS 2012).

*Land transport.* Although the railways remain chronically overburdened, long-haul trucking over the national network of limited-access expressways has added a new dimension to transport in China. The number of trucks rocketed from 0.6 million in 1990 to 2.6 million in 2000 and 10.7 million in 2011; the availability of transport services has expanded briskly, widening the sales horizons of both large and small businesses and undermining the feasibility of local protectionism (NBS 2012). A small manufacturer of steel products in Foshan, Guangdong Province, reports that he often purchases materials from local wholesalers, but can sometimes save money by purchasing steel directly from a state-owned firm in Tangshan, Hebei Province, more than 2,000 kilometers away, and trucking the goods to his plant (July 2012 interview).

### Finance: Access to Formal Finance Still a Challenge

Financing to start up and expand light manufacturing clusters comes mainly from household savings and informal credit arrangements among relatives and friends. In many cases, entrepreneurs have used savings accumulated from trading or from migrant labor to finance initial forays into manufacturing. As clusters expanded and matured, additional sources of funding became available through government-financed market halls and through the emergence of semilegal private financial networks that achieved a large scale in Wenzhou, in Zhejiang Province, and other private sector strongholds (Tsai 2002).

Despite frequent calls for increased bank lending to private business through state-owned banks or the establishment of new institutions, informal arrangements involving the personal networks of entrepreneurs or the underground financial sector contribute the main financial resources for China's private sector, particularly for small and medium firms. The founder of Aiminer, a large shoe manufacturer in Chengdu, Sichuan Province, that has 2,000 workers and produces 6,000 shoes a day, emphasized the role of informal financing:

> We started in 1986 from a small workshop of 20 workers. Our only assets at that time were 600 yuan and a bicycle. In the later development process, whenever we have financial problems, we resort to friends and relatives. (2012 interview)

Recent Chinese press accounts highlight these circumstances:

> Chinese banks, all of which are state-controlled … habitually put privately owned [small and medium enterprises (SMEs)] at the bottom of their lists, a legacy from the planned economy's policies. (Zhou 2011)

> Individual and private businesses account for about 10 percent of the total short-term lending of the country's banks … [even though] the private sector generally generates more than half of the country's GDP [gross domestic product] and accounted for nearly 96 percent of new jobs created in urban areas in 2009.[1]

Citing the profitability of "underground, unlicensed banks" in Zhejiang and Fujian provinces that have benefited from lending mostly to SMEs, a Shanghai financial analyst asks "why not legalize and regulate these underground establishments to give [SMEs] an equal footing … [in obtaining] capital?" (Zhou 2011). In 2012, China's State Council approved a broad package of financial reforms that

> would allow private lenders in Wenzhou, whose legal status has been in limbo, to operate as investment companies to augment the financing available to small and medium-size enterprises. Smaller companies have long complained they have been starved for funds because China's giant state-owned banks favor other state-owned enterprises, whose ability to repay is considered guaranteed by the cash-rich Chinese government.
>
> In addition, the State Council said it is studying allowing Wenzhou residents to invest directly overseas, giving them a way to earn better returns than in Chinese banks, whose deposit rates frequently lag inflation. (Wei, McMahon, and Orlik 2012)

Despite the difficulties in obtaining formal financing, interviews with private entrepreneurs suggest that access to financial resources is not the biggest challenge facing proprietors of new light manufacturing firms. While finding sufficient capital is not easy, our informants emphasize the more challenging tasks of finding a potentially profitable market niche, overcoming technical difficulties to produce suitable products, and finding and retaining customers.

## Trade Logistics: Improvements Led by International and Joint Venture Firms

Conditions at the start of reform were difficult. Physical infrastructure offered limited capacity for shipping goods and materials. China's railways were chronically strained and committed to moving coal, grain, and other items dictated by national economic plans. A World Bank study team in 1980 reported that "pressure on some of the overburdened links in the transport system eased somewhat because of the slowing down of heavy industry and the cancellation or postponement of some major investment projects. … However, ports and many long-haul railway lines remained under heavy pressure" (World Bank 1983a, 279). On ports, the same group wrote that "many berths are very congested, partly because of the shortage of berths and partly because of technically backward materials-handling equipment" (World Bank 1983a, 303). And, on roads, the group noted that "congestion ... is already apparent on many roads, particularly around the cities and in the larger villages, despite the relatively low volumes of motor vehicles" (World Bank 1983a, 367). Inadequate road networks and a shortage of vehicles made it difficult for small manufacturers to move inputs and products. Cars, trucks, and buses, whether standardized by population, total area, or cultivated area, remained scarcer in Fujian Province in 1990 than in Taiwan, China, in 1960 (Parish 1994).

In the Pearl River Delta region, "roads, bridges, electric power, sewage systems, and telephone service lagged badly behind demand. ... Factories ... often had to close two or more days a week; they suffered from blackouts. The problems only worsened until the late 1980s" (Vogel 1989, 165, 209).

Official attitudes compounded the difficulties. An emphasis on national and regional economic self-reliance encouraged local protectionism and underinvestment in transport and communications, as local and provincial governments imposed transport barriers that disrupted shipments across administrative boundaries (see above).

In Fujian during the mid-1980s, businesses faced "a bewildering array of taxes and fees ... [as well as] numerous illegal barriers to trade—notably, inspection stations that stop trucks and demand payment[s] ... sometimes [to] benefit the local community, sometimes only the individuals imposing them" (Lyons 1994, 158).

Individuals transporting bamboo stalks, scrap plastic, scrap wire, and live hogs—materials used in light manufacturing—were subjected to arbitrary and apparently unauthorized roadblocks, resulting in delays, fines, and even confiscation of goods. A 1988 source tabulated 578 fixed inspection stations (plus an undetermined number of mobile operations) of which only 107 had official approval; "at some stations, the scope of inspection is not specified, and there are no standards for imposing fines" (Lyons 1994, 159–63).

Small-scale business operators responded by drawing on the same sorts of behavior that guided private business activity before 1949: using personal networks to create trust-based links to suppliers, wholesalers, and customers and forming beneficial alliances with local government officials.

Knowledge and experience in international commerce were also in short supply. Reviewing Guangdong's early reform experience, Vogel (1989, 67) found that "when [Chinese managers were] held accountable for bewildering tasks like shipping goods to world markets, marketing, insuring, guaranteeing delivery, servicing, and handling errors, [they] usually chose to pass the responsibility to a Hong Kong agent." During the early reform years, visitors observed export merchandise spilling from poorly constructed cardboard boxes even before it left the factory, an invitation to damage and pilferage en route to overseas destinations (1982 interviews).

The long history of self-reliance and of the concentration of trade in the hands of a few state-owned firms isolated potential entrepreneurs from important commercial information. Chinese exporters delivered goods to trading firms without knowing the identity or preferences of eventual buyers. Initial efforts to expand overseas trade were impeded by this lack of contact between exporters and customers. A Shanghai producer of down jackets, for example, emphasized how much he learned on his first overseas trip about color and style preferences, seasonal and regional buying patterns, prices, and selling costs in the U.S. market (1994 interview).

After rocky beginnings, when "long-term neglect of port construction and access transport by means of highway, railway, and inland waterway" made Chinese ports "among the most congested ... in the world" (Ma and Zhang 2009, 189), there have been enormous improvements in transport, communication, and ancillary facilities such as storage. Chinese logistics have been transformed by the rapid influx of leading international vehicle producers to set up joint venture factories, the expansion of urban roads and intercity highways, the creation of efficient telecommunication networks, and the rapid diffusion of computer hardware and expertise. While problems remain, Chinese shipping costs now compare favorably with those in other Asian countries: "China and Thailand offer the lowest inland and international freight rates ... [among several Asian countries studied], much lower than other Asian countries ... [as well as] the lowest ad valorem international and inland transportation costs for all goods" (De 2009, 103).

Trade logistics was seldom cited as a major obstacle to doing business by interviewees at firms in 2010 and 2012.

"The reason that we chose to make the investment here is because of the excellent transportation," said an investor who set up a firm in Jiangxi Province to produce sweetener (September 2010 interview). His company uses raw materials from distant Shandong Province and exports the products to the overseas market from a port in Guangdong Province.

Small manufacturers have benefited from a vast expansion of China's motor vehicle industry. In 1980, World Bank observers reported that "no trucks below 2-ton capacity are regularly manufactured in China." With imports prohibitively expensive, small loads were transported by human porterage, bicycle- or animal-drawn carts, or small (12-horsepower) tiller-type tractors with trailers capable of carrying up to 1,000 kilograms (World Bank 1983a, 366, 370).

Several decades of reform and technical change have completely transformed China's telecommunications sector, which now provides easy access to wired and wireless telephone and fax services and Internet connections. International links are readily available in all urban areas and in most rural communities as well.

### Entrepreneurial Capabilities: Reservoirs of Skill, but Bureaucratic Obstructionism

The long-standing entrepreneurial proclivities of ordinary Chinese have always been particularly evident in the southern coastal provinces, which combine high levels of domestic commercial development with extensive participation in overseas trade and migration: almost 80 percent of the world's population of 30 million overseas Chinese originated in Guangdong Province (Pomeranz 2000; Rawski 1972; Sung 1995). This private entrepreneurial experience provided an indispensable foundation for the creation and expansion of light manufacturing clusters following reform.

Entrepreneurs typically pursue activities in which they can access specialized knowledge acquired through personal experience or personal networks. Earlier case studies of township and village enterprises (TVEs) illustrate the tendency of entrepreneurs to "acquire their technology through an approach combining market and personal arrangements" (Wong, Ma, and Yang 1995, 35). Case studies prepared for this report and our interviews in 2010 and 2012 confirm that smaller private start-ups are even more reliant on personal networks for information and advice. .

The proprietor of a metalworking firm in Foshan, Guangdong Province, explained that he overcame initial technical problems with the assistance of a relative who had worked in a state firm.

> In the early stage I hired my uncle, an engineer, from a famous Guangzhou state-owned enterprise. He did quite well in the metalworking business. When he came here, he trained the employees very well. There are about 50 workers in my factory. (July 2012 interview)

The aluminum-extrusion cluster in Dali, Guangdong Province, illustrates the central importance of personal ties in cluster formation driven by entrepreneurs with limited formal education and technical experience. Because most would-be entrants were individuals without professional training, they relied on experienced elders. As one participant explained: "we learned how to extrude aluminum in the early 1990s through our relatives and close friends" (Li, Bathelt, and Wang 2012, 144).

One interviewee entered the business through his mother's acquaintance with two local industry pioneers. The mother said "my child has nothing to do. Why not give him a cheap machine to let him help you fill some small orders?" (July 2012 interview). Another interviewee obtained an introduction to an "old hardware man" who had "engaged in the metal business since the Great Leap Forward and entered into the aluminum extrusion industry at the beginning of policy reforms. ... We called him 'old master' and asked him for help whenever we had a problem" (2012 interview).

The intensive learning culture that enabled inexperienced beginners to follow local pioneers into the aluminum-extrusion industry in the early 1990s centered on a teahouse in which "nearly 1,000 people gather ... every morning [to] talk aluminum with each other," obtain information about price trends, meet customers and suppliers, and discuss technical issues (Li, Bathelt, and Wang 2012, 143–45).

"When someone makes money, the entire town knows about it," said the owner of a leather company in Wenzhou, Zhejiang Province (September 2010 interview). He said almost all residents in the town were connected by kinship or friendship. There were no secrets.

Information about the textile and garment business in Wenzhou, Zhejiang Province, echoes these observations:

> In Yishan qu [District], ... two brothers overcame the technical difficulty in patterning leftover bits and pieces of acrylic fibers and ... [another individual] spun the regenerated acrylic fiber yarn by modifying a spinning machine. As a result of these two technological innovations, the production of regenerated acrylic fiber fabrics by household industry has increased throughout the entire qu. (Li 1990, 113)

> Chen Anjing, a peasant from Rui'an xian's [county] Hantian cun [village], set up an automobile fittings factory despite many difficulties and setbacks. Following him, many households in that village established factories to produce automobile fittings. (Li 1990, 113)

Many entrepreneurs gained knowledge about business management and marketing through numerous failed attempts. Before setting up his leather firm in 2002, Pan Kefa had tried many businesses. He started out as a farmer and fisherman in rural Zhejiang Province. In 1983, he opened an ice-making factory and later an electrical fan factory. Neither investment succeeded. Nonetheless, he said, he learned how to start and manage a company, what the market needs, and where to get technology and talent (September 2010 interview).

> Some peasants in Wenzhou are very anxious to acquire market information in order to respond to market signals by swiftly producing the goods required. For example, many households in Yishan xian [county] produce nylon clothes with leftover bits and pieces because, first, they see that they can make use of the materials and, second, they see that there is a demand for this kind of cheap clothing. (Dong 1990, 88)

Trade is a frequent pathway to manufacturing because traders have access to market information. Commercially relevant information was scarce in prereform China. Detailed information about prices rarely appeared in open publications. Visitors found their hosts reluctant to divulge information about prices; one official denied even the existence of prices, telling foreign visitors that farmers provided wheat and that local supply agencies provided fertilizer based on mutual respect rather than for money (1975 interviews). Shortly after the start of reform, visitors encountered a well-educated Beijing official who was completely unaware of large regional price differences despite showing a keen interest in shopping (1982 interview).

Under these circumstances, peddlers and traveling salespeople contributed disproportionately to the formation and early growth of light manufacturing clusters. In Wenzhou, they

> travel extensively doing business, concluding contracts, buying raw materials, selling products, and communicating market information. They have become leaders of Wenzhou's commodity economy expansion. Many of these people were previously engaged in small businesses, such as shoe repairing and cotton fluffing, which frequently involved living in other areas. By extensive traveling, they have accumulated a wealth of social experience and respond sharply to information. They are familiar with a great many areas' local customs, consumption habits, and market conditions; they are highly proficient in commodity business. … They bring contracts, market information, technical knowledge and raw materials to household industries, enabling them to produce according to market conditions and obtain better economic returns … [because] there are so many peasants doing commercial business … raw (and other) materials and all sorts of commodities flow in an unceasing stream from all over the country into these [local] markets and then into the multitude of households [engaged in small-scale production]. (Zhang 1990, 99)

Our case studies and interviews confirm the importance of networks and trading as valuable preparation for starting a light manufacturing business. The co-owner of a Jiangmen metalware manufacturing firm, for example, first learned about the industry while running a trading company specializing in importing stainless steel:

> In the mid-1980s, I imported stainless steel through a trading company. … In selling it, I got to know some entrepreneurs in the metalworking business and gradually got to know how to make stainless steel. Then, I did some simple processing. In the end, I entered the business. (July 2012 interview)

Although there are no comprehensive national statistics on cluster formation, some recent papers have documented the trend toward clustering in China (Long and Zhang 2011, 2012). The hundreds of clusters in Guangdong and Zhejiang provinces that have contributed substantially to GDP, industrial production, and exports are also of great importance in China's economic boom (chapter 3).

Officials deserve recognition as entrepreneurial participants in the emergence and growth of light manufacturing clusters in China. The Great Leap Forward of the late 1950s deepened the responsibility of subnational officials for implementing the priorities established by the central government. During the Great Leap Forward and continuing into the 1960s and early 1970s, the entrepreneurial activities of these officials were harnessed to politically inspired initiatives that inflicted profound costs on the economy. The reform regime gradually revised national objectives to focus on economic growth. Once the new priorities took root, local and provincial officials quickly understood that promotion and bonuses awaited leaders who could deliver outstanding performance.

Nonetheless, many officials were ill suited to promoting economic growth. Foreigners trying to do business in China "had a reservoir of stories about Chinese bureaucrats who excelled in inefficiency, bureaucratism, personal profiteering … and poor understanding of the needs of international business" (Vogel 1989, 135).

This obstructionism was visible in the special economic zones that were intended to accelerate China's foray into global markets. One researcher reported that "China lacked personnel sufficiently knowledgeable about foreign economic development to inform leaders about the experience of other countries with export zones" (Vogel 1989, 125). Visitors were surprised to discover, for example, that the director of the special zone at Xiamen, in Fujian Province, while pledging to build the zone "to suit the needs of foreign businesses," had never traveled abroad and spoke no English. Chinese businesspeople investigating opportunities in the Xiamen zone left in dismay after finding that zone officials could not provide specific information on the prices of land, water, or electricity. One manager at a large plant insisted that he did not know the unit cost of his product; another, asked to explain the presence of numerous idle workers, said "if we didn't employ them, where would they go?" (1982 interviews).

Following three decades of centrally planned investment and semiautarchic growth, promoting private business was risky. Political attacks on private business were common, and some entrepreneurs were accused of being rightists or capitalists.

Provinces that encouraged private business, such as Guangdong and Zhejiang, were among those that had benefited least from decades of planned economic growth (table 2.3). Their shares of fixed investment

**Table 2.3 Regional Concentrations of Investment and State Industry in the Planned Economy, China, Various Years to 1980–81**

| Province | Percentage shares of national totals | | | | Ratio of percentage shares | | | |
| | | | | | Fixed investment | | Industrial output | |
| | Population, 1981 | GDP, 1978 | Fixed investment, 1953–80 | State industrial output, 1980 | To population | To GDP | To population | To GDP |
|---|---|---|---|---|---|---|---|---|
| Anhui | 5.0 | 3.3 | 2.8 | 2.6 | 0.57 | 0.85 | 0.53 | 0.79 |
| Beijing | 0.9 | 3.2 | 5.2 | 4.9 | 5.76 | 1.65 | 5.40 | 1.55 |
| Fujian | 2.6 | 1.9 | 1.6 | 1.5 | 0.63 | 0.84 | 0.57 | 0.76 |
| Gansu | 2.0 | 1.9 | 3.1 | 1.8 | 1.60 | 1.67 | 0.95 | 0.98 |
| Guangdong | 5.2 | 5.5 | 4.4 | 3.7 | 0.75 | 0.82 | 0.63 | 0.69 |
| Guangxi | 3.6 | 2.2 | 2.0 | 1.6 | 0.55 | 0.91 | 0.43 | 0.71 |
| Guizhou | 2.8 | 1.4 | 2.2 | 1.0 | 0.79 | 1.65 | 0.34 | 0.72 |
| Hebei | 5.3 | 5.3 | 4.7 | 4.5 | 0.88 | 0.88 | 0.85 | 0.84 |
| Heilongjiang | 3.3 | 5.1 | 5.9 | 5.1 | 1.80 | 1.16 | 1.57 | 1.01 |
| Henan | 7.4 | 4.7 | 4.6 | 4.0 | 0.62 | 0.98 | 0.54 | 0.84 |
| Hubei | 4.8 | 4.4 | 6.0 | 4.6 | 1.25 | 1.36 | 0.96 | 1.04 |
| Hunan | 5.4 | 4.3 | 3.3 | 3.4 | 0.62 | 0.78 | 0.64 | 0.80 |
| Jiangsu | 6.0 | 7.2 | 3.6 | 6.8 | 0.60 | 0.50 | 1.13 | 0.95 |
| Jiangxi | 3.3 | 2.5 | 2.1 | 1.8 | 0.63 | 0.83 | 0.54 | 0.71 |
| Jilin | 2.2 | 2.4 | 3.1 | 2.7 | 1.38 | 1.30 | 1.21 | 1.14 |
| Liaoning | 3.6 | 6.7 | 8.0 | 9.4 | 2.25 | 1.20 | 2.63 | 1.41 |
| Neimenggu | 1.9 | 1.7 | 3.0 | 1.2 | 1.59 | 1.81 | 0.62 | 0.70 |
| Ningxia | 0.4 | 0.4 | 0.7 | 0.3 | 1.73 | 1.71 | 0.81 | 0.80 |
| Qinghai | 0.4 | 0.5 | 1.2 | 0.3 | 3.06 | 2.60 | 0.79 | 0.67 |
| Shaanxi | 2.9 | 2.4 | 3.8 | 2.4 | 1.32 | 1.62 | 0.82 | 1.00 |
| Shandong | 7.4 | 6.5 | 4.8 | 5.9 | 0.64 | 0.73 | 0.79 | 0.90 |
| Shanghai | 1.2 | 7.9 | 3.7 | 13.5 | 3.16 | 0.47 | 11.51 | 1.70 |
| Shanxi | 2.5 | 2.6 | 3.8 | 2.5 | 1.50 | 1.48 | 0.99 | 0.98 |
| Sichuan | 10.0 | 7.1 | 6.6 | 5.5 | 0.66 | 0.92 | 0.55 | 0.78 |
| Tianjin | 0.8 | 2.4 | 2.6 | 3.9 | 3.39 | 1.08 | 5.12 | 1.64 |
| Xinjiang | 1.3 | 1.1 | 2.3 | 0.9 | 1.77 | 2.05 | 0.71 | 0.82 |
| Yunnan | 3.2 | 2.0 | 2.9 | 1.3 | 0.89 | 1.45 | 0.41 | 0.66 |
| Zhejiang | 3.9 | 3.6 | 1.8 | 2.9 | 0.48 | 0.52 | 0.75 | 0.81 |

*Source:* NBS various years.

*Note:* Tibet is omitted. Gross domestic product (GDP) is calculated by the expenditure method. Fixed investment is the sum of basic construction and renovation. State industrial output refers to the total output value of state-owned industrial firms.

and state industry output were well below their shares in overall population and GDP. The share of state industry in Guangdong's GDP trailed every province except backward Yunnan. The ratio of the investment share to the population share (and therefore cumulative fixed investment per person) in Zhejiang was the lowest of any province. Other provinces, by contrast, particularly Beijing, Tianjin, and five northern and northeastern provinces (Heilongjiang, Jilin, Liaoning, Neimenggu, and Shanxi), had concentrations of investment and state industry that were consistently higher than their shares in population or GDP.[2] Beijing is the extreme case: its share of both investment and state industry output is more than five times its population share and more than 50 percent above its share in GDP.

### Worker Skills: A Reorientation to Serving Customer Needs

China entered the reform era with a labor force that was generally healthy, literate, underused, and eager to exchange hard work for a chance to attain higher living standards. The 1982 population census reported a rate of 95 percent literacy among youth aged 15–24. China's development of light manufacturing thus benefited from a favorable combination of low wages and a well-educated cohort of young workers, as had been the case in Japan; in the Republic of Korea; and in Taiwan, China, in earlier decades.

Despite the spread of basic education, two decades of international isolation had deprived Chinese workers of many types of economically useful knowledge and information. In addition, the era of central planning had dulled incentives by separating effort from reward and inculcating a culture of slacking and corner-cutting. A study of Guangdong's early reform experience found that "China lacked staff who could use, maintain, service, and repair modern machinery, let alone install, adapt, improve, and redesign it as personnel ... in other East Asian countries could" (Vogel 1989, 144).

Despite frequent repetition of slogans such as "serve the people," decades of socialism had severely eroded the notion of customer service. Personnel in stores and restaurants were typically rude, even abusive, to patrons. In industry, poor service took the form of widespread neglect of quality, specifications, delivery times, and other customer requirements. Shipping products with small defects was standard practice.

Enterprise managers attributed persistent quality problems to a combination of outdated technology and a lack of incentives. Managers at a Shanghai manufacturer of industrial sewing machines that had imported a highly automated Japanese assembly line complained of difficulties getting local suppliers to meet exact specifications for components and referred frequently to inadequate equipment and obsolete processes. They also criticized worker incentives in their own firm, a shareholding company, claiming that worker motivation there was not much better than in state enterprises (1995 interview).

U.S. managers of a Beijing-based joint venture manufacturer of auto parts expressed similar concerns, remarking on deficiencies in equipment and incentives. Chinese-made furnaces, for example, did not allow users to control either the temperature or the duration of heat treatment, both essential to quality. Steel supplied by Beijing's Capital Steel, a major state-owned producer, varied in quality: shipments would meet standards for several months, then drift outside specified limits. Plant managers agreed that Capital was capable of maintaining quality standards, but sometimes neglected to do so. Leaders criticized their own operations, saying that their firm was "not good at preventive maintenance" and that "our people lack [quality control] discipline ... [and] don't follow blueprints. ... [I]f the plans call for 1 millimeter tolerance, some people think that 1.25 millimeters is OK" (1996 interview). The Beijing managers saw slow equipment as an important source of such difficulties. Waiting for machines to complete tasks that better equipment could have finished more rapidly was encouraging a culture of loafing (1996 interview).

Facing this combination of strengths and shortcomings, private firms, foreign joint ventures, and, eventually, foreign-owned companies led the way in reorienting Chinese manufacturing from a plan-era focus on quantity to more market-oriented attitudes aimed at satisfying customer requirements.

Poor equipment, deficient materials, and limited experience meant that start-ups in light manufacturing clusters typically began operations at the low end of the price-quality spectrum. Researchers at the Chinese Academy of Social Sciences reported that, immediately after moving into new apartments during the late 1990s, they replaced the cheap, low-quality electrical switches that the builder had procured from small rural firms (interviews). Some firms concentrated on serving China's large, but declining market for inferior goods. Others specialized in fraud. In Wenzhou, for example, some producers substituted leatherette and cardboard for standard materials, manufacturing shoes that earned a "reputation for having a 'one week life expectancy'" (Wang 2010, 157).

The growth of export sales, particularly to high-income markets in which buyers expect high quality standards, pressured China-based firms to upgrade products and processes. Rising Chinese incomes pushed manufacturers in the same direction. Foreign firms often led the way in raising quality, exposing millions of Chinese managers and workers to advanced methods of quality testing and management in the process. Large numbers of Chinese enterprises, including many small, privately owned light manufacturing firms, followed this lead, and standards rose, gradually at first, but then more rapidly as new methods diffused across sectors and regions.

Local governments actively supported these efforts.[3] Official contributions included the following (July 2012 interviews):

- Setting quality standards and providing equipment and training to assist firms in achieving them
- Sponsoring overseas tours to acquaint local entrepreneurs with international market conditions
- Encouraging local schools to offer training oriented to the technical requirements of local businesses
- Introducing local businesses to government, industry, and academic researchers whose knowledge might assist in resolving technical problems in local factories

"We walk with two legs," said an official in Jiangxi Province, referring to the combination of training within enterprises and the expansion of vocational education (September 2010 interview). He said both the central government and local governments have increased their efforts to support vocational schools and encourage enterprises to improve training methods and increase the number of trainees.

## Notes

1. "For a Stronger Private Sector," editorial, *China Daily*, U.S. edition, August 1, 2012, http://www.chinadaily.com.cn/opinion/2012-08/01/content_15636687.htm.

2. Chinese statistics treat the cities of Beijing, Chongqing (since 1997), Shanghai, and Tianjin as province-level units.

3. Local governments do play a key role in facilitating quality upgrades. However, the timing matters. In the incipient stage of cluster development, local government policies are mostly oriented to quantity expansion. Interventions aimed at upgrading quality often become more relevant only after a quality crisis. See Ruan and Zhang (2010) on this point.

# References

CADZ (China Association of Development Zones). 2010. *Zhongguo kaifaqu nian-jian 2010* [China development zones yearbook 2010]. [In Chinese.] Beijing: China Financial and Economic Publishing House.

China Light Industry Federation. 2010. *Zhongguo qinggongye nianjian 2010* [China light industry yearbook 2010]. [In Chinese.] Beijing: China Light Industry Yearbook Press.

De, Prabir. 2009. "Empirical Estimates of Transportation Costs: Options for Enhancing Asia's Trade." In *Infrastructure's Role in Lowering Asia's Trade Costs: Building for Trade*, edited by Douglas H. Brooks and David Hummels, 73–112. Cheltenham, U.K.: Edward Elgar.

Dinh, Hinh T., Vincent Palmade, Vandana Chandra, and Frances Cossar. 2012. *Light Manufacturing in Africa: Targeted Policies to Enhance Private Investment and Create Jobs.* Washington, DC: World Bank. http://go.worldbank.org/ASG0J44350.

Dong, Fureng. 1990. "The Wenzhou Model for Developing the Rural Commodity Economy." In *Market Forces in China, Competition and Small Business: The Wenzhou Debate*, edited by Peter Nolan and Fureng Dong, 77–96. London: Zed Books.

Donnithorne, Audrey. 1967. *China's Economic System.* New York: Praeger.

EAAU (East Asia Analytical Unit). 1997. *China Embraces the Market: Achievements, Constraints, and Opportunities.* Canberra: EAAU, Australian Department of Foreign Affairs and Trade.

EBCPY (Editorial Board of the China Price Yearbook). 1996. *Zhongguo wujia nianjian* [China price yearbook 1996]. [In Chinese.] Beijing: China Price Press.

———. 1997. *Zhongguo wujia nianjian* [China price yearbook 1997]. [In Chinese.] Beijing: China Price Press.

Findlay, Christopher, ed. 1991. *Challenges of Economic Reform and Industrial Growth: China's Wool War.* Sydney: Allen and Unwin.

Guo Jianying. 1995. "Proportion and Changes for Three Types of Prices." *Zhongguo wujia* [China price] 11: 10–12.

Li, Peng-fei, Harald Bathelt, and Jici Wang. 2012. "Network Dynamics and Cluster Evolution: Changing Trajectories of the Aluminum Extrusion Industry in Dali, China." *Journal of Economic Geography* 12 (1): 127–55.

Li Shi. 1990. "The Growth of Household Industry in Rural Wenzhou." In *Market Forces in China, Competition and Small Business: The Wenzhou Debate*, edited by Peter Nolan and Fureng Dong, 108–25. London: Zed Books.

Long, Cheryl, and Xiaobo Zhang. 2011. "Cluster-Based Industrialization in China: Financing and Performance." *Journal of International Economics* 84 (1): 112–23.

————. 2012. "Patterns of China's Industrialization: Concentration, Specialization, and Clustering." *China Economic Review* 23 (3): 593–612.

Lyons, Thomas P. 1994. "Economic Reform in Fujian: Another View from the Villages." In *The Economic Transformation of South China: Reform and Development in the Post-Mao Era*, edited by Thomas P. Lyons and Victor G. Nee, 141–68. Cornell East Asia Series 70. Ithaca, NY: Cornell University Press.

Ma, Liqiang, and Jinkang Zhang. 2009. "Infrastructure Development in a Fast-Growing Economy: The People's Republic of China." In *Infrastructure's Role in Lowering Asia's Trade Costs: Building for Trade*, edited by Douglas H. Brooks and David Hummels, 182–229. Cheltenham, U.K.: Edward Elgar.

Naughton, Barry. 1995. *Growing Out of the Plan*. New York: Cambridge University Press.

NBS (National Bureau of Statistics of China). 2012. *China Statistical Yearbook*. Beijing: China Statistics Press.

————. Various years. *China Statistical Yearbook*. Beijing: China Statistics Press.

Parish, William L. 1994. "Rural Industrialization in Fujian and Taiwan." In *The Economic Transformation of South China: Reform and Development in the Post-Mao Era*, edited by Thomas P. Lyons and Victor G. Nee, 119–40. Cornell East Asia Series 70. Ithaca, NY: Cornell University Press.

Pomeranz, Kenneth. 2000. *The Great Divergence: China, Europe, and the Making of the Modern World Economy*. Princeton, NJ: Princeton University Press.

Rawski, Evelyn S. 1972. *Agricultural Change and the Peasant Economy of South China*. Cambridge, MA: Harvard University Press.

Rawski, Thomas G. 1980. *China's Transition to Industrialism*. Ann Arbor, MI: University of Michigan Press.

Ruan, Jianqing, and Xiaobo Zhang. 2010. "Made in China: Crisis Begets Quality Upgrade." IFPRI Discussion Paper 1025, International Food Policy Research Institute, Washington, DC.

Sung, Yun-Wing, ed. 1995. *The Fifth Dragon: The Emergence of the Pearl River Delta*. Boston: Addison-Wesley.

Tsai, Kellee S. 2002. *Back-Alley Banking: Private Entrepreneurs in China*. Ithaca, NY: Cornell University Press.

Vogel, Ezra F. 1989. *One Step Ahead in China: Guangdong under Reform*. Cambridge, MA: Harvard University Press.

Wang, Jici. 2010. "Industrial Clustering in China: The Case of the Wenzhou Footwear Sector." In *Building Engines for Growth and Competitiveness in China: Experience with Special Economic Zones and Industrial Clusters*, edited by Douglas Z. Zheng, 151–79. Washington, DC: World Bank.

Watson, Andrew, Christopher Findlay, and Yintang Du. 1989. "Who Won the 'Wool War'?: A Case Study of Rural Product Marketing in China." *China Quarterly* 118 (June): 213–41.

Wei, Lingling, Dinny McMahon, and Tom Orlik. 2012. "China Tests Financial Relaxation in Wenzhou." *Wall Street Journal*, March 28. http://online.wsj.com/article/SB10001424052702303404704577309051957346004.html.

Wong, John, Rong Ma, and Mu Yang. 1995. *China's Rural Entrepreneurs: Ten Case Studies*. Singapore: Times Academic Press.

World Bank. 1983a. *The Economic Sectors: Agriculture, Industry, Energy, Transport, and External Trade and Finance*. Vol. 2 of *China: Socialist Economic Development*. 3 vols. Washington, DC: World Bank.

———. 1983b. *China: Socialist Economic Development*. 3 vols. Washington, DC: World Bank.

Zhang, Lin. 1990. "Developing the Commodity Economy in the Rural Areas." In *Market Forces in China, Competition and Small Business: The Wenzhou Debate*, edited by Peter Nolan and Fureng Dong, 97–107. London: Zed Books.

Zhou, Feng. 2011. "Give SMEs a Fighting Chance." *China Daily*, U.S. edition, August 4.

# 3

# Major Policy Tools

## Introduction

China's success in expanding the production and export of light manufactures and in using this success to launch higher–value added activities
invites consideration of the policies that have supported and encouraged
these developments. This chapter looks at three major policy tools that
have contributed to China's success: industrial parks, industrial clusters,
and trading companies. China is not the first to implement these policy
tools. Japan; the Republic of Korea; Singapore; and Taiwan, China, did
the same earlier, with similar success. These policy tools are not, however, usually found in the standard toolkits of development economics.

## Industrial Parks: Vehicles to Advance Light Manufacturing

Industrial parks have been a key vehicle for investment in China by
overseas manufacturing firms. The inflows of foreign direct investment (FDI) account for only modest shares of capital formation (see
chapter 1, table 1.3). Their greater impact has been qualitative.

The first economic zone in China was established in Shenzhen,
Guangdong Province, in 1980. In the spring of 1992, following Deng
Xiaoping's tour of southern China and his reaffirmation of China's

commitment to economic reform, the relaxation of the controls over foreign trade and investment was gradually expanded to large cities and the entire coastal area, and the establishment of economic and technical development zones picked up. Some zones contributed significantly to regional growth and local government revenues. Success encouraged other provinces to establish and promote their own zones and to overcome obstacles in the business environment by building infrastructure and improving policies in targeted areas. A development zone rush took China by storm. By the end of 1992, more than 2,700 development zones had sprung up across the country, 23 times the number in 1991.

Since then, government entities at every level have built development zones. As of mid-2012, there were 5 special economic zones (Hainan, Shantou, Shenzhen, Xiamen, and Zhuhai), 90 national economic development zones, 88 national high-technology industrial development zones, 22 duty-free zones, and 15 border economic cooperation zones.[1] All enjoyed special treatment by the national government. Local and provincial governments support more than a thousand other industrial development zones. In 2010, national-level economic development zones contributed 7 percent of gross domestic product (GDP), 11 percent of manufacturing output, and 15 percent of foreign trade. They also accounted for 29 percent of FDI (CADZ 2010).

The industrial parks were established as experimentation zones to test the potential of new methods of administration by concentrating limited investment on infrastructure. The idea was to invite foreign investment, introduce elements of market allocation (for example, by allowing enterprises to select their own workers, thereby avoiding the assignees of labor bureaus), and free local officials from "established administrative and management systems" so that they could become empowered to adopt unorthodox policies (L. Li 2009, 112–13). The intent was clearly to test the proposition that China's socialist system was "fully capable of utilizing and assimilating the material wealth and management methodology created by capitalism" (L. Li 2009, 113).

These experiments amply fulfilled Chinese leader Deng Xiaoping's hope that they would "blaze a new trail" for the entire Chinese economy (L. Li 2009, 93). The special zones and industrial parks rapidly increased the production and export of manufactures, contributed to capital and foreign exchange accumulation, and expanded employment opportunities. Initially, the zones emphasized export processing, using mostly imported materials because domestic suppliers had limited capabilities and were often difficult to access. Speed offered an additional reason to favor imports over domestic supplies; thus, managers in Shenzhen complained that procuring materials from Chinese firms caused troublesome delays (1982 interview).

Early foreign investors were mostly overseas Chinese manufacturers whose profits from operations in Hong Kong SAR, China, as well as in Taiwan, China, were slipping because of rising labor costs. Because low wages were a major attraction to foreign investors, early investment was concentrated in garments, toys, and other labor-intensive products. As a result, newly arriving foreign firms typically created more employment per unit of investment than did domestic firms.

While providing important short-term investment, employment, and foreign exchange benefits, industrial parks also helped China pursue strategic long-run objectives, including technology and skill transfers, multiplier effects for regional development, and the expansion of upstream and downstream industrial links. As Deng Xiaoping noted, the intent of this openness policy was to use "international capital and advanced technology to assist in our economic development" (NBS 1985, 106). The gradual opening from the coast to the interior paralleled the step-by-step transition from a plan system to a market economy.

Industrial parks offered the quickest route to profits and technology acquisition in an environment where sweeping economy-wide reforms were not feasible because of the continuing strength of socialist ideology and the entrenched interests of officials and bureaucracies associated with the plan system. Even partial, localized reforms, including the proposed creation of a handful of small special economic zones, drew considerable opposition:

> Controversy was buzzing. ... Some equated the zones with "colonies,"
> "revived old foreign concessions," or a downright "restoration of capital-
> ism." ... Leaders of some State Council departments were worried that
> the zones might slip onto the capitalist road ... [and] rob national trad-
> ing corporations of old clients and market channels. (L. Li 2009, 114, 135)

Thus, when the balance of political forces opposes the first-best option of sweeping initiatives aimed at openness, marketization, and deregulation, second-best policies—in this case, limiting reform initiatives to a small segment of the economy—can still usher in beneficial change (chapter 11). The success of early small-scale reforms in China helped shift elite opinion and quickly inspired growing numbers of localities to embrace the opportunities offered by the reforms. By 1992, the Chinese power elite had coalesced around Deng's reformist agenda, paving the way for the new long-term goal of a "socialist market economy with Chinese characteristics."

### Industrial Parks and the Major Constraints to Industrialization

Industrial parks helped China circumvent several constraints to the development and competitiveness of light manufacturing, including the lack of inputs, industrial land, finance, trade logistics, and entrepreneurial and worker skills (chapter 2).

**Input industries.** If domestic input markets are underdeveloped and inputs must be imported, import tariffs raise costs. Yet, the removal of the tariffs on all the inputs used in domestic production, while improving the global competiveness of local producers, is generally opposed because it lowers the protection for incumbent suppliers and reduces government revenue. China used industrial parks to avoid these disadvantages by limiting any allowed tariff exemptions to inputs that are imported, processed, and then reexported as part of the final output produced within the parks. China also sought to accelerate technology transfers by allowing duty-free imports of industrial machinery for export-oriented firms in the special zones and industrial parks. Chinese industry benefited from such substantial protection in the years prior to the country's accession to the World Trade Organization (WTO).

**Industrial land.** Manufacturing requires access to affordable land. In the early 1980s, industrial land with efficient infrastructure was in short supply, even in the more developed coastal regions. To circumvent this constraint, local officials provided fully serviced land in industrial parks, sometimes with plug-and-play factory shells that allowed entrepreneurs to commence production without having to build factories. Eventually, local governments facilitated access to industrial land throughout the domestic economy. Government entities gradually developed policies that enabled smaller firms to expand organically or through industrial parks that eased land and infrastructure constraints.

As local industries grew and paid taxes, local governments could afford to upgrade the industrial infrastructure and expand the area of industrial parks. Local officials exercised their power of eminent domain to take over agricultural land at minimal cost and then resell the land use rights to manufacturing or real estate development firms at a large profit. While providing ample land for business expansion, this approach provoked widespread protests among dispossessed farmers and residents (Hsing 2010).[2]

Industrialization and urbanization are reducing the land available for production and commerce. Relocating enterprises to industrial parks or economic development zones is the major channel for obtaining new land. Industrial parks, normally developed by local governments, offer roads, utility connections, and standard workshops. By convincing firms to move into industrial parks, local governments also hope to group firms in the same sector so as to reap the benefits of agglomeration and clustering.

**Finance.** China's banks lend largely to borrowers with strong ties to the public sector and discriminate against small and privately owned firms of the type found in light manufacturing clusters. Some local governments have used land as collateral to obtain funds for developing light manufacturing.[3] Local officials have also used their networks and influence to assist firms in gaining access to external finance.[4]

**Trade logistics.** By locating industrial parks in coastal areas with access to domestic transport and port facilities and with long pre-Communist histories of international trade, China's rising export sectors enjoyed adequate trade logistics from the start. As manufactured exports expanded, investments in export-related transport and port facilities became more attractive. Industrial park administrations also streamlined customs formalities for entrepreneurs.

**Entrepreneurial and worker skills.** Industrial parks provided permanent space for overseas and local investors, thus attracting entrepreneurs with the managerial and technical skills needed to run successful businesses. Reform leaders emphasized "using the money and technology of overseas Chinese and allowing them to run factories" in the southern provinces of Fujian and Guangdong, the home provinces of most emigrants from China (L. Li 2009, 93). As local industries grew, so did the local pool of experienced workers and the availability of ancillary services and goods, including domestic supplies of material inputs. These developments reinforced one another and raised the productivity of local industry.

## How Industrial Parks Evolved in China

Industrial parks in China have gone through three stages. During the first stage (1980–91), industrial parks were components of the special economic zones that were set up to test new methods of attracting FDI and developing export-oriented manufacturing. During the second stage (1992–98), these reforms were scaled up to the national level. The number of industrial parks quickly multiplied, as local governments joined what became a national competition for growth. During the third stage (1999–present), following the Asian financial crisis of 1997–98 and China's entry into the WTO, Beijing initiated the Great Western Development Strategy, which features large-scale investments to help the western provinces catch up with the more prosperous coastal areas. The focus on developing labor-intensive manufacturing shifted to the hinterland, while industrial parks in coastal areas began to shift to capital- and technology-intensive industries.

**Stage I (1980–91): Establishment and exploration.** Long before China tested the waters of economic reform, many of its neighbors, including Korea; Malaysia; Singapore; Taiwan, China; and Thailand, had experimented with export processing zones. These economies had come to realize the benefits of an export-oriented development strategy and the critical role of FDI and to embrace them. The interventions took place in an environment marred by pervasive distortions. Low wages and limited capital, technology, and skills steered initial efforts toward light manufacturing. Hong Kong SAR, China, rapidly emerged as a regional center of export production because of its traditions of entrepreneurship, its laissez-faire policies, and its excellent port facilities.

By the 1970s, rising labor costs forced businesses in Hong Kong SAR, China, to scout for new locations for labor-intensive production. These firms responded enthusiastically to news that China was preparing to allow Guangdong Province to experiment with export processing. In 1979, the first joint venture between local Chinese producers and these investors—the Taiping Handbag Plant—was established in Dongguan, a city near Hong Kong SAR, China.[5] The number of joint ventures began multiplying even before the formal establishment of the first special economic zones.

The decision by Chinese reformists to expand foreign trade and permit imports of foreign capital and technology followed overseas visits that revealed how far ahead of China other Asian economies had advanced. After learning that annual output per worker averaged 94 vehicles at Nissan, but only 1 at China's First Auto Works, Deng Xiaoping commented "now I know what modernization means" (L. Li 2009, 59). High-level visits to Germany, Singapore, and the United States, reminiscent of the international travels of Japan's 19th-century Meiji leaders, revealed other gaps in China and spurred reformers to push aside strenuous opposition and begin experimenting with new policies (L. Li 2009).

*Siting the special economic zones.* Southern China was selected as the site for the first four special economic zones for several reasons. The location would help attract overseas Chinese entrepreneurs, most of whom had originated in the area. The intention was to capitalize on their money, managerial skills, and knowledge of advanced technology. Shenzhen and Zhuhai border Hong Kong SAR, China, and Macao SAR, China (map 3.1), while Shantou and Xiamen have connections to Hong Kong SAR, China; to Taiwan, China; and to the Chinese diaspora in Southeast Asia. The people in these areas have strong links overseas and a tradition of interaction with the outside world. Even though the infrastructure was weaker there than in Dalian, Qingdao, Shanghai, and elsewhere, foreign investors could be more confident that the zones would maintain a market-like environment if they were farther from China's main industrial bases and farther from entrenched interests that might oppose the changes.

**Map 3.1  Location of Special Economic Zones and Selected Open Areas, China, Mid-1980s**

*Source:* World Bank, adapted from Wang and Bradbury 1986.
*Note:* SEZ = special economic zone.

*Types of special economic zones.* The first four special economic zones reflected two contrasting models. Shenzhen and Zhuhai were developed as large, comprehensive economic development zones that would use incentives and preferential treatment to engage foreign investors in manufacturing and a range of other economic activities, from primary production to services. The Longhu District in Shantou and the Huli District in Xiamen, areas with established economies and high population densities, were designated as small export processing enclaves specializing in manufacturing.

As the special zones evolved, it became apparent that the pure export processing model, as implemented elsewhere in Asia, could be extended to production activities and services aimed at the domestic market. Thus, the export processing zone model gave way to large, comprehensively developed economic zones modeled after Shenzhen and Zhuhai. The Longhu District was expanded from 1.6 square kilometers to 52.6, and the Huli District from 2.5 square kilometers to 125.5. The range of economic activities increased correspondingly. By the mid-1980s, all four special economic zones were emphasizing comprehensive development in their respective regions (Wong 1987).

To advance the contribution of special economic zones as bridges to foreign capital and advanced technology and as laboratories for experimentation with economic reforms and free-market mechanisms, China began to abandon its earlier hostility toward foreign business. Reflecting a fairly liberal attitude, China's new policies allowed multiple forms of foreign investment, but initially only in the special economic zones (Wong 1987):

- Sole proprietorship or wholly foreign-owned subsidiaries
- Equity joint ventures between foreign and local investors
- Cooperative joint ventures, in which a foreign firm contributes capital, equipment, and technology, and the Chinese partner supplies land, buildings, and labor
- Compensation trade, in which the foreign investor receives a share of finished goods in return for providing equipment, technology, parts, and components
- Intermediate processing, in which a Chinese partner uses materials provided by the foreign partner to produce finished goods in exchange for a processing fee

Each type of foreign investment had advantages and drawbacks. Processing imported materials created employment and provided foreign exchange without requiring extensive marketing knowledge or management skills on the Chinese side, but it offered little prospect for technological transfer and left most profits in the hands of the foreign participants. Starting in the mid-1980s, Chinese authorities began to steer prospective investors toward joint ventures, using access to China's growing domestic market as a bargaining chip (Wong 1987). Table 3.1 shows foreign investment in three of the initial special economic zones by type of ownership structure.

All four special economic zones enjoyed dramatic growth in the 1980s, with Shenzhen leading in both total industrial output and output funded with foreign investment (figure 3.1).

The central government invested heavily in the four new zones. The Shenzhen special economic zone absorbed Y 4.6 billion ($1.2 billion) in capital assets over 1980–89, more than 90 percent from the state sector (CADZ 1989).[6] With investment funds pouring in, infrastructure in the zones quickly surpassed that in the domestic economy, attracting even more foreign and domestic investment. After four years of massive urban infrastructure development, exports in the Shenzhen special economic zone soared from $5 million in 1982 to $19 million in 1984, then more than doubled to $43 million in 1989.

The industrial geography of the newly established city of Shenzhen quickly became complex, with industrial zones both inside the Shenzhen special economic zone and in other parts of the municipality

**Table 3.1 Forms of Foreign Investment in Three Initial Special Economic Zones, China, 1980–84**

*percent and U.S. dollars, millions*

| Special economic zone | Sole proprietorship | | Equity joint venture | | Cooperative production | | Other | | Total | |
|---|---|---|---|---|---|---|---|---|---|---|
| | Amount | % | Amount | % | Amount | % | Amount | % | Amount | % |
| Shenzhen | 46.42 | 22.5 | 78.19 | 37.8 | 59.76 | 28.9 | 22.26 | 10.8 | 206.63 | 100.0 |
| Zhuhai | 0.08 | 0.1 | 9.07 | 8.2 | 100.85 | 91.2 | 0.54 | 0.5 | 110.54 | 100.0 |
| Shantou | 2.70 | 34.3 | 1.27 | 16.1 | 3.90 | 49.6 | 0.00 | 0.0 | 7.87 | 100.0 |

*Source:* Statistical Bureau of Guangdong Province 1985.
*Note:* Most investments (72 percent) occurred in 1984. The table refers to realized foreign investment.

Figure 3.1 Industrial Output in the Four Initial Special Economic Zones, China, 1989

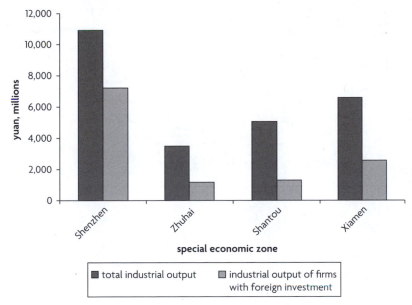

Source: CADZ 1989.
Note: In 1989, $1.00 was roughly equal to Y 3.80.

(Bao'an, Buji, and Longgang in map 3.2). The Shekou industrial zone, the first to open to foreign investment, occupied some 10 square kilometers in the southwestern corner of the Shenzhen special economic zone. Run as a wholly owned subsidiary of the China Merchants' Steam Navigation Company—a state-owned entity based in Hong Kong SAR, China—Shekou downplayed light industry in favor of shipping and navigation, ship breaking, marine engineering, and the production of steel, oxygen, acetylene, marine paint, fiberglass, cargo containers, and ships. Nine other major industrial districts, occupying 14 square kilometers, were established in the Shenzhen special economic zone. Most were in the zone's central and western districts, and most were comprehensive industrial districts for export processing (table 3.2).[7]

Export processing zones also appeared in other parts of the Shenzhen municipal area. Some were run by a development corporation under the township government. These zones attracted small overseas investors in light industry production, mostly from Hong Kong SAR, China.

**Map 3.2  Shenzhen Special Economic Zone, China, 2009**

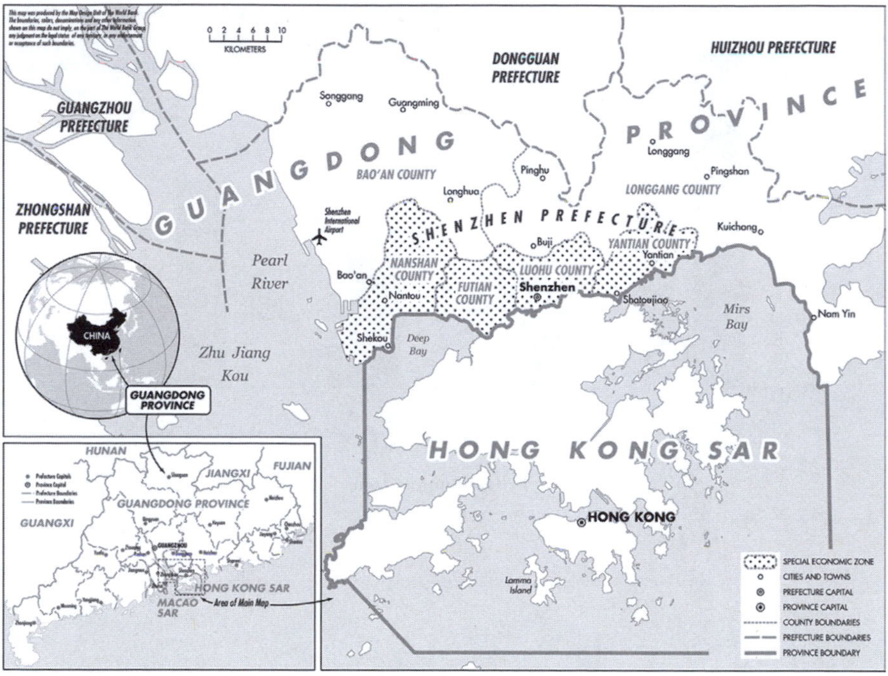

Source: World Bank Cartography.

**Table 3.2  Industrial Districts in the Shenzhen Special Economic Zone, China**

| District | Area, square kilometers | Major type of industry |
|---|---|---|
| Shekou | 10.0 | Shipping and navigation |
| Futian | 4.8 | Comprehensive |
| Chegongmiao | 2.0 | Comprehensive |
| Nantou | 1.5 | Comprehensive |
| Shangbu | 1.4 | Electronics |
| Bagualing | 1.0 | Comprehensive |
| Shahe | 1.0 | Comprehensive |
| Houhai | 1.0 | Comprehensive |
| Liantang | 0.8 | Light industries, textiles |
| Shuibei | 0.5 | Metal and machinery |

Source: Wong and Chu 1985.
Note: "Comprehensive" indicates industrial zones that did not focus on specific industries, but provided standardized plants that could be used in different assembly activities in light manufacturing, such as clothing, toys, consumer electronics, shoes, and so on.

Most projects took the form of compensation trade and intermediate processing. The Chinese partners handled only the processing and reexport of imported materials, while the foreign partners oversaw procurement, logistics, and marketing.

Areas near the Shenzhen special economic zone took advantage of their access to rapidly improving water, electricity, telecommunications, and transport services to set up their own export processing zones. Local control allowed better access to low-paid rural migrant workers because firms based in locally managed zones could avoid the stringent labor regulations applied within the special economic zones. In addition, local governments simplified investment procedures and assigned officials to guide foreign investors through import and export licensing, foreign exchange settlement, company registration, and so on. Investors in export processing projects also enjoyed a wide range of incentives, some more favorable than those in the special economic zones. Besides production facilities, the export processing zone authorities provided services for worker recruitment and accommodation and assistance with customs clearance. Generally, the foreign investors paid the zone authority processing fees for these services and did not have to share profits with the local partners: an attractive arrangement for overseas investors.

The Buji export processing zone, a small (0.25 square kilometer) zone developed in 1981 by a former rural people's commune, is located outside the northern fence separating the Shenzhen zone from the rest of the country. The funds for initial development came mainly from bank loans. Finding that incentives and facilities at Buji compared favorably with those inside the Shenzhen zone, 14 export processing firms based in Hong Kong SAR, China, including 9 producers of garments, textiles, and toys, occupied all available slots by 1986 and employed 9,200 workers to perform sewing or simple assembly tasks (Sun 1989).

*Diffusion of practice.* From the beginning, competition spurred the expansion of investment opportunities in export processing zones and industrial parks. It quickly became evident that foreign investment was a potent catalyst for accelerating growth in employment, production, exports, and tax revenues. Growing numbers of provinces and localities clamored for permission to follow the lead of their southern neighbors in wooing foreign investors. This competition quickly emerged as a major driver of reform. Almost immediately, rival local governments began bending rules and streamlining procedures to attract foreign investors. These incentives were effective in Fujian, Guangdong, and other provinces with strong historical ties to overseas Chinese, but with poor access to investment resources under the plan system. The new zones also signaled to domestic and foreign audiences that China intended to pursue its agenda of policy reform and opening.

Even state-owned enterprises, which had produced 78 percent of industrial output in 1978 (NBS 1999), quickly took advantage of the opportunities arising from the new zones. Although these zones absorbed a third of China's inflow of FDI during the 1980s, only a third of Shenzhen-based industrial firms had any foreign investment (CADZ 1989). The majority of investment funds came from state enterprises in China's hinterland. The new zones rapidly became transmission belts, extending the impact of the technology, equipment, funds, and management expertise of foreign investors beyond the narrow confines of the initial zones (L. Li 2009).

Government policies had a significant impact on the overall investment landscape. Governments improved the physical infrastructure by building roads, power plants, and telecommunications facilities. They also improved the regulatory environment. Intergovernmental competition led to the simplification of official procedures. Township authorities in Shenzhen sought to attract investors by providing one-stop shopping so that investors could readily procure all necessary clearances and licenses at a single location.

The successes of the initial special economic zones encouraged the central government to add zones in other regions and spurred provincial and local governments outside Fujian and Guangdong to campaign for access to the new arrangements. In 1984/85, the new approach was extended to 14 coastal cities, Hainan Island, the Yangzi River Delta, the Pearl River Delta, and the south Fujian triangle area. Between 1984 and 1988, the State Council approved national economic and technological development zones in Caohejing, Dalian, Fuzhou, Guangzhou, Hongqiao, Lianyungang, Minhang, Nantong, Ningbo, Qingdao, Qinhuangdao, Tianjin, Yantai, and Zhanjiang.

The new zones were small plots of land carved out of coastal urban areas. Like the special economic zones, these national economic development zones were designed as bases for initiating regional opening, attracting investment, and promoting exports, high-technology development, and economic growth. An official of the Guangzhou economic development zone noted that the zone "aim[ed] to attract [FDI] and develop export-oriented manufacturing" (July 2012 interview).

The new zones offered preferential treatment for foreign investors similar to that in the special economic zones, but received little investment from the central government. Most used bank loans to fund infrastructure development (see above). Many ran into trouble because of the limited availability of funds and because foreign investors were leery of China's political environment. In the Guangzhou zone, for example, "during the early 1980s it was very hard to attract investment. So the zone welcomed every investor who wanted to come. The zone started with garments, electronics, beverages, and toys" (July 2012 interview).

**Stage II (1992–98): Competition for growth.** During the late 1980s, China's reform momentum stalled as inflation spiked and mass demonstrations erupted in Beijing and other cities and were violently suppressed. The setback in reform was short-lived, however. Deng Xiaoping rekindled reform momentum with a widely publicized southern tour in 1992, which included a visit to Shenzhen. During his travels, Deng attacked reform skeptics, emphasized the necessity of rapid economic development, and insisted that market allocation was fully consistent with China's socialist orientation. Deng's strong, unambiguous stance heartened reformers and sparked renewed experimentation with market-linked arrangements, including a major expansion of development zones and industrial parks.

*Unprecedented growth.* In 1992 and 1993, the central government authorized the creation of national development zones in 20 localities: Beijing, Changchun, Chongqing, Dayawan, Dongshan, Guangzhou, Hangzhou, Harbin, Huizhou, Kunshan, Nansha, Rongqiao, Shenyang, Urumqi, Weihai, Wenzhou, Wuhan, Wuhu, Xiaoshan, and Yingkou. While coastal locations continued to dominate, the inclusion of sites in China's central (Changchun, Harbin, Wuhan) and western regions (Chongqing, Urumqi) reflected the leadership's desire to accelerate development nationwide.

The national development zones grew rapidly. Annual FDI inflows jumped from $0.4 billion in 1991 to $4.7 billion in 1998; industrial production expanded rapidly; and exports surged from $1.1 billion in 1991 to $11 billion in 1998 (Zheng 2008).

***The tournament system.*** By 1992, besides the national zones, various central government ministries had created 70 zones in pursuit of specific policy aims. These included high-technology zones, duty-free zones, border economic cooperation zones, and others. Provincial governments rushed to participate: by 1998, almost every prefecture-level city in China had at least one economic development zone.

Fiscal reform in 1994 unified the procedures for sharing the revenue from industrial and commercial taxes between central and subnational governments, sharpening the incentives for local governments to pursue economic expansion. With economic growth now a key determinant of both local revenues and the performance evaluation of local and provincial officials, subnational governments intensified their efforts to attract foreign and domestic investment. The number of economic development zones grew rapidly as this tournament system emerged whereby county, municipal, and provincial governments competed to attract investment and promote industrial development (Zhou 2009) (figure 3.2).

**Figure 3.2  Growth in the Number of Newly Added Provincial Economic Development Zones, China, 1984–2006**

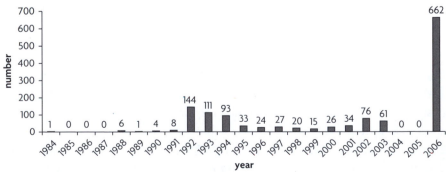

*Source:* G. Li 2009.

Development zones became a key local policy tool for accelerating growth. The willingness of banks to accept land as collateral allowed local administrators to use eminent domain to acquire land cheaply for new zones, obtain bank loans to finance infrastructure, and then apply the revenue from the sale of the developed land and the tax payments from the newly established factories to repay the loans and provide seed money for new growth initiatives (see above). Provinces eventually gained the right to establish new zones without prior approval from the central government. An administrator of a provincial development zone in Chengdu, Sichuan Province, explained how the zone was created, as follows:

> The establishment of the zone and its rating [municipal level, provincial level, and so on] is approved by the provincial government. The concrete policies are made mainly by local government (municipal and district government) based on local fiscal strength, human resources, and industrial foundation. (July 2012 interview)

With the huge increase in economic development zones came intensifying competition for large projects and funding. A government official at a provincial zone in Guangdong explained it this way:

> The zones compete with each other when there is a national program. For instance, the central government initiated a "Guangdong–Hong Kong–Macao Cooperation Program" with funding of 30 million yuan. Enterprises from many zones applied to participate, and the winners received these funds. (July 2012 interview)

Qipai Motorcycle in the Jiangmen development zone in Guangdong Province received a certificate as a high-technology firm with the help of the local government:

> Before 2009 national economic development zones had the right to issue the certificate of high-tech firms. However, in 2009 the Ministry of Science and Technology created a Torch Center, which took over the right to issue certificates from the national economic development zones. So now local government can only help firms like Qipai prepare materials for the application. (July 2012 interview)

Increasing competition highlighted the importance of regional comparative advantage in attracting investment and boosting industrial output. Industrial development zones in the eastern coastal areas, building on their

**Figure 3.3 Growth in the Number of Provincial Economic Development Zones, by Region, China, 1985–2003**

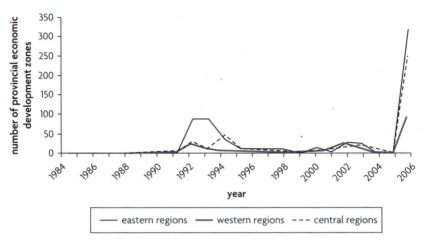

*Source:* G. Li 2009.

proximity to ports, generally superior infrastructure, a more well educated workforce, and more business-oriented administrations, absorbed the bulk of incoming FDI and generally grew more quickly than zones in less well favored locations (G. Li 2009). The disparities among zones were more evident as well (figure 3.3). In 1997, the top four national economic development zones (Tianjin, Guangzhou, Dalian, and Kunshan—all in coastal areas) accounted for 47 percent of the industrial output of all 32 national economic development zones (Ge 1999; Peng 1999).

**Stage III (1999–present): Restructuring and upgrading.** Rapid growth continued until the 1997–98 Asian financial crisis, which sharply reduced export sales throughout Asia. Growth rates of industrial output, foreign investment, and exports in China's industrial parks all slowed. Soon thereafter, China launched the massive Great Western Development Strategy (see above). The short-term goal was to substitute domestic demand for the falloff in overseas demand; the longer-term goal was to enable the poor western regions to reap a larger share of the economic benefits of China's opening and thereby reduce China's large and growing regional income disparities. The program included plans for constructing new national-level economic development zones in the capital

**Table 3.3  Statistics on 90 National Economic Development Zones, China, 2010**

| Statistic | National total | 90 national zones | 47 zones, eastern region | 21 zones, central region | 22 zones, western region |
|---|---|---|---|---|---|
| GDP, yuan, billions | 397.98 | 26.85 | 19.14 | 4.76 | 2.96 |
| Total industrial output, yuan, billions | 707.77 | 77.54 | 57.88 | 12.96 | 6.70 |
| Export value, yuan, billions | 15.78 | 2.54 | 2.35 | 0.11 | 0.08 |
| Export, high-technology products, $, billions | — | 1.64 | 1.56 | 0.07 | 0.01 |
| Inward FDI, $, billions | 1.06 | 0.31 | 0.24 | 0.05 | 0.02 |
| Cumulative foreign investment, $, billions | — | 2.37 | 1.92 | 0.35 | 0.10 |
| Foreign-invested firms, total | — | 2,205 | 1,923 | 205 | 77 |
| Developed area, square kilometers | — | 23.93 | 16.80 | 3.97 | 3.16 |
| Employees, millions | — | 8.98 | 6.12 | 1.64 | 1.21 |

Source: CADZ 2011.
Note: In 2010, $1.00 was roughly equal to Y 6.80. — = not available. FDI = foreign direct investment; GDP = gross domestic product.

cities of hinterland provinces and autonomous regions and for upgrading selected provincial zones to the national level.

By mid-2012, the number of national economic development zones had risen to 116. The coastal (eastern) region still dominated, as shown by 2010 data on 90 national-level zones that report statistical data to the China Association of Development Zones (table 3.3). The coastal region accounted for 68 percent of the 2010 employment and 79 percent of the incoming FDI among the 90 zones.

***Regional disparities.*** Like many other countries, China has been unable to roll back regional economic inequalities that are deeply rooted in geography and history. Despite the movement of tens of millions of workers from western villages to coastal cities, a full decade of large-scale infrastructure development, and strenuous efforts to lure foreign and domestic investors to China's western region, the west's share in development has scarcely changed. In the 90 zones reporting to the China Association of Development Zones, only 3.5 percent of foreign-invested firms are located in western zones, which received only 4.2 percent of incoming FDI in 2010 (see table 3.3).

While the Great Western Development Strategy effectively equalized incentives across regions and allowed large fiscal transfers from the central government to China's western provinces, the coastal development zones have retained their long-standing competitive advantage. Their success no longer depends on favorable policy treatment, but arises from scale economies, growing engagement with global value chains, and accumulations of knowledge and skill. Enterprises in China's coastal development zones have responded to steep increases in wages, land prices, and regulatory costs by deploying their rising capabilities to upgrade their product mix and by performing higher–value added functions such as research and development (R&D) and marketing. Because thousands of firms are pushing in these new directions, agglomeration effects and improved efficiency have lowered costs and enhanced productivity, allowing the coastal regions to maintain their dynamism despite the erosion of the cost advantages. The director of a development zone summarized this upgrading process as follows:

> There are differentiated solutions for industry upgrading. Introducing hi-tech business and moving the traditional business to other locations is one of them. But we can also upgrade some traditional industries and make them more technology-intensive so that they can meet the new demands. However, for those that are really not suitable for the current society and economy, we should let them go and follow the course of development. It sounds painful, but it might be a new opportunity. (July 2012 interview)

*Areas of specialization.* The differences across development zones at various levels have narrowed. To reallocate resources on a large scale, local governments have reorganized the industrial zones under their jurisdiction and tried to form clusters of specialized enterprises around key industries (table 3.4). The Guangzhou economic development zone, begun in the early 1980s with low-cost, labor-intensive industries, has moved far up the value chain. A local government official described the recent cluster promotion strategies and visualized the future of the zone as follows:

> After years of development [the cluster] has moved upward along the value chain. Some industries were knocked out, while some went from strength to strength, such as refinery chemicals, which started with the landing of P&G [Procter & Gamble, a U.S. multinational in consumer goods] and has developed to an industry with annual output of 70 billion

**Table 3.4  Top Priority Industries in Province-Level Development Zones, by Region, China, 2006**

| Industry | East (n = 660) | | | West (n = 242) | | | Center (n = 444) | | |
|---|---|---|---|---|---|---|---|---|---|
| | Number | Share of total, % | Rank | Number | Share of total, % | Rank | Number | Share of total, % | Rank |
| Machinery | 292 | 44.2 | 1 | 82 | 33.9 | 2 | 155 | 34.9 | 2 |
| IT, electronics | 199 | 30.2 | 2 | 31 | 12.8 | 7 | 56 | 12.6 | 8 |
| Textiles | 159 | 24.1 | 3 | 26 | 10.7 | 8 | 97 | 21.9 | 4 |
| Medicines | 127 | 19.2 | 4 | 91 | 37.6 | 1 | 166 | 37.4 | 1 |
| Biotechnology | 59 | 8.9 | — | 33 | 13.6 | — | 27 | 6.1 | — |
| Food | 119 | 18.0 | 5 | 64 | 26.5 | 4 | 133 | 30.0 | 3 |
| Chemicals | 115 | 17.4 | 6 | 60 | 24.8 | 5 | 97 | 21.9 | 5 |
| Transportation equipment | 110 | 16.7 | 7 | 17 | 7.0 | 9 | 54 | 12.2 | 10 |
| Automobiles | 85 | 12.9 | — | 13 | 5.4 | — | 54 | 12.2 | — |
| Garments | 102 | 15.5 | 8 | 6 | 2.5 | 16 | 56 | 12.6 | 9 |
| Agricultural products | 77 | 11.7 | 9 | 73 | 31.0 | 3 | 81 | 18.2 | 6 |
| Construction materials | 71 | 10.8 | 10 | 57 | 23.6 | 6 | 76 | 17.1 | 7 |
| Metal processing | 63 | 9.6 | 11 | 15 | 6.2 | 10 | 32 | 7.2 | 11 |

*Source:* G. Li 2009.

*Note:* The table covers development zones that identified the sector as a lead industry in the China Development Zone Audit Announcement 2006. Each economic zone can have more than one specialized industry; as a result, the total number of zones across industries exceeds the total listed for each region. IT = information technology; n = number; — = not available.

yuan ($11 billion). At present, the government is building six industrial clusters: information technology, LED (light-emitting diodes), biotechnology (hundreds of companies), new materials, refinery chemicals, and modern services, with "Knowledge City" as a platform. The goal is to foster six clusters ... with annual output of 100 billion yuan [$15 billion] each, and develop LED, culturally creative industries, and IOT (Internet of Things) into clusters with annual output of 50 billion yuan ($7.5 billion) each, 1 enterprise with annual output of 100 billion yuan [$15 billion], 4 companies with annual output of 50 billion yuan [$7.5 billion], and 10 with annual output of 10 billion yuan [$1.5 billion]. In the future, the zone will build a Science Town, a Biological Island, and a Knowledge Town. (July 2012 interview)

### Lessons from China's Experience with Industrial Parks

Before the reforms, industrial activity focused on raising output volume, especially for goods that contributed to investment and national defense. The reform policies gave new impetus to light manufacturing, which benefited from the expansion in industrial parks, foreign investment, new export opportunities, and rising domestic demand.

**Incentives and competition.** China's successful parks and clusters incorporate major elements of a market economy, most notably, incentives and competition. The accomplishments of the reforms owe much to policy changes that aligned the goals of the national government with the aspirations of citizens. Deng Xiaoping's widely circulated comments extolling ambition ("to get rich is glorious") and rejecting egalitarianism ("let some people get rich first") summarized the shift away from the emphasis on political loyalty and class struggle in pithy epigrams that every citizen could understand. Equally important was an unusual feature of Chinese public administration: the reform policies linked the incomes and career prospects of public officials, particularly at the local level, to the growth of economic activity in the districts under their jurisdiction.

Local governments throughout China were strongly motivated to accelerate growth, but the regional variations in local history and economic structure channeled their efforts in different directions. In southern coastal areas such as Guangdong and Zhejiang, the combination of the limited development of the state-owned sector and close overseas links motivated the local governments to embrace market approaches, promote private sector start-ups, and welcome overseas investment. Without these characteristics, the governments in these areas would have had no chance of delivering rapid growth. Promoting industrial parks fit readily within their agenda of encouraging new firms and new industries. In northern and hinterland areas, meanwhile, the stronger state-owned economy and the lack of numerous overseas links inclined local governments to protect and nurture state firms, sometimes at the expense of pursuing reform initiatives, and to neglect or even oppose the growth of private business ventures.

Competition played a larger role as the reforms unfolded. Incentives favoring growth fueled competition across jurisdictions at every level: village, district, county, city, prefecture, and province. China's system of identifying, recognizing, and rewarding outstanding performers intensified the rivalry, as firms and localities worked to achieve the recognition and financial benefits tied to officially established benchmarks, such as annual sales of Y 1 billion or exports of $100 million. The competition had many dimensions: among firms in specific industries, between local and regional governments, among rival parks and clusters, and so on.

**Cooperation between private entrepreneurs and public officials.** The government contributions, at different levels, to the development of light manufacturing in China have included efforts to prepare the ground for private sector initiatives by providing a stable macroeconomic environment, enforcing contracts, and ensuring the availability of utilities and transport. However, the evolution of industrial parks in China also reveals a history of dynamic interaction between private entrepreneurs and public officials. Local governments have become more entrepreneurial over time and have supported industry in many ways. Local governments and entrepreneurs have responded quickly to changes and shifts in the strengths of local producers, the obstacles to continuing development, and the success of entrepreneurs and officials in expanding their own capabilities.

Nonetheless, at times, determined government officials have pushed hesitant entrepreneurs toward goals that were overly ambitious or that failed to match market realities. Some entrepreneurs expressed their dissatisfaction with local governments by moving their businesses elsewhere. Others reluctantly went along, only to see their undertakings fail (chapter 5).

To achieve the dynamic balance between private initiative and government leadership that maximizes opportunities to achieve sustained development, public authorities must be sensitive to markets and the daily pressures affecting private entrepreneurs. Officials are more likely to understand these matters in regions already strongly oriented toward private sector development (Luo 1990). In 1999, for example, visitors to Guangdong encountered people who carried two business cards, one identifying them as local officials and the other as company directors (1999 interview).

Although the recent trend among industries to relocate from coastal to inland areas provides·opportunities for local governments in central and western China to communicate and collaborate with the private sector, it is still unclear how smooth this process will be given that many government officials in these industrial frontiers will be confronting economic and industrial management issues for the first time.

## How Industrial Clusters Helped Light Manufacturing

The agglomeration within a limited geographical area of enterprises and institutions that are involved in similar or related business or production activities has long been recognized as an important part of building an economy (Marshall 1920). The beneficial dynamics of such cluster-based regional development is emphasized in the literature on economics, business management, geography, and other disciplines. In the China context, this takes on a regional competitive advantage.

A cluster strategy can help overcome the constraints on the access to inputs, industrial land, finance, trade logistics, entrepreneurial skills, and worker skills that affect business and industrial development in low-income economies (Dinh and others 2012). Once a few firms in a specific industry have formed a cluster in a local community, the entry costs for followers are lower because of positive external economies (Fujita, Krugman, and Mori 1999). Still, because the solutions offered by a cluster strategy are unique to each country and because firms in particular industries may grow in different ways to break free of local constraints, a cluster strategy must be tailored to the specific features of an economy.

### The Evolution of Industrial Clusters in China

In the 1980s, when clusters began to develop in China, communities lacked capital, the technical knowledge to run a factory or sell a product, and the market links to start and maintain a business. These barriers were overcome by mobilizing friends, relatives, and resources inside and outside local communities. The process fostered the gradual formation of clusters.

**Informal financing overcomes the initial capital constraint.** Most early entrepreneurs in China came from rural areas and had little savings and no property to serve as collateral for formal loans. So, entrepreneurs borrowed from their relatives and friends. A survey of 140 local firms in the Wenzhou footwear cluster reveals that, on average, 66 percent of the initial investments were provided through the personal savings of the founders, 25 percent through the savings of relatives and friends, and 3 percent through formal financial institutions (Huang, Zhang, and Zhu 2008).

The spatial proximity and close relationships mean that trust—an important element especially in the early stages of cluster formation—is essential among the initial participants. However, only small amounts of capital can be raised in this way. Because their start-up capital was limited, most of these early entrepreneurs undertook simple, labor-intensive activities, using small secondhand machines to produce textiles, garments, shoes, and other light manufactures that could be readily sold nearby. The pattern of initial capital accumulation thus supported an organic reliance on comparative advantage in the development of light manufactures.

This approach not only befits the shortages in start-up capital, but also encourages clustering (Long and Zhang 2011). Because of the division of labor in local communities, entrepreneurs do not need to build large, integrated enterprises that handle material procurement, product design, mold casting, product manufacturing, marketing, and logistics. In Puyuan, a cashmere sweater cluster in Zhejiang Province, some entrepreneurs even lack physical assets because they are able to purchase raw materials and subcontract all the production processes—dyeing, finishing, printing, and ironing—to local enterprises (Ruan and Zhang 2009).

**Learning from social networks.** In the early stages of cluster formation in China, most nascent entrepreneurs did not have business experience in a specific industry. However, many communities had pioneering entrepreneurs who had been technicians in the planning system, were familiar with various technical fields, and knew how to produce simple products. In traditional villages and small towns, most of these pioneering entrepreneurs lived in the same community as their relatives and friends, who were able to tap into this experience. For example, many firms in the Nanhai metal industry learned the necessary production techniques through local social networks that included pioneering entrepreneurs.

Early entrepreneurs in clusters in Guangdong and Fujian provinces often acquired business and technical expertise through relatives and friends who worked in businesses abroad or in Hong Kong SAR, China. For example, an entrepreneur in the Nanhai metal cluster explained how he started his business:

> We started in 1993. At that time my son graduated from college and worked for one of my relatives in Hong Kong in a factory in Dongguan. My relative in Hong Kong ran a business producing steel pipes for export. My son learned how to do business from the relative. After Deng Xiaoping's South China tour in 1992, Shenzhen developed fast. Many buildings were in construction, which brought a huge demand for steel pipes. So we developed. (July 2012 interview)

**Spin-offs and labor mobility.** In the 1980s and early 1990s, as clusters were developing, state enterprises and township and village enterprises (TVEs) were more technically advanced than private firms. Under the plan system, state ownership of all profits, along with rigid price and wage controls, sapped personal incentive and stifled production efficiency. The reforms instituted profit sharing and established bonuses in state enterprises, where, however, strong internal pressures limited the growth of pay differentials. This meant that private firms could readily tap into the talent and expertise available in the state sector, first by hiring retirees or contracting part-time consulting services with "Sunday engineers" and, later, by recruiting people away from state-owned enterprises. There were frequent complaints about such poaching. Thus, for example, big state banks would train computer specialists at considerable cost only to have them resign to take up better paying jobs in private Chinese or foreign firms.

Because of the business culture of the plan system, government intervention in business decisions had numbed public sector firms to market signals. In particular, state-owned enterprises had difficulty avoiding across-the-board pay increases and emphasizing performance-based incentives. Because private firms, hungry for personnel with business skills and technical experience, had no compunctions about generously rewarding talented personnel, many managers and technicians resigned or retired from state-owned and collective enterprises to take up positions in private firms (or to start their own businesses) once the transition to a market economy began to accelerate. In many cases, management groups took over former state firms. An entrepreneur in the Haining warp knitting cluster (see below and chapter 5) explained the transformation at his firm:

> Our factory dates to 1982. At that time, we were a state-owned enter-prise. After I graduated from high school, I went into this company and worked in every department of the firm. In 1997, when I was already a deputy general manager, the company operated at a loss. So I raised money, bought the company out, and turned it into a private enterprise. (July 2012 interview)

**Finding clients through networks.** Clusters oriented toward the domestic market did not have trouble finding customers in the 1980s and early 1990s because two decades of rationing and shortages had created a backlog of unmet demand for most light manufactures. Moreover, the early economic reforms focused on heavy industry, thereby exacerbat-ing the severe shortages in light manufactures in the 1980s (Lin, Cai, and Li 1996). In addition to the large urban market inherited from the central planning system, demand was high in rural areas in the 1980s and early 1990s following the rise in rural incomes generated by agri-cultural reforms. Many domestic market–oriented clusters owed their rapid growth to the favorable macroeconomic environment at the time.

Finding customers was more challenging for export-oriented clusters, such as those in Guangdong Province. Some small firms collaborated with trading companies to find markets and facilitate exports (see the section below on trading companies). For many other firms, however, trading firms served only as logistics agencies; finding customers was still up to them. One strategy was to work through social networks of entrepreneurs. At a time when organizational trust had not yet developed because small firms had no track record of delivering good-quality orders on time, per-sonal relations made the difference, reducing transaction costs and uncer-tainty. An entrepreneur in the Nanhai shoe manufacturing cluster that exported all its production to Italy described how she found her customers:

> I knew an Italian designer who was looking for a factory [to produce shoes]. We have known each other for more than 10 years. So he found me, and I started my business. (July 2012 interview)

**Examples of the sequence in cluster formation.** The footwear cluster in Wenzhou, Zhejiang Province, originated in local family workshops that produced low-quality shoes, but, by 2005, it had grown to 4,000 firms and more than 400,000 workers, and its output accounted for one-eighth of global footwear production (Wang 2010).

The Wenzhou footwear cluster is by no means unique. Data for 2008 show 312 large industrial clusters in Zhejiang Province, each with annual sales of more than Y 1 billion. These clusters accounted for 54 percent of provincial industrial sales revenue, 56 percent of industrial employment, and 62 percent of export sales. The shares would be larger still if smaller clusters (on which data are unavailable) were included. Light manufactures figure prominently in the output mix of clusters: among the 26 largest clusters, 5 (including the 2 biggest) are in textiles, 2 in garments, and 1 each in metal products and small items.[8]

A tradition of production is not a necessary condition for the success of a cluster. Thus, although clustered manufacturing activities have a long local history in many places in China, modern production clusters emerged only during the reform period, when private enterprise was recognized as legitimate. For example, Foshan, in Guangdong Province, and Jingdezhen, in Jiangxi Province, have been producing ceramics for more than 1,500 years. While such clustered manufacturing activities certainly exerted an influence, modern ceramics clusters based on mass production are a rather new phenomenon and bear little resemblance to the craft production of the past. The mass production of ceramics has been driven by the more recent stable supplies of power and increasing domestic and international demand. The traditional mode of production based on a fine division of labor among workshops focusing on antiques and crafts is, nonetheless, still vibrant in Jingdezhen. Many other successful clusters started without any traditional experience, such as information and communication technology in Shenzhen, buttons in Xitang, and laptops in Suzhou.

Because of the consistently low priority that the plan system assigned to investment and industrialization in Guangdong and Zhejiang, rapid development seemed unlikely without resort to unconventional means. Guangdong, which is close to Hong Kong SAR, China, and which has historic ties to many overseas Chinese communities, worked actively to attract foreign investment. Zhejiang focused on supporting small private businesses.

Light manufacturing clusters began to form in Dali, Wenzhou, and elsewhere when pioneering entrepreneurs succeeded in identifying, producing, and marketing products that could be made with readily available materials, equipment, and techniques and then sold at a good profit. Volume gave rise to specialization, subcontracting, and the division of labor, and success invited imitation.

Even at this early stage, cluster formation depended on official cooperation. Opening and expanding marketplaces, developing transport facilities and commercial infrastructure (restaurants, hotels, teahouses) to accommodate growing volumes of passenger and cargo traffic, and providing electricity and water all required government support. At the least, local governments had to avoid potentially ruinous transaction costs by controlling disruptive and punitive inspections and the excessive collection of taxes, fees, and fines. Such support was not automatic during the late 1970s when China was emerging from a period of tight control.

Zhejiang's experience illustrates the importance of "active intervention from the local government" even at the early stages of cluster development (Ding 2010, 278). Numerous case studies describe the contributions of local administrations in constructing and managing market facilities, classifying commodities, urging private operators to shift from trading to manufacturing, and focusing on quality control and upgrading the product mix of local firms (Ding 2010). In Yiwu, for instance, the local office of the Administration of Industry and Commerce built a new market structure and then, to encourage specialization, required market participants to deal exclusively in a single product (rather than trading several of the 16 products). Traders, concerned that this restriction would reduce profitability, initially declined to apply for licenses. The local officials then "approached some of the leading merchants. ... In the end, most of the booth-keepers were registered ... [and] the situation ... underwent a dramatic change, resulting in the industrial cluster formation" (Ding 2010, 274–75).

There were few foreign entrepreneurs in the early stages of cluster formation in Zhejiang. In Guangdong, however, investors from Hong Kong SAR, China, and from Taiwan, China, many with years of experience in light manufacturing, were a key driver of sectoral growth. Toy production illustrates the importance of outside entrepreneurs. Toy manufacturing began in Shanghai in the 1930s and expanded over the following decades, with Beijing and Shanghai in the lead. By 1975, Shanghai's 20-some firms employed 6,000 workers and accounted for 70 percent of nationwide production; Beijing's 9 firms employed 1,700 workers (China Light Industry Federation 2010). Once reform began, Guangdong rapidly eclipsed Shanghai as China's toy capital. Entrepreneurs in Hong Kong SAR, China, were key drivers in this change:

> Toy firms from beyond our borders shifted operations to China, of which Hong Kong firms moving to the Pearl River Delta were the first and most numerous. The Hong Kong toy entrepreneurs brought capital, brought technology, brought equipment, brought management, and brought customers to Guangdong. They ran their own plants, joint venture plants, co-operative plants, compensation trade plants operating under all kinds of forms, with Guangdong supplying the land, labor, structures, and transport services. Under the reform and opening up policy, the arrival of overseas toy-makers coupled with the local government's activism drove the rapid development of Guangdong's toy sector. Between 1985 and 1987 the number of toy factories in Shenzhen shot up from around 300 to 840, inaugurating a rapid growth spurt. Beginning in 1988, the Hong Kong operators shifted from renting buildings to buying land and building factories in Shenzhen. (China Light Industry Federation 2010, 630)

By 2009, China produced more than 70 percent of global toy output, including sophisticated products, as well as the low-end items that dominated earlier production. Within China, Guangdong towered over all other regions, churning out 79 percent of China's toy exports in 2005 and 67 percent in 2008 (China Light Industry Federation 2010).

Traders and manufacturers based in Hong Kong SAR, China, and in Taiwan, China, who initially organized and managed light manufacturing exports from Chinese-owned producers brought knowledge of overseas demand patterns, customs requirements, shipping, financing, and distribution networks: information that was virtually unknown to Chinese small-scale operators at the start of the reform era. An entrepreneur in the Haining warp knitting industry in Zhejiang Province emphasized the benefit of collaboration with trading firms:

> In the early days, we started to export through trading firms. In 2004, we got a license to export and import, but we still collaborated with trading firms because they have networks. (July 2012 interview)

Later on, European, Japanese, and U.S. retailers such as J. C. Penney, Macy's, Uniqlo, and Walmart established networks linking Chinese light manufacturing exporters with overseas retailers. In the past 10–15 years, Chinese exporters, bolstered by their growing experience, have jumped into market research, product design, materials procurement, quality control, shipping, and other value chain segments formerly the sole purview of foreign entrepreneurs. Increasing numbers of Chinese firms have shifted from producing goods following client specifications and marketed under the brands of the clients to designing or selling the products under their own brands (such as Haier Appliances) or brand names purchased from overseas firms (such as Hoover vacuum cleaners or Ryobi power tools).

## The Interactions between Clusters and Constraints

In clusters, a production process is divided into many incremental steps, which lower capital entry requirements. In addition, because of proximity and repeated transactions, people are more likely to form relationships of trust, which, in turn, facilitate trade credits and ease working capital constraints (Huang, Zhang, and Zhu 2008; Ruan and Zhang 2009).

**Inputs.** An individual firm can gain access to stable input supplies either by locating in a resource-abundant area or because it is big enough to contract regular supplies affordably at a distance. The first solution works only for some industries in some areas, and the second is not an option for newly established private firms. Clusters provide a unique approach to overcoming input restrictions. The agglomeration of similar firms generates a relatively large local demand for similar inputs, gradually making input supply a profitable separate business within the clusters, whether through trade or local production. Specialized suppliers located in the clusters not only provide reliable inputs, but can also interact with local firms to make swift changes in content or design, thereby enabling firms to adjust rapidly to changes in demand.

**Industrial land.** Pioneering entrepreneurs in clusters generally start their small businesses in family workshops because they lack sufficient capital for larger investments. Only in the later growth stage of clusters does industrial land become an urgent need. Successful developing economies usually build industrial parks with good utility services to meet the needs of growing firms. Infrastructure investments, typically by a local government, can take advantage of the scale economies in industrial parks. Although not all industrial parks house clusters, industrial parks are more likely to succeed if they include clusters because a large number of firms are required to make infrastructure investments worthwhile. (See the discussion of the Haining warp knitting industrial park below.) Similar firms agglomerated in clusters tend to have similar infrastructure requirements, which makes construction more economical and easier to plan.

**Finance.** Finance constrains entrepreneurs at all stages of growth in developing countries. A cluster strategy helps start-ups overcome the financial constraint in two ways. First, clusters lower the capital requirements for new firms (Long and Zhang 2011). Because there is a deep division of labor, entrepreneurs are able to focus only on the activities in which they have a comparative advantage. Other firms in the local community make complementary investments. Therefore, clusters enable local entrepreneurs to start up from simple and specialized activities (Fleisher and others 2010).

Second, start-up capital can be more easily accessed in clusters, where entrepreneurs share tight social networks. A cluster is a local phenomenon; so, initially, many of the entrepreneurs are from the same community or from nearby areas. Informal financing gradually develops in clusters through personal and organizational trust. Borrowing may not be limited to friends or relatives. At the later stages, many migratory entrepreneurs who previously worked as front-line workers or managers and who have socialized in the local communities begin to set up their own businesses. In mature clusters, the prevalence of trade credit among local enterprises, both native and migratory, suggests that the social networks have expanded and that proximity and repeated transactions can also facilitate informal finance (Ruan and Zhang 2009).

**Logistics.** At the beginning of cluster formation in developing countries, when market information is scarce, traders are instrumental in building territorial production systems, as illustrated in China and in Japan (Huang, Zhang, and Zhu 2008; Yamamura, Sonobe, and Otsuka 2003).

Traders acquire technical knowledge of manufacturing processes, enabling them to transition from trading to manufacturing. Gradually, professional firms begin to provide logistics services in clusters. As local industries develop, large supply chain enterprises and professional trading companies set up subsidiaries in the budding clusters (see below on trading firms).

**Entrepreneurial skills.** Clusters can spur entrepreneurship even if the level of educational attainment of the population is low. Investigations of clusters in China, Ethiopia, and Vietnam find that few of the early entrepreneurs had finished high school (Vu, Sonobe, and Otsuka 2009; Huang, Zhang, and Zhu 2008; Sonobe, Akoten, and Otsuka 2009). An entrepreneur at Huaqiang Oil and Chemical Equipment Co., Ltd. in Foshan, Guangdong Province, described her business and background:

> Now we make the biggest storage tanks for oil in Nanhai [a city near Guangzhou], over 10,000 cubic meters. We also provide equipment used in the Shenzhen subway. I was a farmer and learned some metalworking skills in a production team [under the plan system]. So my employees trust me. I designed this plan myself. I do not have much education and only went to school for three years. It is just because I do not have education that I am bold [to try new things]. (July 2012 interview)

Entrepreneurial learning, whether technical expertise or management skills, comes mostly from interactions within dense social networks. A pioneering entrepreneur may know how to run a business in a specific industry and, so, sets up shop. Friends and relatives are soon inspired to learn from the pioneer and later build their own business. After a period of working in these early firms, workers and managers are ready to create new firms.

**Worker skills.** In the cluster community, as people observe, chat, and engage with each other, knowledge is quickly diffused. A worker who encounters some technical difficulty can often find the solutions in discussions with others in the cluster. Workers can also move easily to other firms in the cluster within the same industry, expanding their professional learning and helping new firms by leveraging their skills.

Clusters can thus be viewed as laboratories for learning skills. Marshall (1920, 225) described this vividly:

> When an industry has thus chosen a locality for itself, it is likely to stay there long: so great are the advantages which people following the same skilled trade get from near neighborhood to one another. The mysteries of the trade become no mysteries; but are as it were in the air, and children learn many of them unconsciously.

Besides such incidental learning opportunities in clusters, local governments can build vocational schools or collaborate with universities to provide training programs targeting specific industries.

## Expanding and Upgrading Clusters

As entrepreneurs overcame deficiencies of knowledge, entrepreneurship, capital, and market intelligence, they began forming clusters in many rural villages and small towns. As more firms began to produce light manufactures, supply soon outpaced domestic demand. A change in market structures with globalization and the mass entry of multinational corporations into China altered the development of small and medium enterprises (SMEs).[9] The clusters weathered these external changes and grew into vertically and horizontally organized businesses.

**A deep division of labor.** In Adam Smith's 1776 tale (1904) of the pin factory, the technical division of labor according to a sequence of tasks increased efficiency in the manufacturing process. In clusters, the division of labor also occurs across firms in the local community. The agglomeration of similar firms creates a critical level of demand for specialized inputs and services. Clusters mature with the formation of upstream suppliers and downstream service providers in the local community. For example, in the Chengdu footwear cluster (chapter 5), some 1,000 shoe manufacturers are supported by 3,000 material suppliers, equipment manufacturers, logistics firms, and other producer service firms. The deep division of labor among firms in the local community enables cluster firms to respond flexibly to market changes at low cost. Because local suppliers are available, cluster firms can subcontract urgent orders to other local firms without previous additional investment for expansion. The convenience of doing business in clusters makes some firms reluctant to relocate, despite increasing labor and land costs. An entrepreneur who built his shoe factory in Shantou, a noncluster area in Guangdong Province, and then moved it to the Nanhai shoe cluster explained the reason for the relocation:

> Shantou is too far from the center of shoemaking. Materials, infrastructure, they [are] all concentrated in Guangzhou. When we moved to Nanhai, it was so much more convenient. (July 2012 interview)

**Horizontal expansion.** During the first stage of cluster growth in China, imitation led to the formation of groups of similar firms. This early horizontal expansion within clusters created rising demand for inputs and services to supply the firms in each industry. This horizontal growth reflected the strict division of labor that characterized the clusters. As the clusters matured, agglomeration economies started to attract similar firms from other areas, as well as multinational corporations, which set up affiliates or acquired or merged with cluster firms. This first stage of horizontal and vertical expansion was almost exclusively local. An example is Colgate's acquisition of Sanxiao, a leading firm in the Yangzhou toothbrush cluster (chapter 5). The relocation of firms from other areas consolidated the competitiveness of the clusters. If a leading multinational firm builds branches in a cluster, other corporations usually follow. When Coca-Cola came to the beverage cluster in Guangzhou, Pepsi-Cola followed, and, when the beverage firm, Uni-President, in Taiwan, China, came, another leading soft drink firm in Taiwan, China, Master Kang, followed.

**Learning through links outside the cluster.** As the clusters in China matured, local resources and knowledge were no longer sufficient to support growth. To gain access to advanced technological knowledge and market information, cluster firms built links beyond the clusters, including learning from international equipment manufacturers, hiring technicians from foreign competitors, and attending international fairs.

As cluster firms expanded, secondhand equipment became increasingly less useful for raising output and improving quality. Cluster firms began to replace old machines with modern equipment from international machinery manufacturers in Germany, Japan, and other developed countries. International machinery manufacturers often sent technicians to help cluster firms learn to use the new equipment. From the advanced technical knowledge embodied in the equipment, cluster firms learned how to use the equipment to increase efficiency.

Yet, cluster firms also needed access to innovative ideas on organization and product development. Firms began to send representatives to international trade fairs, on their own initiative sometimes, but, sometimes, only after efforts by ambitious and supportive local officials to alert unsophisticated businessmen to the benefits of expanding horizons. At these worldwide gatherings of related companies, cluster firms gained information about new products, new markets, advanced technical information, and new orders. They also learned about emerging trends in consumer demand in developed countries. For example, the head of an enterprise in the Shenzhen garment cluster that exports to the European Union (EU) and the United States attends annual fashion fairs in New York and Paris, where she learns about current styles in the two countries. Local governments provide information on trade fairs and sometimes offer financial support as a means of encouraging firms to participate.

Cluster firms also gained advanced knowledge by hiring technicians from foreign competitors. Retired managers and technicians in developed countries have decades of working experience and can advise cluster firms on technological development and organizational management. Some retired professionals are altruistic about helping firms in developing countries. For example, a retired Japanese manager has worked for more than a decade as a volunteer advisor to a Haining warp knitting firm managed by a Chinese friend.

**The upgrading strategy.** The upgrading process in China has involved enterprises that have progressed from original equipment manufacturers (OEMs) to original design manufacturers to original brand manufacturers. (An OEM is a firm that manufactures products or components purchased by another company and retailed under the purchasing company's brand name.) Cluster firms in China have also upgraded by strengthening their links with global buyers. Global retailers such as Sears and Walmart and branded marketers such as Nike and Reebok often control the marketing channel in developed countries for light manufactures such as garments, footwear, and toys. Cluster firms in these buyer-driven value chains frequently receive design samples from global buyers, along with specific requirements on order size, product price, and delivery time. If the cluster firms can meet these requirements, they may receive orders to produce the products under the global buyer's brand. As OEMs, they are responsible for manufacturing only. In doing business with global buyers, cluster firms develop their own manufacturing capabilities.

As cluster firms demonstrate their manufacturing skills, global buyers may help them learn to design products. Cluster firms gradually increase their design capabilities, as well as their production expertise, transitioning from OEMs to original design manufacturers. A few cluster firms even take the next step of developing their own brands to increase the added value of their products in international markets.

This upgrading strategy describes the trajectory of light manufacturing industries in the newly industrialized economies in East Asia, including China's industrial clusters (Gereffi 1999). The transformation of a large bra firm in the Shenzhen garment cluster illustrates this upgrading process. The firm started in 1998 as a supplier of bra pads and rose up the value chain to produce bras for branded marketers, such as Victoria's Secret. In supplying bras to Victoria's Secret, the firm gradually built its design capability. It now sells bras under its own brand in more than 10 franchised stores in the domestic market. The general manager of the firm explained how the upgrading took place:

> Victoria's Secret is our biggest client. It has a design team in the United States and launches new styles four times a year. Previously, either we flew to the United States, or their designers flew to us to discuss new styles. This model works slowly. Now they moved the design team to Hong Kong, and we meet every week. They provide us with market information, based on which we design new products to meet their requirements. (July 2012 interview)

## Public and Private Sector Leadership and Cooperation

Cluster growth and upgrading have been largely an outcome of market mechanisms, as entrepreneurs, based on mutual advantage, have creatively mobilized knowledge, resources, and capital within and outside local communities. However, the creation of industrial clusters in a developing country with a small knowledge pool, inadequate infrastructure, and limited technological expertise and labor skills also requires active government involvement. In China, different levels of government have worked in parallel in designing and implementing cluster policies.

Public sector leadership resulted in good outcomes in Jiangsu Province, where local officials took pride in the orderly management of small enterprises, thereby offering a favorable contrast with what Jiangsu officials viewed as chaotic conditions in nearby Zhejiang (see below). This public management of rural enterprises gave way to the rapid privatization of local government-owned collective enterprises in the late 1990s (Sato 2003).

In Guangdong Province, local governments have sought to shape and nurture industrial clusters since the 1990s on the principle of one town (*zhen*), one sector. Light manufactures, including garments, toys, and metal products, have played leading roles in the development of specialized industrial clusters. Data for 2011 show a province-wide average of 1,130 enterprises in such local clusters, rising to 2,286 in clusters in the highly industrialized Pearl River Delta region; 326 local clusters accounted for nearly a third (31 percent) of the province's GDP.[10]

However, as one official explained, the government did not want to "run the economy" or "take risks," and, so, it sought to turn loss-making enterprises over to private operators "before the losses mounted" (July 2012 interview). The official compared profitable enterprises to "beautiful daughters ... marry them off before it is too late."

Public sector leaders in Guangdong sought out émigrés, especially those based in Hong Kong SAR, China, and invited them to invest in their home regions. Parts of Guangdong with larger numbers of former residents (and their descendants) living overseas grew more quickly than the rest, suggesting the importance of overseas investment (Johnson 1994).

Private sector leadership has been most evident in the rapid expansion of industrial clusters in Zhejiang Province, where development began through private sector initiatives and then continued through gradually increasing official support and, sometimes, guidance as clusters grew (Zhang and Ruan 2011). This trajectory is linked to Zhejiang's long and rich tradition of private entrepreneurship, the absence of large-scale state industries or state investment in the province, and limited local access to overseas investment (which began to arrive only after cluster-led development was well under way). Private start-ups, which first produced for the domestic market and then for export, provided the foundation for Zhejiang's growth. This combination of circumstances paved the way for public-private partnerships. Political leaders were eager to promote growth. Encouraging small private start-ups, though politically risky at the onset of the reform period, offered the only hope for rapid development in Zhejiang. The absence of large external investments from either the state or foreign sources meant that growth could be based only on locally available resources.

In Zhejiang, initial efforts often took the form of handicraft work or production in individual households using simple machines. These household units, tiny and lacking access to external finance, found it difficult "to manufacture finished products completely and independently—each ... needed labor division and cooperation with others" (Wang 2008, 10). Facing financial constraints, entrepreneurs were ingenious in figuring out ways to circumvent them. In the absence of legal protections for private assets and contract enforcement, households naturally "sought to establish cooperation and minimize trading uncertainties by relying on family relationships and friends ... at the pioneering stage of private sector development" (Wang 2008, 10).

This cooperative approach to manufacturing in Zhejiang caught on rapidly in a region with poor agricultural prospects and long-standing traditions of handicraft production and petty commerce (Bramall 1989). Eager to escape two decades of persistent hunger, villagers grasped opportunities to cooperate with entrepreneurial relatives and neighbors and rushed to imitate successful operators. As these activities multiplied and expanded, the map of Zhejiang was soon populated by a diverse array of light manufacturing clusters; table 3.5 provides a partial list.

**The role of the central government.** The strong commitment of the central government to a market economy was critical to the formation of the first generation of private firms in China, while the fiscal reforms beginning in 1994 created strong incentives for local governments to foster clusters.

In the transition from a plan system to a market economy, local entrepreneurship can be too risky if it does not have organizational legitimacy. To invest, entrepreneurs needed some assurance that the central

**Table 3.5  Leading Products of Light Manufacturing Clusters, Seven Localities, Wenzhou, Zhejiang Province, China**

| Base, commodity production | Principal products | Raw materials | Use of products | Main markets |
|---|---|---|---|---|
| Qiaotou | Buttons | Glass, plastics | Clothing accessories | Shoe and clothing units across the country |
| Liushi | Low-tension electrical appliances | Metal, cooking wood | Accessories for enterprise equipment | Small enterprises run by townships or lower levels |
| Yishan | Regenerated acrylic fiber clothing | Leftover bits and pieces from clothing factories | General consumption | Rural and mountain areas |
| Jinxiang | Badges and labels | Plastics, aluminum | Office use | Enterprises and institutions across the country |
| Xiaojiang | Regenerated plastic woven bags | Waste plastics | Product packing | Chemical fertilizer factories and cement plants |
| Xianjiang | Shoes, plastics, and leatherette | Plastics | General consumption | Rural and mountain areas |
| Shencheng | Elastic cords | Cotton yarn, rubber bands | Clothing accessories | Clothing units and shops |

*Source:* Li 1990.

government would permit private enterprises to develop. Starting in the mid-1980s with the dual-track price system, private and family enterprises grew steadily as entrepreneurs gained confidence that their activities would not be quashed (Wu and Zhao 1987). The number of TVEs increased from 12 million to 23 million from the mid-1980s to the mid-1990s; most of these were private, household firms (figure 3.4). Since the mid-1990s, with the maturation of the market economy, many collective TVEs have been privatized.

While the transition to a market economy permitted private enterprises to form, more was needed to encourage cluster growth. To incentivize local governments to promote clusters and stem growing fiscal deficits, which, between 1990 and 1994, rose from Y 1.2 billion ($0.25 billion) to Y 35.5 billion ($7.4 billion in 1990 U.S. dollars) (figure 3.5), the central government negotiated a tax-sharing system that split the tax revenue from enterprise income; 60 percent now went to the central

**Figure 3.4  Number of Collective, Private, and Household TVEs, China, 1985–2002**

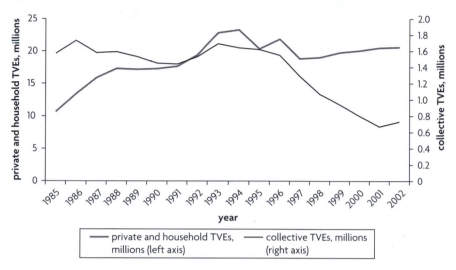

*Source:* Ministry of Agriculture 2003.

**Figure 3.5  Central Government Revenue and Expenditure, China, 1985–2002**

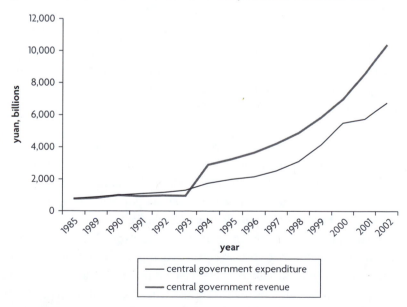

*Source:* NBS 2003.

government, and 40 percent to local governments. Local governments could thus benefit directly from the development of industrial clusters. Before 1994, all taxes had been channeled to the central government. By establishing a tax-sharing system, the 1994 reform introduced a hard budget constraint on local governments in that they were now financially responsible to provide most public services within their jurisdictions. However, the reform also provided a legitimate means for local governments to raise revenue by promoting local industries, which had to pay land and income taxes, and local governments began aggressively championing local business to benefit. The fiscal reform, by encouraging such growth, also led to a substantial increase in central government revenue.

To encourage local governments to promote cluster development, the central government gradually implemented a new performance evaluation system for local government officials that was consistent with the country's transition to a market economy (Li and Zhou 2005). Besides political loyalty, local GDP is a decisive component of the system.[11] Promotions among local government officials are greatly dependent on whether regional economic growth can catch up to or outpace the economic development of other areas in China. The central government established the system to enhance its political legitimacy through economic growth. The new system set in motion ferocious competition among local governments in nurturing entrepreneurship and attracting investment. By the early 1990s, local governments were acting as if they were professional corporations, providing financial and political support to enterprises (Oi 1992).

**Provincial governments.** Compared with the central government, provincial governments play a more active and specific role in regional cluster development. They affect the formation and upgrading of clusters in two main ways: land allocation and cluster development planning.

Because China has little cultivable land relative to the large size of the population, the central government strictly controls the conversion of land from agricultural to industrial use. Each province is notified of an annual quota of industrially convertible land that it may allocate among various industries. In the highly industrialized coastal areas, such as Guangdong and Zhejiang provinces, land is the scarcest production factor because there is almost no idle land suitable for industrial use. In recent years, there has been fierce competition for land among industries. Low-technology industries and industries that generate fewer jobs are at a disadvantage in this competition, and the land allocation decisions of provincial governments have become tools of an industrial policy that tends to favor high-end clusters over less-competitive ones.

Provincial governments use their market information and networks to identify exemplary clusters and design and implement cluster upgrading and development plans to support them. In Guangdong and Zhejiang, the provincial governments have established departments dedicated to such upgrading. Both governments have initiated projects to identify and support innovative clusters. They have also designed cluster development plans to promote collaboration and mutual learning among clusters, to facilitate the construction of joint research centers by universities and cluster firms, and to encourage cluster firms to explore international markets. In 2010, the Guangdong provincial government initiated a large project, One Specialized Town Cluster, One Upgrading Strategy, to encourage each cluster, whatever its stage of development, to plan for structural transformation in the wake of the recent global economic crisis. Table 3.6 illustrates some of the cluster upgrading strategies.

**Table 3.6 Upgrading Strategies among Selected Clusters, Guangdong Province, China**

| Cluster | Stage in cluster life cycle | Upgrading strategies |
|---|---|---|
| Hardware industry in Xiao Lan | In transition from a development to a mature stage | Regional rebranding; shift from exports to the domestic market |
| Lighting industry in Gu Zhen | In transition from original design manufacturer to original brand manufacturer | Develop light-emitting diode and photovoltaic lighting technology; build national marketing channels |
| Woolen textiles in Da Lang | In transition from original design manufacturer to original brand manufacturer | Help leading firms build international brands; strengthen design capabilities |
| Ceramic industry in Nan Zhuang | In deindustrialization stage | Build a ceramic service cluster and a low-carbon economy after manufacturing activities move out |
| Shoe industry in Huang Bu | In transition from OEM to original design manufacturer | Increase the mechanization of shoemaking; build design capabilities |

Source: Data of the Guangdong provincial government [in Chinese] (accessed August 14, 2012), http://www.zhyz.gov.cn/zyzyzycList.htm?clsId=141.
Note: OEM = original equipment manufacturer.

**Local governments.** Local governments are directly connected to clusters, which generally account for most of the economic activity in a village or town. By focusing on individual clusters and communicating frequently with local entrepreneurs, regional governments can devise policies to assist the development of specific local clusters.

*Nurturing clusters from an existing industrial base.* Successful clusters are rarely planned from scratch (Braunerhjelm and Feldman 2006). Entrepreneurs build clusters; governments nurture them, supporting the most profitable local industries. This industrial base can consist of private firms or state enterprises, such as the Chengdu shoemaking industry (chapter 5). Potential entrepreneurs learn from successful pioneer enterprises and form spin-offs. Local government officials in Haining explained how and why they picked the warp knitting industry to support as a strategic industry (chapter 5):

> At the beginning, we here had several small warp knitting firms. After some analysis, we felt these products had a good market potential. ... We had four or five firms. From this, we discussed with these entrepreneurs and decided to develop [the industry]. ... Among the four or five firms, there is one called Zhejiang Jinda Materials Co., Ltd., which trained a lot of professionals in the local warp knitting industry, from front-line workers to technicians to middle-level managers. After acquiring some skills, these professionals started their own businesses. (July 2012 interview)

Some local governments have encouraged trading or sales agents to move into manufacturing to develop clusters. The Nanhai metal cluster evolved from a group of scrap metal recycling and trading businesspeople in Guangzhou, Guangdong Province.

*Building industrial parks.* Since most clusters develop organically, cluster firms are usually scattered across many villages or small towns. Rural areas are a good place for start-ups because the cost of land is low, but they are less advantageous for growth because there is no industrial infrastructure. If local governments target a specific industry, they can build industrial parks with good infrastructure and concentrate firms within the parks (see above). Such firms benefit from favorable policies on land acquisition, taxes, and duty drawbacks. Local governments may not be selective in the early stages of industrial parks, but, as more firms relocate into the industrial parks, local governments become more selective, and many parks gradually focus on firms in specific industries, thus becoming clusters. Clusters often expand rapidly after the construction of the industrial parks. In 2000, for example, after the local government in Haining chose warp knitting as a strategic sector for local development and built an industrial park with good infrastructure expressly to cultivate a warp knitting cluster, only 15 warp knitting firms moved in when the park opened, but, as the number of firms grew from 15 in 2000 to 367 in 2009, the warp knitting industry flourished (figure 3.6). The Haining industry developed into the world's largest warp knitting center, with 2009 sales revenue of Y 15 billion ($2.2 billion). A similar process occurred in the Chengdu shoemaking cluster and the Yangzhou toothbrush cluster (chapter 5).

*Creating special platforms for specific industries.* As firms develop from family workshops to modern factories, they need hard infrastructure, but also soft infrastructure such as new systems of organizational management, technological R&D, and market exploration. Local

**Figure 3.6  Warp Knitting Firms, Haining Industrial Park, Zhejiang Province, China, 2000–09**

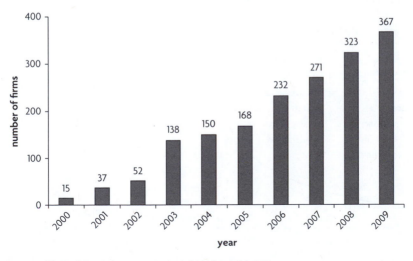

Source: Field trip of the study team in Haining industrial park, July 2012.

governments often set up special platforms for specific industries. There are many examples of creative collaboration between the public and private sectors in this endeavor. In the Haining warp knitting cluster, the local government created professional platforms in science and technology, social services, cultural promotion, international communications, training, trading, finance, and business consulting. Thus, the park cooperates with Shanghai Jiaotong University to provide high-level management courses for local executives; the park also built an experimental factory to offer training programs for front-line workers and technicians. Some platform services are provided by companies set up by local governments. In Haining, the administrative committee of the warp knitting industrial park established a firm specializing in financial guarantees (*danbao*) to help firms obtain bank loans.

*Tailoring policies to the life cycle of firms and clusters.* Local governments can tailor their industrial policies to suit needs that evolve with the life cycle of local enterprises and clusters, from start-up to growth and maturity (figure 3.7). In the beginning, local governments may provide start-up funding and technology for local enterprises. As enterprises grow, cluster policies can focus on developing supply chains in

**Figure 3.7  Dynamic Cluster Policies Implemented by the Guangzhou Municipal Government, China**

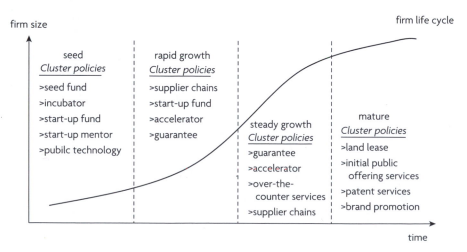

Source: Field trip of the study team in Guangzhou economic and development zone, July 2012.

the local communities. Governments may offer loan guarantee services to help firms obtain funds for expansion. As enterprises enter a steady state of growth, local governments supply over-the-counter services. Finally, when firms reach a mature stage, local governments can encourage cluster firms to go public, build their own brands, upgrade products and processes, and transfer labor-intensive manufacturing activities elsewhere. In this stage, it may be possible to create new clusters in other developing areas or even in other developing countries. In sum, a successful cluster policy focuses less on bringing firms together and more on helping firms overcome barriers to growth.

## Trading Companies and the Development of Light Manufacturing

Under the plan system, exports were controlled by the state, which viewed them as a means to generate foreign exchange. Through a series of reforms, the government gradually opened the door to more international trade, and exports began contributing significantly to national development. Light manufacturers occupied a leading role during the early stages of this process and have retained a substantial position ever since.

Without trading companies, enterprises involved in light manufacturing would have had little opportunity of breaking into overseas markets. Operating at a critical juncture of the market, these companies provide trading services for the import of inputs and the export of final goods. They act as vital matchmakers between importers and local suppliers and manufacturers and between producers and foreign buyers.

They reduce transaction, search, negotiation, and information costs by maintaining networks of suppliers, thereby offering enhanced access to imports of materials and components, which helps a wide array of domestic firms control costs and improve the quality and variety of their products and also forces domestic producers to compete more effectively with imports.

They create economies of scale and scope in overseas distribution by subcontracting and leveraging knowledge about foreign markets and export processes across multiple client firms and products, resulting in the manufacture of products that are more competitive internationally.

They facilitate communication among firms, find ways to gain access to finance, assist in organizing production lines and quality control, help firms discover missing markets and stay abreast of new technologies and new trends, and provide for the shipment of goods from suppliers and to buyers.

Historically, intermediaries have played a major, often unrecognized role in facilitating trade. Japan; Korea; Taiwan, China; Thailand; Turkey; and the United States are among the long list of economies that have benefited from trading companies to improve trade deficits (see Cho 1987 for a survey).

The reasons firms rely on trading companies vary. Based on productivity, firms may choose to export directly, or they may choose to export indirectly through intermediaries.[12] Productive firms that can afford to establish their own distribution networks export directly; less productive firms may export indirectly, while the least productive firms target the domestic market. A model constructed by Ahn, Khandelwal, and Wei (2011, 76) predicts that the "share of exports through intermediaries is larger in countries with smaller market size, higher variable trade costs, or higher fixed costs of exporting." They use firm-level data on China's trade to provide empirical evidence for this view, showing that Chinese firms that export indirectly through intermediaries are more likely to export directly later on.

These model predictions are in line with the business literature on trading companies, which relies on transaction cost theory to analyze trading companies. Transaction cost theory focuses on the actual costs incurred in the process of economic exchange. These costs typically result from "the bounded rationality of decision makers, [the] uncertainty and complexity of the environment, and [the] asymmetric distribution of information between parties to an exchange" (Peng and York 2001, 329). Within this framework, "economic agents select those contractual mechanisms that minimize the sum of production costs and the costs of contracting" (Levy 1991, 162).

The benefits of trading firms vary with the products being traded and the volume of the trade (Roehl 1983, cited in Jones 2000). For some standardized products and bulk commodities, the use of export intermediation might be more beneficial than internalization because trading companies can reduce the transaction costs of both buyers and sellers. In contrast, firms are more likely to choose direct trade if the volume of trade is high, supply and demand are stable, specification is more complex, and quality assurance is difficult (Jones 2000). Also, Ahn, Khandelwal, and Wei (2011) find that intermediary firms in China are focused more on particular countries, while direct exporters tend to focus on particular products, which adds support to the view that intermediaries are a means to overcome the market-specific costs related to international trade.

## Then and Now

In recent decades, China's foreign trade system has undergone various changes. Until 1978, the foreign trade system was highly centralized and subject to strict administration. The central government administrated the flow of tradable goods and capital through a dozen state-owned foreign trade companies (FTCs) and their subsidiary ports, each monopolizing specific types of commodities.[13] The system's main aim was to export sufficient quantities of goods to obtain the foreign exchange needed to fill gaps—notably, in food grains and capital equipment—that threatened to undermine the fulfillment of national economic plans. This system not only cut off the link between manufacturing companies and international markets, but also held back the country's economic development by overlooking the potential benefits of pursuing China's latent comparative advantage, especially in labor-intensive light manufactures.

In anticipation of its accession to the WTO in 2001, China increased its openness to the outside world, gradually lifting the public monopoly on imports and exports, cutting tariff levels, and removing nontariff barriers to trade. The reforms in foreign trade rights have allowed more manufacturing enterprises to explore opportunities in international markets either through direct engagement in the import and export business or through trading intermediaries. In 2010, customs recorded more than 234,000 companies with yearly export volumes of $1 million to $15 million each; 38 percent of these companies were small or medium in size. Intermediaries accounted for 22 percent of the export value (table 3.7) and 18 percent of the import value in 2005. Similar trends have emerged even where trade restrictions remain, such as in natural rubber, timber, plywood, wool, acrylic acid, steel, and steel products. In 2000, for example, 159 companies were authorized to import steel and steel materials.

**Table 3.7  Exports by Value and by Type of Exporting Firm, China, 2000–05**

| Year | Total value, $, millions | Direct export value, $, millions | Intermediary export value, $, millions | Intermediary value share, % |
|---|---|---|---|---|
| 2000 | 249,234 | 163,047 | 86,187 | 35 |
| 2001 | 290,606 | 198,003 | 92,603 | 32 |
| 2002 | 325,632 | 230,740 | 94,892 | 29 |
| 2003 | 438,473 | 323,541 | 114,931 | 26 |
| 2004 | 593,647 | 450,813 | 142,835 | 24 |
| 2005 | 776,739 | 608,926 | 167,813 | 22 |

| Year | Firms, number | Direct exporting firms, number | Intermediary firms, number | Intermediary firm share, % |
|---|---|---|---|---|
| 2000 | 62,768 | 53,759 | 9,009 | 14 |
| 2001 | 68,487 | 58,672 | 9,815 | 14 |
| 2002 | 78,612 | 67,750 | 10,862 | 14 |
| 2003 | 95,688 | 81,724 | 13,964 | 15 |
| 2004 | 120,590 | 100,172 | 20,418 | 17 |
| 2005 | 144,027 | 121,928 | 22,099 | 15 |

*Source:* Ahn, Khandelwal, and Wei 2011.

The following subsection discusses how this transition took place and how it has affected the development of light manufacturing in China.

## The Evolution of Foreign Trade Firms

**Processing trade activities.** Following the initial reforms, China adopted policies to reward exporting firms. Exporters were allowed to retain a portion of their foreign exchange revenues, and exporting enterprises and trading firms could also receive bank loans at favorable terms.

The first four special economic zones, which were established in Zhuhai, Shenzhen, and Shantou in Guangdong Province and Xiamen in Fujian Province in 1979, enjoyed the benefits of favorable policies and considerable import and export autonomy, including exemption from import tariffs on inputs for firms that were processing products for export. All types of enterprises—state-owned enterprises, collectively owned enterprises, township enterprises, and even individually owned businesses in the coastal areas—were allowed access to processing trade. Processing trade became a major pathway for private firms to become involved in international trade. Overseas investors provided equipment, raw materials, and samples and were responsible for selling the final products abroad; Chinese firms provided the plant locations and labor in return for processing fees. The introduction of foreign investment enabled China to take advantage of overseas capital and its own abundant labor resources, while reducing the learning costs and operational risks associated with the country's lack of experience in international markets.

**New incentives: Separating ownership and management in FTCs.** Over the years, China has introduced multiple reforms that have affected trading companies by first pushing the incumbent state trading companies to undertake more commercial operations and then allowing new entrants to add fresh export and import channels, thus intensifying the pressure on firms to adopt commercial behavior.

In particular, in 1988, the State Council began enforcing a contract management responsibility system in the foreign trade sector across the country. The system included a division of revenues and expenditures between central and local governments and held each responsible for balancing its own budget. As a result, local governments were obliged to shift more attention to earning profits and more effectively managing the financial subsidies provided from the center.

The central government eliminated, as of January 1, 1991, direct budgetary subsidies for export losses among FTCs.[14] Trading companies, now held fully responsible for their own profits and losses, were obliged to enhance their management practices and their performance. Pilot initiatives were launched to test the new mechanism in light industry, especially arts and crafts and garment manufacturing.

Beginning in 1999, through pilot reforms, state-owned foreign trade enterprises were gradually transformed into joint stock corporations. FTCs have since been paying taxes and duties, as in the case of other types of enterprises, and are no longer subject to import and export quotas.

Additional steps have also been taken to allow the more flexible management of foreign exchange.[15] In 1994, the government integrated the dual-track exchange rate system and adopted a managed floating exchange rate system based on market supply and demand.

Moreover, in 1985, the government introduced export tariff rebates. It has since modified and improved the policies on export rebates and on credit to promote exports, established an import and export bank, and set up a development fund and a venture fund for exports. In the early years of the first decade of the 2000s, it also initiated an extensive customs clearance system to promote exports.

**Ending state trading monopolies and facilitating the entry of producers and traders.** In 1978, the government initiated the reform and opening-up policy, which emphasized economic reform and the importance of foreign trade. It ended state monopolies through a series of gradual reforms and allowed private companies to conduct foreign trade transactions. Reforms were piloted in the special economic zones and then extended to coastal regions before being adopted throughout the country.

In 1979, Fujian and Guangdong were the first provinces granted foreign trade authority, followed by Beijing, Shanghai, and Tianjin. The government has since delegated the right to engage in foreign trade to all provinces. Through this reform, local governments could now establish FTCs to handle the trade in their jurisdictions. Both provinces and special economic zones are allowed to open foreign trade ports. Approval has also been given to national production ministries and large state enterprises to establish FTCs. By 1985, the Ministry of Commerce had licensed the establishment of more than 800 FTCs. By the end of 1988, about 5,000 state-owned FTCs and 10,000 manufacturing enterprises had the right to export (Yu 2008). Meanwhile, through the Foreign Investment Law of the late 1970s, foreign-invested enterprises were entitled to import production inputs and to export final products. In the 1990s, the government extended direct trading rights to more manufacturing enterprises, joint ventures, and, eventually, private trading firms. Starting in 1998, the eligibility requirements for foreign trade licenses were reduced several times and began being waived in 2004.[16]

**Eliminating mandatory export targets and import plans.** In the 1980s, the government gradually reduced the number of commodities subject to mandatory foreign trade plans and began allowing enterprises to make import and export decisions about most commodities based on market forces. Starting in 1999, the government no longer issued mandatory and directive import plans. Then, in compliance with the WTO accession agreement, China eliminated import licensing requirements and phased out all import quotas during the first five years after the accession (2001–06). The implications were significant. The share of import commodities subject to state control declined from 90 percent in 1980 to 40 percent in 1988 and 11 percent in 1998 (Wang 2008). By 2001, only a few commodities—crops, rapeseed oil, sugar, tobacco, crude oil, petrochemical products, fertilizer, cotton—were being traded exclusively by designated state-owned FTCs. (Petroleum was limited to a few state enterprises.)[17]

**Reducing tariffs.** The government has gradually reduced import tariffs to boost processed exports. In the context of trade liberalization, foreign-owned companies and joint ventures have benefited from a preferential policy and are exempt from import duties on raw materials, intermediate goods, and capital goods (Branstetter and Lardy 2008). The government expanded the tariff exemption in 1987 to all raw materials, parts, and components used to produce export goods. In 1997, it again expanded tariff exemptions for many imported goods for domestic institutions and firms, such as scientific equipment for research and teaching institutions and technology, accessories, and spare parts for software companies. The share of imports subject to import duties fell substantially over 2000–05, to less than 40 percent of total imports (Lardy 2002).

**Positive legislation on foreign trade.** Another reform area was legislation to liberalize trade. The Foreign Trade Law promulgated in 1994 established, for the first time, the legal principles of foreign trade and the rights and responsibilities of foreign traders (here equivalent to FTCs). The law was amended in 2004 in line with commitments associated with accession to the WTO. The main trading rights provisions include provisions that have transformed the authorization procedure to engage in foreign trade from a licensing system to a registration system and provisions that allow entities to engage agents to conduct foreign trade.[18]

## The Current System

**Types of firms engaged in foreign trade services.** There is a multiplicity of firms specializing in trade. Currently, three main types of firms provide intermediary trade services in China: FTCs (trading companies), service providers (service-specific agencies), and representative offices.

***Trading companies.*** Most of the trading companies and agencies are private or foreign owned (subsidiaries of trading companies located in Hong Kong SAR, China, or in Taiwan, China), while state-owned trading companies are responsible for trade in regulated commodities, such as steel, acrylic acid, and timber. Figure 3.8 depicts how local manufacturers link up with foreign buyers and describes the services provided by trading companies.

**Figure 3.8  How Foreign Buyers and Local Manufacturers Connect, China**

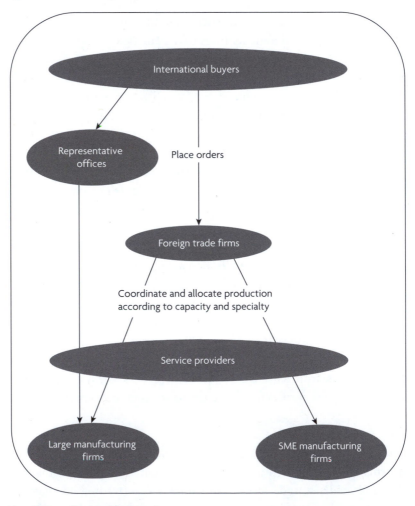

*Note:* SME = small and medium enterprise.

The FTCs are involved exclusively in trade. They are divided into two types based on the mode of operation: trading firms operating under the buy-and-sell model and trading firms operating under the agency model. The first type includes conventional trading firms that purchase commodities from input suppliers or manufacturers, sell them to manufacturers or groups of overseas buyers, and profit from the difference in the purchase price and the selling price (the buyout operational model).

The second type includes trading companies that earn commissions by providing information on market demand for manufacturing companies, assist in negotiations between suppliers and buyers, and supervise the delivery of goods. The commission ranges from 0.8 to 3.0 percent of the market value of the goods (July 2012 interviews with manufacturers). This process does not require a large amount of capital and is therefore the major business model for small and medium trading firms.

Both types of FTCs provide similar services to foreign buyers and manufacturers (figure 3.9). Thus, trading companies help foreign buyers identify potential manufacturers and play an auxiliary role in securing good-quality products, coordinating with suppliers, and guiding and supervising production.

Trading firms perform three core functions that facilitate trade and have helped China become an export powerhouse. First, trading firms usually maintain a network of manufacturing firms and also subcontract orders based on the capacity and technology of these firms. If required, they search for new production units and help the units currently in their networks expand production. For instance, the manager of INOX, an enterprise in Jiangmen, Guangdong Province, that produces stainless steel bins, noted that

> The trading company [TC] distributes orders according to the complexity of the product and the producing unit's capacity. In particular, if the product is not unique and the collaborating producer does not have the necessary capacity to meet a large order, the TC might subcontract part of the order to other factories. If the product is unique, however, the TC will try to assist the producer by negotiating the time frame with clients and/or assisting in expanding production (providing financial assistance for acquiring a new plant, negotiating with the local administration for a shorter blackout time, and so on). (July 2012 interview)

**Figure 3.9 Services Offered by Trading Companies to Manufacturers and Foreign Buyers, China**

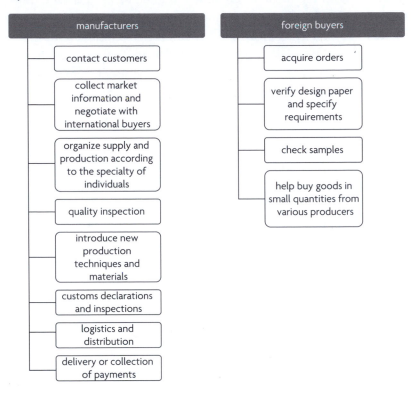

Second, trading firms provide a number of services to manufacturers. They identify potential foreign buyers for the products of their manufacturing clients. They then connect the two parties and help with negotiations and with product development. Trading firms often help guide the production of samples until the two parties agree on the final design and specifications. They help arrange the agency agreement or buyout contract and monitor the production process to ensure that the products are of the desired quality and are produced on time. The trading firm deals with customs declarations, inspections, and logistics and is responsible for the distribution of the final goods and the collection of payment. Trading companies also provide consulting and financial services throughout the process. They supply market information and keep producers up to date on current trends and new materials and technologies.

The trading companies may help provide liquidity to the SMEs by informing them of their financial options and by paying the tax rebate directly, which shortens the receivable cycle for the manufacturers (July 2012 interviews). A representative of Everich Industry Development Co., Ltd., a trading company in Shenzhen, Guangdong Province, illustrated this kind of business:

> We import and export goods that we resell to or purchase from our domestic clients. Nearly 30 percent of our clients are small and medium-size enterprises. If these enterprises want to import some materials, this takes 60 working days and requires the payment of a deposit for storing and shipping these materials. There is thus huge financial pressure on small and medium-size enterprises. We can help them negotiate with customers, and we provide finance and logistics services for them. We specialize in import and export services. (July 2012 interview)

Third, to cope with rapidly growing markets and globalization, some trading companies have expanded their services to include production chain services—along the lines of the well-known model of Everich in Shenzhen and Li & Fung in Hong Kong SAR, China (boxes 3.1 and 3.2)—and production and management consultancy to

---

**Box 3.1  Shenzhen Everich Industry Development Co., Ltd.**

Shenzhen Everich Industry Development Co., Ltd., was established in 2000 by a former employee of a large electronics firm to facilitate the firm's procurement of raw materials. Starting with initial capital of Y 145 million ($17.5 million), Everich has grown rapidly and, by the end of 2011, had total assets of Y 4.5 billion ($697 million). Everich expanded from a simple trading company to a supply chain management firm that provides comprehensive logistics and supply chain services to enterprises in information technology, telecommunications, automotive electronics, energy, chemicals, iron and steel, nonferrous metals, medical applications, precision instruments, heavy equipment, mid-range and high-end appliances, high-end consumer goods, and more. Its main clients are large manufacturing firms, but SMEs account for 30 percent of its electronics firm clients. The company's headquarters are in Shenzhen and Hong Kong SAR, China, but it has branches in all major trading cities in China, including Beijing, Guangzhou, Nanchang, Shanghai, and Wuhan. Everich also has its own warehousing and distribution bases in Hong Kong SAR, China, as well as in the Futian Free Trade Zone.

Everich comprises Everich Industry Development Co., Ltd., a trading company, and Everich Supply Chain Management Co., Ltd., a supply chain management consulting firm. The trading company has three main business segments: logistics, warehouse services, and traditional trading services (export-import). It offers services in customs clearance, warehousing, transport and

*(continued next page)*

**Box 3.1 (continued)**

delivery, procurement, input distribution, and export marketing. The supply chain management consulting firm focuses on improving the efficiency and domestic trading capacities of producer clients. It provides services in distribution processing, value added processing, outsourcing, supply chain information processing, supply chain finance, and virtual production execution. There is some overlap between the two companies, which can benefit clients. For example, the mutual collateral and guarantees the companies can supply enable clients to gain access to larger credit lines from banks.

In addition to professional services, Everich offers financial services by funding projects, supplying loans, and conducting transactions (defrayal processor). Overall, with its diverse team of experts, Everich provides comprehensive one-stop supply chain services for outsourcing noncore business that can be especially useful for small and medium manufacturers.

Small and medium producers rely on the services of trading companies such as Everich for two main reasons. First, such producers often lack the capacity to cover all stages in a value chain and might not have the right to export and import directly. Working with a trading company allows them to outsource part of their noncore business and link with foreign markets to import the raw materials they need and to export their final goods. Second, even if they have the right to conduct foreign trade, direct trade can cost more than indirect trade. In addition, the trading company has more negotiating power and can attract larger orders. Thus, while helping SMEs with export procedures, Everich also provides information on overseas markets (all Everich sectoral experts are experienced in the industries in which the company deals) and offers financial assistance to clients.

Everich helps SMEs by

- Procuring raw materials and inputs. The trading company plays the role of mediator and charges a commission. The main clients are in electronics, coal, and iron.
- Helping find new export destinations. Everich experts introduce new products and technologies to SME clients. Rather than provide R&D, which is a highly specialized and costly service, they link enterprises with sources of information.
- Providing liquidity to small and medium manufacturers by informing them of their financial options and by covering the tax rebate directly in advance, which shortens the delay for the manufacturers, resulting in shorter financial turnover. Everich charges a 1.0 percent commission per unit product if financial support is offered and 0.8 percent otherwise. It makes a profit because of the volume and high capital cash turnover involved in its services.
- Supplying marketing information and consulting free of charge.

Although the types of services supplied are the same, the level of services varies with the ranking of clients within the Chinese system of ranking enterprises by value. The higher a client's ranking, the more cash and logistics services it may receive. Moreover, Everich has established different requirements for smaller manufacturers (lower ranking) than for larger manufacturers (higher ranking). In particular, smaller manufacturers need to provide guarantees and collateral, while larger enterprises tend to receive deeper credit lines.

Unlike some other trading companies, Everich does not subcontract orders to multiple clients because it is difficult to ensure the same quality of procurement, and, in most cases, the products traded by clients are specialized, requiring an individualized R&D effort. However, if a client receives an order, but lacks the necessary technology to produce it, Everich

*(continued next page)*

**Box 3.1 (continued)**

tries to match the smaller enterprises with larger clients or other SMEs in its network that already have the technology. Everich profits on the sales of final goods; so, its sectoral experts have a strong incentive to match clients to produce final goods that can be traded. If there is no company in the Everich network with the necessary expertise, Everich specialists look for companies outside the network. Everich also participates in a government-backed initiative to improve communication between value chain producers and industry associations and offers consulting services to officials in industrial zones on matching companies, industries, and R&D providers.

Everich's biggest risk is the impact of the economic recession. In electronics (the majority of Everich clients are in this industry), 70 percent of small and medium producers go bankrupt annually. Everich is thus becoming increasingly hesitant about taking on start-ups as clients.

Everich offers integrated supply chain solutions. SMEs obtain multiple development benefits from their relationship with Everich, including financial benefits, lower transaction costs, and market information. The relationship can also be profitable for the trading company because small and medium manufacturers can produce innovative products that yield high revenues. In addition, through the Everich matching system, enterprises are introduced to new technologies and materials that help broaden their product range. Finally, though Everich focuses on high-technology products, there are lessons for the role of trading companies in other manufacturing sectors. A network of larger and smaller companies in which producers exchange information and services helps both types of producers become more efficient. Large manufacturers can outsource parts of their production to specialized SMEs, and the smaller companies can gain experience and knowledge of markets, while expanding their production of intermediate goods. The trading company is crucial in bringing these parties together, identifying potential new products, matching producers according to capabilities, performing quality control, ensuring smooth collaboration in the interest of both parties, and marketing and trading the final good.

reduce production costs and enhance manufacturer competitiveness. For instance, Li & Fung is both a manager and a shipper of manufactured products. Customers merely communicate what they think they would like. Li & Fung realizes the product concepts in prototype so that the customer may make a selection, and then the company creates a complete production program specifying the product mix and schedule. The trading group provides all the resources, monitors production, and delivers the final goods. The key to Li & Fung's success is its large network of suppliers and subcontracting manufacturing units in regions around the world, enabling it to break up the value chain and rationalize the production of each component of the final product (Margetta 1998). These practices reduce production costs, enhance the competitiveness of the associated SMEs, and facilitate business upgrading.

### Box 3.2  Li & Fung Trade Company

Li & Fung Trade Company of Hong Kong SAR, China, provides services ranging from trading services to supply chain management. Dating to 1906, the company is well known for innovations in foreign trade. Li & Fung Trade Company (Li & Fung), a professional FTC affiliated with the Li & Fung Group, has, over the years, boldly transformed the business model reflected within its services. According to the evolution of the services and value added provided by the firm, the development of Li & Fung can be divided into five stages: procurement agency, procurement company, borderless manufacturing provider, virtual manufacturing provider, and comprehensive supply chain management agency (figure B3.2.1).

During the first two stages, Li & Fung acted as an intermediary. Taking advantage of its expertise in language communication, its client network, its sources of supply, and its knowledge of the trade policies of different countries, Li & Fung bridged the gap between customers and suppliers. During these stages, commissions were the company's main source of profits. The business model was similar to that of conventional Chinese FTCs.

At the third and fourth stages, borderless provider and virtual provider, the company's role changed dramatically. Li & Fung no longer searched for buyers according to the requirements of suppliers, nor did it search for suppliers according to the requirements of buyers; instead, it became the manager and executive agent for the plans of manufacturing firms. More important, it implemented a service model centered on clients and designed an optimal supply chain for each client. In the borderless production model, by breaking through the existing value chain, Li & Fung

**Figure B3.2.1  The Five Stages of Li & Fung's Development**

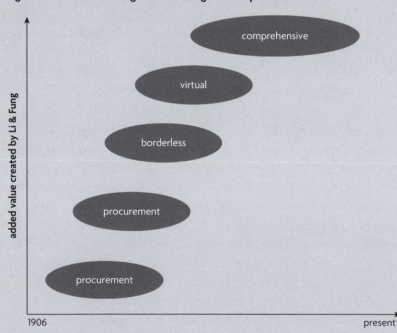

*(continued next page)*

**Box 3.2 (continued)**

became engaged in high–value added activities in Hong Kong SAR, China, such as design and qual-ity control, and allocated the business involved in lower–value added activities to other manu-facturers. In realizing the virtual production model, Li & Fung no longer signed any contracts with suppliers in the name of clients. It acted instead as a supplier itself, signed contracts directly with customers, and provided them with the products they needed. During this stage, Li & Fung expanded its services from intermediary agent to production activities and could thus coordi-nate and optimize the entire supply chain. During the virtual production stage, because Li & Fung signed supply contracts with customers and assumed bigger risks and greater responsibility, it charged higher fees and earned more profit.

Li & Fung is currently at the fifth stage, comprehensive supply chain management. This is also the development orientation the company will be striving to realize in the future. In this stage, Li & Fung provides more comprehensive supply chain services. In addition to a focus on products, Li & Fung is responsible for the planning and management of entire supply chains, breaks down supply chains into segments, and optimizes each segment to maximize the efficiency of the supply chains.

Chinese FTCs have learned from the practices and the experiences of Li & Fung, which oper-ates in a similar economic, cultural, and geographic context and once followed a trade model similar to that followed by Chinese firms. Supply chain companies in Shenzhen and elsewhere are now copying the approach of Li & Fung, while continuing to innovate.

*Service providers.* To their manufacturing company clients, service providers (service-specific agencies) offer services that help ease customs clearance procedures, payment collection, and foreign exchange settle-ments. These service providers are often exporters themselves and make extra profits by taking advantage of their access to export certificates and foreign exchange accounts. They do not provide the comprehensive services of FTCs; rather, the suppliers and the buyers establish their own contacts (directly or through a foreign trading firm) and then hire the agency to provide the logistics.

For example, Baoguang Shoes is a small company in Foshan, Guangdong Province that specializes in high-end women's shoes for the Italian market. An entrepreneur at the shoe firm explained how shoes are exported through trading companies on the agency model:

> When we have a customer, for example, we had an Italian customer the other day, he places the order here. When we finished production of the order, we chose the trading company and directly shipped the shoes to Italy. The trading company [in our case] is actually a logistics company responsi-ble for shipping and does not do the marketing for us. (July 2012 interview)

*Offices of foreign-company representatives.* Many large overseas buyers have set up subsidiaries in China to supply goods for their parent companies and for other clients. Such offices offer services that are similar to those of the FTCs, but focus on the interests of their parent companies. They identify manufacturers and distribute orders according to capacity and specialty. An executive at a bra producer, Chung Tai Garment Factory in Shenzhen, described the system as follows:

> Our clients have their own supply offices that identify manufacturing units, distribute orders, and check quality through their representative office in Hong Kong. For example, our company deals with an agency of Maidenform that gives us orders not just for the Maidenform brand but also for other retailers such as Costco, Walmart, and so on. Also, the agency is responsible for the shipment of goods and the distribution of final goods. Maidenform is both a brand and a leasing agency. The agency [Maidenform's representative office] is very supportive; it helps us upgrade technology and assists in the design process. They have their own designer. … In some cases design firms send their own technical team over to help them. (July 2012 interview)

The director of the trading department of Qipai Motorcycle Co., in Xinhui District, Jiangmen, Guangdong Province, offers a more detailed description of the operations of the department:

> The company has its own trading department, not independent, which focuses on the international market only and not on the domestic one. The department's main responsibility is importing raw materials and, in general, looking for profitable opportunities, such as importing goods unrelated to our products, like electronics, and making a profit by reselling them in the domestic market. In terms of procedure, we compile the feasibility study, pass it to headquarters to raise capital, and conduct the trade. In addition, we find clients through trade fairs and our parent company's network and help with trading logistics. (July 2012 interview)

**The role of government.** The government has played a key role in creating markets for trading intermediaries by lifting the restrictions that formerly preserved foreign trade as a state monopoly; by liberalizing the access to trade, thereby creating the environment necessary for fair competition and allowing trading intermediaries to take full responsibility for their profits and losses; and by promoting export-oriented policies. At the local and provincial levels, industrial zone officials have recognized the vital importance of trading intermediaries in matchmaking, and they offer a range of incentives to promote the intermediaries.

Trading intermediaries provide a plethora of benefits for the local economy. They are a great source of revenue for industrial zones. They contribute to tax revenue and, by serving manufacturers in the zones, especially the SMEs, help develop manufacturing, which also increases tax revenue. According to representatives of the Jinguzhou Economic Development Experimental Zone, in Xinhui District, Jiangmen, Guangdong Province, and the Warp Knitting Science and Technology Industrial Zone, in Haining, Zhejiang Province, the incentives offered to trading firms include better infrastructure and facilities (for example, warehouses), favorable conditions in financing and taxation, and help in mitigating exchange rate risks. Industrial parks have established their own trading firms to facilitate exports, as in the industrial cluster for women's footwear at the Chengdu Wuhou industrial park. A park official summarized why trading firms are important for local economic development and how the government has promoted these firms:

> Trading companies do play a very important role in economic development. They help other businesses import raw materials and market products. They also contribute to tax revenue themselves. So we would like to support their development. We try to provide good infrastructure for them, such as bonded warehouses, and insure that they have access to the hardware they need. (July 2012 interview)

**Tackling the major constraints on initial industrialization.** China's experience shows that trading intermediaries are important not only for facilitating trade, but also for overcoming the major constraints on the competitiveness of light manufacturing at the early and middle stages of industrialization. These constraints include problems in the access to and the costs and quality of inputs, access to industrial land, access to financing, poor trade logistics, and a lack of entrepreneurial and worker skills (Dinh and others 2012).

*Logistics.* Each type of firm providing trade services in China—FTCs, service providers (service-specific agencies), and the representative offices—contributes in eliminating the logistics constraint. The service providers specialize in easing customs clearance procedures, payment collection, foreign exchange settlements, and trade logistics. The FTCs and representative offices, depending on their size and business model, may offer similar services or outsource them to service providers. The main objective is the provision of comprehensive services to enhance the export sector, such as connecting manufacturers with foreign clients, production management consulting, quality control, market information, and financial services.

In addition, trading firms are go-betweens and connect producers with potential buyers. They provide a service that is conspicuously absent in many countries. Numerous small and medium manufacturers lack information about potential suppliers or buyers and face language barriers in communicating with overseas clients. Small manufacturers may avoid exporting because they are intimidated by the start-up costs: the up-front costs of establishing in-house channels and developing a knowledge base of overseas markets, including the costs of discovering new markets, developing trust and credibility with foreign customers, and writing, negotiating and monitoring contracts (Ilinitch and others 1994; Peng and York 2001). Exporting through trading companies is more cost effective for many companies than establishing their own marketing and distribution centers. Foreign trade firms maintain their own network of suppliers and buyers, as well as international market information and marketing platforms. In addition, they organize delegations to domestic and international exhibitions, such as the China Import and Export Fair (the Canton Fair), and offer marketing information for free.

***Access to inputs.*** Access to good-quality inputs at a good price can be challenging at the initial stage of industrialization, especially among smaller enterprises. Foreign trade firms offer various solutions for manufacturers. First, trading companies can maintain their own supplier networks or, through their marketing channels, can identify potential input suppliers. Small and medium producers often prefer to procure raw materials through specialized trading companies instead of ordering directly from suppliers because trading firms have more marketing power and can negotiate better prices by, for example, combining the orders of several producers. A metalware manufacturer in Guangzhou noted,

> We procure raw materials from northern China, close to Beijing, because the suppliers there offer lower prices for steel than in Guangzhou. The price in the north is 200–300 yuan lower than local prices, plus 100 yuan for transportation; the suppliers are [state-owned enterprises]. Sometimes we order iron steel directly from suppliers if they offer competitive prices, but recently, because the market is volatile, intermediaries—trading companies—are offering better prices than the suppliers, and we therefore prefer them. (July 2012 interview)

Moreover, trading firms provide quality control and guarantees that the inputs will be delivered on time. A shoe manufacturer in Guangzhou underlined the issue:

> We import raw materials through a Hong Kong trading firm because it offers quality control and ensures that the input products arrive on time. I would rather pay a little bit extra than run a risk. (July 2012 interview)

*Access to finance.* Limited access to credit and shortage of liquidity are two common problems affecting small and medium manufacturing firms. Trading companies help SMEs mainly through two channels: by buying products from them and then selling the products to the buyers (in the case of the buyout model) and by paying value added tax rebates in advance. Trading firms help shorten the cycle by paying the rebate directly to the firm from their own funds.[19] Alternatively, the buyout model enables SMEs to recover payments as early as possible, thereby reducing some of the risks in trade. The larger trading firms have also been offering financial services as part of their service platform.

*Worker and entrepreneurial skills.* Trading companies build their own networks of suppliers and buyers and have their own marketing platforms. Through these platforms, they introduce new products, materials, and techniques to enhance the competitiveness of the SMEs. They match their clients with other enterprises in their networks or with research centers to fill technology gaps. Trading companies profit on the sale of final products; so, they have a strong incentive to link enterprises inside or outside their networks with complementary technologies to ensure the effective production of the final goods required.

Trading firms help develop worker and entrepreneurial skills, usually indirectly, by exposing enterprises to international markets. By collaborating with foreign enterprises, manufacturers can become familiar with the various models of business operation and learn about new products, materials, and technologies. Thus, it is common for trading firms or foreign clients to send designers and technical teams to train and collaborate with producers.[20] More and more trading firms are offering consulting services to identify the core competitive advantages and constraints of each enterprise and help design and implement strategies to improve the competitiveness of their clients (see boxes 3.1 and 3.2).

An entrepreneur at a trading firm in Shenzhen explains part of his business:

> We have a VIP [very important person] center that provides financial, logistics, and networking services to our important clients. We also introduce some foreign buyers to our clients. For example, if some small firms produce selected products, and we have channels or networks in the relevant industry, we can provide business information to these small firms and help them contact potential buyers. (July 2012 interview)

**New opportunities.** Trading departments or subsidiaries can provide third-party services to manufacturing firms in the same or related industries. For instance, the trading subsidiary of Qipai Motorcycle Co., in Jiangmen, Guangdong Province, in addition to importing raw materials, occasionally imports electronics for resell in the domestic market, as the manager of the trading subsidiary describes (see above).

**The origin of trading companies.** The origin of firms engaged in trade services in the reformed system is varied, as follows:

- Large domestic newcomers, such as Everich, that began with a substantial capital base and expanded their business and clientele quickly (see box 3.1)

- Well-established foreign-owned trading firms, such as Li & Fung, especially companies based in Hong Kong SAR, China, and in Taiwan, China, that extended their services to China to take advantage of the new openness in trade (see box 3.2)
- Trading firms that successfully moved from state-owned to corporate status and linked with local and provincial governments or manufacturers (box 3.3)
- Numerous small private start-ups that have emerged throughout the reform period, some of which have expanded; an example is offered by firms in the city of Wenzhou (box 3.4)

---

**Box 3.3  The Haixin Trading Group: Success during the Transition from the Plan System**

The Haixin Group began as the Haixin Food Import and Export Corporation, a state-owned foreign trading agency specializing in the food trade. Established in 1955, the firm formed business relationships with more than 1,000 clients in 70 countries and regions. By 1988, it had about 300 staff and registered an annual export volume worth $60 million. Enjoying a monopoly in the export of more than 80 varieties of food products, the corporation was a star enterprise in Fujian Province. It built a network of suppliers across northeast, northwest, and north China and had its own transportation, storage, and fishing entities.

Until 1988, Haixin was under the administration of local and central government authorities and was bound by the export quotas allocated by the central government. All foreign exchange revenues were transferred to the state. Because of the difference between the domestic price of goods and the export price, the firm registered a loss in its export business every year. The loss was covered by the national budget.

However, everything changed in 1988, when the government reformed the foreign trade system, enforcing three-year export contracts with FTCs, while gradually phasing out fiscal subsidies. The reform threw Haixin into turmoil. At the end of 1990, when its first three-year export contract ended, it had an accumulated loss of Y 50 million (about $10 million). The management had to cut losses and earn profits. Haixin put together a list of all its export commodities with detailed information on cost, market demand, supply capacity, technological content, the geographical distribution of suppliers, market share, client credibility, and selling prices. Haixin used this list to adjust the composition of its export commodities, and it restructured its operating procedures to strengthen efficiency and quality control. By the end of 1991, Haixin had become profitable again.

Haixin was rewarded for its rapid adjustment to the new system. Over 1991–94, it was able to take advantage of the vibrant demand in the international market and the stable supply in the domestic market. It also benefited from the government policy of promoting the export agency system, while newcomers in foreign trade were not yet competitive. The company made additional profits by selling its retained foreign exchange on the swap market. The sharp depreciation of the yuan in 1994 because of the merging of the dual-track foreign exchange system also boosted the export sector. Haixin had wiped out all its losses by the end of 1994. In 1995, it was restructured into a corporate group with more than 30 affiliated firms covering both manufacturing and trading.

## Box 3.4  SMEs in Wenzhou

The city of Wenzhou in Zhejiang Province is a stronghold of China's private economy and a world leader in light manufacturing. Private entrepreneurs in Wenzhou began looking for overseas markets in the early 1980s. A few pioneer firms made the first attempt by attending the semiannual Guangdong Fair. Because foreign trade was mostly monopolized by state enterprises at the time, it was difficult for private firms to obtain space at the fair. In a common maneuver to skirt the barriers, private companies signed agreements with state-owned FTCs whereby the private firms paid the FTCs to lease slots at the fair and sign contracts with overseas buyers. Thus, the FTCs acted as export agents for the private firms. The practice was beneficial for both parties. The FTCs, which often operated at a loss because of poor management, gained a new source of revenue, while the private firms enjoyed access to international markets. In the early 1990s, a manufacturer of lighters erected a 12-meter-long lighter in front of the firm's booth, attracting many overseas buyers and making Wenzhou lighters famous.

After a few years of operation under these sorts of export arrangements, some private Wenzhou firms, having built up a stable client pool and accumulated experience in the export business, lobbied the local government to allow them to undertake foreign trade directly. In 1995, the Wenzhou government gave the local foreign trade authority the right to approve the affiliation between qualified FTCs in the city and export companies. After that, any approved specialized state-owned FTC could sign contracts with firms with export potential, authorizing them to conduct direct foreign trade transactions in the name of the FTC, while the affiliated firms would pay management fees to the FTC.

This indirect agent model provided a stable business relationship between the affiliated export firms and the FTCs and established a clear division in the responsibilities and risks of the export firms and the FTCs. The model became a popular way for private enterprises to access international markets. By 2000, 126 enterprises in Wenzhou were conducting foreign trade in the name of the dozen state-owned FTCs, accounting for two-thirds of the total exports of the FTCs and more than one-fifth of the city's export volume.

In 1999, the government lifted the restrictions preventing private firms from entering foreign trade. Thereafter, private enterprises could compete with state enterprises and foreign-invested companies on an equal footing. Private Wenzhou firms, which had already gained experience in foreign trade, began to export on a large scale.

A study on private enterprises in Wenzhou finds that firms in the city followed one of two separate paths to acquiring access to international markets after the restrictions were lifted.

*Model 1: Cooperation between smaller and larger firms (lighters and eyeglasses)*
Wenzhou produces about 70 percent of the world's cigarette lighters. By the end of 2002, Wenzhou was producing 600 million lighters annually, 80 percent for export. The manufacturing cluster for lighters comprises more than 500 SMEs, mostly family workshops, and a few big producers, such as Dongfang Lighter Co., which was established in 1993 and has businesses in both manufacturing and trading. The company produces more than 8,000 varieties of lighters and exports products to more than 50 countries. In 2002, Dongfang registered an export volume of $5.1 million. A large share of the exports is provided by small producers that have no capacity to explore overseas clients. Through a cooperative arrangement, these trailer firms provide new product samples to Dongfang, which then presents the samples to potential overseas buyers. If the buyers are interested, Dongfang negotiates contracts with the trailer firms to supply the products for export.

The approach in eyeglasses is similar. Wenzhou supplies one-third of the global market. At the sector's peak during the early part of the first decade of the 2000s, more than 1,000 enterprises

*(continued next page)*

**Box 3.4  (continued)**

were producing eyeglasses, and another 500 firms, the majority small or micro firms, were making frames, lenses, and other accessories. In 1998, two local entrepreneurs joined with a state-owned entity and invested Y 150 million ($18 million) to establish the Taiheng Glasses City Group Co., Ltd., the largest eyeglass manufacturer in Zhejiang Province.[a] The corporate group consisted of five closely affiliated firms, three other somewhat closely affiliated firms, and a large number of loosely connected affiliates. Shortly after its establishment, the corporation obtained the right to engage in foreign trade thanks to the new policy allowing private firms to import and export directly. With comprehensive operations in R&D, manufacturing, and trading, the company produced thousands of varieties of glasses, 95 percent for export. By 2003, the company had become Wenzhou's leading exporter of eyeglasses, fulfilling export orders worth $13.6 million, a large portion through subcontractors.

*Model 2: Obtaining orders with the help of the overseas Wenzhou network (shoemaking)*
Wenzhou entrepreneurs are well known for their adventurous entrepreneurship, mercantile culture, and deep attachment to homeland and family. With a long history of migration abroad, overseas Wenzhounese play an important role in promoting the region's foreign trade. In 2003, an estimated 2.1 million Wenzhounese were living outside Wenzhou, 1.7 million in China, and 425,000 abroad. Most of the emigrants were in Europe, half in Italy. This significant diaspora has affected the local economy, not only through the substantial remittances, but, more importantly, because of extensive business networks.[b] It has been estimated that more than 80 percent of the export orders for city industries have been obtained through the business connections of overseas Wenzhounese. By 2005, there were more than 1,000 foreign-invested enterprises, with a total capital of $1 billion, about 80 percent owned by overseas Wenzhounese (Wang and Wu 2008).

Footwear manufacturing, the city's top export sector, has likewise benefited from the international connections of Wenzhounese. Dongyi Footwear Co. is one example. Established in 1986, this family business began by producing shoes for the domestic market. In the early 1990s, it was a popular practice to undertake overseas investments to benefit from the preferential policies toward foreign-invested enterprises and take advantage of the right to export to international markets. Chen Guorong, Dongyi's owner, found a relative in Italy who was willing to collaborate in a joint venture. In 1992, a merchant from Hong Kong SAR, China, who was originally from Wenzhou visited the company. When he returned, he took back a few samples. To the surprise of the shoemaker, on the basis of the samples, the merchant was able to help the company obtain an order from a Belgian enterprise as an OEM. The company has since expanded its overseas markets to include the Russian Federation, the United States, and countries in the Middle East.[c]

Aokang, another major shoemaker, regularly obtained more than 20 percent of its overseas orders through the connections of Wenzhounese abroad. Indeed, many SMEs in Wenzhou undertook foreign trade following an unexpected order from an overseas Wenzhounese. Local entrepreneurs have seized the opportunity and continue to explore potential markets without necessarily undertaking the difficult process of entering the international market from scratch.

a. The three investors were Wenzhou Xinxing Eyeglasses Plant; Wenzhou Xintai Optics Co., Ltd.; and Zhejiang No. 11 Geology Team (a state enterprise).
b. According to the Overseas Chinese Association of Wenzhou Municipality, total overseas remittances reached $2.6 billion (Y 21.3 billion) in 2005, a growth of 28.6 percent over 2004.
c. "Xieye língjūn houxuanrenwu: Chen Guorong de waixiangxing xiejing" [The export-oriented experiences of Cheng Guorong, a leader in the shoe industry] [in Chinese], China Light Industry Information Net, August 29, 2006, http://shoes.clii.com.cn/news/show.asp?showid=116089.

## Conclusion

The trading company system is an important segment of China's economy. Trading companies provide valuable services to firms both large and small, allowing these firms the flexibility either to perform part of their business in house or to contract it out in various combinations depending on the scale, product mix, overseas expertise available, and so on.

Trading companies show a large degree of flexibility and respond to client needs. While trading firms offer the same type of services to both larger and smaller enterprises, the level of services varies. For large manufacturers, the FTCs were useful at the initial stage of the reform period, offering market information and connecting producers with foreign buyers. As manufacturers expanded production and obtained the right to export directly, most established their own trading departments or subsidiaries in foreign countries and managed their imports and exports, mostly without having to resort to trade service firms. However, even large companies use these firms to trade in unfamiliar markets or to minimize the risk in the case of the buyout model. For example, the director of Wanfang Warp Knitting Co. Ltd., in Haining, Zhejiang Province, noted as follows:

> At the initial stage, when we transformed from a [state-owned enterprise] to a private enterprise, we exported through trading companies (a state-owned trading company and through a textile import-export company in Zhejiang Province). We began to export our products in 1997, but we acquired the right to export directly in 2004. But now, we still export through trading companies because they have networks. We still trade through trading companies, for instance, for sportswear exported to Bangladesh (for Walmart) and Vietnam (for Fila). These trading firms buy out our products and resell them to foreign buyers. (July 2012 interview)

Trading firms provide comprehensive consulting and auxiliary services for SMEs. The significance of trading firms for the SMEs can be illustrated by the Warp Knitting Science and Technology Industrial Zone in Haining (chapter 5). The director of the zone emphasizes that

> In this building alone [the administrative building of the zone], there are 30 trading companies. Big producers tend to export through their

affiliated trading companies. Small producers prefer independent trading companies. (July 2012 interview)

China's experience shows that trading intermediaries can facilitate exports and directly or indirectly help overcome the constraints that manufacturers often face in the initial stages of industrialization.

## Notes

1. The five special economic zones are strategically located. Hainan Province includes Hainan Island and is the southernmost province of China. Shantou is in Guangdong Province. Shenzhen, also in Guangdong Province, is next to Hong Kong SAR, China. Xiamen, in Fujian Province, is on the Taiwan Strait. Zhuhai, in Guangdong Province, is next to Macau SAR, China.
2. "Chinese Cabinet Warns over Eviction of Farmers," *China Daily Europe*, Beijing, April 4, 2011, http://europe.chinadaily.com.cn/china/2011-04/04/content_12280375.htm.
3. Although local governments are forbidden to incur debt, "figures from the National Audit Office showed local debt of 10.7 trillion yuan ($1.6 trillion) by the end of 2010, in which local governments are responsible for 70 percent" (Wei and Wang 2012).
4. The firms locating in industrial parks are normally large. They are able to use their fixed assets, including the industrial land in the park, as collateral to obtain external financing from banks. Land banking has also been widely applied by local governments to raise funds for infrastructure investment. A local government first reclassifies the land from agricultural use to industrial use for the public interest and then acquires the land rights cheaply from farmers. It registers a company that lists the land as the major asset. With land as collateral, it can obtain a loan from a bank to finance the construction of an industrial park. To attract investment, industrial land is often offered to investors at a subsidized rate.
5. "Quanguo shoujia sanlaiyibu qiye fengyulicheng" [History of China's first processing trade enterprises] [in Chinese], *Nanfang dushibao* [Southern Municipal Daily], January 21, 2008, http://business.sohu.com/20080121/n254791945.shtml.
6. Under the planning system, investments of state-owned enterprises were controlled by the central government.
7. Comprehensive industrial districts were built to induce various kinds of light industrial manufacturing, such as clothing, toys, consumer electronics, shoes, and so on. They provided standardized plants that could be used in different assembly activities.

8. See Zhejiang Province Economic and Information Commission, 2009, *2009-nian Zhejiangsheng kuaizhuang jingji diaocha baogao* [Survey report of agglomeration economies in Zhejiang Province in 2009] [in Chinese], Index number ZJJX–06–02–201008–00017, http://www.zjjxw.gov.cn/cyfz/yqjd/2010/08/05/2010081100035.shtml.

9. Most endogenously developed clusters started organically in the 1980s, while multinational corporations flocked to China in the 1990s (see Huang, Zhang, and Zhu 2008).

10. "Guangdong Province Unveils Plan to Promote Transformation and Upgrading of Local Industrial Clusters to Attain GDP Contribution of RMB 2.5 Trillion within 5 Years" [in Chinese], *Nanfang ribao* [Southern Daily], Guangzhou, July 20, 2012, http://epaper.nfdaily.cn/html/2012-07/20/content_7106370.htm. See also "GDP of Specialized Towns in Guangdong Will Reach 2,500 Billion RMB in Five Years" [in Chinese], *Nanfang ribao* [Southern Daily], Guangzhou, July 20, 2012, http://www.gd.xinhuanet.com/newscenter/2012-07/20/c_112484469.htm.

11. In recent years, the GDP-centered government performance evaluation system has been widely criticized for promoting environmental degradation and income inequality. The central government has now articulated a philosophy of scientific development intended to give added weight to environmental protection and distributional equity in economic policy making.

12. Ahn, Khandelwal, and Wei (2011) propose a theoretical model to explain the role of intermediaries in facilitating trade. They extend the model of heterogeneous firms proposed by Melitz (2003) to allow for an intermediary sector. In this case, companies can export indirectly through an intermediary firm by incurring "a one-time global fixed cost that provides indirect access to all markets, which allows firms to save on market-specific bilateral fixed costs" (Ahn, Khandelwal, and Wei 2011, 73).

13. No other entity was granted the right to import and export goods. The types of commodities traded, as well as the volume and price of imports and exports, were subject to central planning. Moreover, the state-owned FTCs operated under the national budget, and, as a result, profits and losses were borne by the Ministry of Finance. The exporters were not linked to customers; they were, instead, compelled to sell their products to the FTCs, thereby often incurring losses (1982 interviews). The exchange rate was also fixed and overvalued, and individuals and unauthorized entities could not exchange yuan for foreign currencies.

14. National FTCs continued to receive direct subsidies for any losses incurred on the planned imports of goods sold on the domestic market at subsidized prices, such as food grains and chemical fertilizers.

15. In the 1980s, new policies were implemented to allow FTCs to retain some of their foreign exchange earnings. On January 1, 1991, the central authorities, in accordance with the annual export and foreign exchange plans approved by the State Council, assigned targets to localities and national trading companies

on the value of exports and on the foreign exchange transfers going to the state. The targets remained unchanged for three years. Municipal and provincial trade commissions also began binding foreign trade enterprises under their jurisdictions to contracts. The system provided localities with considerable discretion in the export mix, but not in total export volume. Firms that met the export and foreign exchange targets could retain 70–80 percent of their foreign exchange earnings. The surplus was split between the trade firms (80 percent) and the central government (20 percent). Foreign exchange retention rates were unified across regions. Retained foreign exchange was put at the disposal of the exporters and could be traded at national foreign exchange swap centers (*waihui tiaoji zhongxin*). Over 1986–93, more than 100 foreign exchange swap centers and 15 regional foreign exchange swap markets were established.

16. In 2001, the Ministry of Commerce promulgated the Administrative Regulations for Operation Qualification of Import and Export Corporations. In November 2002, the Administration System for Operation Qualification of Import and Export came into force nationwide. In August 2003, the Ministry of Commerce released the Notice for Modifying the Import and Export Operation Qualification Standards and Approval Procedures, reducing the eligibility requirements for a business to enter the foreign trade sector. To comply with its commitment to liberalize the right to conduct foreign trade, the government amended the Foreign Trade Law in July 2004 to replace licenses for the right to carry out foreign trade with a filing registration system that allowed all businesses to conduct foreign trade, thereby opening the sector to individual entrepreneurs.

17. The annual import total of such commodities had to be approved by the State Council. In addition, several types of products (natural rubber, timber, plywood, wool, acrylic acid, iron and steel, iron and steel products) were considered designated trade items. Although the state imposes no quantity restrictions on the imports of such items, they can only be imported by trading companies designated by the central government.

18. The Foreign Trade Law, as amended in 2004, eliminated the provision in the 1994 law requiring entities to obtain a foreign trade permit from the authorities. Instead, entities desiring to conduct foreign trade needed only to register with the relevant supervisory authority under the State Council. Subsequently, the procedure was changed, and registration was only required with the local foreign trade authority. Moreover, according to the 1994 law, any organization or individual lacking a foreign trade permit may engage a foreign trader located in China as its agent to conduct its foreign trade business. The agent is required to provide the organization or individual with information on market conditions, commodity prices, and clients. The agent is engaged through an agent agreement that specifies the rights and obligations of each party.

19. Normally, the value added tax is 17 percent, and the rebate is 13 percent, but rates can vary by the category of the goods. So, the actual tax burden for manufacturers is about 4 or 5 percent.
20. See the example of the shoe industry in Taiwan, China, presented in Hsing (1999).

# References

Ahn, JaeBin, Amit K. Khandelwal, and Shang-Jin Wei. 2011. "The Role of Intermediaries in Facilitating Trade." *Journal of International Economics* 84 (1): 73–85.

Bramall, Chris. 1989. *Living Standards in Sichuan, 1931–1978*. London: Contemporary China Institute.

Branstetter, Lee, and Nicholas R. Lardy. 2008. "China's Embrace of Globalization." In *China's Great Economic Transformation*, edited by Loren Brandt and Thomas G. Rawski, 633–82. New York: Cambridge University Press.

Braunerhjelm, Pontus, and Maryann P. Feldman, eds. 2006. *Cluster Genesis: Technology-Based Industrial Development*. New York: Oxford University Press. http://www.oxfordscholarship.com/view/10.1093/acprof:oso/9780199207183 .001.0001/acprof-9780199207183.

CADZ (China Association of Development Zones). 1989. *Zhongguo kaifaqu nianjian 1989* [China development zones yearbook 1989]. [In Chinese.] Beijing: China Financial and Economic Publishing House.

———. 2010. "2010 Nian guojian ji jingjijishu kaifaqu zhuyao jingji zhibiao" [Key economic indicators of national-level economic development zones in 2010]. [In Chinese.] Beijing: China Financial and Economic Publishing House. http:// www.cadz.org.cn/Content.jsp?ItemID=1570&ContentID=99806.

———. 2011. *Zhongguo kaifaqu nianjian 2011* [China development zones yearbook 2011]. [In Chinese.] Beijing: China Financial and Economic Publishing House.

China Light Industry Federation. 2010. *Zhongguo qinggongye nianjian 2010* [China light industry yearbook 2010]. [In Chinese.] Beijing: China Light Industry Yearbook Press.

Cho, Dong-Sung. 1987. *The General Trading Company: Concept and Strategy*. Lexington, MA: Lexington Books.

Ding, Ke. 2010. "The Role of the Specialized Markets in Upgrading Industrial Clusters in China." In *From Agglomeration to Innovation: Upgrading Industrial Clusters in Emerging Economies*, edited by Akifumi Kuchiki and Masatsuga Tsuji, 270–89. Houndmills, Basingstoke, United Kingdom: Palgrave Macmillan.

Dinh, Hinh T., Vincent Palmade, Vandana Chandra, and Frances Cossar. 2012. *Light Manufacturing in Africa: Targeted Policies to Enhance Private Investment and Create Jobs*. Washington, DC: World Bank. http://go.worldbank.org/ ASG0J44350.

Fleisher, Belton M., Dinghuan Hu, William McGuire, and Xiaobo Zhang. 2010. "The Evolution of an Industrial Cluster in China." *China Economic Review* 21 (3): 456–69.

Fujita, Masahisa, Paul Krugman, and Tomoya Mori. 1999. "On the Evolution of Hierarchical Urban Systems." *European Economic Review* 43 (2): 209–51.

Ge Hongsheng. 1999. *Zhongguo jingjitequ kaifaqu nianjian 1998* [Yearbook of China special economic zones and economic development zones 1998]. [In Chinese.] Beijing: Reform Press.

Gereffi, Gary. 1999. "International Trade and Industrial Upgrading in the Apparel Commodity Chain." *Journal of International Economics* 48 (1): 37–70.

Hsing, You-tien. 1999. "Trading Companies in Taiwan's Fashion Shoe Networks." *Journal of International Economics* 48 (1): 101–20.

———. 2010. *The Great Urban Transformation: Politics of Land and Property in China*. New York: Oxford University Press.

Huang, Zuhui, Xiaobo Zhang, and Yunwei Zhu. 2008. "The Role of Clustering in Rural Industrialization: A Case Study of Wenzhou's Footwear Industry." *China Economic Review* 19 (3): 409–20.

Ilinitch, A. Y., M. W. Peng, I. Eastin, and D. Paun. 1994. "Developing Intangible Resources: The New Battleground for Export for Small and Mid-Sized Firms." Working paper, School of Forestry, University of Washington, Seattle.

Johnson, D. Gale. 1994. "Effect of Institutions and Polices on Rural Population Growth: The Case of China." *Population and Development Review* 20: 530–31.

Jones, Geoffrey. 2000. *Merchants to Multinationals: British Trading Companies in the Nineteenth and Twentieth Centuries*. New York: Oxford University Press.

Lardy, Nicholas. R. 2002. *Integrating China into the Global Economy*. Washington, DC: Brookings Institution Press.

Levy, Brian. 1991. "Transactions Costs, the Size of Firms and Industrial Policy: Lessons from a Comparative Case Study of the Footwear Industry in Korea and Taiwan." *Journal of Development Economics* 34 (1–2): 151–78.

Li Guowu. 2009. "Spatial Distribution, Growth Process, and Leading Industries of Province-Level Development Zones in China." [In Chinese.] *Chengshi fazhan yanjiu* [Urban studies] 16 (5): 1–6.

Li, Hongbin, and Li-An Zhou. 2005. "Political Turnover and Economic Performance: The Incentive Role of Personnel Control in China." *Journal of Public Economics* 89 (9–10): 1743–62.

Li, Lanqing. 2009. *Breaking Through: The Birth of China's Opening-Up Policy*. Hong Kong SAR, China: Oxford University Press and Foreign Language Teaching and Research Press.

Li Shi. 1990. "The Growth of Household Industry in Rural Wenzhou." In *Market Forces in China, Competition and Small Business: The Wenzhou Debate*, edited by Peter Nolan and Fureng Dong, 108–25. London: Zed Books.

Lin, Justin Yifu, Fang Cai, and Zhou Li. 1996. *The China Miracle: Development Strategy and Economic Reform*. Hong Kong SAR, China: Chinese University Press.

Long, Cheryl, and Xiaobo Zhang. 2011. "Cluster-Based Industrialization in China: Financing and Performance." *Journal of International Economics* 84 (1): 112–23.

Luo, Xiaopeng. 1990. "Ownership and Status Stratification." In *China's Rural Industry: Structure, Development, and Reform*, edited by A. William Byrd and Lin Qingsong, 134–71. New York: Oxford University Press.

Margetta, Joan. 1998. "Fast, Global, and Entrepreneurial: Supply Chain Management, Hong Kong Style; An Interview with Victor Fung." *Harvard Business Review* 76 (5): 102–14.

Marshall, Alfred. 1920. *Principles of Economics*. London: Macmillan.

Melitz, Marc J. 2003. "The Impact of Trade on Intra-industry Reallocations and Aggregate Industry Productivity." *Econometrica* 71 (6): 1695–1725.

Ministry of Agriculture, China. 2003. *Zhongguo xiangzhen qiye tongji ziliao (1978–2002)* [Statistical materials of township and village enterprises in China 1978–2002]. [In Chinese.] Beijing: Zhongguo nongye chubanshe.

NBS (National Bureau of Statistics of China). 1985. *China Special Economic Zones Yearbook 1985*. Beijing: China Statistics Press.

———. 1999. *China Statistical Yearbook*. Beijing: China Statistics Press.

———. 2003. *China Statistical Yearbook*. Beijing: China Statistics Press.

Oi, Jean C. 1992. "Fiscal Reform and the Economic Foundations of Local State Corporatism in China." *World Politics* 45 (1): 99–126.

Peng, Mike W., and Anne S. York. 2001. "Behind Intermediary Performance in Export Trade: Transactions, Agents, and Resources." *Journal of International Business Studies* 32 (2): 327–46.

Peng Sen. 1999. *China Special Economic Zone and Development Area Yearbook*. Beijing: China Financial and Economic Publishing House.

Roehl, Thomas. 1983. "A Transactions Cost Approach to International Trading Structures: The Case of the Japanese General Trading Companies." *Hitotsubashi Journal of Economics* 24 (2): 119–35.

Ruan, Jianqing, and Xiaobo Zhang. 2009. "Finance and Cluster-Based Industrial Development in China." *Economic Development and Cultural Change* 58 (1): 143–64.

Sato, Hiroshi. 2003. *The Growth of Market Relations in Post-Reform Rural China: A Micro-Analysis of Peasants, Migrants, and Peasant Entrepreneurs*. Vol. 1 of RoutledgeCurzon Studies on the Chinese Economy. London: RoutledgeCurzon.

Smith, Adam. (1776) 1904. *An Inquiry into the Nature and Causes of the Wealth of Nations*. 5th ed. Edited by Edwin Cannan. London: Methuen & Co. Ltd.

Sonobe, Tetsushi, John E. Akoten, and Keijiro Otsuka. 2009. "An Exploration into the Successful Development of the Leather-Shoe Industry in Ethiopia." *Review of Development Economics* 13 (4): 719–36.

Statistical Bureau of Guangdong Province. 1985. *Guangdong Statistical Yearbook 1985*. Beijing: China Statistics Press. http://tongji.cnki.net/overseas/engnavi/HomePage.aspx?id=N2011090056&name=YGDTJ&floor=1.

Sun, Yonghong. 1989. "Export Processing Zones in China, Buji: A Case Study." *Economic and Political Weekly* 24 (7): 355–65.

Vu, Hoang Nam, Tetsushi Sonobe, and Keijiro Otsuka. 2009. "An Inquiry into the Transformation Process of Village-Based Industrial Clusters: The Case of an Iron and Steel Cluster in Northern Vietnam." *Journal of Comparative Economics* 37 (4): 568–81.

Wang, Huiyao, and Bin Wu. 2008. "Going Global of Chinese Private Enterprises: Wenzhounese Model and Its Impact on Home Development." Paper presented at the Asia Programs' "China Goes Global" conference, Ash Center for Democratic Governance and Innovation, John F. Kennedy School of Government, Harvard University, Cambridge, MA, October 8–10.

Wang, Jici. 2010. "Industrial Clustering in China: The Case of the Wenzhou Footwear Sector." In *Building Engines for Growth and Competitiveness in China: Experience with Special Economic Zones and Industrial Clusters*, edited by Douglas Z. Zheng, 151–79. Washington, DC: World Bank.

Wang, Jici, and John H. Bradbury. 1986. "Changing Industrial Geography of Chinese Special Economic Zones." *Economic Geography* 62 (4): 307–20.

Wang Zixian, ed. 2008. *The Past 30 Years of China's Foreign Trade and Economic Cooperation*. Beijing: Economic Management Publishing House.

Wei Tian and Wang Xiaotian. 2012. "Direct Local Govt Bonds Halted." *China Daily*, June 27. http://www.chinadaily.com.cn/business/2012-06/27/content_15525212 .htm.

Wong, Kwan-Yiu. 1987. "China's Special Economic Zone Experiment: An Appraisal." *Geografiska Annaler, Series B, Human Geography* 69 (1): 27–40. http://www .jstor.org/stable/490409.

Wong, Kwan-Yiu, and David K. Y. Chu, eds. 1985. *Modernization in China: The Case of the Shenzhen Special Economic Zone*. Hong Kong SAR, China: Oxford University Press.

Wu Jinglian and Zhao Renwei. 1987. "The Dual Pricing System in China's Industry." *Journal of Comparative Economics* 11 (3): 309–18.

Yamamura, Eiji, Tetsushi Sonobe, and Keijiro Otsuka. 2003. "Human Capital, Cluster Formation, and International Relocation: The Case of the Garment Industry in Japan, 1968–98." *Journal of Economic Geography* 3 (1): 37–56.

Yu Miaojie. 2008. "Three Decades of China's Foreign Trade (1978–2008)." Beijing: Peking University, China Center for Economic Research.

Zhang, Xiaobo, and Jianqing Ruan. 2011. *Evolution and Development of Industrial Clusters in China*. [In Chinese.] Hangzhou, China: Zhejiang University Press.

Zheng, Lu. 2008. *China Industrial Development Report*. Beijing: Institute of Industrial Economics, Chinese Academy of Social Sciences.

Zhou, F. Z. 2009. "The Tournament System." [In Chinese.] *Sociological Studies* 3: 54–77.

# 4

# Case Studies, China: Individual Firms and Entrepreneurs

Despite the official condemnation and legal prohibitions affecting private business before the reforms of the late 1970s, private plots, family sideline businesses, and bazaar trade survived on an informal basis, especially in the vast, lagging rural areas of the coastal regions.

The rehabilitation of private enterprise began in 1978, when Deng Xiaoping put forward the concept of "let some people get rich first." Gradual relaxation of the government's hostility toward the private sector followed. In 1978, the government began issuing permits to individual businesses (*ge-ti-hu*) that could hire up to seven employees. Subsequent reforms encouraged the growth of larger "private" firms (with eight or more workers), which began to grow rapidly. Then, private enterprises—including sole proprietorships, partnerships, or limited liability companies—were allowed to set up joint ventures with foreign corporations, thus providing additional opportunities for ambitious entrepreneurs. At the same time, China gradually moved toward an export-oriented strategy that encouraged private and overseas investment in labor-intensive manufacturing. The private sector grew at an unprecedented rate beginning in the early 1990s as the government enacted a series of policy changes and legal steps that gradually enhanced the legitimacy of private business.

Private business, which had come to be regarded as a small, but useful complement to the public sector economy, progressed initially to become recognized as an important component of China's socialist market economy (Zhao 1987). As the economic reforms expanded the scope for private sector operations, China's reformers began to see private business behavior as a good example for state enterprise reform. Thus, market-based commercial practices gradually spread into the operation of state-owned firms, and, soon, private business had become a principal market sector that, according to China's Constitution and laws, qualifies for the same treatment as state, collective, and foreign-owned enterprises.[1]

Thus, over the past three decades, the government has gradually lifted many restrictions on private businesses and reduced the legal and institutional barriers to private sector access to market resources. As a result, the private sector has witnessed remarkable growth. By 2010, China had more than 8.4 million registered private enterprises that employed more than 180 million people (NBS 2011).

Beginning in the late 1970s, the economic reforms created opportunities for the rapid expansion of light manufacturing, where entry barriers are low. By 2005, following the expansion of private firms and the privatization of some state-owned enterprises, the private sector accounted for more than 90 percent of China's light industry enterprises. These businesses produce many types of commodities, from household articles and electronic appliances to stationery and construction materials.

A number of favorable circumstances have contributed to this success. At the global level, steeply rising costs eroded the cost advantage of earlier global export leaders, creating an opening for Chinese exporters. Overseas ethnic Chinese entrepreneurs added capital, commercial expertise, and knowledge of specific technologies and markets for light manufactures to the joint effort with the labor available in China. China possessed an abundance of literate workers eager to trade diligent effort for wages that, from a global perspective, seemed low.

Domestic economic conditions also played a role. China's plan system viewed consumer products as costs rather than benefits and therefore channeled resources away from light manufacturing. As a result, there was pent-up demand for clothing, shoes, and a wide array of other household and personal items, particularly among households in more prosperous urban areas. The immediate success of China's agrarian reforms enhanced the prospects of light manufacturing by boosting rural incomes and, thus, the demand for consumer products, as well as by expanding the supply of raw materials and nonfarm labor. Finally, the main competition to private sector entrants in this growing market for consumer goods came from lumbering state-owned firms with little experience in market dealings.

While these circumstances provided substantial opportunities for private light manufacturing firms to establish profitable niches, the road to success was not smooth. Nonetheless, many new entrants, typically starting with limited capital and expertise, managed to overcome the substantial obstacles and build thriving businesses that employed millions of workers and filled China's empty foreign exchange coffers.

The case studies on China in chapters 4 and 5 cover the five light manufacturing sectors examined in our project: agribusiness, wood products, leather products, apparel (including apparel accessories), and metal products. To illustrate the policy tools discussed in chapter 3, we have also selected additional cases involving industrial parks and clusters.

We present three types of case studies. First are studies of firms or entrepreneurs that focus on the characteristics shared by successful industrial entrepreneurs and show how individuals adapt to changing circumstances. Examples are Jiangxi Youjia Food Manufacturing Company and Yiwu Huatong Meat Products Company.

Second are studies of industries, for instance, Dieshiqiao International Home Textiles Market and Haining Warp Knitting Science and Technology Industrial Zone. These cases are most useful in addressing issues revolving around the binding constraints on manufacturing growth—land, finance, skills—and spillovers.

Third are studies of clusters (buttons, zippers, toothbrushes) that help us understand the nature of agglomeration economies and the dynamics of industrial location.

In this chapter, we discuss the first type, while, in chapter 5, we discuss industries and clusters. We note, however, that some cases contain elements of two or all three types.

In China, as everywhere else, for each instance of success, there are many (unknown) failures. Indeed, the owners, entrepreneurs, and managers we have interviewed have failed many times before finally achieving success.

We have selected the cases for this book according to a number of criteria. First, they represent different subsectors in light manufacturing. Second, sufficient time (measured in years) must have elapsed so that the outcomes may be judged accurately. (Annex table 10A.1 indicates the date of the onset of operation of our enterprises.) Third, as in the non-China cases (part II), we present both successes and failures. Fourth, we have tried to include only cases in which we have been able to interview the owners or managers. The main exceptions are the Yongkang metalware industry and the Yongle economic development zone. All interviews were conducted in 2010 and 2012.

## Yiwu Huatong Meat Products Company Ltd., Zhejiang Province

China's annual output of meat products rose more than sevenfold during 1979–2011, from 10.6 million tons to 79.3 million tons, or nearly 60 kilograms per capita (figure 4.1). Despite the increase, per capita meat consumption is still only half the developed-country average. As China becomes wealthier, a combination of rising incomes, changing diets,

**Figure 4.1 Per Capita Meat Output, China, 1979–2011**

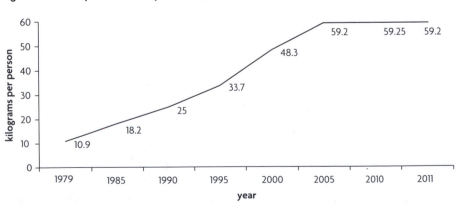

*Sources:* Calculated from data of the National Bureau of Statistics of China; data for 2010 and 2011: NBS 2012.

and urbanization will boost the demand for meat and meat products, and the share of processed meat consumed will rise from today's 15 percent to an estimated 17 percent by the end of 2015 (MIIT 2012).

The output value of China's meat industry totaled Y 923.4 billion ($142.9 billion) in 2011 (NBS 2012). The value of the output, profits, and tax revenues associated with the meat industry was higher by more than a third in 2011 relative to 2010.[2] Meat processing enterprises with annual sales of more than Y 5 million (about $774,000) employed 905,000 workers in 2011. China is now the world's largest meat producer, accounting for more than 30 percent of global meat production, or close to 80 million tons in 2011.

Along with rapid growth and rising scale, the industry faces serious challenges. The number of private companies has multiplied in response to surging consumer demand. Most meat processing enterprises are small and follow traditional slaughtering and processing practices. Quality control is poor. Chinese meat often falls short of international food safety standards. There are frequent reports of tainted or adulterated meat.

One successful company, with annual sales of Y 1.5 billion ($232 million), is the Huatong Meat Products Company, a large agribusiness firm in coastal Zhejiang Province. The company raises and slaughters hogs, processes poultry and pork, and produces animal feed. Huatong Group's tale mirrors that of the province, one that starts with struggle and poverty before the national economic reforms that began in the late 1970s, followed by incremental growth and, eventually, private wealth accumulation on a scale unimaginable before the reforms.

## Origin and Course of Development

Under the prereform planned economy, most agroproducts were subject to the government's system of unified procurement for distribution and resale through state-owned trade and retail networks. While the system aimed to provide a cheap and secure supply of agroproducts to China's urban areas, it offered little incentive for villagers working on the country's collective farms to improve production. Reforms introduced in the late 1970s dismantled collective farming and returned cultivation to individual households. The new arrangement allowed farmers to keep the income generated through their holdings after fulfilling compulsory grain procurement and tax obligations. The restoration of incentives led to an explosive growth in agricultural effort, output, and productivity, freeing up millions of villagers to seek nonfarm employment. Newly abundant supplies of farm products and labor, coupled with new demand stoked by rising household incomes, sparked the rapid growth of rural industry (Brandt and Rawski 2008). The ongoing liberalization of rural marketing created a favorable macroeconomic environment that encouraged potential entrepreneurs to bet on the growing consumer demand for meat, eggs, and other agroproducts.

**Starting from scratch.** Zhu Jianyong, founder of the Huatong Meat Products Company, was among the first generation of entrepreneurs to emerge following China's economic reforms. His early experiences resemble those of many others in the region. Growing up a son of farmers in the 1960s and 1970s, Zhu did not seem destined to lead a multimillion dollar business. Throughout his childhood, the government focused on collective agriculture and forbade the sort of private enterprises that have now emerged as a leading source of China's economic growth.

During Zhu's childhood, living conditions were harsh in urban areas, but harsher still in rural areas. Working to meet state-imposed agricultural quotas, farmers such as Zhu and his family had little opportunity to advance beyond bare subsistence. Then, in the 1960s, came China's Cultural Revolution, which severely disrupted the country's education system, further reducing people's hope for upward mobility.

All this began to change in 1978 as the first economic reforms started to open new possibilities. Agriculture was decollectivized, and households were allowed some leeway to establish small businesses. Zhu's home province of Zhejiang was among the first to implement these reforms.

**Staying in the family.** In 1986, soon after the national economic reforms took effect, Zhu was ready to dive into the new, Chinese-style market capitalism. For capital, Zhu tapped into his family's resources. He and a cousin decided to produce *huang jiu* (yellow wine), a fermented grain alcohol. Between them, they had only Y 400 ($116) and 150 kilograms of rice. Zhu learned from this first foray into private enterprise at age 19 and went on to open a series of businesses that eventually made him the owner of a small meat production empire.

Zhu moved on to an agribusiness that was closer to his roots: hog feed. Inflation in the late 1980s was contributing to disruptions and shortages in the supply of feed. Zhu's family raised several pigs; so, he knew firsthand the difficulties of finding a reliable source of feed. Because the Chinese are enthusiastic consumers of pork, Zhu also knew that demand would be strong. He began work on an animal feed company supplying local hog farmers.

In 1989, Zhu established the Yiwu Grain Animal Feed Company. The firm had about 20 workers, all relatives and fellow villagers. Being new to the sector, Zhu had to learn everything, from acquiring raw materials, technology, and marketing skills to financing and managing the business. With the help of experts in animal husbandry and nutrition, Zhu identified the proper mix of feed and began figuring out how to source it. Raw materials, which included corn, soybean, and other crops, were procured from grain markets nearby or directly from crop processing firms.

**Financing through community support.** Funding for the Yiwu feed company was never a certainty. As remains typical even today, bank lending for start-ups was rarely available, and foreign capital has traditionally gone to well-established operations. Zhu secured start-up capital of Y 2,000 ($530) through friends and family. A friend who owned a local factory offered to put up his own property as a guarantee. Though it seems risky to put one's livelihood on the line to help an inexperienced friend, such reliance on strong social networks represents a legacy of China's past that has carried over into today's business world. With this support, Zhu secured a Y 5,000 loan ($1,330) from the local rural credit cooperative, an early source of credit in farming communities. The government's economic reforms of the 1970s paved the way for these small cooperatives to extend limited, mostly short-term credit to groups of entrepreneurs in situations in which bank loans were largely unavailable. Despite their spotty record (weak governance, a poor administrative and supervisory framework, weak assets), China's rural credit cooperatives helped many start-ups in the early years of reform.

**Collaboration with overseas investors to fuel expansion.** Overseas collaboration marked a milestone for Zhu's Huatong Group on its way to becoming a major meat producer. As with many other small and medium enterprises (SMEs) that emerged from the shadows of China's rural collectives, the initial capital and network were all domestic. As Zhu's company began to grow, it drew the attention of overseas investors. In 1992, Zhu met Lin Zhen Fa, the owner of the Taiwan Chia Tung Development Corporation. Lin was looking for a local partner to invest in animal feed, having witnessed the booming demand accompanying the rapid economic growth in the nearby Yangzi River Delta region. Zhu's business acumen impressed Lin. Local government incentives for agribusiness also created a favorable investment environment. This combination gave birth to Yiwu's first involvement with offshore capital, a $1.4 million joint venture, Zhejiang Yiwu Huatong Animal Feed Company Ltd., established later in 1992.

Overseas collaboration helped Huatong beat the domestic competition. Lin provided an equity investment of more than $1 million, as well as new technology and ideas. In 1999, Huatong bought up a formerly state-owned flour mill, greatly expanding the scale of production. In 2003, Huatong acquired another animal feed company, consolidating its leading position in the local animal feed market. Now, the company faced a pressing new question: where should it expand next?

Based on an understanding of the domestic and international pork industry, Lin suggested that Zhu expand into pig farming and meat processing. Zhu followed this advice. He formulated a five-year plan that mapped out his company's strategy for developing the entire industrial value chain, from animal feed to animal husbandry, slaughtering, and meat processing. Lin brought in a team of seasoned consultants from Taiwan, China, to help Huatong install a modern management system and train Huatong's managers. These reforms have provided key support to the company's sustained development.

Since 1999, Huatong has evolved into a corporate group, spanning the meat industry's entire value chain. The company also established its own research and development (R&D) and foreign trade affiliates.

In 2001, Zhu leased 14 hectares near his village and invested Y 24 million ($2.9 million) to build a hog farm. The farm applied advanced breeding practices, enforced strict standards, and introduced high-quality pig breeds. It eventually produced 60,000 pigs a year. In June 2001, the Huatong Meat Product Company Ltd. opened. Equipped with a German-made automatic production line, the company had the capacity to slaughter and freeze 400,000 pigs a year. The company received Hazard Analysis and Critical Control Point certification for sanitation management and met International Organization for Standardization 14001 standards for ecological management. In 2007, Zhu invested Y 20 million ($2.6 million) in a poultry slaughterhouse capable of processing 4,500 chickens and 1,500 ducks an hour using automated equipment. The company provided technical support to help local farmers maintain quality standards in poultry breeding, feeds, hatcheries, and quarantining.

Zhejiang Province is home to Jinhua ham, a popular pork product with centuries of history. Most local production followed a conventional process marked by poor hygiene standards and low output. It was no surprise then that a food safety scandal happened in 2005 and damaged the reputation of Jinhua ham.

Huatong's management saw the incident as an opportunity. They imported an Italian ham production line in 2008, supported by a loan of Y 50 million ($7.2 million) from the Agricultural Development Bank. The new line features digital systems to control temperature, humidity, and salinity in an isolated environment. Advanced Italian equipment has replaced traditional vacuum chamber packaging, leading to increased productivity, reduced costs, and improved packaging. Advanced-technology refrigeration ensures food safety and quality.

Huatong is now China's largest producer of processed meat. It has received several national prizes, including "most famous agricultural product of China." Decorative boxes of preserved ham, a top domestic seller, are also sold in Hong Kong SAR, China; in Malaysia; and in the Philippines.

## Competitiveness and Binding Constraints

Huatong's success reflects strong entrepreneurship and the company's ability to adapt to a changing business world. As household incomes rise, domestic consumers have become less focused on price and more sensitive to quality. Huatong faces growing domestic and overseas demand for high-quality meat products.

By building its own hog breeding center and collaborating with more than 80 contractor farms in Fujian, Henan, Jiangxi, and Zhejiang provinces, Huatong has secured a stable supply of high-quality hogs and poultry. From feed mills to meat processing, Huatong's quality control now spans the entire supply chain, creating an efficient enterprise with a strong reputation. Furthermore, supported by bank loans and equity investments from its overseas partner, Huatong has maintained food quality by purchasing advanced machinery and controlling inputs and the production process.

The main early binding constraint on Huatong was a lack of entrepreneurial expertise, followed by difficult access to land, financing, and technology. Huatong resolved these constraints mainly through the partnership with the Taiwanese investor, who provided capital and access to new technologies and managerial and technical skills.

Risks remain significant. Maintaining a stable supply of animals is still a major challenge for the company. Huatong and other enterprises are facing pressure to supply products that meet rising food safety standards, while controlling costs. Because animal husbandry is concentrated in small-scale farms that respond quickly to short-term shifts in profit margins, animal output is volatile, following cyclical movements in meat prices (figure 4.2). The meat industry is also sensitive to fluctuations in crop prices (including animal feed) and energy, which have increased steadily over the past few years.

**Figure 4.2  Changes in the Pork Price Index, China, 2005–11**

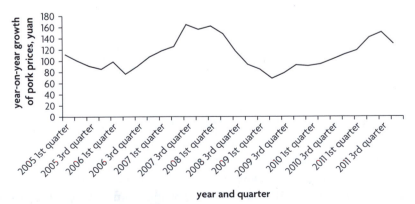

*Source:* National Bureau of Statistics of China.

Agribusiness firms also face rising labor costs. Huatong employs nearly 1,200 people. In 2010, the average monthly salary for a front-line worker was about Y 2,000 ($295); monthly salaries of management staff ranged from Y 5,000 ($739) to Y 10,000 ($1,477). Wage costs in Zhejiang's food processing industry approximately doubled during 2005–10 and continued to rise thereafter.

## The Role of Government

The government helped the Huatong Group succeed in several, mostly indirect ways.

Zhu's business benefited from a local administration that offered entrepreneurs incentives such as low-priced land in industrial parks, subsidized interest on loans, and tax breaks. The local rural credit cooperative loan was a great help to Zhu in the start-up years. The local authorities also supplied training in agricultural best practices to the farmers who supply pigs and poultry to Zhu's processing plants.

To boost agribusiness in rural areas, the government offers subsidies to local farmers who agree to dedicate their land to supplying agribusiness. This enables scattered lots to be joined into units better suited for large-scale production of hogs and other agroproducts.

As the leading agribusiness enterprise in Yiwu City, Huatong has received Y 359 million ($53 million) in bank loans from the Agricultural Development Bank, sometimes at the concessional interest rates offered to designated suppliers of China's national stockpile of pork reserves.

In a broader sense, Huatong's success has also benefited from national policies that encourage commercial relations with Taiwan, China, as well as with other industrially advanced economies. The resulting ties have fostered the kind of mentoring and innovation that foreign investment can bring. Zhu credits China's economic reforms with his success.

"Huatong is a fruit growing under the nourishment of China's reform and opening-up," he says.

## Summary

Huatong demonstrates the possibilities that have become available for expansion among innovative, forward-looking entrepreneurs since China's economic reforms. Zhu started with a rural home-based microbusiness and built it into a massive agribusiness enterprise.

His success has resulted from his diligence, his keen eye for market trends, and support from an overseas partner. The company has benefited from reforms that liberalized the market and opened it to foreign investment, providing access to capital and entrepreneurial skills.

## Jiangxi Youjia Food Manufacturing Company Ltd., Jiangxi Province

With few resources beyond entrepreneurial spirit, many Chinese have ventured into the market and built their own enterprises—often after countless failures—by mastering entrepreneurial skills and the workings of the market through trial and error. Wu Youjia, the owner of Jiangxi Youjia Food Manufacturing Company Ltd., is one of the grassroots private entrepreneurs who have driven the development of south China and turned the region into a global powerhouse in light manufacturing.

As China's living standards and incomes have risen, so has the country's demand for higher-quality food products. In 2011, annual per household food spending totaled Y 2,107 ($326) in rural areas and Y 5,506 ($852) in urban areas, up 181.3 and 188.9 percent, respectively, from 2005.[3] The snack food market has expanded even more quickly, registering sales of Y 96 billion ($14.9 billion) in 2011, up from Y 22.8 billion ($2.8 billion) in 2005 (figure 4.3).

**Figure 4.3  Growth of the Snack Food Industry, China, 2005–11**

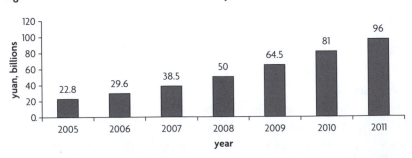

Source: China Food Industrial Net website [in Chinese], http://www.shipin588.com/news/show-32920.html.

## Origin and Course of Development

As China's economic reforms unfolded, the share of state enterprises in industrial output declined steadily; some of these enterprises were closed down or privatized; and others were restructured as corporate entities, while maintaining substantial public ownership. The output share of traditional state-owned firms fell from 77.6 percent in 1978 to 49.6 percent in 1998 and 8.2 percent in 2010 (NBS 2005, 2011). During the reform process, millions of employees were laid off, and competition from imports and from growing numbers of new firms intensified. State enterprise profits fell from 15 percent of gross domestic product (GDP) in 1978 to 2 percent in 1997 (Li and Putterman 2008). Over the same period, the private sector's share rose sharply, benefiting from the country's liberalized policies and a surge of pent-up entrepreneurial energy and consumer demand.

**Before start-up.** The tale of the founder of Jiangxi Youjia Food Manufacturing Company Ltd. is typical of postreform China. When Wu Youjia failed a college entrance exam in 1993, villagers believed that he had lost his only chance to escape farming, the destiny of most people in the area. But, within only 10 years, Wu would become the owner of the top food manufacturing company in Jiangxi Province and the most famous producer of local specialty foods in the province.

Born in the suburbs of Nankang, in Jiangxi Province, central China, Wu received no formal training in business and trade during his formative school years. As China liberalized the economy and encouraged private investment, people around him started opening businesses.

In 1994, Wu joined the sales staff of a state-owned food retailing enterprise in Nankang's Fushi Township. During the year he worked for the firm, he traveled across the province, building connections with people in the food industry. To teach himself about sales, he read all the books he could find on the subject. Meanwhile, the country's deepening reform exposed the weaknesses in Wu's company, which ultimately went bankrupt. The experience earned Wu a skill set that would help him launch his own company.

In the 1980s, villagers in Jiangxi Province began migrating to work in the thousands of private firms and factories in the Pearl River Delta region. In 1995, encouraged by his neighbors' successes and assisted by a government-backed local labor market, Wu joined the migrant workers going to the Shenzhen special economic zone. He had several production and sales jobs. In every position, he worked hard to acquire business management skills and was soon promoted to manager.

**Start-up.** Despite his comfortable life as an employee, Wu had greater ambitions: starting a business. When he returned to Nankang in 1996, a careful study of the market convinced him of the great potential for snacks, particularly traditional food created by the local Hakka people. Hakka cuisine is enjoyed the world over, but few Chinese knew about traditional Hakka snacks, which are mostly homemade. Wu noted that

> You could not find those traditional snacks with our special flavor anywhere in China. But most producers were very small, and food quality was inconsistent. In addition, few people outside the province know about those snacks because they were only sold locally and there was no brand-name product. (September 2010 interview)

Wu determined to start with *dou-ba* (crispy crust), one of the most popular snacks in southern Jiangxi, made using local rice, wheat flour, peanuts, and sesame. He moved quickly to realize his investment plan. In 1996, with Y 30,000 ($3,608), his entire savings, plus money borrowed from relatives, Wu rented a 300-square-meter workshop and established the Nankang Tongxing Food Plant. The workshop, staffed by a dozen employees, mostly relatives and immediate family members, used the same processes and equipment used by households to produce traditional dou-ba. The processing equipment was simple and could be bought locally.

By the 1990s, food processing and manufacturing were growing into one of the top industries in Nankang City and received support from the local government. Wu wanted his product to be of higher quality than products already on the market. He hired local food preparation masters and a food specialist from Ganzhou, in southern Jiangxi Province, to improve flavor, appearance, and freshness. His new dou-ba (called *yue-liang-ba*, moon crust) was thinner, crispier, and packaged more effectively to preserve freshness. By tapping into the network of contacts from his days at the state enterprise, Wu was able to launch a niche product in a growing market.

In a trial run, Wu's workshop manufactured 300 cartons of yue-liang-ba. He pitched his product to dozens of wholesalers, retailers, supermarkets, and vendors in Ganzhou and Nankang who were eager to sell his product. Yue-liang-ba was soon popular in the local market, and outside wholesalers started placing orders. Wu's production scale was too small to meet the rising demand. Moreover, his household workshop, with its antiquated processing methods and equipment, operated on a low-input, low-returns model that would not long survive the growing competition. Indeed, one year later, Wu's turnover had declined. Wasting no time, Wu made a bold decision: he would close the workshop and open a new, larger firm with greater product variety.

His relatives and family warned Wu that he could lose all the money he had earned and go into debt if the new investment failed. Wu remained determined. More and more firms were rushing into the market, attracted by the simple techniques, low capital requirements, and growing demand for snack food. Wu was convinced that the way to respond to the increased competition was to boost the scale of production and upgrade quality.

For his company headquarters, Wu raised Y 300,000 ($36,236), half from the savings of his company and the rest from bank and private loans, and, in 1998, rented a 4,000-square-meter building in a township industrial park. The new location offered ample space for expanding production and adding convenient logistics services. In addition to yue-liang-ba, the company developed other snacks, including pumpkin cakes and dried bamboo shoots. All these products were registered under the brand Youjia and marketed as healthful "green" food.

## Competitiveness and Binding Constraints

Wu faced several constraints as he worked to get his new company off the ground.

**Managerial skills.** As his business expanded, Wu began to feel that his lack of formal training in running a large-scale company was holding the company back. He explained as follows:

> This type of household business normally could not fly high. To sustain the growth of the company, it had to be restructured into a modern corporation. (September 2010 interview)

In 2000, he surprised everyone again, taking a leave of absence to pursue an executive master of business administration degree at Peking University. During his year at the university, Wu regularly attended lectures by visiting scholars, economists, and entrepreneurs, in addition to his regular coursework. He consulted with them on how to improve the management of his company. The degree program introduced him to advanced concepts and skills in business management. Perhaps more important, it also added to his already extensive network of connections.

On returning home, Wu plunged right in, applying what he had learned to his business. He restructured the company along the framework of a modern corporation and relocated the headquarters to Ganzhou, the central city in southern Jiangxi Province. He also established a distribution network across China's major cities.

Youjia Food Company Ltd. has expanded rapidly since 2002, growing a stunning 80 percent a year in the first few years. By 2009, the company had 140 employees and produced 800,000 cartons of yueliang-ba, 600,000 cartons of pumpkin paste, and 200,000 cartons of hot pepper paste annually, registering yearly income of nearly Y 40 million ($5.9 million) and profits of Y 3.6 million ($526,977) (September 2010 interviews). The company now manufactures more than 20 products in four major categories and has a 60 percent share in the provincial market for puffed foods. In 2004, the company won exclusive rights to produce *Defuzhai* pumpkin paste, a traditional brand-name product and a local cultural gem.

**R&D.** Youjia Food was a pioneer in several areas. It was one of the first food processing firms to register a brand name in Ganzhou, the first to adopt vacuum packaging and innovative nontoxic packaging materials, and the first to invest in automated machinery. Recognizing that technological innovation is important to maintaining a competitive edge in the food business, Wu invested heavily in new technologies, processes, and materials to upgrade product quality and standards. He hired professionals in the Food Engineering Department of Nanchang University as R&D advisers. He also established collaborative relationships with other universities and research institutes to research and develop new products and techniques, positioning the company as an industry leader.

**Labor.** Youjia's snack products are sold mainly in local markets. Most employees are from the area, which has an abundant supply of low-skill labor. Of Youjia's 140 employees, unskilled workers account for about 73 percent, skilled workers for 10 percent, marketing staff for 12 percent, and research and managerial staff for 5 percent. About two-thirds of the workers have an elementary or lower-middle-school education; about 20 percent are graduates of high schools or secondary technical schools; and only 13 percent have college degrees. New employees are trained at the company or in vocational schools.

The average monthly base salary for a front-line worker was about Y 1,500 ($222) in late 2010. Workers could earn more depending on their productivity. Labor costs have risen steadily in the past few years, though more slowly at Youjia than at similar companies in the coastal region. In 2010, labor costs accounted for 15 percent of total costs, raw materials for 55 percent, and other inputs for 15 percent. The gross profit margin was 15 percent, higher than in most manufacturing sectors. Like many other businesses in the sector, Youjia Food must overcome the rising costs of raw materials and energy, as well as shortages of workers, particularly senior management staff and skilled workers.

## The Role of Government

Like many small-business owners in southern China, Wu received no direct government support when he started his business. He began with capital from his own savings and from family loans. However, Wu did benefit from indirect government support. First, the local government–sponsored labor market helped him find a job in the coastal region, offering him a chance to learn entrepreneurial skills. The government's job-matching service also enabled Wu to strengthen his human capital and develop his skills.

Second, the local government takes a laissez-faire attitude toward private investment, encouraging entrepreneurs to venture into all industries that are not expressly forbidden.

Third, the government helps provide businesses like Youjia Food with cheap land and standard services in local industrial parks.

Fourth, the local government encourages SMEs such as Youjia to become more competitive. After a few years of rapid expansion, the Nankang municipal government identified Youjia as an enterprise with good growth potential, which qualified the firm for government support in financing and technological upgrading. In 2009, Youjia Food received a Y 10,000 ($1,464) award for its rapid growth, making it eligible to borrow from the government-backed credit guarantee agency for SMEs (Nankang Municipal Government 2010). For firms with high growth potential, the local government also brokers professional assistance to help the firms solve technical and managerial problems.

To help SMEs improve managerial and worker skills, the local government organizes free training programs and invites university experts to give lectures to mid-level management. Because Youjia is a leading food producer in the region, it received preferential treatment in bidding on the brand name Defuzhai, a locally renowned brand (see above). The local government wanted to assign the brand to a local firm.

### Summary

Wu Youjia typifies the sort of grassroots entrepreneurs in China who have eagerly seized the business opportunities made possible once the government liberalized the economy. Wu and many others picked up basic knowledge and skills as state enterprise employees. The market experience was critical in determining which sector to enter. To keep their companies growing, many of these entrepreneurs pursued formal training. Successful entrepreneurs recognized the importance of building a professional network and consulting with outside experts. They also understood the importance of innovation (expanding product varieties, adopting new technologies) and modern management systems. Many of them, like Wu, also benefited from government support in multiple ways.

## Fudebao Furniture Company, Wenzhou, Zhejiang Province

Most entrepreneurs in Wenzhou, Zhejiang Province, come from small communities with mercantile traditions. Few have received formal training in manufacturing, business management, or commerce. Most have relied on their own savings or on money borrowed from family and friends for initial capital and have learned their skills in the market.

Furniture is among China's most dynamic labor-intensive sectors. Growing at an annual rate of more than 15 percent over the last decade, with a large capacity to absorb labor, the industry has expanded to meet increasing domestic and international demand. China's furniture exports were valued at more than $20 billion in 2011.[4] The country has overtaken Italy as the world's largest furniture exporter. More than 15,000 enterprises and many unregistered workshops produce furniture for Chinese and foreign markets. Low labor costs and rising demand have attracted investment to the sector.

Furniture production in China, initially based on volume, now focuses more on quality. Large enterprises have developed well-integrated supply chains and complete product lines. Private small and medium firms have proven resilient, but they lack modern technology and innovative practices and design. A growing share of timber—44 percent in 2011—is now imported (NBS 2012). The industry is clustered geographically along the key river deltas and adjoining cities in four provinces: Zhejiang (26 percent), Guangdong (23 percent), Fujian (16 percent), and Shandong (10 percent). Production in the Pearl River Delta and the Yangzi River Delta is mainly for export.

One of the pioneering enterprises is Fudebao Furniture Company, now a top furniture producer in Zhejiang. With capital of Y 31.8 million ($4.7 million) in 2010, the company had more than 100,000 square meters of manufacturing workshops producing about 150,000 pieces of furniture for hotels and homes. In 2009, annual output hit Y 200 million ($29 million), and retail sales totaled Y 420 million ($61.5 million). The company exports about 15 percent of its output.

## Origin and Course of Development

**Start-up.** Fudebao was founded in 1988 by Lin Panwu. Lin was born in Wenzhou, where his parents worked in state-owned factories. Lin's father often invited friends over for homemade wine, a popular drink in Zhejiang. Lin would sit beside the table and listen to their conversations about what they could do to make more money and improve their lives. He resolved to become rich one day and make his family proud.

As the eldest son, Lin shared responsibility for supporting his family. At age 13, he left school and apprenticed as a carpenter to his uncle. After six years of rigid training, Lin learned to make furniture and build wooden house frames. He decided to branch off on his own. He recruited five apprentices and traveled around Wenzhou looking for business. For eight years, he and his apprentice carpenters worked from dawn to dusk, making furniture by hand.

One day, Lin happened upon a retail store of the state-owned Wenzhou Furniture Factory. Several pieces of furniture caught his eye. Lin learned that they were made of new materials using equipment imported from Japan. At the time, the furniture industry was innovating rapidly, with new Japanese-style frames and veneers coming into the country from all over the world. Lin was taken by the new designs. He visited the furniture factory and decided to set up his own workshop. He borrowed Y 6,000 (about $1,612) from relatives and friends and leased a 600-square-meter plot next to his house to build a simple factory. On March 28, 1988, his 26th birthday, he opened the Lucheng Jimei Furniture Plant. That first plant had only six employees, including two master carpenters. Its major products were sold through the retail stores of other factories.

**Growing bigger.** The income from Lin's business kept him and his family out of poverty, but his dream of wealth was still distant. Sensing that the government's commitment to economic reform was firm, Lin decided, in 1991, to pursue bold expansion. In a neighboring village, he acquired user rights to 0.13 hectares of land with a 2,000-square-meter workshop to provide a robust manufacturing base for his business. Ready to switch to mechanized production, Lin purchased electric saws, three drill presses, and a cold press machine made in Shanghai. The company opened its first retail store in a residential complex in 1991. In 1993, Lin registered the Fudebao brand for his products.

To explore the new and growing market, Lin joined the first national furniture exposition in 1994. At the time, Guangdong Province led the country in furniture production, well ahead of Zhejiang Province. Although Lin obtained few orders at the event, he absorbed a lot of information. The more he saw, the more he felt it was urgent to upgrade and diversify his products. He decided to learn from the leading international producers. In late 1995, Lin registered for an international furniture exposition in Cologne. Only a dozen people applied to join the Chinese delegation because of the travel costs. Lin considered the trip worth every yuan. He was enthralled by the great variety of furniture designs. He walked the exhibition halls, gathering material and ideas.

He filled a sack with 50 kilograms of brochures he had picked up at the exhibit booths. At night, while other team members went out on the town, Lin stayed behind to study the materials.

Motivated by the trip, Lin decided to expand. He worked with his master carpenters to break down the designs of the overseas furniture producers, adapting the designs to the tastes of his Chinese consumers. The new products were a big hit and generated large profits. In 1995, Lin moved the factory to the Xinqiao Gaoxiang industrial area in Ouhai District in Wenzhou. It now covered 5 acres, and the factory was 5,000 square meters. Lin invested Y 300 million ($36 million) in machines imported from Western Europe. This was Lin's first fully modern factory.

In 1996, following further expansion, turnover reached almost Y 100 million ($12 million), and Lin renamed his company Wenzhou Fudebao Furniture Company Ltd. That year, Lin reserved a 200-square-meter booth at a Beijing furniture exhibition to promote his new products. The results surpassed expectations. By the end of the exposition, the company had Y 6 million ($721,660) in new orders.

"When I saw the orders, I felt like I was flying," said Lin. Encouraged by the strong market demand, Lin invested a further Y 300 million ($36 million) in imported furniture-making machines and manufacturing process upgrades. Most of the cost was financed through bank loans.

In 2000, the company moved into a larger space, covering 45 acres. The space included a 50,000-square-meter factory with a flow-line operation. That year, the company participated in the Singapore International Furniture Fair. In 2002, Lin became chairman of the Wenzhou Furniture Association. Two years later, he established a wholly owned subsidiary, with initial turnover of Y 40 million ($4.8 million). In 2008, the company began building its 10,000-square-meter Fudebao showroom. Fudebao is now one of southern China's top furniture companies.

Fudebao, like other wood product manufacturers in China, benefited from the furniture supply chain in coastal areas. Guangdong Province to the south has the largest furniture cluster in China, offering a wide range of raw materials and other furniture inputs. Fudebao acquires hardwood boards, plywood, and other materials mostly from markets in

Guangdong, but also, in small numbers, from the Beijing and Shanghai areas.

## Competitiveness and Binding Constraints

Lin and Fudebao overcame several constraints to become competitive in the furniture business.

**Worker skills.** The biggest constraint has been the lack of skilled workers to operate the new production line and the lack of senior management and sales personnel. As Fudebao expanded and quality improved, it needed to scale up its staffing. In 1997, Lin attended a marketing lecture by Lu Wei, a professor at Shanghai Transportation University. The lecture helped Lin realize that he needed advisers who could help him work out a long-term strategy and modernize the company's marketing and governance practices. Lu became Lin's senior marketing adviser. Following Lu's suggestions, Lin revamped the company's marketing strategies and invested heavily in promoting his products at large furniture expositions, bringing his company greater name recognition. Lin also worked on building a nationwide retail network, using a franchise model. Fudebao applies a standard—the terminal franchise technology system—to help franchises market their products with the support of the company's training, logistics, and after-sales service networks. Fudebao now has a network of more than 700 franchised retail agents, allowing Lin to expand production in both domestic and foreign markets.

By 2010, Fudebao had 1,400 employees, 80 percent of whom were migrants from rural areas. Half the employees had only a primary school education. All new workers receive 10 days of training on company rules, values, manufacturing processes, and operations. According to Lin, staff training accounts for about 10 percent of the company's expenditures.

Lin also uses other methods to upgrade staff quality. Since 1997, all new marketing recruits have had to undergo a week of military-like training, regardless of the weather. The aim is to improve teamwork and endurance. In recent years, many coastal regions have experienced a shortage of both skilled and unskilled workers. The average monthly salary for an unskilled worker was about Y 2,000 ($295) in 2010, more than double the salary three years earlier. The company provides free meals and housing subsidies to attract workers, as well as free housing for managers.

The company imports most of its machines (70–80 percent), mainly from Germany and Italy. Chinese-made machines are not yet as precise as foreign-made equipment. The suppliers train workers in operating the machines.

**Industrial land.** The Pearl River Delta area pioneered land reform in China. In 1979, land use rights were, for the first time, converted into shares in joint ventures. Even foreign firms were allowed to buy land use rights. In 1987, Shenzhen introduced the country's first land auction.

However, markets for industrial land use rights are a recent development. In the early phase of reform, many local governments used cheap land to attract investors, granting land use rights at little or no cost. These investors realized tremendous gains as city expansion and growing economic activities caused land to appreciate. Land is also important as collateral for bank loans.

Access to land was likewise important in Fudebao's development and expansion. As Fudebao grew, Lin moved operations to successively larger plots, enabling the company to expand assembly line production. As a star enterprise and a major tax contributor in the region, Fudebao benefited from preferential access to land through the local government.

**Finance.** Like most other private entrepreneurs, Lin started his business with money borrowed from relatives. Later, he borrowed more from family and friends to expand the company. Once the company became larger and had acquired land, bank loans became available. To build new workshops in 1995, Lin used land as collateral for a Y 1.7 million ($203,568) loan from the Agricultural Development Bank (September 2010 interviews).

**Competition.** Lin worked tirelessly to upgrade products through new designs and better functionality, as well as through effective marketing strategies. He participated in trade fairs and relied on his network for market intelligence. To compete successfully in the international market against other Chinese enterprises, Lin targeted a market niche, closely studied the demand, preferences, and consumption habits of consumers in the niche, and customized products to meet the needs of these consumers.

Fudebao's resilience and aptitude for reinvention became ever more evident after the 2008 global crisis. Demand for furniture dipped considerably in both the domestic and the international market after 2008 following the financial crisis and implementation of domestic policies aimed at cooling China's urban real estate market. After thorough investigation, Lin modified the company's marketing strategy, shifting attention from large cities to counties, which were less affected by national government macroeconomic policies and had maintained strong demand because of rapid urbanization. The strategy has helped the company maintain sales and market share.

"Our goal is to be the IKEA of the market," says Lin.

## The Role of Government

As a leading Chinese furniture manufacturer, Fudebao has received support from the local government in gaining access to land and worker training and has benefited from central government tax breaks for technological upgrading.

In 1998, the local government granted the company user rights to 3 hectares of developed industrial land in an industrial park, marking the start of the firm's take-off. The park organizes regular training events to introduce advanced concepts in management and operation, information on new technologies, and basic knowledge on safety and production methods. In 2002 and 2005, when the firm was at a critical point for business expansion, it won government approval and tax breaks for two technological upgrading projects with investments of Y 15 million ($1.8 million) and Y 5 million ($0.6 million). The company also became eligible for fiscal subsidies and subsidized bank loans.

## Summary

Like most Wenzhou entrepreneurs, Lin came from a small community with a mercantile tradition. He had no formal training in manufacturing, business management, or commerce, but managed to pick up the necessary skills while gaining experience in the market. He relied on his own savings and on money borrowed from family members and friends for his initial capital investments. Lin combined shrewd business intelligence with diligence and innovation.

## Julong High-Tech Company Ltd. (Stevia), Ganzhou, Jiangxi Province

At the end of the 1970s, China's rural reform began to improve agricultural productivity and free up large numbers of farm workers. The capital obtained through the heightened agricultural productivity fed the emergence of rural enterprises that catalyzed rural growth. Julong High-Tech Company Ltd., one of China's largest producers of the stevia extract stevioside, a natural sweetener used widely in food, beverages, medicines, wine, cosmetics, and many other consumer products, was part of this growth, transforming agricultural products into processed outputs.

Since the reforms, China's agroprocessing sector has grown at an average annual rate of 13 percent, outpacing GDP growth. By 2011, agroprocessing output exceeded Y 15 trillion ($2.3 trillion), nearly 18 percent of the country's gross industrial output. Agroprocessing enterprises with an annual output of more than Y 5 million ($0.8 million) employed a total of 25 million people (Ministry of Agriculture 2012).

An early stevia processor, China now accounts for 80 percent of the global supply of stevioside. Stevia cultivation covers more than 200,000 hectares across China; Jiangsu, Jiangxi, and Shandong provinces are the largest producers. Some 30 companies have an annual processing capacity of more than 50 tons. In 2011, China's stevia extract output was more than 4,000 tons, 80 percent of it for export. Exports have grown rapidly, surging from less than $1 million in value in 2000 to $84 million in 2009 (figure 4.4).

### Origin and Course of Development

**Start-up.** Xie Ruihong, the founder of Julong, grew up amid the chaos of the Cultural Revolution and received little education when he was young. After retiring from the military in 1982 at age 21, he worked at the state-owned Jiangxi Air Compressor Factory. This was stable employment, but Xie found that it lacked excitement. In 1992, Xie was appointed sales manager in a rare earth mining company. He later

**Figure 4.4  Export Volume and Growth of Stevia Extract, China, 2004–09**

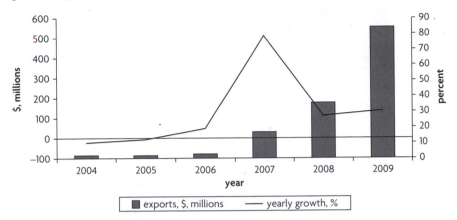

Sources: China Chamber of Commerce of Medicines and Health Products Importers and Exporters; China Stevia Producers Association, http://www.doc88.com/p-993284639783.html [in Chinese].

established his own trading company selling rare earth and other mineral products.

In the winter of 2001, Xie learned through a friend that the Third Jiangxi Sugar Refinery, a local state enterprise, had gone bankrupt and was selling its stevioside workshop. The company had invested more than Y 20 million ($2.4 million) in 1995, with support from the Gan County government, in a stevioside production line. To support the company, the local government had ordered local farmers to plant stevia. However, the Asian economic crisis in 1997–98 weakened the major market for stevia, and China's burgeoning stevia industry was hit hard. Many companies, including the one in Gan County, went bankrupt, and stevia farmers suffered severely.

Xie was confident that this was an opportunity he could not afford to miss. Consulting several experts, he learned that, in many countries, stevia is considered a healthy sweetener. Stevia is 200–300 times sweeter than sucrose (table sugar), but has only 1/300 the caloric content. Despite the temporary slump in the market, stevia was still in great demand in Japan and the Republic of Korea, and other countries were beginning to use it. Years of trading experience told Xie that this was a strong growth market. He got in touch with the Gan County government and visited the factory and farming areas where stevia was grown. After a thorough assessment, he decided to acquire the refinery and establish a new stevioside company. Along with Li Shangwang, an engineer from the Third Jiangxi Sugar Refinery who led technology support for the new company, and another partner, Xie established Julong.

**Business expansion.** Xie and his partners knew that, to survive in the market, the company had to lead in both quality and the scale of production. This meant a large investment was required to upgrade technology and build new production lines. However, other than its working capital, the company had no funds to purchase raw materials and maintain operations. So, Xie started to look for new funding.

In 2005, Stevian Biotechnology Corporation, a Malaysian company that processed and traded stevioside internationally, offered to partner with Julong in a joint venture. The Malaysian company acquired 25 percent of Julong's shares for $2 million and transferred the proprietary technique for crystallizing stevioside to the joint venture. The funds helped Julong install three new production lines and build capacity to process 15,000 tons of stevia leaves and produce 1,000 tons of stevioside a year.

Global demand for stevia extract continued to grow rapidly. With its superior purity, Julong's stevioside products dominated the market. Several multinational food and beverage producers, including Coca-Cola, Nestlé, and Pepsi-Cola, ordered 5,000 tons of stevioside over a five-year period. To meet this demand, the company needed to expand once again. To acquire funding for a fifth production line, Xie and Li sold another 30 percent of their shares to Stevian and became minority shareholders. Later in 2007, Stevian was listed on the London Stock Exchange as PureCircle SDN BHD, with Julong as a subsidiary. Xie and Li sold 40 percent of the company shares in exchange for an undisclosed amount of stock in the listed firm. By then, Stevian had become the majority shareholder of Julong. The listed mother company invested $7 million into Julong to build the fifth production line and lent Julong another $43 million for technological upgrading and operations.

In 2008, a foreign shareholder cashed in 10 percent of the company stock without informing the Chinese partners. When Xie questioned the action, he was told that, as a minority shareholder, he would not be consulted for such transactions. There was also a disagreement over company operations with the Malaysian management, which escalated as the company grew.

The frictions eventually resulted in the breakup of Xie's team. Seeing that he had lost control of the company, Xie cashed in his remaining shares and resigned from his management position late in 2008. Li, his former partner, became Julong's general manager. After several rounds of negotiations, Xie's right to use the name Julong High-Tech was recognized, and he established another company under that name in 2009. The original Julong was renamed Jiangxi PureCircle Biotechnology Company.

## Competitiveness and Binding Constraints

The government supported agroprocessing through finance, help with land acquisition, and technology, relieving some of the major constraints on Julong.

**Financing.** Capital was a major obstacle in expanding the business. With personal savings and bank loans secured with land and equipment as collateral, Xie raised Y 4 million ($0.6 million) to buy the bankrupt state enterprise. He went to the local government and made an innovative proposition.

"If I pay you every penny I possess to acquire a bankrupted company, I won't be able to get loans from the bank in the future, and I'll end up with nothing to operate the company," he explained. "But if you can sell it to me for 3 million yuan, I'll revive the company and run it as my lifelong business."

In the end, the local government agreed to sell the workshop to him for a bit more than Y 3 million ($0.44 million).

The new company was established in January 2002 with only one production line and fewer than 100 workers. The average annual salary for a front-line worker was about Y 800 ($97).

**Inputs.** An adequate supply of stevia was critical for sustaining operations, as this was the primary raw material. Because the local supply was too small to meet the company's processing capacity, Xie had to buy raw materials from other provinces, not an easy task for a new company. In Shandong Province, farmers greeted him with suspicion. A few years before, local farmers had suffered heavy losses when another company broke its promise to buy harvested stevia. Xie explained the company's operations in detail and assured farmers that they would get the promised returns. He signed supply contracts at a fixed price of Y 5,200 ($628), about Y 1,000 ($121) higher than the going price. He also promised farmers free technical assistance. Through careful negotiations and marketing efforts, Xie secured additional supplies in Anhui, Heilongjiang, and Jiangsu provinces.

Shortly after start-up, Julong ran into a serious food safety crisis. In March 2002, media in Hong Kong SAR, China, as well as media in Singapore published stories questioning the safety of stevia as a food sweetener, triggering panic among domestic and overseas consumers and food manufacturers. Demand for stevioside crashed. By the end of 2002, Xie's company had recorded a loss of Y 1 million ($120,817). Many stevia companies closed their doors. Xie decided to hang on amid great difficulties.

Fortunately, the crisis soon ended. The market revived in late 2003, and prices again rose quickly. In 2004, the company received a large order from Stevian Biotechnology Corporation SDN BHD. Seizing the opportunity, Julong resumed full-scale operations. That same year, it installed a third production line. By year's end, it had expanded and achieved total sales of Y 30 million ($3.6 million), with a profit of Y 5 million ($604,098).

**R&D.** Julong's success stemmed from its strong R&D capacity. Xie knew that a superior product was essential for beating the fierce competition in the stevia market. The company registered more than a dozen patents, some of which were acknowledged by the Ministry of Science and Technology and nominated as projects to be sponsored by the ministry's special innovation fund for SMEs. In addition to its own R&D team, the firm cooperated with several universities to upgrade its techniques for extracting stevioside.

By August 2010, the company had production lines capable of producing 1,100 tons of stevioside and 1,500 tons of high-purity crystallized stevioside products annually. Another two production lines were expected to be put into operation in 2011.

"Our mid-term target is to achieve a production capacity of 3,300 tons a year by 2012," said Xie.

### The Role of Government

Located in Gan County's industrial park, Julong had initial capital of Y 220 million ($32 million), with a total investment of Y 760 million ($111 million). Popular among local government officials for being a top tax revenue contributor in the region, Julong received strong local government support in land and capital. The park administration allocated 12 hectares to Xie's firm for workshops. Initially, Xie could raise only Y 30 million ($4.4 million), not enough to build the workshops and buy the required equipment. Without sufficient manufacturing scale, Xie knew Julong would fall behind. Taking advantage of his close relationship with the local government, he obtained the support of a government-sponsored guarantee company, which enabled him to obtain bank credit on favorable terms.[5]

Julong also benefited from the local government's support for stevia cultivation. In 2008, Gan County set up a special Y 4 million ($575,879) fund to expand the cultivation of high-quality stevia, upgrade planting technologies, and promote new techniques. Although the fund did not go directly to Julong, it ensured the company's access to a stable supply of raw materials.

By 2011, the company had about 300 employees, more than 40 of whom had college or advanced degrees. The monthly salary for unskilled front-line workers had increased to Y 1,600–Y 1,800 ($248–$279). The company provides regular training for its staff. Annual staff turnover is below 4 percent thanks in part to a management system that emphasizes personal value and skill improvement. Once all six production lines were in full operation, the company aimed to achieve annual sales of Y 2 billion ($310 million).

### Summary

Julong's success validated the persistence of an entrepreneur who often faced high risks on both the input side and the output side. The government and foreign direct investment (FDI) helped reduce the risks by providing access to land and to finance. FDI, in particular, not only opened the door to financing, but also access to international markets, new ideas, and new technologies.

# Aihao Writing Instruments Co. Ltd., Wenzhou, Zhejiang Province

The center of world pen production has shifted from Western Europe to southern China. The pen cluster in Wenzhou is one of China's largest centers for the production and export of pens. More than 200 Wenzhou firms produce some 12 billion pen parts annually, or nearly two pens for every person in the world. The annual output value is about Y 3 billion ($443 million in 2010 U.S. dollars), one-third of the country's total in this industry, while annual exports amount to Y 1.8 billion ($266 million).[6] Aihao Writing Instruments Co. Ltd. is the world's largest producer of roller ball pens (using water-based ink) and exemplifies the success of Chinese light manufacturing.

Wenzhou, a pillar of Chinese light manufacturing, is known worldwide as the birthplace of the Wenzhou model, which refers to rapid economic growth and industrialization arising from vibrant private investment in small-scale manufacturing.[7] The region is a leader in the manufacture of lighters, shoes, sweaters, neckties, eyeglasses, low-voltage electronic equipment, valves, pumps, locks, and razors, as well as pens and many other light industrial products.

## Origin and Course of Development

Aihao Writing Instruments Co. was started by a budding entrepreneur who had not finished elementary school and could not even write his name well. Zhang Hanping and his team in Wenzhou worked hard to produce well-designed, high-quality pens using imported technologies and ideas to meet strong global demand.

Wenzhou, located in a hilly area with limited agricultural resources, has a long history of trading with the outside world. Many people left their villages to come to Wenzhou to be peddlers, carpenters, shoe repairers, masons, or cotton fluffers, exploiting niche markets. Between 1949 and 1978, China's planned economy concentrated investment spending elsewhere, offering little support to this region. Traditionally, many household workshops have produced simple metalwares, shoes, and other small commodities. Despite harsh crackdowns, free-market trading and underground manufacturing never stopped in Wenzhou, and the city became a national pioneer in free enterprise. Since the area had few state enterprises, China's postreform push to accelerate economic growth encouraged local officials to welcome the efforts of small-scale entrepreneurs such as Zhang Hanping to explore new markets.

As a child, Zhang dropped out of school to help support his family. He collected used bits of plastic and sold them for recycling, learning a great deal about plastics in the process. He was among the first to start a business in the early days of the economic reforms. In 1978, agricultural reforms divided much of the rural land into private plots, and, in many villages, agricultural machinery no longer used for collective production was sold to individuals. Sensing an opportunity, Zhang joined with some partners to set up an agricultural machinery station in his village. The plan was to use the workshop and tools to produce plastic parts for electronics. Each partner contributed Y 720 ($428) to buy a plastic injection molding machine. The annual output was about Y 6,000–Y 7,000 ($3,564–$4,158).

However, in the late 1970s, support for private enterprise was still limited, and markets were underdeveloped. Zhang's business failed after two years, leaving him with less money than he had at the start. In the early 1980s, the market began to open up, particularly in the Wenzhou area. In line with central government reform policy, the local government encouraged household-based workshops and traders, and the demand for small products grew quickly. Local villagers, who had experience peddling during the slow agricultural seasons, saw an opportunity. By 1985, there were more than 130,000 household workshops with more than 330,000 workers in the Wenzhou region.

At that time, Zhang borrowed money from friends and relatives to buy another plastic molding machine for small items such as toys, umbrella handles, and buttons. Many villagers followed suit. Finding too many producers and too small a market, Zhang moved on to another business: pens. He believed that the rising number of students and the boom in commercial activities would greatly boost the demand for pens. In 1986, he joined with eight partners to raise about Y 800,000 ($232,912) to set up the Longwan Changsheng Pen Company; Zhang had one-third ownership.

## Competitiveness and Binding Constraints

**Input markets.** The manufacturing clusters for low-voltage electronics, hardware, and plastic products that had emerged in Wenzhou laid a solid foundation for the pen industry. Market liberalization in China made it easy for pen makers to obtain stainless steel, plastics, and other raw materials locally. Within a few years, a complete supply chain for pens had formed in Zhejiang, including manufacturers of pens, accessories, pen molds, and packing and printing materials. For example, Wenzhou pen makers bought high-quality ball-point pen refills from Yiwu and nearby areas until 1998, when a local stationary company began producing similar products in Wenzhou. Of the 200 pen companies, about 10 percent now produce accessories, such as ink cartridges, pen points, boxes, caps, colors, packaging, and stationery.

At first, companies such as Aihao relied on domestic networks for technical assistance, but copied the designs of Western pens, particularly German and Italian pens, and produced low-quality versions for the domestic market.

"My pen-making business started from a household workshop," recalls Zhang. "At that time, almost all households in the village produced something related to pens. If we had any technical difficulties, we went to Shanghai to talk to an expert."

Product quality improved over time with the deepening of specialization as the company moved up the learning curve. As quality improved, export production increased. This climb up the quality spectrum occurred at Aihao, as it did at thousands of Chinese companies, in less than two decades.

The Longwan Changsheng Pen Company was dismantled in 1992 because of disagreements among the owners, including Zhang. By then, the company had assets of Y 10 million ($1.8 million). Zhang decided to stay in the pen business because of the strong and growing international demand. In 1995, he invested all his savings in a new plant.

The new company started with several hundred workers producing 3,000–5,000 pens a day. Zhang soon had to expand production capacity to meet the demand. In 1996, he invested Y 1 million ($120,277), mainly from retained profits, to expand and buy more equipment. By 2000, Aihao had 12,000 square meters of workshops, more than

500 employees, and 100 pieces of specialized equipment. Annual output exceeded Y 30 million ($3.6 million).

In 2002, the local government allocated 33 hectares of land inside an industrial park to build a pen manufacturing center called China's Pen Capital. It invested Y 600 million ($72 million) to build 480,000 square meters of workshops and office buildings and sold or leased them to 45 pen manufacturing companies at the market rate. Aihao obtained about 20,000 square meters of space.

Aihao continued to grow and now produces eight categories of pens in nearly 400 varieties in more than a dozen series. For writing, there are gel ink pens, ball-point pens, fountain pens, roller ball pens, and carbon pens. For marking documents, there are highlighting pens, marker pens, and fluorescent pens. For drawing, there are crayons and felt-tip pens. The company's most popular product is its roller ball pen, which uses pen tips supplied by Premec (Switzerland) and ink imported from Mikuni Corporation (Japan) and National Corporation (United States). Many of Aihao's products are exported, and the brand is well respected internationally.

After China entered the World Trade Organization (WTO) in 2001, Zhang's company benefited from lower tariffs and a more open global market. The company produces a staggering 1.8 million pens a day, or more than 600 million a year, of which more than 80 percent are exported to around 100 countries, especially in North America and Western Europe. Over the years, Aihao has received many awards and titles, including "China's Master of Pens" and "Famous Zhejiang Brand." The company has 25 design patents and has registered the Aihao brand in more than 100 countries.

**Marketing.** Early on, many pen producers in Wenzhou relied on commodity markets in Yiwu and other nearby cities to reach customers at home and abroad. Almost all the top pen firms in Wenzhou have sales branches in Yiwu, China's largest market for small products. Aihao set up a retail store in Yiwu in 1998. In 2007, the company sold an estimated Y 40 million ($5.3 million) in products at the Yiwu commodity market.

Regional and global trade fairs are important marketing channels for pen producers. Zhang and his team attend trade fairs and expositions organized by local governments and trade associations. Aihao was selected as a pilot for an e-commerce platform sponsored by the Wenzhou Pen Manufacturers Association and funded partly through government grants.

**Technology.** To beat the competition, Zhang was determined to make superior products. He tapped into his growing network to identify suitable machinery for expanding production. Learning about the latest international market developments from overseas clients, Zhang imported seven automated assembly lines from Korea and gradually phased out manual pen assembly. Pen quality improved.

Good molds are key to a pen's look and structure. In 1999, Zhang invested more than Y 10 million ($1.2 million) to build a mold manufacturing center that would become a high-technology tooling facility. He installed cutting-edge machines and sophisticated inspection equipment from Japan and Taiwan, China. He also imported the world's most advanced high-precision forming machines from GF AgieCharmilles (Switzerland), a clamping system from Erowa AG (Switzerland) and Fadal Machining Center (United States), and a Mitutoyo projector measuring system (Japan). Zhang's center leads the country in sophisticated mold manufacturing technology.

To keep up with trends in the international market, the company set up its own R&D center in 2008, investing more than Y 90 million ($13 million) in technology development and in upgrading pen designs, structure, and functions. In 2010, Aihao invested Y 30 million ($4.4 million) to build the country's largest stainless steel ball-point pen workshop, producing stainless steel ball-point pens with 24-station Swiss composite machine tools. Over time, Zhang focused more on the design of his pens so as to respond to growing consumer sophistication. The company has registered more than 200 patents.

## The Role of Government

The pen industry in Wenzhou grew largely outside the regulatory orbit of the government, as thousands of private entrepreneurs took advantage of new market opportunities. Yet, the government has played an important role in creating a favorable investment climate and helping businesses upgrade technology and products. To foster a pen industrial cluster in the region, the Longwan District Authority built a pen manufacturing center, China's Pen Capital. In the first phase, 45 pen firms, including Aihao, moved in.

Pen firms also receive government support in marketing and technology. Companies that invest in building new workshops, renovating old ones, or setting up new production lines receive tax breaks on the investments. To reduce the cost of pen tip and ink imports, the Wenzhou Pen Manufacturers Association arranged for Wenzhou University to set up an R&D lab to solve key technological bottlenecks in pen tips, ink, ball points, and automatic assembly. The local government and Wenzhou University jointly invested Y 20 million ($2.4 million) to build the lab. These investments have made it easier and cheaper to obtain inputs domestically. The local government has also invested in building commodity markets that reach across the region and the country and that help match emerging enterprises with buyers.

In recent years, pen manufacturers in Wenzhou have faced mounting labor shortages and rising labor costs. Despite annual wage increases in the 20 percent range, with monthly wages rising from Y 600 ($72) in the early 2000s to more than Y 2,000 ($310) in 2011, the new generation of workers, most of whom are migrants from the inland provinces, are not attracted by the long working hours and poor working conditions. To stabilize the labor force for the industry, the local labor authority, in a step coordinated by the Wenzhou Pen Manufacturers Association, joined with universities in establishing a training center in 2007 to attract, train, and certify pen professionals. The association issued policies on professional titles, salaries, and social security to provide incentives for technical talent. The center holds regular training sessions for senior and mid-level employees with specific skills. These programs aim to raise the share of skilled workers to a quarter of the sector's workforce.

## Summary

The first generation of Chinese postreform entrepreneurs generally received no formal training in business management and development. They acquired entrepreneurial skills through imitation and by learning from failures. Influenced by a deep-rooted regional commercial culture, local entrepreneurs are not cowed by failure, but keep trying until they succeed.

Aihao is a model success story. As with thousands of private firms in the region, the success of Zhang's business can be attributed to a solid supply chain and the well-developed input market in the coastal area. Private enterprises also benefit from local government policies to facilitate business start-up and upgrading. Zhang tapped into existing networks, identified market niches, adopted new technologies, and constantly innovated to make Aihao a world-class company.

## Notes

1. See the report of the 13th National Congress of the Communist Party (Zhao 1987). The report of the 15th National Congress of the Communist Party positioned the private economy as an important component of China's socialist market economy (Jiang 1997). The report of the 16th National Congress of the Communist Party noted that all legitimate income, from work or not, should be protected and that the legal system should be improved to protect private property (Jiang 2002).
2. "A Review of Food Industry Performance in 2011 and Prospects for 2012" [in Chinese], China Food Industrial Association, Beijing, http://news.xinhuanet.com/food/2012-05/18/c_123153878.htm.
3. See NBS (2006). See also China Statistical Database, National Bureau of Statistics of China, Beijing, http://219.235.129.58/welcome.do#.
4. UN Comtrade (United Nations Commodity Trade Statistics Database), Statistics Division, Department of Economic and Social Affairs, United Nations, New York, http://comtrade.un.org/db/.
5. To address the credit constraint facing most small firms, many local governments allocate funding to support credit guarantee companies that help small firms qualify for bank loans by pledging their own or a third party's capital as loan collateral. At the end of 2009, there were 5,547 credit guarantors nationwide, 27 percent of which were backed by government agencies.
6. Data of the Zhejiang provincial government.
7. Wenzhou has 240,000 individually owned businesses and 130,000 private enterprises, of which 180 are group companies, 4 are among China's top 500 enterprises, and 36 are among the top 500 private enterprises in the country.

## References

Brandt, Loren, and Thomas G. Rawski. 2008. "China's Great Economic Transformation." In *China's Great Economic Transformation*, edited by Loren Brandt and Thomas G. Rawski, 1–26. New York: Cambridge University Press.

Jiang Zemin. 1997. "Hold High the Great Banner of Deng Xiaoping Theory for an All-round Advancement of the Cause of Building Socialism with Chinese

Characteristics into the 21st Century." *Beijing Review*, Beijing. http://www
.bjreview.com.cn/document/txt/2011-03/25/content_363499_3.htm.

———. 2002. "Build a Well-off Society in an All-Round Way and Create a New
Situation in Building Socialism with Chinese Characteristics." Xinhua News
Agency,    November    18.    http://news.xinhuanet.com/english/2002-11/18/
content_633685.htm.

Li, Weiye, and Louis Putterman. 2008. "Reforming China's SOEs: An Overview."
*Comparative Economic Studies* 50: 353–80. http://www.palgrave-journals.com/
ces/journal/v50/n3/full/ces200831a.html#bib27.

MIIT (Ministry of Industry and Information Technology, China). 2012. "The 12th
Five-Year Plan for the Meat Industry." [In Chinese.] February 24, MIIT, Beijing.

Ministry of Agriculture, China. 2012. "Processing of Farm Products Accounts for
17.6% of Gross Industrial Output," [In Chinese.] XinhuaNet, July 1. http://
finance.qq.com/a/20120701/000567.htm.

Nankang Municipal Government. 2010. "Brief Report on Nankang Municipal
SMEs for the First Quarter of 2010." [In Chinese.] Nankang Municipal Bureau
of   SMEs,   Nankang,   China.   http://xxgk.nkjx.gov.cn/bmgkxx/zxqyj/gzdt/
zwdt/201004/t20100429_20534.htm.

NBS (National Bureau of Statistics of China). 2005. *Xin Zhongguo wushiwunian
tongji ziliao huibian 1949–2004* [China: 55-year compendium of statistics
1949–2004]. [In Chinese.] Beijing: China Statistics Press.

———. 2006. *China Statistical Yearbook*. Beijing: China Statistics Press.

———. 2011. *China Statistical Yearbook*. Beijing: China Statistics Press.

———. 2012. *China Statistical Yearbook*. Beijing: China Statistics Press.

Zhao Ziyang. 1987. "13th National Congress of the Communist Party of China."
Beijing Review Publications, Beijing.

# 5

# Case Studies, China: Industrial Parks and Industrial Clusters

This chapter focuses on China's industrial parks and clusters. Industrial clusters and parks are two of the special policy tools used to support light manufacturing in China (see chapter 3). Both are also interesting from the perspective of agglomeration economies and the dynamics of industrial location. Therefore, even though some of the clusters covered here are not in light manufacturing, they offer valuable policy lessons.

## Women's Shoes, Wuhou Industrial Park, Chengdu, Sichuan Province

The Wuhou industrial park in Sichuan Province is a leading footwear producer. Located south of downtown Chengdu, the park is home to one of China's largest footwear clusters; women's shoes are the major product. In 2002, in a 6.1-square-kilometer area, the park and its surrounding facilities hosted about 1,100 manufacturers. The number of shoemaking enterprises in Chengdu hit 1,360 in 2004, but dropped to 550 in 2011 because of the impact of the global economic recession as well as the relocation of business to other regions. The output value increased from Y 2.4 billion ($290 million) in 2000 to Y 13.3 billion ($1.9 billion) in 2011 (table 5.1). Over time, Wuhou has developed a complete supply chain that spans backward and forward links, from upstream shoemaking machinery and spare parts, leather and fabric, heels, soles, accessories, and other auxiliary materials to the downstream manufacturing and distribution of shoes, as well as design, research and development (R&D), logistics, and other services. It also has a raw materials market and 160 logistics corporations, 10 shoemaking apprentice training schools, around 300 registered shoe trademarks, and nearly 100,000 employees. Chengdu's shoe firms have a staggering production capacity: 100 million pairs of shoes a year, which are sold in 120 countries. About 95 percent of the production is women's shoes. Chengdu's women's shoes account for 10 percent of China's footwear industry and 7 percent of the world's, ranking behind only the footwear clusters in Guangdong and Zhejiang provinces.

Rising labor and land costs have encouraged growing numbers of footwear firms to leave China's coastal cities. Many have chosen to move to Chengdu because of its pivotal location in southwestern China, its good industrial foundation, its rich supply of raw materials, and its abundant labor.

Chengdu firms produce four basic kinds of footwear products. One is low-end shoes for domestic sales. The demand for these shoes is high, but the quality and price are low. Sold mainly in rural and inland areas through wholesale markets, these shoes are produced primarily by numerous small private family workshops.

**Table 5.1 Development of the Shoemaking Industry, Wuhou District, Sichuan Province, 2000–11**

| Indicator | 2000 | 2001 | 2002 | 2003 | 2004 | 2011 |
|---|---|---|---|---|---|---|
| Enterprises, number | 607 | 710 | 824 | 1,020 | 1,360 | 550 |
| Enterprises with annual sales of more than Y 5 million | 22 | 53 | 92 | 139 | 198 | — |
| Foreign exchange earned through exports of major products, $, millions | 62 | 69 | 73 | 82 | 100 | 223 |
| Product output value, Y, billions | 2.4 | 3.1 | 3.6 | 4.5 | 5.8 | 13.3 |
| Enterprises with complete quality system, % | 24.5 | 27.3 | 29.4 | 30.0 | 30.7 | — |

*Sources:* RIME and DRC 2009; Wuhou New District Administration Committee, http://www.chinaleather.org/special/show.php?itemid=3821.
*Note:* — = not available.

The second category is mid-range products for domestic sales in malls, supermarkets, and franchised stores. Production capacity for firms in this category is at least 100,000 pairs a year. The producers have stronger technical capacity and better equipment than family workshops, and almost all have their own brands.

The third category is export products, sold mainly in the Russian Federation and countries in Central Asia through trading markets in Beijing, Urumqi, and other cities. This type of product is in high demand and relatively low in quality. Most of the shoes are produced by enterprises with a relatively large scale of production.

The fourth category is higher-quality shoes produced through original equipment manufacturers (OEMs), mainly for international brand-name shoe firms or large retailers. Only a handful of enterprises have the advanced manufacturing facilities and upgraded technology to fill such orders and deliver them on time.

## Origin and Course of Development

In the late 1970s, when China's economic reforms began, light industrial products were in short supply, and most products were rationed. Leather shoes represented a luxury good. This situation changed quickly as the government gradually lifted the ban on private businesses in retailing and light industry.

Chengdu enjoys a long tradition of leather production and shoemaking. During the 100 years from the late Qing Dynasty to the early 1950s, Wuhou was the major leather production base for Chengdu's shoemaking industry. In the 1980s, Wuhou developed a large leather market, as the dozens of shoemaking firms turned into hundreds, partly because of the relocation of firms from other areas. Subsequently, more firms moved to Wuhou to take advantage of the agglomeration effects.

Since the 1990s, this traditional industry has demonstrated renewed vitality thanks to a burst of support from the local authorities. In 1994, Wuhou District started to build a trade zone for private leatherworking businesses, and, in 1999, it held the first Western Footwear Industry Fair, attracting merchants from home and abroad to exhibit or place orders. Chengdu's footwear industry soon entered the international market.

In 2000, the central government launched the Great Western Development Strategy. Sichuan Province received fiscal support to expand infrastructure and to promote social and economic development. The business environment improved; rapid urbanization and industrialization brought unprecedented wealth; and the demand for consumer products exploded.

Rapid urbanization led to land shortages that affected small and medium footwear companies, forcing many of them into suburban areas. Some companies even moved several times because of the frequent confiscation of land for new construction.

The Wuhou District government recognized the importance of supporting footwear enterprises as a platform for industrial growth and development. At the beginning of 2002, a large-scale footwear industrial park was planned. Provincial leader Zhou Yongkang endorsed the idea and announced that Wuhou should learn from Wenzhou, home of a large shoe cluster, and turn itself into the "City of Shoes." With the government's support, Wuhou District set up an industrial park for western China's shoe sector. In 2007, Chengdu was selected as one of the pilot cities for urban reform, providing Wuhou District with opportunities for land reassignment and industrial restructuring. Chengdu's 2007 Development Plan for the Chengdu Shoemaking Industrial Cluster proposed building Wuhou into a women's shoe manufacturing cluster consisting of two industrial parks and an R&D base, as well as a center for trade, communications, exhibits, and training.

## Competitiveness and Binding Constraints

The Chengdu footwear industry cluster consists mainly of private small and medium enterprises (SMEs). Box 5.1 recounts the tale of one private footwear company's rise.

**Logistics and the supply chain.** Chengdu is southwestern China's largest transportation hub and largest manufacturing and commercial center. The city has several huge distribution markets from which commodities are traded and shipped to the western provinces. Sichuan Province is rich in raw materials and is an important agricultural and livestock producer, generating abundant leather for the footwear industry. These factors have enabled Chengdu to become the major locus of western China's production and distribution of leather and other shoe materials.

### Box 5.1 Roeblan: From Hand Workshop to Custom Tailor to the U.S. First Lady

The black high-heel shoes worn by the U.S. first lady, Michelle Obama, at her husband's 2009 inauguration, became a popular item; 500,000 pairs were sold within a short time. The shoes were produced by Roeblan, a footwear enterprise in Chengdu.

It took more than a decade for Roeblan to grow from a small family workshop to a modern company.

In the early 1980s, Wu Deguo was the director of a state-owned shoe factory in Sichuan Province. After three years, he left to sell clothes at a local wholesale market. Then he set up a shoe factory in Fujian Province in southern China. When he returned to Sichuan years later, private enterprises in Chengdu were booming. Considering the convenience of setting up a factory in his hometown, he moved his business back home. In 1997, he established Roeblan with a small workshop and a few dozen workers, a typical pattern at the time.

Roeblan expanded and opened a factory in downtown Chengdu. In 2000, because of rapid urbanization, shoe factories started moving to the suburbs. Roeblan did, too. It shifted from manual to mechanized production and modernized its management. The ensuing difficulties remain fresh in Wu's mind. He recalls that, over 1999–2003, the company lost money each year, with losses as high as several million yuan. After inspecting firms in Fujian, Guangdong, and other coastal provinces, he realized that the only way to survive was to standardize his production line. Yet, orders were scattered, and it was difficult to standardize production and management.

"It was a difficult period of time," he recalls. "Many friends tried to talk me out of this attempt." However, he was determined to experiment with the reform. "It's like going across a mine field. If I could cross safely, then others would follow. If I failed, I would be the only one to die."

Wu decided to introduce a mechanized assembly line, becoming the first company to do so in Chengdu. Using the assembly line meant that the company had to dump the old equipment and techniques and had to train workers in new skills. However, it ensured stable quality in the shoes, which generated orders from large overseas wholesalers such as Paramount Footwear Co. In the meantime, with the sponsorship of the local government, company representatives attended expositions overseas to promote their products.

Roeblan's turnaround was complete by late 2003; the firm has earned a profit ever since.

**Technology.** Even before the reforms, state-owned shoemaking factories in Chengdu had developed to some scale and thus provided a source of skills and expertise. Today's shoemaking enterprises in Wuhou are mainly local private companies, some of which were set up and developed by the former management and technical personnel of state-owned factories. In recent years, companies from the coastal areas and overseas have brought not only investment funds, but also the latest technology and concepts in business management and marketing.

**Human resources.** Sichuan is one of China's most populous provinces, with a large labor force of both skilled and unskilled workers. A third of the front-line workers in shoe enterprises across China are from Sichuan. The rapid development of Chengdu's footwear cluster has attracted large numbers of shoemaking workers back to their hometowns, providing high-quality workers and managers. Sichuan has more than 100,000 skilled shoemaking workers. Many production line managers had years of experience in the Guangdong footwear industry before transferring to Chengdu.

**R&D.** As a center of science, technology, and education in southwestern China, Chengdu has many universities, colleges, and research institutes. The Leather and Chemistry Department of Sichuan University and the Sichuan Leather Research Institute have a wealth of scientific research talent. This intellectual support provides training and helps foster innovation in the Chengdu footwear industry.

## The Role of Government

The footwear industrial cluster in Wuhou took off in the 1980s after the central government relaxed regulations on private business. Seeing the industry's potential, the local municipal and district governments adopted measures to foster its growth, from industrial parks to better administrative services.

**Developing an industrial park through corporatization.** In 2007, Wuhou District invested Y 400 million ($53 million) to establish the Chengdu Wuhou Industrial Park Investment and Development Company Ltd., which was responsible for developing and managing infrastructure and public facilities in the industrial park and functions as a large corporatized financing platform to raise funds. The company has initiated business relationships with banks and signed contracts with investment institutions. Through fiscal funding and bank loans, it raised Y 2.3 billion ($302 million) in its first year, securing the funds for future development. The park's management committee promotes investment, supervises investment projects, and collects taxes. It also raises funds, manages land, and builds infrastructure. The Wuhou industrial park, by separating management from operations, has effectively enlarged the industry's capacity to raise funds and provide specialized services.

**Combining government and market roles.** To allow the market to play its proper role, Wuhou industrial park established Sichuan Western Shoe

Center Company Ltd. jointly with Chengdu Zhixin Industrial Group Company Ltd., a shareholding real estate developer. The company was contracted to build the China Women's Shoes Industrial Park, which was expected to become the largest and most advanced specialized market of footwear products in western China. By joining the government's visible hand with the market's invisible hand, the venture not only highlights the government's role as guide, but also helps mobilize the capital and human resources of the market.

**Providing policy support to spur expansion and upgrading.** Several government policies have aimed at intensive development. In addition to the 3.8-square-kilometer Shoe Center Industrial Park in Wuhou District, nearby Chongzhou and Jintang counties have also assigned land to expand shoe production. Financed through a government grant, these specially allocated areas offer cheap land and discounted fees for shoemaking firms, which receive compensation for relocating from other areas into the district's facilities. Meanwhile, at the time the enterprises transfer, the park administration credits their output value and relevant tax payments to the authorities in their previous homes. An incubation area supports small and medium firms, which can buy or lease plants in the incubation area, a benefit for capital-constrained firms. To speed government approval, the park administration has set up a one-stop shop that brings together all the individual departments to facilitate rapid response to investment applications. The park administration offers preferential taxation, financing, and screening for enterprises moving into the zone.

**Building a comprehensive business center and cultivating local brands.** In 2005, Wuhou District launched the Brand Enterprises Base in the Western Shoe Center of China Industrial Park to establish an industrial platform for shoe materials selection, shoe buying and trade, R&D, and international logistics for women's shoes. It used 10.5 hectares inside the park to build an international trade center, a shoe materials center, a logistics supermarket, and a shoe techniques and services center. The Brand Enterprises Base attracts top brands and cultivates local brand-name enterprises. At 4,200 square meters, the international trade center is one of China's largest for shoe products. The center provides the services of purchasing and commission agents and offers assistance in international logistics, as well as training programs for professional and management personnel. All these functions enable face-to-face contact between merchants and manufacturers, lowering costs and enhancing profits.

**Establishing a public platform and exploring international trade channels.** The industrial park encompasses six key centers that supply a series of integrated services, including R&D and testing, a measurement center, a trade center, a training center, a brand exhibition center, and an information and services center. The industrial park helps large coastal shoe buyers link up with local manufacturers, while also helping local SMEs find clients. The trade center taps into international market channels through, for example, the annual International Shoes and Materials Exhibition, which encourages more enterprises to enter the international market. After the global financial crisis of 2008 led to a slump in international demand, Chengdu launched the Wuhou Direct Sales Mall, the Chinese Women's Shoe Center Top Brands Chain Stores, and the National Tour for Chengdu-Produced Women's Shoes to open up more avenues for domestic sales. In 2009, Chengdu established China's first transregional trade market to offer local shoe producers a stable channel for direct sales as an alternative to relying on OEMs. Local producers have already received orders worth millions of dollars. On January 1, 2010, the Association of Southeast Asian Nations–China Free Trade Area was officially established, providing opportunities for Chengdu shoemakers to explore the growing Asian market. Within six months, the export volume to Asia had exceeded $10 million, an increase of 71 percent on a year-on-year basis.

**Building brand names.** To expand business, the Wuhou government sent delegations to learn from the experience of leading footwear producers in Guangzhou, Quanzhou, and Wenzhou. Entrepreneurs in Wuhou realized that the gap between the local shoe industry and the coastal producers derives mainly from the scale of production and branding. The Wuhou government decided to offer incentives to encourage the production of brand-name products. In 2004, it promulgated guidelines to encourage private firms to engage in R&D,

brand-name production, and export. It set up a competition for the title of "Famous Brands" at the municipal, provincial, and national levels, with respective awards of Y 30,000 ($3,625), Y 50,000 ($6,041), and Y 600,000 ($72,492).

**Building harmonious labor relations.** The park administrator has established a special group to oversee labor issues and arbitrate disputes. The group organizes dialogues between employers and employees, provides training for business start-ups, and monitors compliance with labor regulations. Financial and taxation incentives are provided to firms with excellent records in employee relations.

### Summary

The Chengdu footwear cluster grew out of a traditional industry and has benefited from the country's policy of encouraging the westward migration of labor-intensive manufacturing. Despite its great distance from the coast, the cluster has developed a strong export base because of its complete supply chain, competitive production costs, and efficient logistics system. Because of the mounting pressure of the cost of labor and raw materials, the relocation of major labor-intensive sectors from China's coastal regions to the inland provinces and other developing countries will continue and may even intensify in coming years.

## Dieshiqiao International Home Textiles Market, Haimen, Jiangsu Province

Since the 1980s, the locus of world textile production has shifted from northern Europe and the United States to China, where wages are lower and product quality is good. The textile and clothing industry is among China's largest, with more than 40,000 enterprises and 10 million enterprise workers in 2011 alone (NBS 2012).[1] China's share of world output has risen rapidly since it joined the World Trade Organization (WTO) in 2001 and since the Multi-Fiber Arrangement governing world textile trade ended on January 1, 2005. By 2010, China was producing more than 40 percent of the developed world's textile and apparel imports. The value of its fabric and apparel exports exceeded $150 billion in 2011 (NBS 2012).

Textile production has shifted from other developing countries to China because of the greater competitiveness of the Chinese industry. China has moved to the top in the world textile trade thanks to a strong supply chain, an undervalued exchange rate, government support for light industry, an immense pool of young workers who prefer factory work to farming, and a long history of embroidery and textile crafts-manship. Although rising wages in China and slumping demand in North America have hurt the industry in recent years, the fundamentals of the Chinese textile model remain strong.

Textile centers have emerged throughout China in response to chang-ing global market dynamics. Clustered mostly in the coastal south-east, textile firms have grown by leaps and bounds. In less than two decades, there has been a mushrooming of private enterprises relying on increasingly mechanized facilities and an entrepreneurial vision.

### Origin and Course of Development

An important textile cluster is centered on the former village of Dieshiqiao, which is now part of Haimen, a county-level city in Jiangsu Province. The Dieshiqiao cluster specializes in the manufacture, sale, and distribution of home textiles, a category that includes bed linens, curtains, quilts, cushions, and plush toys. Local firms manufacture these products for sale to households and to hotels, hospitals, and schools.

Today, the cluster operates on a massive scale. Activity revolves around the Haimen industrial park, which was established in 2006, occupies 65 square kilometers, and houses over 1,400 home textile enterprises.[2] The park's 2010 output totaled Y 6 billion ($886 million), generating fiscal revenue of Y 500 million ($73.9 million) and foreign investment of $46.5 million. The Dieshiqiao International Home Textiles Market incorporates over 20,000 shops; their combined sales exceeded Y 35 billion ($5.2 billion) in 2010 (figure 5.1), of which over one-third were accounted for by overseas buyers. Dieshiqiao provides an important marketing platform for local producers of home textiles, who typically maintain offices for representatives—their own wholesal-ers or authorized traders—directly at the market. Specialized agencies provide intermediary trade services, such as customs clearance.

Neighboring Zhihao Town, the site of China's largest cloth wholesale market, supplies fabrics made of cotton, polyester, and hybrid materials

**Figure 5.1 Trade Volume, Dieshiqiao International Home Textiles Market, Haimen, China, 2004–10**

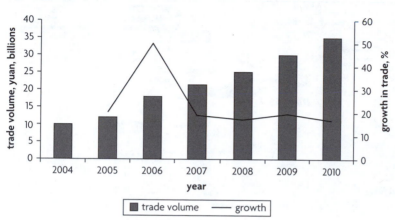

*Source:* National Bureau of Statistics of China.

in limitless varieties and grades, providing local manufacturers with a stable source of inputs. A market, also associated with the park, and the thousands of enterprises clustered nearby form a complete industrial value chain from inputs to final packaging.

How did this imposing cluster, which today enjoys global recognition and incorporates one of China's largest wholesale markets for textile products, originate? The answer reflects a combination of geography, local craft traditions, small-scale private entrepreneurship, and sustained, imaginative, and determined official support, especially at the local level.

**Geography.** Map 5.1 shows the location of Dieshiqiao in Haimen County, east and slightly south of Nantong, Jiangsu Province. Prior to the recent development of transport and communications, this area, situated on the northern bank of the Yangzi River estuary, was rather isolated. Travel times and economic distance from Nanjing, the provincial capital, from the great metropolis of Shanghai, and from the regional economic centers of Changzhou, Suzhou, and Wuxi—all clustered along the south bank of the Yangzi River—were substantial.

Although Jiangsu is among China's most prosperous provinces, a comparison between Haimen and Wuxi, also in Jiangsu, during the

**Map 5.1  Dieshiqiao Home Textile Complex, Jiangsu Province, China**

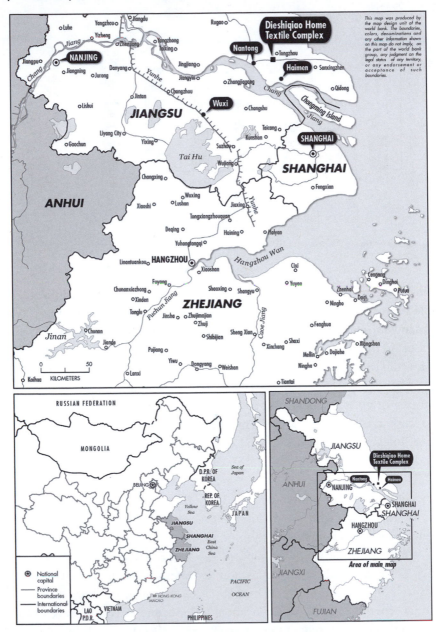

*Source:* World Bank, adapted from maps at "Jiangsu Profile," made-in-jiangsu.com, http://www.made-in-jiangsu.com/info/ jiangsu-profile.html#1.

early years of reform reveals that Haimen was a regional laggard. The data for 1980 shown in table 5.2 indicate that both counties had rural populations of slightly less than one million. Both also had high levels of agricultural productivity, although output per villager was 16 percent higher in Wuxi than in Haimen in 1985. Electricity consumption, however, differed radically: villages in Wuxi used over four times the power available in Haimen. Wuxi was far ahead of Haimen in reducing the labor intensity of farming and shifting farm workers into industry. In Wuxi, visitors in 1975 reported that mechanization had already replaced draft animals, so that threshing and food processing were mostly mechanized, and tractors were being used to plow 90 percent of farmland (Perkins 1977).

In Haimen, as in other isolated and relatively poor localities, the local authorities refrained from the strict enforcement of official antibusiness policies during the 1960s and 1970s. Farmers were allowed to bring vegetables and handicrafts to sell in the Dieshiqiao market, which became a haven where local farmers, private businesspeople, and individuals could trade in local agricultural, industrial, and sideline products. While the local government's hands-off policy benefited entrepreneurs, there was no sign of supportive policies similar to those that emerged during the reform era.

Table 5.2 Two Jiangsu Counties, Haimen and Wuxi, during the Early Reform Period, China, 1980–85

| Indicator | Haimen County | | Wuxi County | |
|---|---|---|---|---|
| | 1980 | 1985 | 1980 | 1985 |
| Village population, thousands | 918 | 807 | 954 | 797 |
| Village power consumption, kWh, millions | 43.6 | 87.6 | 185.2 | 362.0 |
| Net value of agricultural output, yuan, millions at current prices | — | 238.3 | — | 324.5 |
| Power consumption per capita, kWh | — | 109 | 194 | 454 |
| Index, Haimen = 100 | 100 | 100 | 409.1 | 418.6 |
| Net value of agricultural output per capita, yuan | — | 351.0 | — | 407.2 |
| Index, Haimen = 100 | 100 | 100 | — | 116.0 |

Source: NBS 1989.
Note: — = not available; kWh = kilowatt hour.

**Tradition.** Dieshiqiao is located in Haimen, on the outskirts of Nantong City. This area has a long history of cultivating and processing cotton, jute, and silk. Haimen is the home of the prominent scholar-entrepreneur Zhang Jian (1853–1926), a top graduate in national civil service examinations who later became one of China's first industrialists. Jiangsu ranks among China's leading cotton producers.

Nantong, along with other districts in southern Jiangsu Province, was a leading center of the handicraft textile industry during the Qing Dynasty. Jiangsu and Shanghai pioneered the expansion of factory textile production in the decades prior to World War II; their leadership in the manufacture of cotton goods continued after 1949. As a result, the local populace included many individuals with knowledge and experience in all aspects of cotton textiles, from cotton cultivation, yarn and cloth manufacture, embroidery, and other craft skills to distribution and marketing. Local residents who had worked in state-owned textile factories, which maintain a prominent presence in Jiangsu, provided technical expertise at the early stages of cluster development.

Under these circumstances, it is not surprising that small-scale production and trade included activity in the textile and embroidery sectors. Beginning in the mid-1950s, small numbers of villagers were producing, buying, and selling textile materials and products in Dieshiqiao markets. Emboldened by the local government's policy of benign neglect, the budding industry gradually expanded, leading to the spontaneous, unplanned formation of a distribution center for locally made textile-related products. By the 1970s, long before the local government took an active role in promoting local business expansion, Dieshiqiao had developed a burgeoning industrial cluster revolving around the embroidery trade.

**Entrepreneurship.** While we have no detailed accounts of the initial stages of home textile development in Dieshiqiao, information about Mingchao, a local firm that grew from start-up to national and international prominence within 15 years, illustrates the verve and ambition of small-scale Chinese entrepreneurs. Landmarks of Mingchao's development include the following:

- 1992: Mingchao founder Hu Mingliang accumulates Y 1,500 ($272) and assembles a small number of friends and neighbors to undertake a home textile business.

- 1993: Hu purchases equipment, sets up a workshop, and hires an initial tranche of local skilled workers, none educated beyond the junior high school level. The business progresses, from activity as a sales agent for other producers to making and selling original products.
- 1994: Hu's fledgling firm begins to gain traction within local markets.
- 1995: Hu daringly invests Y 20,000 ($2,395) to establish his own national and international wholesale outlet for textiles and fabrics in Yiwu, in neighboring Zhejiang Province.
- 1996: Mingchao, now facing the full force of domestic and international competition, begins to establish a self-contained value chain encompassing supply, production, and marketing.
- 1997: Mingchao rapidly expands its distribution network, recording annual sales growth of 60 percent. As the leading producer of home textiles selling in the Yiwu market, Mingchao seizes the opportunity to move its operations to a new level. The firm raises over Y 1 million ($120,630) to build new production facilities. At the same time, it invests heavily to establish a flagship store in Yiwu.
- 1998: Hu transforms his business into a limited liability company and registers his own Dream brand name, thus taking two big steps forward. In preparation for future expansion, the firm standardizes the operations of its sales agents.
- 1999: Mingchao systematically establishes a distribution network encompassing over 30 regional sales outlets in four provinces.
- 2000: Dream products become the top seller in the Yiwu wholesale market for home textiles.
- 2001: Mingchao managers begin to focus on selling in the rapidly emerging wholesale market in their Dieshiqiao base.

The result for Mingchao was explosive growth: annual sales expansion reached 100 percent during 2002–05 as the marketing effort shifted from regional to nationwide distribution. A second brand, Silky Elegance, helped power Mingchao's sales growth, allowing it to emerge as the national leader in China's home textiles sector.

- 2002: Mingchao centralizes its operations in Dieshiqiao and reorganizes its business under the name Shanghai Mingchao Bedding Co. Ltd.
- 2003: Mingchao ceases production as an OEM and focuses production exclusively on goods to be sold under its own name. The firm pioneers a new line of "summer cool" products intended to provide comfort in torrid weather.
- 2004: The firm pursues a multibrand strategy focused on its upscale Silky Elegance and mass-market Mingchao product lines. It also sets up Sunshine Textiles, a wholly owned subsidiary in Hong Kong SAR, China, while pursuing human resource development on the domestic front.
- 2005: As its corporate offices move into a new building with 5,000 square meters of floor space, the firm's sales channels and its distribution networks continue to mature. The Dream brand is sold in major wholesale markets. The number of Silky Elegance retail shops passes the 100 mark. Mingchao products are on the shelves of major supermarkets and chain stores.

This tale, multiplied by the thousands, has propelled the local economy from regional laggard to provincial leadership. Thus, for instance, the Zhihao fabric market started in much the same way as the Mingchao company: each of 21 local households contributed Y 500 ($91) to support the establishment of a local market that opened in 1992 with 64 stalls. Multiple expansion and upgrading projects increased the number of shops to 360 by 1996 and 1,120 by 2010 and raised the combined annual turnover to Y 64 million ($8 million) by 1996 and Y 12 billion ($2 billion) by 2010.[3]

Expansion attracted the attention of large-scale investors. In 2001, for example, the local government welcomed a private investor who poured Y 500 million ($60 million) into the construction of the Dieshiqiao International Home Textiles Market on 17 hectares of land encompassing 2,000 stores. By 2010, through such initiatives, powered by thousands of small private firms, some of which have evolved into large-scale businesses, Haimen ranked ninth among Jiangsu's cities and counties in terms of both gross domestic product (GDP) and foreign investment.[4] Haimen's explosive growth is not simply the result of private entrepreneurial success, however; the public sector's contribution has also been much in evidence.

## Competitiveness and Binding Constraints

The initial emergence of the Dieshiqiao home textile cluster was built on existing strengths: the local tradition of embroidery and other textile-related handicrafts, local experience in modern textile production, and locally available materials and entrepreneurship. The small scale of early start-ups meant that informal financing sufficed to get fledgling enterprises under way. Many Chinese manufacturers, including several in Dieshiqiao, used processing trade as a means of boosting production with minimal capital requirements. Profits from processing and OEM production could then support the expansion of production facilities, the upgrading of equipment, and investment in brand development without recourse to China's banks, which typically hesitate to extend credit to all but the largest and best known private firms.

As the industry began to expand, three key constraints threatened to limit its growth.

**Logistics.** Prior to the start of the reform era, the Nantong area, although located near some of China's biggest domestic markets, was poorly integrated into major transport networks. As a result, high logistics costs threatened to choke off efforts to expand Dieshiqiao's emergent home textile cluster at an early stage. However, general improvement in transport and communication networks throughout the Yangzi Delta region, especially the extension of major highways to Nantong and adjacent regions along the north bank of the Yangzi estuary and the construction of bridge and tunnel links connecting Nantong to Shanghai's ports and markets, turned the cluster's location into a major advantage.

**Land.** Energetic action by local governments, which used eminent domain to clear substantial tracts for the Haimen industrial park and for the construction of large market facilities for home textile products in Dieshiqiao and for home textile inputs in nearby Zhihao, effectively removed land availability as a major obstacle to the development of the Dieshiqiao cluster.

**Quality and distribution.** Following initial success, the continued growth of output and sales depended on the expansion of sales and distribution networks and on the ability of local producers to upgrade the quality and variety of their goods to match the changing tastes of an increasingly prosperous domestic populace and meet the expectations of overseas buyers. Dieshiqiao firms relied on networks to expand the sales and distribution of their products. Rapidly abandoning the old model of street vendors and peddlers, the industry turned to the increasingly sophisticated commodity market for trading. Some firms, such as Mingchao, established their own wholesale and retail outlets in distant cities.

To raise product quality, local entrepreneurs enhanced traditional hand embroidery techniques and used information from clients and competitors to introduce computers into the production of embroidery products. More than 100 local enterprises have received the International Organization for Standardization (ISO) 9000 quality system certification and the 14000 environmental quality system certification. Firms such as Mingchao and Sanxing Clothes and Embroidery, which registered its Shulian trademark in 1986, shifted from producing generic goods to using trademarks and brands to highlight the distinctiveness of their products. By 2008, Dieshiqiao home textile enterprises had registered more than 600 trademarks. Kailun Home Textiles is another firm that has successfully pursued a branding strategy. After beginning as a small-scale producer, Kailun began to sell goods in rented shops and through agents. When trading volume grew, the firm established its own factory and eventually developed into one of the region's biggest textile enterprises, in part by using expensive celebrity endorsements to promote the Kailun brand.

## The Role of Government

Since the onset of reforms in the late 1970s, official actions have supported local development in two ways: through general interventions that reduce costs and expand opportunities for all sectors of the economy and through actions specifically targeted at smoothing the path for home textiles and other light manufactures.

The first category includes measures affecting logistics and labor quality. The Nantong region, including Dieshiqiao and Haimen, has reaped large benefits from a massive expansion of regional infrastructure.

No longer isolated, Haimen and Nantong are now connected to a network of roads and expressways that provide easy access to Nanjing, Shanghai, and the booming cities along the southern bank of the Yangzi. Bridge and tunnel connections spanning the Yangzi have slashed transit times so that trucks departing from Haimen can now reach Shanghai's ports within one or two hours.[5] Nantong's airport, completed in 1993, allows business travel to major domestic destinations, as do new and expanded airports in Shanghai and throughout the delta region.

The local government has expanded regional economic prospects by extending Haimen's traditional reputation as an educational center. Haimen students taking China's demanding college admission tests attain a 97.6 percent success rate, the highest in Jiangsu. Haimen has three vocational universities and two vocational high schools; its technical schools and continuing education facilities provide training to over 5,000 workers each year. An unusual feature is the use by local governments of financial incentives, tax benefits, and special provisions for the education and health care of dependents to attract businesspeople and technicians to Haimen.[6]

The local government has also implemented specific measures to support the home textile sector. In Dieshiqiao, the local authorities adopted an active supporting role as early as 1982 when they established a market service team to supervise and encourage the nascent Dieshiqiao marketplace for home textiles. Beginning in 1983, home textiles became a focus of the Dieshiqiao government's agenda, resulting in the introduction of policies and preferential incentives affecting land, taxation, industry, and commerce in ways that benefited household producers and eventually led to the creation of the Haimen industrial park.

The government has encouraged local firms to improve product quality and enter new markets. In 1994, for example, it conducted a training course on the export business for 40 local embroidery firms with the objective of upgrading their technology and smoothing their entry into the international export market.

The Enterprise Development Bureau and Enterprise Service Center offer incentives tailored to the development stage of firms. Individual enterprises receive cash rewards for moving to the industrial park (which provides subsidized housing and utilities for firms located within its boundaries) or listing on the stock exchange. They also receive rewards for adopting new, high-technology methods.[7]

The local authorities promote textile-related research by offering R&D grants and helping local enterprises establish cooperative ties with nearby universities and technical institutions. The industrial park administration has invited domestic and international experts to speak to local entrepreneurs and executives about enterprise management and the procedures for listing on the stock exchange.

Through partnerships between the trade association and institutions of higher learning, the local government has sought to attract professional talent, offering favorable arrangements for housing and business facilities. By 2010, specialized design and R&D teams had been established in the region. To help embroidery businesses boost production, the town government cooperated with vocational schools to hold annual training classes on corporation management, long-term development, and brand management. Professional consultancy is also offered in R&D and technological innovation. In addition, the local adult education center conducts annual technical training courses.

The enhancement of innovation through R&D has been a key strategy of the local government. High-technology R&D projects or technology upgrading programs qualify for subsidies. The local government invests only in public R&D platforms rather than specific R&D projects. To encourage the growth of advanced home textile R&D efforts, the industrial park earmarked 20,000 square meters for a new science and technology innovation park in 2011. Firms in the innovation park enjoy preferential policies, such as free rent and utilities.

The local government provides additional services from several interrelated platforms, as follows:

- *Intellectual property rights.* In 2002, a local agency was established to oversee patent registration and copyright protection. As of 2009, the office had registered patents for 6,414 pattern designs and handled 685 copyright infringement complaints. Patent applications have increased more than 10 percent a year. In 2008, the World Intellectual Property Organization named the Dieshiqiao home textile cluster a demonstration case of copyright protection and honored it with a Gold Award for Copyright Initiative.
- *Quality testing.* In 2005, the Home Textile Subcenter of the Jiangsu Textile Product Quality Supervision, Inspection, and Testing Center

was established and certified as a national laboratory. Its eight inspectors, equipped with more than 100 advanced testing machines, conduct some 2,000 inspections each year on request. The center has enhanced the quality of Dieshiqiao home textile products and improved their access to domestic and international markets.

- *Information technology and exchange.* In April 2010, a panel of experts from the China Academy of Engineering gave a green light to the Dieshiqiao home textile index compilation scheme. The index will become a barometer for the entire home textile industry. Dieshiqiao has also constructed an e-government network in the industrial park, an e-commerce network, and a logistics information system.

Recognizing the problem of the chronic shortage of capital confronting small-scale entrepreneurs, local officials have tried to assist by establishing a financing platform. The government serves as an intermediary between banks and enterprises after evaluating companies based on sales volume, market share, and tax contribution. The park authority actively promotes cooperation between banks and financial groups to help enterprises expand their financial channels. It has set up a microfinance agency in the park that provides intermediary financial services for enterprises. The microfinance agency avoids guarantees to ensure that companies remain competitive. In 2010, Haimen City transformed the Dieshiqiao market into a limited liability company. This model of public-private collaboration has mobilized capital from multiple sources and upgraded the management of the market.

Once the scale of activity expanded beyond the capacity of local labor resources, the local government began helping Dieshiqiao firms obtain unskilled and skilled workers by establishing a labor market through which enterprises can recruit workers. The local labor authority has partnered with Anhui and Henan, provinces that provide about 70 percent of the incoming domestic migrants, to recruit more workers. Local labor costs have risen steeply in recent years: the average monthly wage for assembly line workers had risen to Y 3,000–Y 4,000 ($475–$634) by 2012, up more than 20 percent from 2011 and much higher than the nationwide average for similar work. This illustrates the vulnerability of labor-intensive sectors such as home textiles to offshore competition for export and even for domestic sales.

**Summary**

The story of Dieshiqiao International Home Textiles Market, a tale of the successful transformation of a quiet fishing village into a home textile hub, shows how the combination of strong entrepreneurship, dynamic local government, and innovative policy has enabled the home textile cluster to achieve rapid economic growth.

## Warp Knitting Science and Technology Industrial Zone, Haining, Zhejiang Province

Haining, in central Zhejiang Province, is China's largest manufacturing base and distribution center for warp-knit fabric.[8] Haining supplies 70 percent of the warp-knit cloth used in China in light box advertising and 40 percent of the cloth used in geogrids, a construction material. By 2010, Haining had more than 400 warp knitting enterprises (up from 3 in the 1980s), 235 of which had annual sales of at least Y 5 million ($0.7 million) each. Enterprises in Haining own more than 30 percent of the world-class warp knitting equipment in use and produce 325,000 tons of warp-knit fabric annually. Haining's warp knitting industrial value has more than tripled since 2001, rising from Y 2.2 billion ($268 million) in 2004 to Y 7.7 billion ($1.1 billion) in 2008 (figure 5.2).

The warp knitting industry began in China in the 1980s mainly in the production of apparel fabric and cloth for mosquito netting. The industry's rapid development in Haining followed a visionary analysis that recognized the global changes in the industry. In the late 1990s, as the international warp knitting industry relocated from Europe and the United States to developing countries in Europe and Southeast Asia because of rising labor costs, market-sensitive Haining entrepreneurs began to purchase foreign equipment. The returns have been impressive. Warp knitting production and sales have grown substantially through the rapid upgrading of technologies and equipment, a diversifying product mix, and the clear advantages of clustering. Applications of warp knitting products include high-visibility construction projects such as the Qinghai-Tibet railway and the Shanghai-Hangzhou expressway. Half the flags at the Beijing Olympic Games in 2008 were made of high-grade warp-knit cloth produced by Wanfang Warp Knitting Company

**Figure 5.2  Gross Output by Above-Scale Enterprises, Warp Knitting Industrial Zone, Haining, China, 2004–08**

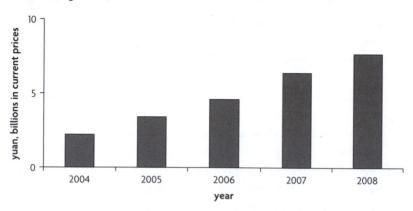

*Source:* Data of the Administrative Commission of the Warp Knitting Science and Technology Industrial Zone, Haining.

*Note:* Above-scale enterprises (*guimo yishang*) is an aggregate that includes all state sector firms, as well as all other firms with annual sales above Y 5 million ($0.7 million) each.

Ltd., a local company. The uniforms of the U.S. National Basketball Association are made of the warp-knit fabric produced in Haining.

Over the last decade, through public-private collaboration, the Haining Warp Knitting Science and Technology Industrial Zone has emerged as a global leader. The zone's management committee set the goal of making the zone China's warp knitting capital and of attaining substantial international market share. By 2009, the zone included an integrated industrial supply chain spanning raw materials, knitting, deep processing, and finished products. Warp knitting in the zone accounts for 70 percent of all warp knitting in Haining and 20 percent of the national total. The warp knitting index, designed and compiled by the zone, has become an important barometer of China's warp knitting industry. The zone registers annual output of Y 920,000 ($134,672) per worker and annual fiscal revenues of more than Y 42,000 ($6,148) per worker, much higher than the national average.

## Origin and Course of Development

The warp knitting industry in China has humble origins. Maqiao, the site of the industrial zone, is a small town under the administration of Haining City. It has a land area of less than 40 square kilometers and a population of less than 30,000. Before the 1990s, the town was dominated by agriculture. Its single warp knitting company used old-fashioned machines to make simple products such as mosquito nets. In 1992, Ye Xuekang, the company's owner, made the bold decision to import a high-end knitting machine at a cost of Y 12 million ($2.2 million). The machine enabled the company to produce high-quality products, and orders flooded in. Encouraged by this success, household workshops began manufacturing warp-knit products on a small scale.

By 1997, several industrial clusters had sprung up in Zhejiang Province and neighboring Jiangsu Province, leaving Maqiao far behind. Shen Shunnian, who was appointed to a leadership position in the town, vowed to identify an industry with great market potential that fit the region's comparative advantage. He and colleagues visited hundreds of enterprises, universities, and research institutes. One college professor they visited extolled the benefits of the warp knitting industry, which was in the process of relocating from Europe and North America to developing countries. Because of the high technological and capital requirements, few enterprises in China could produce high-end products; so, there was little competition in the market.

Warp-knit cloth has a broad range of applications and has a growth future in domestic and international demand. The fabric is used for decorations and exhibits, apparel, shoes, tents, and even automobiles, buildings, and railways. Warp-knit products generate a much higher profit margin than ordinary textiles. The product also has a long value chain of machinery, raw materials, and supporting industries, including dyeing and printing, and, thus, showed strong potential as the focus of an industrial cluster.

After evaluating the market and the region's industrial strengths, Shen and his team eventually identified warp knitting as the industry they would target for development.

In December 1998, a warp knitting industrial park was established to provide better infrastructure and services for enterprises. The warp knitting industry was officially launched in Haining in 1999. Through a loan of Y 3 million ($362,395), the zone was extended to slightly more than 65,000 square meters during the first phase. The land was obtained at a subsidized rate. Along with this government support, the total investment by the five initial enterprises was Y 30 million ($3.6 million).

Zone management adopted a flexible approach that combined market-based commercial operation and government-led investment. Private investors and contractors were involved in the real estate development and the building of infrastructure. The government supported zone development through special funds for industrial restructuring, the application of new and high technologies, energy savings, emission reduction, and guidance for service industry development.

Within a decade, persistence and innovation had enabled the town to become a world leader in warp knitting. Production surged from less than Y 100 million ($12.1 million) to Y 20 billion ($2.95 billion) in 1999–2010. The warp knitting park has won top awards for industrial scale, number of high-speed warp knitting machines, the market share in light box advertising cloth and geogrid textile in China, and the scale of the database of warp knitting products. Secondary industries were established, including services for technology development and consultancy, logistics, trade, and product testing and standardization.

The Haining warp knitting industry now has the capability to produce more than 1,000 kinds of products, ranging from traditional fabric for garments and decorations to high-technology products, including yacht hulls and the blades of wind-driven generators. The number of patents granted to enterprises in the zone reached 300 by 2009, accounting for some 70 percent of the industry's total in China.

## Competitiveness and Binding Constraints

Haining's warp knitting industry has benefited from the region's convenient location, well-developed communication system, and abundant supply of raw materials.

**Logistics and the supply chain.** Haining is located along the southern rim of the Haijiahu Plain in the Yangzi River Delta, on the north bank of the Qiantang River. The city is near the rail line connecting two major cities, Shanghai and Hangzhou. It is connected by a dense transportation network of road, rail, and air links. Goods can be exported overseas through the port at Shanghai, 150 kilometers away.

The take-off of Haining's warp knitting industry has been fueled by the boom in downstream sectors, such as apparel, banner manufacturing, and auto production. China's rapid growth and urbanization have spawned enormous domestic demand for warp-knit fabric, which accounts for more than 85 percent of the industry's output, much of it in the form of intermediate goods sold to domestic industries. For example, in 2010, above-scale Haining firms exported Y 2 billion ($295 million) in warp-knit products, which represented only about 14.5 percent of total sales. A large share of the final output is distributed at wholesale markets in Haining and elsewhere.

Petrochemical materials, which are processed into polyester, terylene, and industrial yarn, are the main inputs for warp-knit fabrics. In the early years, producers had to buy the raw materials from large petrochemical firms, which dominated the market. The sector's expansion attracted more suppliers to the region.

Haining's warp knitting industry has had a strong agglomeration effect. Warp knitting enterprises accounted for nearly 86 percent of the zone's 2010 gross output value. An industrial chain has formed for knitting, affixture, printing, dyeing, and apparel making.

**Technology and R&D.** New technologies and products have fueled the success of Haining's warp knitting cluster. Over 1998–2009, enterprises in the zone invested more than Y 7 billion ($1.02 billion) in technological innovation and introduced 1,500 types of advanced equipment. Haining has a third of the country's advanced warp knitting machinery. Foreign equipment manufacturers recognize the zone as the world's largest concentration of high-grade warp knitting machines. Most of the machines are produced by German companies. They have improved the technological content of the zone's warp-knit products.

While warp knitting firms spend willingly on modern machinery, few invest in R&D. This lack of competitiveness could reduce the sector's long-term competitiveness in Haining. In 2010, only 39 percent of the above-scale companies responding to an enterprise survey reported engaging in R&D activities, 16 percentage points less than the average for all manufacturing in the city. R&D expenditure by warp knitting firms was only 1.5 percent of sales revenue, and less than a quarter of the industry's gross output value was derived from newly developed products, much less than the value in the leather sector, another important Haining industry.

**Capital.** The zone has benefited from strong investment and capital formation through the leveraging of advanced technologies. In recent years, enterprises in the zone have invested about Y 600 million ($88 million) annually in technological renovation. The return on investment has been high. The economic returns among enterprises in the zone have been trending upward. Labor productivity and investment levels are higher in Haining than in other domestic warp knitting centers.

**Labor.** More than 20,000 people work in Haining's warp knitting enterprises. Most are unskilled migrants from inland provinces. In 2010, skilled personnel accounted for only one in four workers in above-scale enterprises.[9] About 11 percent of the workers in above-scale enterprises had university degrees. Professional technical staff made up less than 10 percent of the workforce, and mid-level and senior staff made up only 1.1 percent.

## The Role of Government

Haining's warp knitting industry benefits from the region's comparative advantages in location, industrial legacy, readily available production factors, and government support. Aiming to build the world's best warp knitting cluster, the Maqiao Township government has built a specialized industrial park, promoted industrial agglomeration, and helped enterprises promote their brand-name products and expand their capacity for indigenous innovation.

**Providing services.** The zone authority has reached out to enterprises interested in moving into the zone. The Department of Land Acquisition and Relocation contacts enterprises and guides them through the entry procedures to reduce the application time. The zone administration also handles site-selection proposals, project prereviews, land use licenses, construction permits, feasibility reports, environmental impact evaluation reports, and equipment import and customs forms. The Investment Promotion Department provides intermediation services for the completion of application forms, the preregistration of company names, business licenses, the transfer of money, opening accounts at the People's Bank, and preparing tax registration certificates.

Once an enterprise enters the zone, the authority acts to resolve any difficulties, and the management committee and development company of the zone provide one-stop services to investors, including project applications, land leasing, and registration. The local government emphasizes the park's soft infrastructure, which includes platforms for science and technology, social services, cultural promotion, international communications, trading, finance, business consulting, and workforce training. The park cooperates with local universities and research institutes to help with R&D and staff training.

**Unifying standards.** Warp knitting enterprises in the zone initially suffered because of the absence of unified standards; so, the zone administration invited industry experts to coordinate standards, resulting in the publication of unified standards in 2008. The zone management committee and the industry association supply enterprises with guidance on compliance. The share of low-quality goods has declined substantially.

**Promoting the industrial cluster.** In April 2000, the Haining government announced a 3 percent interest rate subsidy for investments by SMEs in imports of warp knitting equipment. All technological renovation projects moving into the zone receive special land arrangements. The city and the zone offer financial support to projects that contribute to the industrial value chain, industry enhancement, and the relaxation of bottlenecks. The city and the zone authority also grant subsidies to the industry association, which consults on market performance, conducts industry studies, arranges for domestic and foreign exhibitions and exchanges, collects and distributes statistical information, and implements technical standards. Members of Industrial Fabrics Association International have been invited to lecture in the zone on development trends in the international industry.

Strategic investors are welcomed. The zone administration offers special preferences for foreign investments of more than $50 million, domestic investments of more than Y 300 million ($44 million), and new and high-technology projects. Land policy practices aimed at encouraging enterprises to move into the zone include resource integration, remote trusteeship, project cobuilding, and revenue sharing. In 2008, the first initial public offering of a firm in the warp knitting zone,

Zhejiang Jinda Hailide New Material Corporation Ltd., was announced on the Shenzhen Stock Exchange. The zone offers special rewards to newly listed enterprises or to listed enterprises that move into the zone.

**Supporting R&D.** Rewards are given to technological renovation projects that promote obvious social benefits: energy savings; new water conservation products; new technologies, equipment, and processes; and renewable energy.

### Summary

After only a decade, Haining's warp knitting industry is booming, confirming the vision of the Maqiao Township government in promoting this capital-intensive industry. Benefiting from strong and growing market demand as a result of China's economic prosperity, Haining has developed into a world-class industrial cluster. Haining's success shows that, once market forces begin to support the formation and expansion of an industrial cluster, local government can play a key role in guiding and accelerating the process.

## Button City, Qiaotou, Zhejiang Province

When we started building factories like crazy, it was for our own survival; we had no capital. Everything came from the work of our own hands.

—*Chinese entrepreneur in Qiaotou*

Now we need to upgrade our quality and produce more high-quality buttons . . . ; then we can expand to the international market.

—*Chen Jianlin, Communist Party secretary, Qiaotou*

In the wake of liberalization, Zhejiang Province witnessed the emergence of spontaneous capitalism led by private family enterprises and small industrial workshops.[10] This contrasts with the Pearl River Delta region in south China, where success arose largely because of inflows of diaspora capital from Hong Kong SAR, China, and from Taiwan, China.

Qiaotou, in Zhejiang Province, is southeast of Shanghai and some 60 kilometers from Wenzhou, the nearest large coastal city. This small town has come to represent the quintessential Chinese light manufacturing success. Deficient in both economic size and arable land, it has nonetheless become the international center for world button production in less than two decades. Far from railroads or good-quality roads and surrounded by mountains and the sea, the region was forced to trade to survive, taking advantage of its location near the coast and strategic ports. Qiaotou's tale epitomizes China's success in both manufacturing and poverty alleviation.

Like many other manufacturing successes in southern China, Qiaotou shows the power of product specialization and of the geographic concentration of small companies. A one-product town, it shares the manufacturing limelight with similar one-product towns and cities nearby. One neighboring cluster produces most of the world's socks; another makes sweaters; a third produces lighters. With slightly more than 65,000 people in 2010, Qiaotou has revolutionized the world button industry.

Qiaotou's success has much to do with mastering the microeconomics of the business and the existence of a supportive macroeconomic environment. Through a combination of domestic and pooled savings and good access to inputs, domestic entrepreneurs have prospered. Entrepreneurial skills have improved, and a well-lubricated supply chain has helped the local economy take off. As firms grew, the government facilitated their expansion by providing industrial land.

The industry, launched in the mid-1980s, peaked in the 1990s after it had captured more than 80 percent of the national market. Output surpassed $1 billion in 2008. With about 500 factories and 20,000 migrant workers, Qiaotou sold around 15 billion buttons a year over 2007–10, thereby servicing 70 percent of the domestic market and producing roughly 60 percent of the world's buttons (figure 5.3). There was a brief decline in 2009 because of the financial crisis and competition from neighboring cities, but current trends appear favorable. The cluster has developed a substantial supply chain, with access to quality inputs and outlets for its products. The town has established a strong export presence in Europe and the United States. Today, it sells more than 1,000 button varieties, including plastic and glass-bead buttons and metal, ceramic, and decorative fastenings. It has also started to produce zippers.

Qiaotou is the center of a dynamic industry and a vibrant wholesale market. The town's main streets are lined with more than 1,500 button stores. The stores specialize in different kinds of buttons, sold in batches

**Figure 5.3  The Market Share of the Qiaotou Button Industry, China and the World, 2007–10**

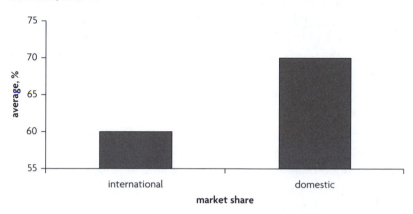

*Source:* Interviews with local entrepreneurs, Qiaotou, 2010.
*Note:* The vertical axis begins at 55 percent; so, the international market share is large.

of 100, 500, and 1,000. Customers are mostly wholesalers for garment companies. Interviews with retailers and factory owners confirm the tale of a dynamic and specialized industry. Factories on the edge of town sell goods on domestic and international markets through trading companies. A web of contracting and subcontracting arrangements keeps production humming. As the industry has grown in recent years, the scale and specialization have become more pronounced.

## Origin and Course of Development

The button industry flourished in the late 1980s and 1990s following economic liberalization. A depreciating exchange rate, high growth, and declining inflation all provided a supportive environment for private industry.

In the early years of reform, a dozen centralized trade corporations controlled the path and direction of China's small overseas trade. High tariffs sheltered China's button industry from import competition. Tariffs averaging 80 percent in the early 1980s were progressively reduced to 10–11 percent in 2000–10 following China's accession to the WTO.

Qiaotou has become a middle-class town thanks to the success of the button cluster. The success owes much to a mixture of entrepreneurship, the mastery of input markets, and accident. In the late 1970s,

Qiaotou was a dusty village surrounded by hills and mountains that had no natural resources. It suffered from frequent flooding; incomes were low. A few households were making plastic products and small handicrafts. The lack of farming opportunities and land shortages meant that trading and the town's proximity to Wenzhou, one of the most dynamic centers of capitalism and private sector industry in the country, were Qiaotou's only comparative advantages.

Qiaotou's astonishing rise began modestly. In the 1970s and 1980s, entrepreneurial villagers began buying buttons elsewhere to sell them from their bicycles throughout the city. These peddlers, who came from families with a tradition of small-scale trading, were looking for promising business opportunities.

Peddling had gone underground during the commune era, but eventually resurfaced through the activities of craftspeople and small-scale traders. It turned out there was money to be made in this low-technology product, buttons. Margins were larger in buttons than in other products, sometimes reaching more than 10 percent. Because the garment industry was expanding in China in the 1980s, the demand for buttons was exploding. Their small size and light weight simplified transportation. Following their initial successes, many peddlers opened small shops and imported simple machines from Taiwan, China, using their own and pooled savings. Family and personal networks were also important in obtaining market information and capital to feed expansion.

Because of the high profits and limited barriers to entry in the early years, the industry grew through a strong demonstration effect. Itinerant peddlers spread the word. Machines were imported from Taiwan, China, through a network of connections, and knowledge and techniques were disseminated through the same network, contributing to entrepreneurial skill formation. Capital was acquired through personal savings and the pooled funds of relatives and neighbors.

The button market in Qiaotou opened in 1983 and soon became a well-known center for the products. By the mid-1980s, more than 400 local enterprises were making buttons. The center of town came to be filled with button stores. The industry grew in tandem with garment factories, which sent representatives to buy buttons in bulk. Demand was huge, and soon almost every villager was making buttons.

Qiaotou's development was driven by the private sector. The entrepreneurs, factory outlets, and agents were mostly local, and the factories and businesses mostly self-financed. There were no state-owned enterprises in the area, and most businesses were established with local capital. Later, businesses from Hong Kong SAR, China, and from Taiwan, China, set up joint ventures and brought with them technical knowledge, market information, managerial skills, training, and finance. The state intervened indirectly, but it was not a major force early on. The firms transitioned from craft workshops to industrial districts to clusters of SMEs. The industry acquired more advanced machinery and slowly scaled up.

As Qiaotou developed, its reputation spread. In the 1990s and the first decade of the 2000s, local trading companies began to link up with the growing international market. Most buttons from Qiaotou were delivered to these trading companies for export, though there was also a growing indirect export market. The ratio of export to domestic production has varied with the industry's responses to changing market signals, but the efficiency and flexibility of the private sector eventually helped Qiaotou establish a commanding presence in the world button industry.

## Competitiveness and Binding Constraints

The emergent Qiaotou cluster made a big splash in the button industry because it had lower production costs and access to cheaper labor than traditional firms.[11] Before Qiaotou's rise, buttons made in Italy; Taiwan, China; and the United States dominated in manufacturing. New York City's garment district had a range of suppliers producing high-quality buttons for the apparel and textile industry. In China, a few state firms produced low-quality buttons at high cost, mostly in the south. These firms received government subsidies, which were phased out after the reforms. Our enterprise interviews confirm that operating costs were significantly lower in private enterprises than in state firms, and, thus, the private firms could offer competitively priced products. The average monthly income for a rural button worker in Qiaotou in the 1990s was about Y 335 ($50), compared with Y 400 ($60) for urban workers in state button factories. The state firms had to provide housing, medical insurance, and pensions, while the Qiaotou button factories relied on local and migrant workers who lived in their own settlements.

Several early movers confirmed that they could sell their buttons at one-third the price charged by state firms. Furthermore, with the purchase of good machines in the 1990s, the Qiaotou entrepreneurs rapidly moved up the quality scale. As the buttons became more sophisticated, Qiaotou's competitors began going out of business.

The Qiaotou entrepreneurs demonstrated remarkable resilience in overcoming constraints in access to land, inputs, and finance. Though land was owned by the state, there were grey areas in the law that allowed family industrial workshops to develop during the 1980s, coinciding with Qiaotou's ascent. For historical reasons, state intervention in the economy was weak, and the regulatory environment relatively relaxed. Households could thus use their land to build a vibrant industry, with the implicit support of the local government. Unlike many small enterprises, the Qiaotou entrepreneurs sourced their inputs—mostly metals, nylon, and plastic—domestically. Our interviews with local entrepreneurs confirm that the factories in Qiaotou obtained their raw materials from suppliers throughout the country, especially in Guangdong and Nanjing.

Some entrepreneurs in Qiaotou had family who had emigrated to Taiwan, China, and who shared their expertise in the button industry and helped them import machines. The early entrepreneurs peddled the buttons by bicycle, traveling across the province on marketing missions and purchasing inputs.

One of our interviewees provided low-cost marketing and purchasing services for some of the button manufacturers, picking up information and skills. He would ask around about the kinds of buttons in demand, the colors and materials in fashion, and the sorts of buttons preferred in different countries. He visited customers and trading companies and attended seminars. Through his relationship network, he facilitated business development, providing information on products, prices, and market demand to nascent entrepreneurs.

When the Qiaotou button industry was expanding, some entrepreneurs traveled to Italy to learn about the button industry there and to purchase additional machinery. In the first decade of the 2000s, a button association was created to supply market intelligence and serve as an intermediary between the local government and the industry.

The Qiaotou button industry grew largely by accumulating capital and reinvesting profits, hiring and training low-cost, semiskilled workers, and using good inputs and machines. Most entrepreneurs we interviewed used local savings to invest in their businesses and then financed expansion through retained profits. Many button factories had grown from 100 to 1,500 workers within a few decades and increased output more than 20 percent annually. The low entry barriers encouraged new entrants. There was a great imperative to expand production quickly. Scaling up was easy because of the efficient supply chain. Profit margins are several cents per bag, and they are greater on metal buttons than on plastic ones. Through the creation of a fairly stable market and distribution network and assistance from the local government, the button cluster managed to expand and develop a reputation for efficiency, low cost, and quality. In recent years, the Qiaotou button industry has withstood growing competition, especially from neighboring towns and from factories in Guangdong Province, as well as macroeconomic shocks, including the financial crisis and exchange rate appreciation.

The history of Qiaotou's button cluster shows how specialization can lead to economies of scale. There was a proliferation of different types of enterprises, with each specializing in a particular kind of plastic, metal, or hybrid button. The specialization has evolved organically, as new entrants have emerged in response to market signals. As of late 2010, the industry had about 150 big firms with more than 200 workers each, 150 medium firms with about 35 workers each, and about 300 small firms with fewer than 15 workers each.

Some procedures, such as coloring and glossing, are outsourced. Many larger firms subcontract parts of the production process to smaller firms to reduce costs. Subcontracting also facilitates the rapid fulfillment of large orders. As buttons become more complex, production, especially of metal buttons, can involve as many as five different factories. As the industry has expanded and more orders have come in, buyers have requested greater sophistication and more rapid delivery, and the industry has responded promptly. Companies maintain little inventory, but are nonetheless able to keep up with the imperatives of the business.

## The Role of Government
As was common in much of south China in the early postreform years, Qiaotou businesses faced an uncertain policy and regulatory environment. Entrepreneurs feared that the government would take over

successful enterprises as had occurred during the 1950s. Enterprises took a variety of measures to ensure their survival amid the uncertainty. Quite a few early button factories in Qiaotou registered as collective enterprises (a practice known as borrowing the red hat) to avoid the state's regulatory net. Some firms sought to avoid the regulatory net by staying small.

Prior to the rise of the local button cluster, Qiaotou's economy saw little in the way of direct government support. Fiscal transfers to the area were negligible—only half the national average—during the 1953–78 plan era.

Once reform began in the late 1970s, the button industry emerged mainly from the spontaneous activities of many private enterprises that received no official subsidies. However, though the local and provincial governments did not engage in product selection or the more common practice of picking winners, there was some help. Following the onset of economic reform, an export duty drawback system was put in place to refund the duties paid on the imports used in producing exportables. Instead of provincial and city governments deciding on the quantity of raw materials to be imported and on the allocation of the raw materials, button manufacturers could obtain what they needed through the market, reducing the costs along the supply chain. A system of foreign exchange retention rights enabled Qiaotou entrepreneurs to keep the foreign exchange they earned from overseas sales.

There had always been some interplay and a web of connections between local government officials and peasant entrepreneurs. Now, as the industry evolved, the local government began to assume a more active role. The local government engaged in regulation, taxation, and administrative support of the industry during its expansion. Business registration and customs clearance policies were simplified. The decentralization of the licensing authority to local levels of administration allowed Qiaotou entrepreneurs to deal directly with local authorities. None of the entrepreneurs we interviewed complained about long clearance times at customs offices. Doing business had become easier.

The local government began pursuing a series of smart policy interventions to help expand the industry. Because fiscal revenue depended heavily on the sector's prosperity and growth, local leaders made every effort to facilitate the sector's expansion. They had a vested interest in promoting the industry in Qiaotou because the career prospects of officials benefited if the local economies under their jurisdiction achieved unusually rapid growth.

In the mid-1990s, the government provided subsidized land for factories. During the 1990s, collateral requirements were somewhat relaxed, especially for trade credits and the use of tax rebates as collateral for loans.

In the early 2000s, the provincial government designated Qiaotou as a specialized town for clothing accessories. The local government championed the expanding industry especially by facilitating trade logistics and improving the fiscal regime.

In 2005, the local government provided land and helped in the financing of the construction of Button City in the center of town, a two-level structure on a 20,000-square-foot site that housed 771 stalls and 53 shops. Now jointly run by the town government and the industry and commerce association, Button City has facilitated marketing and reduced the cost of trade logistics. The government's decision to help build a special facility to house the button market signaled official recognition of the sector's central role in the local economy.

After 2005, the government decided to build a new industrial park to help button manufacturers scale up. The project is currently under construction, with close to 50 larger button factories signed up. There is some concern that the policy discriminates against smaller button enterprises.

The interaction between the public and private sectors deepened as the industry gained world renown. The town government itself proposed the establishment of a button trade association to manage and standardize the market.

Access to finance has also been a concern, though there are now local branches of the Industrial and Commercial Bank and the Agricultural Development Bank. An important ingredient of China's economic success has been the undervalued exchange rate, which has been maintained through prudent macroeconomic policies and high private savings rates. The undervalued exchange rate catalyzed export growth in the button industry. The Chinese currency lost about 70 percent of its value against the U.S. dollar over 1980–95 as measured by the trade-weighted real effective exchange rate index, making Chinese button exports cheaper than those of competitors.[12] Because the real exchange rate is the key relative price determining the international competitiveness of a country's exports, the devaluation of the yuan was a critical contributor to export growth in light manufacturing enterprises.

As the button cluster developed, taxes were kept low, and administrative procedures were simplified. Minor tax evasion was tolerated, and the Qiaotou government exerted little energy collecting formal tax revenues.[13] Since 1994, however, the fiscal regime has tightened through a value added tax of 17 percent and a sales tax of 4 percent, spurring some firms to leave the industry.

Like other industries, the button industry in Qiaotou must confront structural change. Wages are rising, and many workers are looking beyond the factory jobs that pay them only about Y 1,540 ($250) a month. Several button entrepreneurs complain of the difficulties finding skilled labor. Insufficient cash flow and weak orders led to a decline in 2008, and a number of button firms went bankrupt. However, the industry has recovered somewhat in recent years.

## Summary

Qiaotou has become the button capital of the world through a combination of local entrepreneurship and local government support. It has developed a successful business model combining low wages and good machines.

## Weihai Zipper Company Ltd., Yiwu, Zhejiang Province

Asia has emerged as one of the world's largest zipper markets, and China has become the world's largest zipper manufacturer. The Chinese zipper industry sells to downstream manufacturers of clothing and apparel, sporting equipment, luggage, shoes, and bags. As these industries have evolved, zipper companies have adapted and kept pace, evidence of the supply chain's interconnectedness. Together with southern China's other dynamic specialty enterprises, the zipper clusters have become more well developed and specialized.

Weihai Zipper Company Ltd., in Yiwu, Zhejiang Province, exemplifies the success of the Chinese zipper industry. Founded in 1982 and formally launched in 1995, the company was one of the industry's

**Figure 5.4  Daily Production, Weihai Zipper Company Ltd., Yiwu, Zhejiang Province, China, 2010**

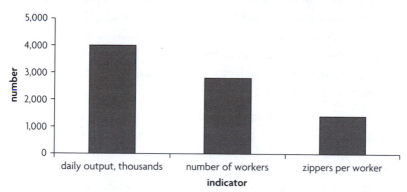

*Source:* Interviews with a zipper entrepreneur, Yiwu, 2010.

early movers and is now widely recognized as one of China's top zipper brands.

Weihai employs 3,000 workers and has an estimated daily output of 4 million zippers (figure 5.4). It is a key player in the Chinese zipper industry, which now consists of more than 2,000 manufacturing enterprises with sales of more than Y 20 billion ($3 billion). Weihai's zippers sell for one-third the price of zippers produced by international competitors. The plant covers 240,000 square meters and has more than 5,000 machines. Because of the growth of garment and sporting goods industries in China, the country's zipper production has increased enormously, accounting for more than half of global supply. The average annual growth in China's zipper output is expected to remain above 20 percent.

Weihai's success reflects a combination of domestic entrepreneurship, steady access to high-quality inputs and markets, and good-quality industrial land. Small-scale entrepreneurs have used government-subsidized land to upgrade, recruiting good workers and reinvesting profits into the industry. Over time, their mastery of the supply chain gave entrepreneurs the ability to beat out their international competitors and establish a strong global presence in the industry.

## Origin and Course of Development

Our discussions with the founding entrepreneurs illuminate the industry's early days.

In the 1980s, a vibrant trading network evolved into workshops run out of people's homes. Because neighbors traded multiple products, entrepreneurs could compare the profitability of each. They decided to focus on zippers, the most profitable product. Without access to formal finance, Weihai's founders used their own savings and the savings of friends to set up their initial factory. Wang Yue, one of the first movers, explained as follows:

> We were poor and we had to produce something. In those years in China, it was difficult to get two meals a day, and we were very happy when we got that. At the beginning there were no factories in this place and no money to start factories. We had to come up with some ideas for export…. [W]hat appealed to us about zippers was that the product was easy to transport and was giving lots of profit when we peddled it. A lot of industries were taking off in China in those days, especially shoes and clothing. So we figured out that there would always be a strong demand for zippers. It was new and the cost was low. We decided to trade zippers and see what happened. We tested it by trial and error and then decided that we could make a lot of profit with it. (September 2010 interview)

Rather than remain simple family businesses, the Weihai founders expanded dramatically by relying on their trading relationships and customer networks. In 1994, they moved to an industrial park to capitalize on government support for light industry. There, they benefited from access to industrial land and a steady and predictable supply of utilities, especially water and energy. Setting up the factory cost about Y 3 million ($350,000), which was paid out of personal savings and retained earnings. The factory had about 400 workers and close to 30 machines. Lack of collateral made it difficult to qualify for bank loans. By 1998, the enterprise directors had expanded the business, increased the size of the factory, and diversified zipper production (nylon, plastic, and metal). As the company grew, the directors decided to import machines from the Republic of Korea; from Taiwan, China; and from elsewhere. They focused on acquiring a level of technological sophistication that would allow them to meet the orders of trading companies.

A key to Weihai's success has been its connections with an entrepreneurial network in Taiwan, China, that provided invaluable technology and information. In the late 1970s, industrial zipper technology was brought from Taiwan, China, resulting in marked improvements in quality and technology. The Taiwanese also brought innovation, professional expertise, and efficient management, helping Weihai develop and scale up. Weihai has had an OEM contract with Taiwanese firms since the mid-1990s.[14] Although Weihai started as a domestic enterprise, foreign investment freed it from the constraints of long-standing deficiencies in education, technical knowledge, finance, managerial skill, and market information.

## Competitiveness and Binding Constraints

China's success in the world zipper industry grew out of the dynamism of local entrepreneurs. While some producers manufactured on a large scale from the start, Weihai is one of several large zipper manufacturers that began as family workshops and that used personal savings to acquire simple equipment and commence production on a small scale.

Weihai now exports $15 million in zippers to about 60 countries. In both scale and product specialization, the company is an important player, exporting more than 1,000 types of zippers. The firm benefits from a large clustering of the zipper industry; more than 500 local enterprises specialize in zipper production. Despite China's rising labor costs, the 2008 global recession, and the recent appreciation of the yuan, which forced Weihai to sell more product domestically, the company has remained vibrant and innovative.

Governments, particularly at the local level, provided access to land in a local industrial park. The land allowed Weihai to scale up and to house its workers. The company expanded from 400 workers to more than 2,000 within 10 years, and its production skyrocketed.

Without the Yiwu industrial park, the scale and degree of specialization achieved by Weihai and other companies would not have been possible. In addition to providing infrastructure and utilities, the park assists with employee training, logistics support, and financing, all important in an environment with pervasive distortions. The government made abundant industrial land available at preferential rates starting in the 1990s, offering Weihai an incentive for moving into the industrial zone.

Easy access to inputs allowed Weihai to grow and specialize. In the 1980s, when there were no major subsidies, the Chinese operated at the small end of the scale in a market with strong competition from Taiwan, China. As Weihai has improved its responsiveness to international orders, its products have diversified.

Weihai has traditionally done well in recruiting a good-quality workforce and upgrading worker skills. Workers in the Chinese zipper industry are typically migrants aged 18–25 from inland areas. Most are women who are hard working and disciplined. The firm recruits these workers through its networks. Manufacturing costs are low, and the workers were paid less than $0.50 an hour (as of mid-2010). The company makes several cents in profit on a set of 100 zippers. According to the managers, low-cost, productive labor has been one of the great assets in scaling up.

In recent years, however, manufacturing wages have been rising, and many workers are looking beyond factory work to jobs that earn more. Many entrepreneurs in the zipper industry complain about the difficulty of finding skilled workers. The flow of migrant workers has slowed since the onset of the global financial crisis, and the direction of the industry is uncertain. However, China's zipper industry continues to be robust. In 2010, it produced more than 30 billion zippers, more than 75 percent of the global production, and employed more than a million people. Despite international competition, wage differentials remain large, insulating China from competitors (figure 5.5).

**Figure 5.5  Hourly Wages in the Zipper Industry, by Country, 2009**

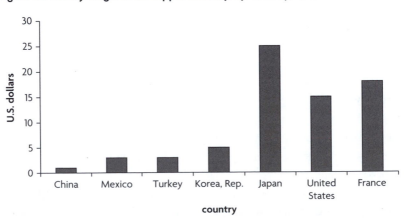

*Sources:* Chinese government statistics; industry estimates.

Weihai initially focused on the domestic market, especially nearby cities. Then, in 1998, it started exporting through trading companies. Foreign companies eventually requested that Weihai produce a certain kind of quality zipper. By the first decade of the 2000s, Weihai had 3,000 workers, more than 1,700 of whom were women. The rising cost of labor in China and the appreciation of the yuan have led the company to increase its focus again on domestic production. In 2010, Weihai exported only 30 percent of its zippers, selling the rest in the domestic market.

## The Role of Government

Weihai's success has derived from strong entrepreneurship, coupled with government help as the company scaled up. The government helped the industry reach global scale by maintaining a probusiness environment and building infrastructure. Weihai entrepreneurs affirmed the vital role of government. The success of Weihai parallels that of Zhejiang's economy, which can be characterized as small firms and big clusters (*xiaoqiye, da jiqun*), and reflects the importance of SMEs in catalyzing economic growth.

Several government policy decisions have had a strong impact on Weihai's development and helped lower the costs of logistics and inputs. First, in 1982, the local government created the four permissions policy (*sige xuke*), which allowed Yiwu residents, including Weihai's founders, to engage in local and long-distance commerce, to enter businesses formerly monopolized by state-owned enterprises, and to establish local commodity markets. This provided the first catalyst for the Weihai founders.

Second, in 1985, the local government helped build and develop the Yiwu commodity market.[15] It also took measures to manage transactions in the Yiwu market and establish a managing committee representing local government departments. In 1994, a market-management company, China Commodity City Group, helped develop the Yiwu market. The market is managed by a group of small producers, small buyers, and a public sector management committee.

The rise of this market was a major catalyst for Weihai and the zipper companies in adjoining areas. It reduced the cost of trade logistics and enabled Weihai and other companies to exchange information regularly.

China Commodity City is now considered Southeast Asia's largest zipper distribution market. Weihai and other companies have benefited from the network effects. While local governments in southern China have emphasized innovation and technology for the survival of the zipper industry in a highly competitive market, their greatest contribution has been to connect zipper companies, which allows the companies to cross-fertilize their experiences. As its international exposure deepened, Weihai expanded its product base to encompass a wider range of zippers and other products. Weihai has become known for its variety.

By 2005, close to 500 zipper companies had located in and around Yiwu, along with various subcontractors and suppliers. Because the value chain is important in zipper production, the creation of China Commodity City has promoted a natural clustering of similar companies, while easing transport costs. It also allowed Weihai to scale up to meet rising demand and a greater interest in quality in the late 1990s and the early part of the first decade of the 2000s. The company is now one of the biggest in China producing zippers used in the production of garments, suitcases, and tents and has developed a strong international brand.

The local government continues to assist with quality control and regulations to prevent substandard products from entering the market. The Yiwu government has worked to ensure that regulations on investment, product quality, and standards remain uniform and meaningful to the industry. It provided guidance when Weihai introduced world-class equipment and called in technical experts from Korea; Taiwan, China; and the United States. As a result and with the assistance of local government experts, Weihai passed the International Organization for Standardization quality system certification in 1999, one of the most important tests for any enterprise in the industry.

In 1994, the Weihai entrepreneurs decided that relocating to an industrial park would change the microeconomics of the business and allow them to scale up. In 2003, Weihai obtained additional land at a subsidized rate of one-third the official price, giving it space to expand. As the company broadened its range of activities to include molding, weaving, sewing, dyeing, casting, and painting, it benefited from the business environment in the industrial zone. Customs formalities have been streamlined in the industrial park, facilitating export shipments.

As elsewhere in southern China, the local government has implemented policies favorable to SMEs and made efforts to alleviate financing constraints. It provided fiscal incentives through tax holidays for companies in the zone. It cleared land for the development of the industrial zone and engaged private developers to provide the facilities and services. Local governments in places such as Yiwu generally refrain from interfering in the management and operations of private companies, but make money from land sales to developers and corporate income taxes. In recent years, rising costs, limited land availability, and increasing environmental requirements have made it more difficult for the local government to provide the same set of incentives to other businesses, but the government continues to create a foundation for industry expansion.

The Yiwu Zipper Association has been an important source of industry best practices and has linked zipper enterprises with local governments. The zipper association is financed through a combination of private sector subscriptions and budgetary subsidies from local authorities. Over the years, the association has helped companies such as Weihai expand. Recently, the association set up a zipper quality testing center. The website of a trade early warning demonstration system has helped zipper enterprises overcome technical problems, improve product quality, and cope with trade barriers. Weihai has benefited greatly from the association and, in turn, contributed to it.

In parallel, the government has helped the zipper industry develop through its trade policies. In the early reform years, high tariffs sheltered the zipper industry, as well as other light manufacturing sectors. Tariffs averaged 80 percent in the early 1980s, but fell dramatically in anticipation of China's 2001 accession to the WTO (WTO 2011). As with the button industry, 1993 was a turning point for the zipper industry because tariffs fell even further (figure 5.6).

## Summary

The Weihai Zipper Company exemplifies the triumph of creative entrepreneurship and the assistance of the local government in building on substantial market intelligence and networks to complete the value chain and expand to the global market.

**Figure 5.6  Tariffs on Zipper Imports, China, 1992–2009**

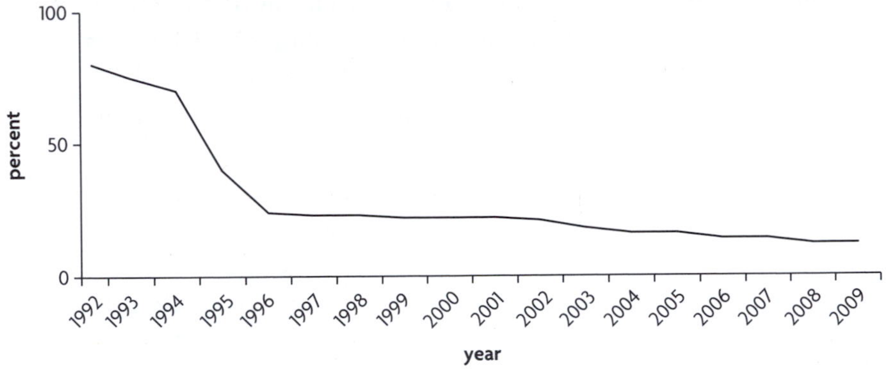

*Source:* WTO 2011.

## The Toothbrush Cluster, Yangzhou, Jiangsu Province

In Hangji, the air is saturated with the smell of toothbrushes.

*—Professor Wang Jici, Beijing University*

The supply, production, and sale of toothbrushes, from raw materials to packaging and transportation, have long been an integrated process within Hangji Township.

*—Secretary-General Kong Fanlin, Hangji Toothbrush Association*

Hangji has adopted a method that incorporated foreign capital, private capital, state capital, various inputs, and multilayered development. Opening up means sailing into unchartered waters for the people in Hangji, who in turn deepened their understanding of competition and cooperation.

*—Director Xie Kemin, Hanjiang Economic and Trade Bureau*

Hangji, a small town in the eastern suburb of Yangzhou, Jiangsu Province, has emerged as a world-class manufacturing center for toothbrushes, dental floss, and dentures. In a 36-square-kilometer area, with 10 administrative villages and about 36,000 residents, the township achieved industrial output of Y 10.2 billion ($1.5 billion) in 2009. With a per capita GDP of more than Y 66,640 ($9,755), Hangji ranked among the top towns in the province. The township now has more than 80 toothbrush manufacturing enterprises, which produce 6 billion toothbrushes a year. These enterprises supply 80 percent of the domestic market, more than 90 percent of China's toothbrush exports, and 35 percent of the global market. Hangji's toothbrush industry, which emerged spontaneously and developed into an industrial conglomerate with a huge share of the global market, has drawn the interest of policy makers and economists alike.

## Origin and Course of Development

In 1978, the Chinese government kicked off reform in rural areas, making it clear that private plots, side businesses, and trading were allowed as complements to the central planning mechanism. As the government continued to move away from its prereform hostility to private entrepreneurial activity, household and commercial manufacturing entities, as well as township and village enterprises (TVEs) owned by local governments in rural areas, sprang up across the coastal regions.

Toothbrush manufacturing in Hangji can be traced to the 19th century, when Liu Wanxing made the first ox bone toothbrush in Yangzhou. His apprentices carried on the technology, and many of them started businesses in large cities. In 1963, a toothbrush factory was set up in Hangji, making toothbrushes out of ox bone and pig bristles. Many people made a living by peddling the toothbrushes outside the area.

The industry took off in the 1980s when the government eased restrictions on private enterprise. Family workshops began to make toothbrushes manually and sell them in the local market. In the early 1990s, Hangji introduced a development strategy based on TVEs. Since 1997, more than 100 new household enterprises and 80 private firms have been set up each year. Registered capital has risen nearly twentyfold with the emergence of major enterprises such as Mingxin, Qionghua, Sanxiao, and Wu-ai.

Over 1987–2006, the value of Hangji's economy grew from Y 100 million ($27 million) to Y 6.8 billion ($995 million). Some Hangji enterprises expanded from toothbrushes to disposable personal care articles, household chemical products, hygiene articles, and new packaging materials. The township now has more than 1,100 enterprises manufacturing toothbrushes and personal care products, supplying more than 60 percent of the domestic market. TVEs sell more than Y 1 billion

($146 million) in items for the hotel industry alone. Hangji has created the country's largest industrial cluster specializing in the production, supply, and marketing of personal care products. In 2003 and 2008, Hangji Township was named China's Toothbrush Capital and China's Capital of Hotel Toiletries by the China Association of Light Industries.

## Competitiveness and Binding Constraints

Hangji is competitive thanks to economies of scale and agglomeration effects, which attract outside investment, cheap and readily available inputs, and a large pool of skilled and unskilled labor. More than 20,000 migrants work in Hangji, which has a resident population of only 36,000. These workers have made it possible for companies such as Sanxiao Group to expand rapidly because of a cost advantage. Over time, Hangji enterprises have increased the range of their oral hygiene products and broadened the scope of their businesses. In recent years, the local household chemical products industry has also grown rapidly.

The industrial park established in the eastern suburbs of Yangzhou in 2001 has facilitated enterprise expansion and conglomeration, which are vital for sustainable growth. The current stage of the construction of Hangji industrial park covers 8 square kilometers. Along with factory buildings, the park now includes facilities for marketing, distribution, exhibitions, packaging materials, quality control, and R&D. Sales from the park's 480 enterprises totaled Y 24.2 billion ($3.6 billion) in 2010.

**Supply chain.** Enterprise Road in Hangji is filled with shops and the offices of service providers, raw material suppliers, and equipment suppliers. Professional assistance is available at each link in the supply chain, from manufacturing to package printing and machinery maintenance. Many large buyers have established offices in Hangji. The entire production process, from the purchase of raw materials to the distribution of final products, can be completed in Hangji, and this has lowered the threshold for new firms to enter the industry. For example, in the past, companies had to go to Chongqing, 1,500 kilometers away, to source the titanium powder to dye toothbrushes. Then, with Y 300 ($44), a Hangji housewife opened a business producing powder for local toothbrush firms. The investment benefited both sides.

"The supply, production, and sale of toothbrushes, from raw materials to packaging and transportation, have long become an integrated process within Hangji," said the secretary-general of the Hangji Toothbrush Association to our interviewer. All along the production chain, the town attracts firms: packaging firms from Anhui, bag makers from Zhejiang, textile firms from Nantong, towel makers from Huai-an. It has also attracted prominent multinational investors, such as Johnson & Johnson and Procter & Gamble (P&G).

**Finance.** The Hangji toothbrush industry was launched based on personal investments, including family savings and money borrowed from friends and relatives. By the late 1990s, foreign investors had become interested in Hangji. The township government adopted preferential policies to encourage local enterprises to seek foreign investment and set up joint ventures. In 2000, Sanxiao Group, a company in Hangji that accounted for 70 percent of the country's toothbrush market, sold 75 percent of its equity to the U.S. Colgate Company for Y 120 million ($14 million). Colgate relocated its global toothbrush production base to Hangji, and Sanxiao received access to the high-end international market. With capital from Colgate, Sanxiao diversified its business and expanded into real estate, shoe polish, mosquito repellent incense, and women's hygiene products. Many enterprises, including Qionghua and Wu-ai, have set up joint ventures with companies from the European Union (EU), Korea, and the United States. Companies have also obtained capital for business upgrading and expansion through venture capitalists, mergers, acquisitions, and, in the case of the Qionghua Hi-Tech Company, from a 2004 initial public offering on the Shenzhen Stock Exchange.

**Trade logistics.** Hangji Township is at the intersection of the Yangzi River and the Grand Canal, next to Yangzhou's international port. It has water on three sides. Before the Nanjing-Nantong Highway was built in 1996, only a local road linked the town to the outside world. With the establishment of Hangji industrial park, logistics improved considerably. Cargo trucks travel around the clock to the nearby port, reducing transport costs. Many manufacturing firms have also extended their business activities upstream and downstream. Sanxiao Logistics, an affiliate of the toothbrush producer, has become one of China's largest logistics firms.

**Technology.** Over the last decade, the cluster has benefited from industrial upgrading. Under pressure from mounting competition and changing market trends, firms have been forced to shift to products with more high-technology content and value added to boost productivity. Several R&D centers have emerged in Hangji as a result, and collaboration between enterprises and research institutes has intensified.

**The brand-name effect.** Sanxiao Group, established in 1992, was the first firm to introduce its own brand. Within a few years, Sanxiao brand toothbrushes had captured half the domestic market. After Colgate bought the Sanxiao brand in 1999, the joint venture, Colgate-Sanxiao, reaped much higher profits relative to the old firm, though the techniques, equipment, materials, and workers were the same. Other firms have since registered their own brands and patents. By 2011, there were more than 420 registered toothbrush brands and 350 patents. Meanwhile, the regional brand, the Capital of Toothbrushes, brought great value to the toothbrush industry in Hangji, attracting more up- and downstream enterprises.

**Sanxiao Group: The epitome of the Hangji model.** The tale of Han Guoping, the founder of Sanxiao Group, and of the development of his company is a microcosm of Hangji's experience. Starting as a family workshop, Sanxiao grew into the country's largest toothbrush producer. By the end of 2011, the company had total assets of Y 1.6 billion ($248 million), more than a million square meters of space, and 7,000 employees producing more than 100 varieties of oral care, household chemical, and personal care products.

Han was born into a family of six children. His childhood was one of hunger and poverty. Like many other villagers in and around Hangji, he learned to make toothbrushes when he was young. In 1974, the 20-year-old went to work in Lankao County, in Henan Province, to support his family. He set up a small toothbrush factory, where he managed production, supply, marketing, and machinery maintenance. He also had a family workshop in Hangji, traveling back and forth to keep both going. These ventures brought him good returns.

In 1988, when private businesses started to grow in his hometown, Han returned with more than Y 800,000 ($214,932) saved from his business in Henan. He acquired a small factory that had gone out of business and established Yangzhou-Bridge Toothbrush Factory, recruiting dozens of villagers to work for him. Only two of the employees had a high school education. Over the next three years, he labored alongside his employees, eating the same food and living under the same roof, though his house was only a few hundred meters from the factory. The company focused on oral care products, including toothbrushes. By 1995, sales exceeded Y 100 million ($12 million), a more than tenfold increase.

In 1995, the company went on the fast track. To meet strong demand, Han upgraded production capacity by introducing more advanced equipment. When Han attended a household chemical products exhibition in Beijing, he saw German toothbrush-making equipment priced at Y 3.6 million ($431,085). Impressed, he decided to buy it. Despite some opposition within his company, Han was convinced that the investment would pay off. He was right. Within a few years, the company became China's largest toothbrush producer, occupying more than two-thirds of the domestic market and one-third of the global market. The company subsequently diversified into shoe polish, air freshener, insecticides, and more. In 1999, Sanxiao's sales exceeded Y 1.4 billion ($169 million).

This stunning growth put Sanxiao's multinational competitors on notice, particularly Colgate in the United States. Han welcomed Colgate's proposal of a merger. In 1999, the two companies established a joint venture, Colgate-Sanxiao Company Ltd., with the foreign investor holding 70 percent of the shares. Han sold his shares to Colgate for $14 million; Colgate obtained the right to use the Sanxiao brand for 50 years. The deal aroused considerable controversy. Han was roundly criticized for selling a successful brand to a foreign investor, but he had good reasons. As Sanxiao expanded, it ran into serious bottlenecks because of low technical capacity and poor labor quality. Han realized that the company was at a critical juncture. Unless the company's management and production were upgraded to prepare it for the emerging market risks, its long-term development could be jeopardized. Han's decision benefited the market's long-term development, however, because Sanxiao's retreat left more space for small firms to grow.

Using the capital from the merger, Han established a new Sanxiao Group. After careful market analysis, he decided to produce mosquito repellent incense. He imported automatic drug injection and packaging lines to produce the Good Sleep brand. In 2001, he purchased three additional factories to create a complete production line. This project cost more than Y 100 million ($12.1 million), included 80,000 square meters of modern factory buildings, and created more than 2,000 jobs. The mosquito repellent incense had sales of Y 200 million ($24.2 million) in 2001. In 2005, Han's firm invested Y 250 million ($30.5 million) to establish a factory to produce women's sanitary napkins, achieving total sales of Y 250 million ($30.5 million) in the same year. The company established manufacturing bases in several other cities by acquiring and collaborating with local firms. In 2010, the company returned to the oral care market.

## The Role of Government

The industrial cluster in Hangji was formed through the spontaneous emergence of thousands of private businesses, which grew without much government support. The local government's hands-off policy and the availability of basic public facilities and services were essential for the toothbrush industry to take off in Hangji.

**Hands-off policy.** In the early 1980s, the central government relaxed its restrictions on private enterprise. Nonetheless, the environment was still somewhat hostile, and many people continued to consider private ownership to be contrary to the country's socialist framework. The local government in Hangji pragmatically proposed a dual-track system of collective and individual enterprises. It improved industrial supply and marketing facilities and provided services for private enterprises, including issuing referral letters, providing receipts, accepting entrusted funds, and purchasing raw materials. It also helped private firms settle contract disputes and offered loan guarantees.

These measures boosted the local private economy. By the end of the 1980s, there were more than 2,000 household enterprises and 3,000 sales workers in the township. Competition intensified along with development, as companies sought lower-cost suppliers. The local authorities joined with private companies in establishing the Toothbrush Industry Association to formulate rules and norms and ensure order in the industry.

**Privatization.** After rapid growth in the 1980s, many TVEs became mired in difficulties in the 1990s because of the ambiguous ownership structure and inadequate management. To help local firms ease bottlenecks, Hangji decided, in 1992, to reform the enterprise system. Collectively operated TVEs were gradually privatized, and their workshops and equipment were sold or leased to private individuals. In May 1997, the township ceased regulatory control of TVEs.

**Industrial park.** In 2001, with the aim of building the township into a global toothbrush production base, the government established Hangji industrial park. Inside the park, preferential policies on land acquisition and taxation prevail. Investors are exempt from or pay reduced district and township tariffs and are eligible for financial subsidies; the preferential policies have encouraged foreign investment.

**Support for business upgrading.** The Hangji and Yangzhou governments have implemented several innovation and development projects since 2004. To speed decisions, a special coordination agency convenes regular meetings involving multiple government departments. By 2006, the local government had authorized 331 projects and issued Y 52 million ($6.5 million) in loans. The local government also rewards enterprises for establishing their own brands and gives priority in setting up technical research centers to enterprises with provincially and nationally recognized brands. It directs resources to leading enterprises and helps them set up product standards and quality tests. It encourages leading enterprises to restructure and reorganize their up- and downstream affiliates to optimize returns. It supports the establishment of enterprise associations and promotes the dissemination of information and network marketing. It encourages toothbrush firms to upgrade their technology and provides information on industrial development to strengthen the global competitiveness of these enterprises.

## Summary

In a tale repeated among light industries throughout coastal China, the toothbrush industrial cluster sprang up spontaneously and flourished after reforms unleashed market forces and the entrepreneurial spirit of private investors. The local government generally gave a free hand to local businesses and encouraged innovation and brand naming among larger companies. As the sector expanded, the government provided an enabling environment for private businesses by improving infrastructure and services. Hangji shows that, by facilitating entrepreneurship and creativity, a city can develop rapidly, even as the wider investment climate remains deficient.

## The Metalware Industrial Cluster, Yongkang, Zhejiang Province

As China became a global manufacturing powerhouse, the metals industry grew considerably. Already the world's largest steel producer, with close to 45 percent of world output, China has increased its production capacity in aluminum, iron, copper, and other metals. Demand for metal inputs has been increasing not only from heavy manufacturing industries, such as automobiles and shipbuilding, but also from light industries that produce consumer metalwares, such as tools, locks, hinges, security doors, thermal cups, and cutlery. Several hardware clusters have emerged in the coastal regions. In central Zhejiang Province, Yongkang, which enjoys a prime location and good logistics, has developed thanks to strong entrepreneurship and preferential government policies.

Since the onset of reform, Yongkang's economy has developed rapidly on the strength of the traditional hardware industry and the advantages of a flexible private ownership system. The numbers point to a dynamic and thriving industry. By 2011, Yongkang had nearly 10,000 hardware enterprises, 95 percent of which were SMEs. More than 300,000 people work in the sector.[16] The hardware industry has become a force in the local economy, accounting for more than 90 percent of industrial output, 60 percent of GDP, about 80 percent of tax revenues, and close to 50 percent of employment in the city.

The sector produces more than 10,000 metal product lines in eight major categories: electric tools, measuring apparatus, nonferrous metals, household appliances and kitchen utensils, stainless steel products, security doors, electric automobiles, and motorized scooters. Each year, Yongkang firms produce 200 million cups (80 percent of the country's total), 4.5 million recreational vehicles (electric scooters and bicycles, accounting for 70 percent of the country's total), and 9 million security doors (70 percent of the country's total). Yongkang firms also produce more than half the country's stainless steel utensils, nearly half its measuring tools, and a third of its electric tools. Much of the output is exported to more than 130 countries, including Australia, Brazil, Japan, Russia, and the United States. The city is China's largest exporter of electric razors and a major exporter of electric scooters.

## Origin and Course of Development

Yongkang has a tradition of metalworking and hardware manufacturing. The region has more people than the land can support; so, there has also been a long history of relying on itinerant craft labor. The modern hardware industry was started by a group of blacksmiths and coppersmiths who made a living from their handcraft skills.

Before 1978, industrial development in Yongkang was slow, but nonetheless sufficient to lay a foundation for future progress. In the early 1970s, a local Yongkang official conducted field investigations that convinced him of the need to develop industry, in addition to agriculture, because arable land was scarce. He boldly wrote to Mao Zedong suggesting that the central government should support the development of TVEs in the area. Unexpectedly, the letter was well received and was publicized at a national conference, greatly encouraging local support for TVE expansion. The Yongkang metalware industry subsequently boomed after China initiated economic reforms in the late 1970s.

Since China's reforms, Yongkang's hardware industry has undergone four stages of growth.

**The start-up stage, 1979–84.** Family businesses began to grow in Yongkang in response to rising demand for kitchen knives, keys, thimbles, and tools. Many craftspeople became enterprise directors or managers. Yongkang's GDP grew rapidly, and the number of manufacturing enterprises rose from 240 to more than 1,400.

**The growth stage, 1985–91.** Private companies grew rapidly and started to produce more sophisticated products, such as tractors, electric tools, valves, aluminum pistons, and steel barrels. Many companies bought used equipment from state-owned enterprises and hired retired technicians from large enterprises to acquire the needed technologies. They leased houses to build factory workshops and relied on networks of friends and relatives to identify potential markets. Development was market-led, primitive, and spontaneous. An industrial agglomeration took shape, comprising tens of thousands of small private firms scattered across the region. Many towns and villages built industrial zones. Local GDP expanded fourfold between 1985 and 1991.

**The development stage, 1992–96.** During this period, the most dynamic for the growth of the metalware industry, Yongkang enterprises became more specialized. They upgraded production processes, built new plants, acquired new equipment, and recruited and trained technical staff. Profits came mainly from domestic sales of thermal cups, electric tools, scooters, security doors, motorcycles and accessories, farm vehicles, solar water heaters, and other, similar products. In 1992, the local government built China's Hardware City, the country's largest trading market for hardware products and metal materials. Four years later, the city government joined with the National Hardware Products Association of China to host the annual China Hardware Fair. Within a few more years, the city had become the country's largest trading center for metalware products.

However, the metalware workshops scattered across the region created serious pollution and environmental damage. Also worrisome, many of the products had low value added and a short life span. For example, a thermal cup enterprise entered the market in 1995, and, within only two years, its output in Yongkang dropped to one-eighth the peak, as competitors rushed into the market. The process became a vicious circle: a new product was introduced; thousands of imitators followed; and the market withered.

**The second start-up stage, 1997–present.** In 1999, the local government established the Yongkang Science and Technology Industrial Park, consolidating more than 100 scattered industrial zones across the city. In 2002, the industrial park was expanded and upgraded to the Yongkang economic development zone. During several years of expansion, the zone has grown from 8.6 square kilometers to 46.6 square kilometers. Now, the largest of the 20 industrial parks in Zhejiang, it provides a platform for the development of Yongkang's metalware industry and serves as a center of technical innovation. Bolstered by good infrastructure and multifaceted support from the local government, the industry has achieved stunning scale and sophistication over the last decade. Since the park's launch, the value of industrial output has grown 35 percent annually; export delivery has grown 36 percent; and tax revenues have jumped 32 percent. In 2011, the value of the industrial output of the Yongkang economic development zone reached Y 69.6 billion ($10.8 billion). The zone has attracted more than 500 enterprises with annual sales above Y 5 million each, 90 percent of which are metalware producers. Enterprises based in the Yongkang zone own 2 prominent Chinese brands, 12 well-known trademarks, and more than 4,800 patents.

In recent years, Yongkang's metalware industry has undergone a critical transformation, shifting from the production of conventional, low–value added hardware products (small hardware) to the production of modern high–value added hardware products (big hardware) by boosting quality and expanding the product range. By encouraging high–value added sectors, the park has achieved output of Y 7.4 billion ($1.1 billion) per square kilometer, ranking among the most productive industrial parks in Zhejiang Province. Among firms with an annual output of Y 500 million ($77 million) each, the share of enterprises producing traditional small hardware products has dropped to around 22 percent. The park hosts more than 100 enterprises engaged in automobile assembly and the manufacture of key components and parts, with a total output of Y 21.5 billion ($3.3 billion) in 2011.

## Competitiveness and Binding Constraints

One of the world's largest hardware manufacturing clusters has emerged in a small Zhejiang city with virtually no metal resources. Success has been possible because of hardworking craftspeople, entrepreneurs, and workers.

**Entrepreneurship.** For generations, Yongkang's youth learned metalworking skills and traveled outside the area to practice their trade during the slow farming seasons. People in Yongkang are known for their hard work, resilience, and entrepreneurial spirit. Almost all firms in Yongkang started out small and tried out may different products, acting swiftly to meet changes in market demand.

The Superman Group is one of China's largest producers and exporters of electronic health and beauty products, such as electric razors and hairdryers. When the company started producing electric razors, the general manager led a team to observe customers at urban department stores. Based on the information they collected, the general manager identified the varieties of razors to produce and drew up plans to improve quality.

Scooters represent another example of the determination and creativity of people in Yongkang. Kick scooters became popular in the United States in the late 1990s. Initially, producers in Guangdong Province in the Pearl River Delta manufactured most of the scooters. Once Yongkang entrepreneurs discovered this market through their extensive networks of clients and friends, local firms quickly began to produce copycat versions. The cost was much lower than that of the competitors in Guangdong; so, many overseas clients turned to Yongkang.

One of these Yongkang companies was Buyang Group, established in 1992 and now one of China's largest producers of security doors. The firm started by supplying cast components such as oven burners for cookware firms in Guangdong and then expanded into binoculars, security doors, and auto parts. In 2000, observing the surging overseas demand for scooters, the company's owner made a quick decision to manufacture scooters. Demand was so great that the company had to build a new warehouse every two months. By 2003, the company had built 20 assembly lines for the manufacture of scooters, all for export (Buyang Group 2012). To fill overseas orders on time, Buyang started outsourcing part of its production. This approach not only reduced company costs and inventory, but also enabled the company to concentrate on filling orders for large retailers such as Walmart, which has high quality requirements.

**Trade logistics.** Yongkang is 350 kilometers from Shanghai and 200 kilometers from Hangzhou, Ningbo, and Wenzhou, putting it within reach of important domestic and foreign markets. In 1992, Yongkang established China's Hardware City. The market, covering 670,000 square meters and containing more than 4,600 shops, attracts some 10,000 visitors and trades more than 1,000 tons of commodities daily. It is a regional marketing and demonstration platform and an important information exchange; it has played a key role in the upgrading and specialization of hardware enterprises and has become the main force in industrial conglomeration in the area.

Since the late 1990s, the share of exports in total production has gradually picked up. In 2009, exports accounted for 22 percent of industrial output in the Yongkang economic development zone. Most metalware producers in Yongkang are small and have little bargaining power with large overseas clients. Instead, the firms take orders from large international trading firms, becoming OEMs for overseas companies. Only a handful of the large enterprises have registered brand names with overseas marketing branches. Many companies take the first step toward international sales by attending trade fairs in Guangdong Province and in Hong Kong SAR, China, and export to the international market through the latter, thereby attracting trading companies from around the world. Some companies have also set up sales branches in Hong Kong SAR, China.[17] Trading companies serve as intermediaries between small producers and large buyers. In recent years, however, as production costs have risen and profits have shrunk, more producers are seeking to circumvent trading companies and reach final buyers directly.[18]

Buyang Group, for example, sells through two main channels. Direct orders come from large clients such as Walmart, which identified Buyang as a candidate supplier in 2002 and increased its orders in the following years. Along with other local companies, Buyang also pursues clients through e-commerce because of the convenience, speed, and low cost.

The European Union and the United States were the main initial export markets. When demand fell after the 2008 global financial crisis, Buyang and other local companies looked to new markets in emerging economies in Eastern Europe, the Middle East, and South America. Russia and Ukraine have supplanted Germany and Italy as the two largest European importers.

**Supply chain.** Yongkang's hardware cluster benefits from a well-developed local supply chain. Supplies of needed materials and components can be delivered within two hours. Most equipment can also be procured locally. Enterprises in the zone tend to have fixed suppliers. The high demand among local hardware producers has led many nonlocal suppliers to set up offices and warehouses near their clients in Yongkang to be able to ensure timely deliveries.

"Links between firms along ... the value chain are close and flexible," said a manager of Buyang Group during our interview in 2012. "When there is a problem, we only need to call the supplier and help will arrive within one hour." The company once found a problem with a plastic part for its scooters. A call brought the supplier to the site immediately, and the technicians found a solution in only a few hours. The supplier firm was soon producing the improved part.

Whenever Yongkang firms start to produce something, a complete supporting supply network will emerge, the manager explained. As a result, the firms enjoy a cost advantage that can hardly be beaten by competitors in other areas.

**Raw materials.** The availability of low-cost metal materials is another advantage of metalware firms in Yongkang. While there are no metal mines in the region, Yongkang has developed the country's largest recycling center for metal waste. Almost all the raw materials for producing metalware products in Yongkang are derived from recycled metal. Some 10,000 people are involved in acquiring used metal and shipping it to Yongkang for smelting. In 2006, between Y 6 billion and Y 7 billion ($753 million–$878 million) in metal waste was traded in Yongkang. Taizhou, about 160 kilometers away, is the country's largest center for the disassembly of used electrical engines; each year, it produces 160,000–200,000 tons of used copper, 120,000 tons of used aluminum, and 1.4 million tons of used steel. Much of the recovered metal is shipped to Yongkang.

More than 200 smelters produce 250,000 tons of aluminum alloy and 200,000 tons of copper each year.

**Labor.** Metalware manufacturing is labor intensive. The sector employs about 300,000 workers in Yongkang, most of them rural migrants from other provinces. In addition, Yongkang firms hire an estimated 10,000 skilled workers each year. Turnover varies, running 8–30 percent, according to a 2010 survey of two private firms.[19]

Demographic change and rapid economic growth in the inland provinces have intensified the competition for labor. To attract workers, many firms have had to raise wages. In early 2012, the average monthly wage was Y 4,000 ($634), compared with less than Y 2,000 ($295) in early 2010. The city has set up 36 recruitment centers in 10 cities and provinces to reach migrant workers in other regions. To meet the need for skilled workers, the municipal government has built 28 training centers for local villagers. In cooperation with local vocational schools, these centers processed nearly 90,000 trainees, of whom 36,000 passed the training exams and obtained employment in local hardware firms.[20]

**Technology and R&D.** In Yongkang's hardware industry, a critical problem is the low technological content and value added. Local firms produce few original products; most products are copies. When a popular product emerges, firms rush to grab a share of the profits by cutting prices and lowering quality. As a result, the market saturates quickly, and consumers lose confidence in the product. In global markets, metalware products from Yongkang are supplied mostly as OEM orders; so, the profit margins are thin. Because of the rising cost of labor and raw materials, many Yongkang companies are struggling.

Some firms are working to reverse the situation. One solution is to extend operations up- and downstream. Buyang Group, for example, has increased R&D investments, while building its brand name through commercials on China Central Television.

By 2008, there were 34 technology renovation projects in the industrial park. Of these, 7 represented investments of more than Y 100 million ($14.4 million), while 22 represented investments of more than Y 10 million ($1.4 million).

## The Role of Government

From the beginning, Yongkang's hardware industry has received the full support of the local government. Even in the early 1970s, local officials allowed family-based metalware workshops in the villages. These workshops formed the foundation of the industrial cluster that emerged in the 1980s and 1990s. As the sector expanded, the local government provided support and guidance to help the enterprises grow.

**Building industrial parks to upgrade the metalware cluster.** The emergence of the metalware cluster in Yongkang was unplanned. The industry brought wealth to local people, but it also generated problems, such as inefficient competition, wasteful consumption, and ecological damage, which began threatening the sustainability of the industry as the years went by.

In 1999, the local government established the Yongkang Science and Technology Industrial Park, consolidating more than 100 industrial zones across the city. In 2002, the industrial park was expanded and upgraded to form the Yongkang economic development zone. To meet the needs of enterprises in the zone more effectively, the administration invested over Y 6 billion ($725 million) to build 10 platforms: corporate headquarters, exhibitions, logistics, science and technology innovations, customs clearances, inspections, concepts and design, human resources, international trade, and molds. The platforms are designed to direct the growth of the Yongkang hardware industry in strategic rather than reactive directions. The factory buildings now have a uniform light steel structure that looks tidy and attractive.

The park administration conducted a feasibility study of Yongkang's medium-term economic development and worked out a zoning plan that established specific areas for industry, R&D, and housing. Enterprises were relocated to designated areas according to their products. This reorganization improved the zone's layout, environment, and infrastructure.

The industrial park has a well-developed logistics network, extending to medium and large cities in China and surrounding areas.

**Strengthening the capacity for technical innovation.** Yongkang is considered a model cluster for industrial upgrading. To sustain the market competitiveness of Yongkang's hardware industry, the local government has strengthened quality and environmental standards. To foster their growth, it also provides financial incentives for large tax contributors, producers of brand-name products, high–value added industries, and big exporters. Large firms are urged to help design national and international trade standards and products. The development zone has a reward system to encourage enterprises to increase R&D investments, strengthen technological innovation, and raise the technological content of products.

**Gaining access to finance.** Most metalware firms in Yongkang are small or medium. They often face financing difficulties that can slow technological innovation and expansion. In 2008, the Yongkang government launched a program to promote collaboration among the government, banks, and enterprises. Under the program, the local government recommends promising projects and firms to financial institutions for loans.

In 2009, the local tax authority joined with local bank branches to create a platform for information exchange and resource sharing. For loans at local banks, the city recommended SMEs with good credit histories, annual tax payments of more than Y 200,000 ($29,277), and growth rates in tax revenue of more than 10 percent. In the first half of 2010, 921 SMEs were on the list, and 735 of them obtained loans totaling Y 1.59 billion ($235 million) (China E-Commerce Research Center 2010). This contrasts with the general pattern in China whereby banks hesitate to make loans to small private firms.

**Simplifying administrative procedures and improving services.** The local government has opened a one-stop service window at the industrial park to assist firms in navigating official administrative procedures. A green channel provides expedited services for priority projects, such as the investment projects of multinational companies and enterprises with famous brands, as well as high-technology projects.

**Promoting a regional brand.** The Yongkang economic development park has promoted the brand name Yongkang Hardware City. The Yongkang economic development zone sponsored a commercial, "China Hardware City in Yongkang, Home to Hardware," on major television channels.

**Fostering trade associations and professional agencies.** The growth of Yongkang's metalware industry is linked closely with the support of the Yongkang Hardware Industry Association, which has helped crack down on counterfeit and shoddy products, formulate industrial standards, and impose discipline to curb unfair competition. To assist local firms in improving competitiveness, the association sponsors the annual China Hardware Fair, introduced the Top Ten Credit Project, formulated five-year plans for the hardware industry, promoted exchanges among enterprises, and sought to reduce administrative burdens on enterprises. During the recent global financial crisis, the association helped SMEs meet challenges such as antidumping filings and technical barriers.

The Yongkang Hardware Productivity Promotion Center Company Ltd. provides for-profit and not-for-profit technical intermediary services. It was established in September 1999 through the merger of two institutions affiliated with the Science and Technology Commission. In May 2001, the new center became an independent private enterprise. In July 2002, it received International Organization for Standardization 9001:2000 quality management system certification, the first in Zhejiang.

## Summary

Yongkang's hardware industry cluster is one of a multitude of indigenous industrial clusters that sprang up spontaneously across China after the launch of the economic reforms. The cluster is a product of the region's social, economic, and cultural endowments and received little government support in the beginning. As the sector grew, the government played a facilitating role through the creation of an enabling environment for private businesses by improving infrastructure and services and by instituting sound urban planning. Yongkang demonstrates that giving full play to local entrepreneurship and creativity can help a city achieve industrial development even if the investment conditions are less than optimal.

## Qinye Industrial Company Ltd., Ganzhou, Jiangxi Province

A key driver of China's stunning economic growth over the past three decades has been the country's strong export performance. As part of the economic reforms that were undertaken in the late 1970s, a number of special economic zones and open cities were set up in Fujian, Guangdong, and other coastal provinces, thereby offering a favorable environment for foreign investors engaged in export-oriented manufacturing (chapter 3).

In the mid-1980s, entrepreneurs in Hong Kong SAR, China, who were attracted by the lower factor costs began shifting manufacturing facilities to these areas, where they produced mostly labor-intensive products such as garments, shoes, toys, and electronics. The connection to Hong Kong SAR, China, brought new technology, modern management practices, and critical links to global markets, in addition to needed capital (Panagariya 1995). Thus, for example, China now exports about $10 billion in toys each year, a large share of which are shipped through Hong Kong SAR, China.

As rising wages in the coastal areas led to escalating production costs in the early years of the first decade of the 2000s, many firms established manufacturing operations in inland locations, despite the less attractive trade logistics conditions, to take advantage of cheaper land and labor.

Qinye Industrial Company Ltd. is one such firm.

## Origin and Course of Development

Toy manufacturing is a new sector in Jiangxi Province, where metallurgy, food, textiles, and construction materials are the major industries. Ganzhou, the province's second-largest city, has the biggest toy manufacturing cluster in Jiangxi. Over the past decade, several toy companies from nearby Fujian and Guangdong provinces have relocated to Jiangxi, concentrating mainly in Ganzhou, home to one of the largest Hakka communities in China. The Hakka, Han Chinese from northern China, are renowned for their entrepreneurial spirit. Since 2003, when the first toy company was established in the city, more than 20 toy producers have located in the vicinity; most are transplants from coastal regions. These firms produce a total annual output of Y 800 million ($118 million) and account for 80 percent of the province's toy exports. Most of the toy firms are OEMs for foreign-invested export companies along the coast.

Qinye Industrial Company Ltd. is Jiangxi's largest toy producer. A wholly owned subsidiary of the Tsuen Lee Group (Holdings) Ltd., an OEM based in Hong Kong SAR, China, Qinye was established in 2005 in Ganzhou's industrial park with an initial investment of $15 million. Major products include plastic, plush, and electronic toys, gifts, consumer goods, and household items. The company has 6,000 employees and an annual output of Y 250 million ($37 million). Like other toy producers in the region, the company exports all its products to overseas clients such as Fisher-Price and McDonald's. In 2010, it paid Y 20 million ($3 million) in taxes.[21]

## Competitiveness and Binding Constraints

Qinye's decision to relocate to Ganzhou proved prescient when economic problems subsequently led to the bankruptcy of several major Guangdong toy producers—for example, Smart Union, which folded in 2008—and forced others to relocate to interior areas because of rising wages and land costs, the gradual appreciation of the yuan, and a slump in global demand following the 2008 global economic crisis.

**Input markets and location.** Toy companies planning to move inland face obstacles such as the lack of an integrated supply chain, the scarcity of skilled workers, higher logistics costs, and complex customs clearance procedures. Jiangxi is still far behind the coastal regions in the availability of a complete value chain, including equipment for toy manufacturing, cloth and plastic components and molds, and packing and transport facilities. Many inputs must be shipped from Guangdong. To export toys, companies first need to transport empty containers from neighboring Guangdong, fill the containers in Ganzhou, and then transport them back for shipment overseas. Transport costs are estimated at 20 percent higher relative to the coastal regions.

Nonetheless, manufacturing in Ganzhou offers benefits that frequently outweigh the costs. Cheaper labor and land represent the main attractions.

"The availability of trade services such as customs and convenient transportation [compared with other inland cities] is the key reason for us to locate in Ganzhou area," said Zhang Guangming, chief executive officer of the Tsuen Lee Group (Holdings) Ltd. "The city has a conspicuous advantage in the investment climate compared with other inland cities."[22]

In comparison with other inland locations, Ganzhou benefits from a central geographical position. It borders Hunan Province to the west, Guangdong Province to the south, and Fujian Province to the east. It is adjacent to the Pearl River Delta region, China's largest manufacturing and export base, and is within a few hours of major seaports, as well as Hong Kong SAR, China, and Macao SAR, China. It is connected to a vast network of highways, railways, river shipping lines, and airways. The region has drawn the interest of coastal investors, and manufacturing has grown rapidly since the Beijing-Kowloon Railway opened in 1996.

**Labor.** Abundant labor was another reason Tsuen Lee Group decided to set up the Qinye manufacturing base in Ganzhou. Toy production is labor intensive. With 8.5 million people, Ganzhou offers abundant labor at lower cost than in the coastal areas. In 2008, the average wage of an unskilled worker in Ganzhou was around Y 1,000 ($144) a month, about half that in Shenzhen.[23] The difference is narrowing, but Ganzhou wages are still lower. In 2009, the high transport costs—shipments to Guangzhou or Shenzhen cost about Y 3,600–Y 4,000 ($527–$586) per container—were offset by the lower wages, preserving the competitive advantage of the Ganzhou industry.

In recent years, the rapid development inland has created a labor squeeze, particularly among skilled workers. Most mid-level and senior management staff and research staff in Ganzhou toy firms are hired from outside the city. To attract workers, Qinye sent a performance team to visit local villages and perform Hakka-style shows. Many people have learned of the company in this way.

Early in 2009, shortly after the financial crisis began depressing global demand, Qinye surprised many people by expanding employment. The company was diversifying its international market by shifting from Europe and the United States to new markets such as Australia, Canada, and the Middle East. The company was also expanding its product varieties to appeal to domestic consumers. In addition to toys, the company produces plastics, electronics, and housewares. Because of its strong quality control and competitive production costs, the company was able to wrest customers from firms along the coast, many of which went bankrupt. These steps enabled Qinye's business to grow during the financial crisis.

**Logistics and customs.** Reliable transport services and streamlined customs clearance are critical for Qinye. Although located in a landlocked area, Ganzhou has developed an administrative system for dealing with overseas trade, including customs and inspection, foreign exchange, trade facilitation, and port clearance. Goods can be exported directly to foreign markets through integrated railway, truck, and sea transport services.

"For export enterprises, timely fulfillment of orders is critical," said Wu Yukun, chief of the Longnan customs office, in our interview (September 2010). "What we can do is improve efficiency and speed the customs clearance process. By doing so, we can also attract more business volume."

The Longnan customs office collaborates with peers in Guangdong to expedite the commodity transfer and customs clearance service between Guangdong; Jiangxi; Hong Kong SAR, China; and Macao SAR, China. An agreement reached with customs offices in Guangdong allowed Ganzhou enterprises to submit customs declarations at the local office, even though the containers were inspected at the coastal customs stations. This means export shipments undergo only one declaration and one inspection instead of two (at the place of origin and at the departure port), reducing customs clearance for a cargo vehicle originating in Ganzhou from 10 to 4 hours. Customs clearance costs also plunged from Y 300 ($44) per vehicle to about Y 2 ($0.30). Qinye management estimates that the expedited customs clearance system is saving the firm Y 200,000 ($29,544) each year.

The cost of utilities is also low in Ganzhou. Electricity costs Y 0.55–Y 0.76 ($0.08–$0.11) per kilowatt hour, compared with Y 1.2 ($0.30) in Guangzhou. Water costs Y 1.2 ($0.17) per ton, compared with about Y 3 ($0.44).[24] Thus, low factor costs offset increased transport costs, making industries in the landlocked areas more viable.

## The Role of Government

Qinye benefits from good infrastructure and a favorable policy regime in the Ganzhou economic development zone. To attract investors from the coastal regions, Ganzhou has implemented policies to improve the business environment that cover the supply of land, infrastructure, utilities, and financing and include tax breaks and low administrative surcharges.

"The preferential policies offered by the local government are unbeatable," said Lai Zengnong, vice-president of Qinye, in our interviews (September 2010).

**National policy.** Jiangxi Province benefits from the central government's favorable policies under China's Great Western Development Strategy, including lower corporate income tax rates, customs exemptions on imported equipment, and preferential terms on land use, mining ventures, and foreign investment.

The Ministry of Commerce has designated Ganzhou as a beneficiary of policy and grant support for the relocation of processing firms. This allows preferential treatment for processing companies that relocate from the coast.

In May 2009, Ganzhou was included in the Taiwan Strait region economic zone, which covers 9 cities in southeastern Fujian Province and 11 in three neighboring provinces, including Jiangxi. The intent is to provide central government support to promote economic and social development in the region and expand cross-strait economic cooperation.

**Provincial policy.** Under provincial policies, key export and high-technology firms enjoy preferential tax treatment, and firms that engage in qualified technological upgrading projects are exempt from tariffs on imported equipment.

**Municipal policy.** City and county governments are required to provide subsidies for the acquisition of land by companies moving into Ganzhou's industrial park.[25] They are also required to invest at least 20 percent of their land revenues into improvements in park infrastructure. Relocated enterprises enjoy priority consideration in the supply of land. The government offers land discounts, exemptions from administrative fees, and tax refunds to encourage private investors to construct warehouses in the park.

To subsidize their logistics expenditures, the government provides refunds to firms new to the parks for 60 percent of the value added taxes and corporate taxes they pay to the local tax authority. Firms located in the park receive discounts of about 10 percent on social security contributions.

Firms in the parks are exempt from surcharges levied by the city government, while surcharges levied by the provincial and national governments are assessed at the minimum rate. Service charges are half the standard amounts.

Migrant workers with labor contracts for two consecutive years can send their children to local schools without charge. Married workers who have worked in the park for more than three years are eligible for low-cost public housing. Senior staff who purchase homes in the city receive income tax refunds. Firms can use 7 percent of the industrial land allocated to them to build residential facilities for senior management staff and employees. The local government also offers free professional training for employees. Each district, city, and county is required to build at least one public technical training center.

The municipal government provides generous support to a financial guarantee company that offers services to enterprises within the industrial cluster. The government also provides subsidies of up to Y 2 million ($0.3 million) in the form of equity for leading enterprises that invest in business expansion. Subsidies are likewise offered through favorable loan interest rates. The municipal government has worked to improve the transparency and efficiency of administrative approval mechanisms.

## Summary

The advantages of the lower costs in Ganzhou, in inland Jiangxi Province, became evident during and after the global financial crisis of 2008. The Qinye company was less affected by the market slump than were many rival firms located in coastal areas. Qinye's success in increasing output and sales after the crisis arose from a combination of entrepreneurial skill, the favorable location, and strong links with foreign investors through the OEM system. Qinye's experience shows that competitiveness can be maintained in locations outside the coastal region provided the supply chain is well managed. Lower wages, cheap land, and official subsidies and concessions can trump the higher logistics costs to make an industry viable, at least in the short to medium term.

# Zhengzhou Economic Development Zone, Zhengzhou, Henan Province

Established in 1993, the Zhengzhou economic development zone is in southeast Zhengzhou, the capital of Henan. China's most populous province, Henan has been one of the country's largest sources of migrant labor since the economic reforms of the late 1970s. For example, in a factory in Zhengzhou technology park owned by Foxconn, the world's largest electronics OEM, 157,000 of the more than 800,000 employees are from Henan.[26] Zhengzhou also has a transport advantage because it is a major railway hub and has China's largest marshaling station. Two arteries of the national railway system, the Beijing-Guangzhou and Longhai railways, intersect in Zhengzhou.

Despite these advantages in labor and logistics, the Zhengzhou zone grew slowly until the early 2000s, when the central government elevated it to a national economic development zone, thereby allowing the zone more management autonomy. Development was slow for three reasons. First, the national development strategy during the 1980s and 1990s emphasized the coastal areas. Because Zhengzhou is in an interior region, its policy environment was poorly suited to the increasing competition for investment among industrial parks.

Second, Zhengzhou's substantial complement of large state-owned firms absorbed much of the local government's resources and created an unfavorable business environment for domestic and foreign private investors.

Third, until around 2005, the growth of wages in China was slow because of the steady supply of surplus labor. This encouraged investors to focus on the coastal region, which enjoyed greater transportation advantages and agglomeration effects relative to interior cities such as Zhengzhou. Since then, however, the rise in wages in the coastal areas has made Zhengzhou more attractive as a destination for light industry investment.

**Origin and Course of Development**

In the early 1980s, the government authorized the establishment of four special economic zones and planned to use them as a testing ground for economic reform. During 1984–86, 14 economic and technological development zones were created in coastal cities. They were open to overseas investment. The experiment was a great success, prompting the government to extend the model across the country. Because of their good infrastructure, efficient administration, and favorable business terms, industrial parks have become the major vehicle for attracting foreign and domestic investment, encouraging technology transfer and adaptation, and promoting advanced manufacturing and high-technology sectors. By 2006, Henan's 275 industrial parks accounted for 24 percent of provincial GDP, 52 percent of foreign investment, and 35 percent of exports (Henan Provincial Bureau of Commerce 2007).

In 1992, Zhengzhou and 19 other coastal and inland provincial capitals were opened to foreign investment and permitted to establish economic development zones. Zhengzhou's zone was launched in 1993, two years after the city's first industrial park, which focused on high-technology industries.[27] The new Zhengzhou zone was at a considerable disadvantage in the competition for external investment because it was not favored with the preferential policies that applied to the nearby high-technology park. Neither the city's location nor its preponderance of state-owned firms was attractive to foreign investors. As a result, the new development zone grew slowly despite its relatively low labor costs and land prices.

**Preferential policies of the central government.** An opportunity for change came in the late 1990s, when the central government launched the opening-up policy, which emphasized balanced regional development. The government allowed more ports and cities in coastal and inland regions to accept foreign investment. Over 2000–02, the State Council raised 17 economic zones in inland provinces, including Zhengzhou's, to the level of national economic zones. This administrative upgrade qualified the Zhengzhou zone for important new benefits:[28]

- *Administrative autonomy:* The zone administrative authority received project approval and management powers equivalent to those of a provincial commercial authority (rather than a local government). This allowed it to approve foreign direct investment proposals with a value up to Y 1.8 billion ($266 million).
- *Financing:* The new arrangement provided access to interest subsidies on infrastructure loans, special funds for foreign trade development, and international aid funds. Furthermore, investment projects in the zone now received priority consideration by the State Development Bank as well as state-owned commercial banks.

- *Land:* The administrative upgrade allowed the Zhengzhou zone
  to benefit from central government guarantees that provide additional land to zones that achieve industrial agglomeration and scale
  economies.[29]

Seeking to build the Zhengzhou economic development zone into an
engine of industry, a window on the outside world, and a base of modern manufacturing, the Zhengzhou municipal government issued a
revised development plan for the zone in 2003. The plan enabled the
zone to control the administration of 26 surrounding villages, expanding its size to 80 square kilometers, including 55,000 permanent residents and 100,000 workers.

**The reform of state-owned enterprises.** Zhengzhou is home to a
substantial population of state enterprises, many of which were deeply
in debt. As part of the country's Great Western Development Strategy,
the government expedited the reform of state-owned enterprises in the
early 2000s. In 2002, Zhengzhou adopted a new strategy for transforming the city's economic structure by shifting the emphasis from heavy
industry to commerce. With the intervention of the municipal government, state enterprises located in the city's central district sold their
downtown land parcels and moved their operations to suburban industrial parks. The municipal government then resold these valuable plots
to commercial developers. The relocated companies used the proceeds
of their land sales to pay off debt and upgrade technology.[30]

For example, Zhengzhou Baiyun Electrical Equipment Company
(the former state-owned Zhengzhou Trailer Plant) moved from the
city center to Zhengzhou economic development zone in 2001. The
enterprise sold its downtown premises for Y 40 million ($4.8 million).
Supplemented by bank loans, the company invested Y 110 million
($13.3 million) to build a new plant in the zone. The company was
restructured as a shareholding company through a management buyout
and has grown steadily ever since.

While some restructured companies have thrived in the market-based
environment, many have failed. A prominent example is Zhengzhou
Shuangta Paint Company (the former state-owned Zhengzhou Paint
Plant), which moved to the zone in 2003 and built a new factory with

Table 5.3 Economic Performance, Zhengzhou Economic Development Zone, China, 2005 and 2010

| Indicator | Ratio, 2010 value/2005 value | Annual growth rate, % |
|---|---|---|
| Gross demestic product | 3.0 | 20.6 |
| Total industrial output | 3.8 | 28.0 |
| Investment in fixed assets | 3.2 | 26.0 |
| Total government revenue | 4.8 | 37.0 |
| Foreign investment | 8.0 | 51.8 |
| Trade volume | 9.8 | 51.8 |

Source: Zhengzhou Economic Development Zone Administration.

the Y 80 million ($9.7 million) it had obtained by selling the old factory and a fresh loan of Y 20 million ($2.4 million). However, the new company never became competitive.

Despite such failures, the Zhengzhou zone has continued to attract investment to improve infrastructure. The eventual agglomeration of industrial enterprises has had a strong impact on the local business environment.[31]

The growth of the economic development zone has accelerated since 2006 (table 5.3) because of the arrival of major companies such as Hainan Mazda Automobile, Nissan Automobile, Henan Coalbed Gas, and AnFei Electronic Glass. The zone administration has concentrated on developing five sectors: automobiles and spare parts, machinery, food processing, electronics and information technology, and logistics. More than 3,000 enterprises now populate the zone, including 1,500 industrial companies, 205 foreign-invested firms, and 31 listed firms. The expansion of the zone exploded in 2011 after the State Council issued a directive assigning priority to regional development in China's central plains region, which includes Henan province, with emphasis on industry, urbanization, and agricultural modernization.

In 2011, the gross industrial output of the zone totaled Y 55 billion ($8.5 billion) (figure 5.7). The scale of foreign investment was also impressive, totaling Y 2 billion ($310 million) in 2011. The average investment per project receiving foreign investment increased from Y 8.2 million ($1 million) in 2005 to Y 58.2 million ($9 million) in 2010.

**Figure 5.7  Growth, Zhengzhou Economic Development Zone, China, 2000–11**

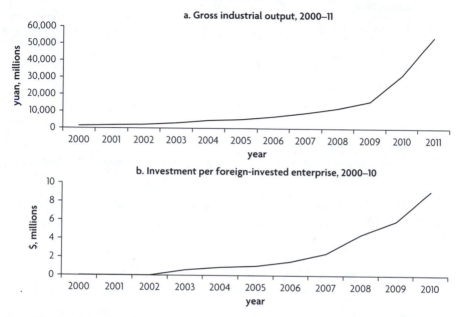

Source: China Association of Development Zones.

## Competitiveness and Binding Constraints

Although Henan has a long history as a major crossroads of politics, culture, and transport, an abundant labor force, and substantial resources in raw materials, it also has a scarcity of arable land and an uneven record in industrial development linked to the heavy concentration of state enterprises.

**Trade logistics.**  Henan Province is far from the coast, and this has long been a disadvantage in attracting foreign investment and in the development of exports. Today, the province's central location attracts investors interested in expanding to serve China's growing domestic market. Zhengzhou also enjoys reasonably good infrastructure despite lengthy delays in customs clearance (table 5.4). The province is connected to China's largest urban areas, including Beijing-Tianjin-Tangshan and the Yangzi and Pearl River Delta regions, and to other inland provinces by a network of railways, highways, air routes, and telecommunications links. The Zhengzhou economic development zone is 41 square

**Table 5.4 Distances and Delays, Zhengzhou Economic Development Zone, China, 2010**

| Distance or delay | Measure |
| --- | --- |
| Average time for customs clearance | 12.7 days |
| Distance to major highway | 4 kilometers |
| Distance to the closest freight railway station | 5 kilometers |
| Distance to the closest passenger railway station | 5 kilometers |
| Distance to the closest cargo port | 500 kilometers |
| Distance to the closest airport | 30 kilometers |

Source: China Location website [in Chinese] (accessed September 30, 2012), http://www.cnlocation.com/Zone/index.aspx?id=88.

kilometers in area. It has benefited from investments of Y 43 billion ($7 billion) on fixed assets, Y 5 billion ($739 million) of which has gone for building infrastructure.

**Input industries.** Henan Province is a major supplier of agroproducts, including wheat, cotton, oilseeds, and tobacco. It boasts one of China's largest food processing industries. It has reserves of petroleum, coal, and other minerals.

Despite Henan's ability to supply materials for light manufacturing, China's state industries in Henan followed plan directives and focused on priority sectors during the prereform decades. There was no incentive to build links between the state companies and private producers. Because Henan society lacked the entrepreneurial élan visible in China's coastal provinces, light manufacturing clusters of the sort observed in Guangdong and Zhejiang provinces were slow to appear.

During the initial stage of the Zhengzhou economic development zone's growth, enterprises in the zone lacked connections to each other and attachment to the local economy. Most operated independently, with little division of labor or collaboration. The local government stressed efforts to attract foreign investors and paid little attention to local SMEs. After this strategy failed to improve productivity or lead to engagement with the local economy, the zone authority modified the strategy to focus on fostering industrial clusters in the five targeted sectors. In recent years, Foxconn, the world's largest electronics OEM, and other large international firms have moved into the zone, along with some of their suppliers.

**Labor supply and skills.** An abundant supply of skilled and unskilled labor has been one of Zhengzhou's biggest advantages (table 5.5). Henan is one of the largest suppliers of migrant labor in China. In recent years, more investors have relocated their factories inland to escape the rising cost of labor and the land shortages in the coastal regions. Despite a steady increase in wages (figure 5.8), the average labor cost is still lower in the Zhengzhou zone than in the coastal provinces.

Henan is home to a number of research institutes and universities, but the level of human capital, though much improved over the course of the reform era, remains modest. While the typical resident of the

**Table 5.5  Educational Attainment, Permanent Residents, Zhengzhou Economic Development Zone, China, 2010**

| Education | Measure |
| --- | --- |
| Illiterate, % | 2.2 |
| Primary school graduates, % | 16.3 |
| High school graduates, % | 35.5 |
| Middle specialized school graduates, % | 19.3 |
| College graduates, % | 18.9 |
| Graduates with master's degrees or above, % | 0 |
| Research institutes and universities, number | 179 |

*Source:* China Location website [in Chinese] (accessed September 30, 2012), http://www.cnlocation.com/Zone/index.aspx?id=88.

**Figure 5.8  Average Monthly Salary of Workers, Zhengzhou Economic Development Zone, China, 2001–10**

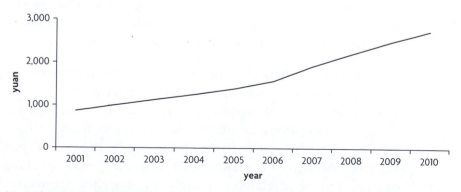

*Source:* China Location website [in Chinese] (accessed September 30, 2012), http://www.cnlocation.com/Zone/index.aspx?id=88.

territory administered by the Zhengzhou economic development zone is a high school graduate, none have postgraduate degrees (table 5.5). Educational attainment among the migrants who dominate in the zone's workforce is surely much lower.

**Industrial land.** In 2003, the Zhengzhou municipal government issued a revised development plan for the zone. Under the new plan, the zone took over the administration of 26 surrounding villages and expanded to 80 square kilometers. The zone lacked adequate funds in the early years to invest in necessary infrastructure. Having been granted higher autonomy, the administration actively sought solutions to expand financing channels, including establishing an investment entity to raise funds for infrastructure construction by issuing bonds and trust financing.

## The Role of Government

Government policies have strongly influenced economic growth in the inland regions, which have less private sector dynamism and less favorable logistics conditions than the coastal areas. Growth began to take off once the central government elevated the Zhengzhou zone to a national-level zone.

**National policies.** The Zhengzhou economic development zone benefited from an administrative upgrade that expanded the zone's autonomy and provided preferential treatment in financing and land supply. It then received additional benefits linked to Beijing's initiatives for accelerating development in the country's western and central plains regions. These efforts to boost growth in lagging regions brought concrete advantages in the form of supportive policies affecting taxation, finance, investment, industrial development, and land supply (State Council 2011).

**Provincial policies.** China's hierarchical system of governance requires local and provincial governments to support national policy initiatives. Thus, both Henan and Zhengzhou took steps to boost Beijing's regional development initiatives, generating further benefits for the Zhengzhou economic development zone. For example, in 2005, Henan instructed local governments to foster a favorable business environment by cutting red tape, reducing government intervention, promoting information technology, strengthening infrastructure, enhancing financial support, facilitating the inflow of professional talent, offering greater autonomy to zone authorities, encouraging foreign investment in high-technology sectors, and emphasizing rational planning and land use.[32]

**Municipal and other local government policies.** Taking its cue from the provincial and national authorities, Zhengzhou's municipal government also sought to offer support. Local governments are allowed to set up special funds for building infrastructure, carrying out major investment projects in economic development zones, and covering investment promotional costs. Zone authorities can issue incentives in targeted areas, such as inducing students studying overseas to return, servicing the outsourcing sector, selecting candidate firms for stock exchange listings, and supporting start-ups. Accordingly, the zone administration issued a comprehensive policy package in 2009 to help firms in the zone deal with the fallout from the global economic crisis, as follows:[33]

- *Encouraging enterprises to explore domestic and foreign markets:* Firms participating in trade fairs at home and abroad are reimbursed for their expenses. Firms with good business performance and export records receive bonuses. Urban construction projects financed by the government have to procure raw materials and products from enterprises in the zone. Agency and resident purchases of products and vehicles produced in the zone are subsidized.
- *Expanding financing channels:* The zone authority hosts meetings to build partnerships between enterprises and banks. Financial institutions and guarantee firms that increased their financing to firms in the zone by Y 100 million ($15 million) in 2009 received awards valued at 0.1 percent of the loans. The administration also subsidizes the losses of the guarantee firms it sponsors. Firms are encouraged to apply for stock exchange listings.
- *Strengthening support for key investment projects:* Enterprises investing in designated projects receive priority in land allocations, the supply of utilities, subsidies for technical innovation, and renovations to enhance energy efficiency.
- *Encouraging innovation:* The zone administration organizes events to facilitate partnerships between enterprises and research institutes. Firms that build their own R&D centers receive subsidies from

the zone administration. Firms that develop successful brands also receive rewards.

- *Reducing fees.*
- *Subsidizing staff training during slack periods.*

## Summary

The case of the Zhengzhou economic development zone demonstrates government's critical role in attracting labor-intensive industries to the interior regions. These regions generally have a less dynamic private sector and less favorable logistics conditions than the coastal areas. Growth began to take off once the central government elevated Zhengzhou's economic development zone to a national-level zone. The development of industrial parks in China also depends on policy alignment between the central government and other levels of government, including local governments.

## Auto Industry, Yinchuan, Ningxia Province

A city without an automotive sector is a city without a manufacturing industry.

—*A Chinese official*

For lagging regions like us, whose main strength lies in abundant resources, the only way to attract investors is to provide subsidies and preferential policies, that is, to sacrifice the immediate benefits for the long-term returns.

—*Deputy Director Chen Wei, Administrative Committee,*
*Yinchuan Economic Development Zone*

Ningxia Hui Autonomous Region, in northwest China, enjoys abundant land, low-cost labor, and cheap energy. Yinchuan, Ningxia's capital, had a per capita income in 2009 of Y 21,777 ($3,190), ranking 19th among China's 31 provincial capitals. The Yinchuan economic development zone was originally established as the Yinchuan Provincial-Level High-Technology Industrial Development Zone in 1992, with a planned area of 7.5 square kilometers. At that time, agricultural technology was targeted as a key field for development to serve the region's food, herbal medicine, dairy, and wool sectors.

The State Council elevated the zone to national-level standing in 2001, leading to the expansion of the zone to 32 square kilometers and a change in strategy, which now targeted more sophisticated industries, such as machinery manufacturing, new energy, new materials, software, animation, service outsourcing, and fine chemicals (figure 5.9). At the end of 2009, the zone housed 2,350 firms, including 366 industrial enterprises. In that year, the zone's GDP reached Y 6.5 billion ($1 billion), and gross industrial output amounted to Y 13.2 billion ($2 billion).[34] The zone has hosted several rapidly growing machinery manufacturing firms, such as Little Giant Machine Tool Company Ltd., with investment from LGMasak, a prominent Japanese firm. The company supplies nearly 20 percent of the domestic high-end digital control machine tools. About 40 percent of the orders come from major Chinese automakers.

Ningxia is one of 10 provinces with no substantial automotive industry. Since 2007, the local government has been striving to attract outside investors, to little effect. In November 2010, the province's first vehicle assembly project, with a planned investment of Y 1.8 billion ($266 million) and annual production of 90,000 vehicles, was terminated because of the investors' inability to obtain a production license. Close examination reveals that the local government failed to properly assess the conditions facing a potential automobile cluster in Yinchuan.

**Figure 5.9  Industrial Structure, Yinchuan Economic Development Zone, China, 2009**

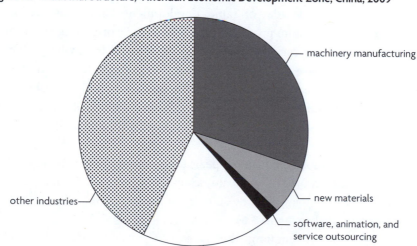

*Source:* Data of the Administrative Committee, Yinchuan economic development zone.

### Origin and Course of Development

China's modern automobile industry, started with help from the former Soviet Union in the 1950s, began by creating vertically integrated auto firms. The Sino-Soviet split of the 1960s cut the links to Soviet technology. Strict centralized controls of investment and production were then combined with a location preference for remote peripheral regions because of the defense-orientation of the industry (Sit and Liu 2000).

Auto manufacturing subsequently became a national priority industry. Following the economic reforms of the late 1970s, the auto sector grew rapidly, drawing on foreign investment and technology. In 1994, the government issued the first industrial policy for the auto sector, making it clear that "the state encourages enterprises to develop the auto industry by utilizing overseas investment."[35] Joint ventures with foreign firms supplanted early domestic leaders as the sector's dominant producers. In 2004, China issued a new auto industrial policy, which encouraged mergers and restructuring.

Beginning in 1986, China imposed a protective tariff on automobiles: 180–220 percent for assembled vehicles and 20–50 percent for auto parts.[36] These high tariffs blocked most imports, and rising domestic demand spurred local governments to build their own automobile industries.

After three decades of rapid development, China has become a global leader in auto production, as well as the world's largest national market for new cars. To meet the rising demand for civilian vehicles, automakers have concentrated production in more developed regions in central and eastern China. There are now 30 major automobile producers in China, manufacturing 13 million cars in 2008 (figure 5.10). The number is projected to hit 31.2 million by the end of 2015 (NDRC 2010).

The automobile industry appeals to local governments because of its visibility, high profits, long value chain, and potential for raising GDP growth and employment. By 2009, 23 of the 31 provinces had their own large automakers (table 5.6).

Ningxia was among the laggards, causing local officials to search for a path to enter this prestigious industry. The growth of

**Figure 5.10  Automobile Production, China, 1978–2008**

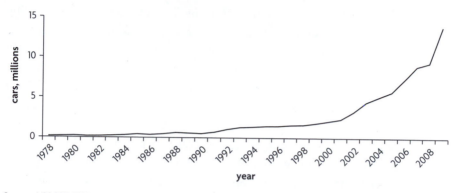

*Sources:* NBS 2011, 2012.

**Table 5.6  Automobile Production by Province, China, 2011**

| Province | Number of vehicles | Province | Number of vehicles |
|---|---|---|---|
| Shanghai | 1,915,700 | Zhejiang | 306,300 |
| Chongqing | 1,666,400 | Fujian | 186,400 |
| Jilin | 1,556,800 | Heilongjiang | 181,700 |
| Beijing | 1,504,600 | Hunan | 161,900 |
| Guangdong | 1,502,800 | Hainan | 152,000 |
| Guangxi | 1,423,500 | Sichuan | 128,600 |
| Hubei | 1,319,000 | Yunnan | 97,200 |
| Anhui | 1,170,300 | Inner Mongolia | 36,500 |
| Jiangsu | 803,800 | Gansu | 20,600 |
| Shandong | 762,900 | Guizhou | 12,800 |
| Tianjin | 756,900 | Shanxi | 6,100 |
| Liaoning | 755,400 | Xinjiang | 1,100 |
| Hebei | 721,100 | Tibet | 0 |
| Shaanxi | 556,700 | Qinghai | 0 |
| Henan | 365,800 | Ningxia | 0 |
| Jiangxi | 343,500 | *China total* | *18,416,400* |

*Source:* NBS 2011.

Yinchuan's machinery sector encouraged the officials to introduce vehicle manufacture into the economy. The goal was to woo a leading auto company and its suppliers. In 2007, the administration of the Yinchuan economic development zone hired a consulting firm to evaluate the zone's suitability for developing an automotive sector. The report concluded that demand in northwestern China could support auto production in the Yinchuan zone and that trucks could become a key product. The administration acted on these recommendations, assembling a team to search for a potential investment partner. The team visited auto producers in 18 provinces without success: established producers expressed concerns about the limited market demand, the high logistics costs, and the shortage of local suppliers.

Chengdu New Land Auto Company, a producer of low-end cargo trucks and sport utility vehicles based in Chengdu, Sichuan Province, finally expressed an interest in investing. The company determined that demand for light, medium, and heavy-duty trucks would be strong because Ningxia and the surrounding areas had abundant agricultural and mineral resources, and most cargo would have to be transported by road.

Yinchuan's prospective partner, Li Zihao, president of Chengdu New Land, was not an auto manufacturing professional. Originally from Shunde, Guangdong Province, Li was known for adventurous capital undertakings. He started in business in the 1990s with a trading company. After accumulating some capital, he expanded to southwestern China and acquired a local truck company on the brink of bankruptcy, naming it Chengdu New Land Auto Company. In 2001, the company signed a deal with the Korean auto producer Ssangyong to introduce a sport utility vehicle model, the Musso. The sport utility vehicle was rarely seen on the roads or on the market. In 2008, Li acquired an auto firm in Jiangsu Province that was listed on the Hong Kong Stock Exchange, but that had been sustaining heavy losses. In late 2009, Li became the focus of media attention when he acquired a Chilean iron mine for Y 15 billion ($2.2 billion).[37]

Li's diversified business portfolio and his lack of core industry experience had helped divert the attention of his company from automaking and diluted its capital. Although Chengdu New Land Auto is officially certified to develop, produce, and sell passenger vehicles, trucks, and sport utility vehicles, it has not done so since 2008. Instead, it has authorized smaller auto producers to use its brand.[38]

In September 2007, Chengdu New Land signed a formal contract with the Yinchuan economic development zone and promised to invest Y 1.8 billion ($237 million) in a subsidiary company with an annual production capacity of 90,000 trucks and passenger vehicles. In December 2007, Ningxia New Land Auto Company Ltd. was established as a subsidiary of Chengdu New Land. Secured by the land he had acquired in the Yinchuan economic development zone, Li obtained Y 30 million ($4 million) in bank loans, but these funds were never invested to establish auto production in Yinchuan.

A grand celebration was held to announce the zone's production of the first four red heavy-duty vehicles branded *Da-Di* (grand land).

"History has been made," the local media proclaimed. "Ningxia has built the 'flagship auto industry in Western China.'" Not a single vehicle has been produced since.

The plan was to build an auto manufacturing cluster, with Ningxia New Land Auto at the center and surrounded by auto parts manufacturers. In April 2009, the Yinchuan economic development zone signed an agreement with the China Auto Parts and Accessories Corporation for the joint construction of an auto parts manufacturing base in Yinchuan. The cooperation plan did not include any specific investment, but provided more channels for the Yinchuan economic development zone to communicate with auto parts manufacturers.

A sudden disconnect between provincial and national policy halted this effort. In 2008, the central government, fearing excessive expansion, declared that approval of new auto manufacturing projects would henceforth be limited to acquisitions by or mergers with existing local auto producers. As there was no auto company in Yinchuan, it became impossible for Ningxia New Land Auto to obtain the license needed to establish automotive production in Yinchuan. In November 2010, the project was cancelled, to the distress of the local government.

## Competitiveness and Binding Constraints

Yinchuan is located on the fertile Ningxia Plateau. The Yellow River winds through the city, providing the area with abundant irrigation water despite limited precipitation. Yinchuan is one of China's sunniest cities, with 2,800–3,000 hours of annual sunshine. This combination of factors makes Yinchuan an important agricultural production base in northwestern China. Ningxia also has rich coal reserves, but it lacks the industrial foundation to support an auto industry, which requires large capital investments, sophisticated technologies, significant R&D capacity, a vast supply network of parts and components, and a large pool of professionals and skilled workers.

**Input industry.** Automobile assembly firms rely on sophisticated supply networks among components and parts manufacturers. Such networks have evolved in some areas of China, where they have been led by joint ventures between state-owned enterprises and foreign automakers, attracted dozens of international component producers, and developed multiple layers of subcontracting suppliers, including hundreds of private domestic SMEs. Ningxia is distant from these areas. The cost of shipping the inputs needed to assemble a truck would be higher in Yinchuan than in regions with a sound foundation in automobile manufacturing. Only a handful of companies producing auto-related machinery, equipment, and components are located in Yinchuan. Most of these companies are small.

**Trade logistics.** Ningxia is far from the main suppliers of auto parts, which are concentrated in China's coastal and northeastern regions. The cost of establishing an input supply chain would be much higher in Ningxia than in regions that already have an auto parts supply chain and a good machinery sector.

**Labor skills.** Skilled and experienced managers, engineers, and workers are critical in the automobile industry. All major auto clusters in China are in regions with leading universities and institutions for engineering technology and sciences, such as Beijing, Changchun, Chongqing, Guangzhou, Shanghai, and Wuhan. Ningxia has a small population of 6.3 million people, an area of 66,400 square kilometers, and limited education resources. Most skilled workers are from neighboring provinces, such as Inner Mongolia and Shaanxi. Ningxia's remote location and weak educational system makes it unappealing to the engineers and managers whose participation would be key to building a competitive auto sector.

**Technology.** China's auto sector is becoming a competitive battleground, and auto producers have to be prepared to upgrade rapidly and innovate. Because there is no local auto producer in Yinchuan, all technology has to be provided by outside investors. Chengdu New Land Auto Company Ltd., the investor selected by the local government, was a weak partner that did not have the expertise or technological strength to compete with established auto and truck producers.

## The Role of Government

The Yinchuan economic development zone was a beneficiary of China's Great Western Development Strategy. Supported by the grants and preferential policies of the central government, Yinchuan has greatly improved its infrastructure and business environment. Because the performance assessment of local administrators is tied to GDP growth and investment inflows, local officials strive to attract as much investment as possible. Local governments find automobile production especially appealing as it has contributed to rapid regional growth and rising tax revenues, thanks to buoyant demand and government interventions that have created large rents.

The local government attempted to develop an auto industry in Yinchuan to spur the region's growth. The project was planned by the Yinchuan municipal government (including the zone authority), which announced supportive policies such as tax holidays and land subsidies in the hope of attracting investors. However, the local government ignored the issue of regional comparative advantage and failed to recognize the realities of China's auto market. Its policies led it to cooperate with an ill-prepared partner who was more interested in subsidized borrowing than in long-term industrial development.

While the automobile project in the Yinchuan economic development zone was already burdened by many flaws, the death blow was dealt by the central government's 2008 policy adjustment that rejected new auto manufacturing except for projects built around acquisitions or mergers involving existing local automakers. The policy was intended to cool the overheated automobile industry in China, to consolidate fragmented output capacity, and to prevent the sort of ill-considered initiative described in this section.

### Summary

The automobile project in the Yinchuan economic development zone failed mainly because of premature local and provincial government-led efforts to build an industrial cluster from scratch for a sophisticated manufacturing product, the automobile. The major lesson is that directives from above are not sufficient to create a viable cluster. Cluster development builds on private initiatives that can endure market tests. Policies that attempt to circumvent comparative advantage by providing preferential treatment to investors can encourage moral hazard and damage the local economy. This case illustrates the dangers of policies linking the evaluation of local administrators to local GDP growth and investment outlays. While such policies have the merit of promoting competition and spurring public-private partnerships, they also have the capacity to encourage incautious decision making and wasteful public spending.

## Yongle Economic Development Zone, Beijing

Located in southeast Beijing, the Yongle economic development zone was established in 1992 with a planned area of 4.6 square kilometers.[39] At the heart of the Bohai Economic Circle, a major metropolitan area that includes Beijing, Tianjin, and other population centers adjacent to the Bohai Gulf, Yongle is close to Beijing and Tianjin (the largest seaport in north China). However, in contrast with the rapid growth of nearby development zones, such as the Beijing economic development zone (about 30 kilometers north of Yongle) and the Langfang economic development zone (directly adjacent to Yongle, although located across the provincial border separating Beijing and Hebei), the Yongle zone failed to catch on (table 5.7). Only 23 enterprises had set up there as of 2010, with total industrial output of Y 180 million ($27 million) and annual growth of less than 6 percent, well below the average growth rate in the Beijing zone or in the surrounding region.

**Table 5.7  Comparison of Three Economic Development Zones near Beijing, China**

| Indicator | Beijing | Langfang | Yongle |
|---|---|---|---|
| Administrative level | National | Provincial | Provincial |
| Main industries | Information and communication technology, biotechnology, automobile, and machinery | Machinery, electronics, food, construction materials, textiles, medicine | Machinery, electronics |
| Planned area, square kilometers | 46.8 | 69.5 | 4.6 |
| Firms, number | 3,870 | 1,491 | 23 |
| Cumulative investment | Y 166 billion ($24 billion) | Y 30 billion ($4.4 billion)[a] | Y 0.9 billion ($112 million) |
| Total industrial sales revenue | Y 378 billion ($55 billion) | Y 33.7 billion ($4.9 billion)[b] | Y 351 million ($51 million) |

*Sources:* BJStats and NBS 2011; Hebei Provincial Bureau of Statistics 2010.

a. Investment data refer to stock accumulated from 1992 to 2010 for Beijing and Yongle and from 1992 to 2009 for Langfang.

b. Total industrial output.

## Origin and Course of Development

The Yongle zone was part of the boom in the establishment of economic and technical development zones that followed Deng Xiaoping's 1992 tour of southern China. It seemed to have bright prospects because of its proximity to major population centers.

**Early period, 1992–97.** During the early period, the Yongle zone was subordinate to the authority of the Beijing General Company of Agriculture, Industry, and Commerce (formerly, the Beijing Management Bureau for State-Owned Farms).

Established in the 1950s, state-owned farms in Beijing focused on agricultural development, including farming, food production, and light industries that relied on agricultural inputs. The intention was to guarantee the capital city a secure food supply. However, under the plan system, the state-owned farms had little incentive to solicit customers outside the state-owned sector. They had few business relations with local farmers or outside investors.

The Yongle zone's initial management achieved little commercial success. Although real estate development is a key task for any new zone, Yongle only managed to attract a single real estate firm during its first six years. Meanwhile, industrial development was moribund.

**Modest expansion, 1998–2004.** To introduce competition and provide incentives to attract enthusiastic local government support, Beijing's municipal government transferred control over the floundering zone to the Tongzhou District government (Beijing Municipal Government 1998). This change brought an acceleration of Yongle's development: 20 firms moved in. In 2004, the zone had a total industrial output of Y 70 million ($8.5 million) and tax revenues of Y 30 million ($3.6 million). After a failed attempt by the Tongzhou District authorities to expand the Yongle zone in 2003, the zone reverted to its previously planned area in 2004. However, the development zone failed to identify a clear development plan and an effective strategy that could help it take advantage of its natural endowments and proximity to the vast market in north China, while mitigating its disadvantages. Because of the slow development of infrastructure and lack of supportive business services in the zone, many investors chose to establish companies in the parks in Beijing and Langfang.

**False start, 2005–08.** In another experimental move, a 2005 agreement with the privately owned Beijing Zhujiang Housing and Real Estate Development Company initiated a joint investment to establish the Yongle Economic Development Zone Development Company. Of the investment, 80 percent was provided by Zhujiang Real Estate, and 20 percent by the zone administration committee. The company was to be in charge of building infrastructure and operating the zone. Zhujiang Real Estate appointed the company president; the former director of the administration committee became vice president.

While trying to introduce a partnership with the private sector, the zone administration had difficulty sharing control and making decisions with private participants.

"Under a model in which private developers are involved in the primary land development, we often lose control of the infrastructure construction process due to various delays caused by the private partner," complained a local official. Among the problems he cited were the intentional delay of the project by the private developer to obtain a huge premium from the increase in land value; disputes between the private developer and farmers over the compensation in the process of land acquision and relocation; delays in construction caused by disagreement among shareholders or changes in shareholders; and so on. These problems led to the adoption of a new policy by the Beijing municipal government in 2008 that forces private developers to withdraw from the primary development of urban land.

The real estate company expected to obtain the right to develop virgin land and sell it for a profit once the infrastructure was built. The withdrawal of private developers from the primary development of urban land after 2008 thus derailed the joint venture between the zone administration and Zhujiang. In an atmosphere of extreme uncertainty about local policies, the zone's infrastructure and industrial development stagnated, and industrial output reached only Y 110 million ($15.8 million) in 2008. When the cooperation agreement with Zhujiang collapsed, management of the Yongle zone reverted to the Tongzhou District government.

## Competitiveness and Binding Constraints

**Input industry.** Beijing's role as a national economic center was de-emphasized to strengthen its position as a national political, cultural, and education center. Labor-intensive manufacturing was deemed unsuitable for Beijing. In any case, high labor costs and strict environmental controls ruled out industrial development in the city. As a result, Beijing's input industries for manufacturing remained underdeveloped. Industrial parks close to downtown Beijing attracted domestic and foreign clients who wanted to locate corporate headquarters (rather than factories) in Beijing. However, Yongle was too far from the city center to draw in such tenants.

**Trade logistics.** Despite its superior location adjacent to several large metropolitan areas and seaports, the Yongle economic development zone managed to invest only Y 70 million ($10.3 million) by 2010 to build infrastructure in a 1.5 square kilometer area. The zone has 13,400 meters of road, 158,800 square meters of green area, three deep water wells, 9,448 meters of water supply pipes, two boilers that can heat an area of 25,000 square meters, one transformer station, and one telephone station to meet the needs of telecommunications and a broadband network. The developed area was only a small portion of the planned zone.

**Finance.** Efforts to engage private investors in developing the zone failed. The propensity of the Beijing municipal government to implement unexpected rule changes imposed high risks that encouraged private investors to pursue quick profits rather than long-term development. But the development of an industrial park takes time, involving the creation of infrastructure and the nurturing of nascent industries.

Land development is highly capital intensive. It is estimated that the cost of land development averaged Y 500 million ($77 million) per square kilometer to level the land and install utilities in the Tianjin development zone and was as high as Y 600 million ($92.8 million) in the Suzhou industrial park in 2010. The cost has risen in recent years. Entities wishing to participate in initial land development had to supply 35 percent of the financing. To obtain a bank loan, a developer needs to provide adequate real estate assets as collateral. It normally takes at least five years for an economic development zone to see profits once the land development is complete and enterprises move in. Without any guarantee of a stable business environment, private investors are unlikely to risk the losses associated with a bad long-term investment.

There are five industrial parks in Tongzhou District, in addition to Yongle. As a result, the local government had to concentrate its limited resources on a few priority parks. Yongle, located on the edge of the district, did not obtain financial support from the local government.

## The Role of Government

**Planning.** Inadequate planning by the local government and an inefficient administrative structure are the fundamental reasons for Yongle's failure. There was a lack of clear and systematic planning, including a failure to identify priority sectors, promote investment, and prepare a comprehensive development strategy. The local authorities never conducted a comprehensive analysis of the region's endowments and comparative advantage.

Although the general plan for the zone was approved by the local government in May 1993, it was not until 2003, a full decade later, that a planning institute produced a detailed scheme for land use, transportation, and public service facilities in the zone's 4.6 square kilometers. With no plans for targeted industries, the general plan provided only broad guidance. Fatally, an organically developed cluster never emerged; so, the plan was not based on demonstrated success on the ground.

**Administration.** Because the Yongle zone was situated within Beijing, literally across the road from Hebei, and close to the large metropolis of Tianjin, there was ambiguity about who would administer the zone. Multiple administrative changes disrupted the development strategy and investment promotion efforts and resulted in inadequate inputs in infrastructure development. Furthermore, the zone administration had been granted little autonomy in management and decision making, leading to the zone's weak capacity in investment promotion.

**Partnership with the private sector.** While the change in local policies, which mandated the leading role to local government in primary land evelopment, directly led to the collapse of the partnership between the zone administration and the private investor, the lack of coordination and trust was another profound reason for the collapse. On the one hand, local officials welcomed private investment in infrastructure, which would speed up the development process and spread the risks of investment from the government to the private sector. On the other hand, the same local officials did not trust the private investor and were reluctant to let go of their power or authority.

**Investor services.** Inadequate administration and lack of support from the local government led to poor services for potential and incumbent investors in Yongle. In this regard, the Langfang economic development zone has proceeded differently. The Langfang administration received strong support from the local government and was able to do all they could to woo projects into the zone; the zone managers learned on the job (first, they accepted all comers, and, then, they started to focus on target industries) and provided good services to firms that moved into the park. The consistent service provided by the Langfang administration has facilitated the growth of enterprises in the park. These enterprises have raised their investments and gradually expanded their production scale. For example, a food processing firm increased its capital by seven times in five years. The firm owner told our interview team that, aside from market factors, the meticulous service provided by the Langfang administration was an important factor for the firm in expanding investment in the zone.

## Summary

With fierce competition among local governments over investment for industrial development, an industrial park cannot succeed based simply on good location. A clear design for both the physical infrastructure and the administrative structure, based on an in-depth understanding of the park's competitiveness and comparative advantage, is crucial. To invest for the long term, private developers also need government support to encourage their confidence in the stability of the business environment.

## Notes

1. These figures refer to above-scale enterprises, that is, those with annual output of more than Y 5 million (around $800,000), and include the manufacture of textile fibers and fabrics, clothing, shoes, hats, leather, and furs. For the significance of above-scale enterprises, see the note to figure 5.2.

2. See "Haimen Industrial Park," Haimen Municipal Committee of the Communist Party of China and Haimen Municipal Government, Haimen, China (accessed January 2, 2013), http://www.haimen.gov.cn/default.php?mod=article&do=detail&tid=183794.

3. See www.xhby.net [in Chinese] (accessed January 4, 2012), http://zl.xhby.net/system/2008/10/29/010365641.shtml.

4. *Zhongguo xianyu jingji nianjian 2011* [China county-level economy yearbook 2011] [in Chinese]. Beijing: Zhongguo dadi chubanshe.

5. *Zhongguo xianyu jingji nianjian 2011* [China county-level economy yearbook 2011] [in Chinese]. Beijing: Zhongguo dadi chubanshe.

6. *Zhongguo xianyu jingji nianjian 2011* [China county-level economy yearbook 2011] [in Chinese]. Beijing: Zhongguo dadi chubanshe.

7. According to a policy that went into effect on January 1, 2010, enterprises benefiting from foreign investment of more than $5 million or with registered capital of more than Y 10 million receive preferential treatment in the supply of land. Firms with provincially or nationally recognized brands receive an award of Y 50,000–Y 300,000.

8. In warp knitting, the yarn zigzags along the fabric to provide greater strength and endurance. The technology is used to produce a wide assortment of products, including apparel, home goods, sporting goods, and industrial and highly engineered applications.

9. "Development Status, Existing Problems, and Proposed Solutions for the Warp Knitting Industry in Haining" [in Chinese], Haining Statistical Information Net (accessed December 29, 2011), http://tjj.haining.gov.cn/tjfx/201112/t20111229_203297.htm.

10. From the late 1970s to the end of 2005, Zhejiang gained 304,000 SMEs, or about 99.6 percent of the total enterprises established during the period. In the first half of 2008, private enterprises in Zhejiang contributed 70 percent of the province's total output, 60 percent of its tax revenue, and 70 percent of its exports. Almost all the jobs in the province are in private enterprises.

11. The average income of a state textile worker was Y 7,000 ($1,050) in the 1990s, while that of a township and village enterprise (TVE) worker in a Shanghai suburb was Y 3,000 ($450). A worker in Qiaotou would have earned even less.

12. International Financial Statistics (database), International Monetary Fund, Washington, DC, http://elibrary-data.imf.org/FindDataReports.aspx?d=33061&e=169393.

13. Since 1994, China has separated local and central government taxes and tax administration. The central tax bureau collects value added taxes and special consumption taxes, while the local tax bureaus are responsible for business income taxes and other taxes.

14. The OEM arrangement is a common one between Chinese and Taiwanese firms.

15. Ding (2006) finds that there was a substantial transformation of the market over 1992–97 because a large number of merchants from other regions began operating in the Yiwu market, the number of comparatively well-educated and young merchants in the Yiwu market increased, and the booth keepers in the Yiwu market gradually built up sturdy business relationships with producers.

16. "Interview with the Vice Mayor of Yongkang City" [in Chinese], *Zhejiang News*, November 28, 2011, http://zjnews.zjol.com.cn/05zjnews/system/2011/11/28/018030561.shtml.

17. "Yongkang Enterprises Go Overseas Via Hong Kong" [in Chinese], *Jinhua Daily*, July 5, 2012, http://biz.zjol.com.cn/05biz/system/2012/07/05/018633865.shtml.

18. "Yongkang Metalwork Firms Go Around Traders to Meet Buyers" [in Chinese], Zhejiang Online, July 14, 2011, http://news.hexun.com/2011-07-14/131435619.html.

19. "Different Experiences in Hiring Workers of Two Private Enterprises in Yongkang" [in Chinese], Zhejiang Online, February 26, 2010, http://finance.sina.com.cn/roll/20100226/09567464004.shtml.

20. "Yongkang Trains Rural Workers to Become Hardware Specialists" [in Chinese], *Zhejiang Daily*, April 17, 2006, http://www.clii.com.cn/news/content-170013.aspx.

21. See jxnews.com, May 21, 2009 [in Chinese], http://bbs.jxcn.cn/dispbbs.asp?boardid=6&ID=254739; Ministry of Commerce of Ganzhou [in Chinese], http://www.gzwsxh.com/hyzq/fhzqy/2011-05-25/107.html.

22. *Gannan Daily* [in Chinese], May 20, 2009, http://local.jxwmw.cn/system/ 2009/05/20/010136125.shtml.

23. "Toy Companies Relocating to Inland" [in Chinese], *Economic News Daily*, February 11, 2009, http://finance.ifeng.com/news/industry/20090211/363204 .shtml.

24. XinhuaNet [in Chinese], August 23, 2008, http://www.xinhuanet.com/ chinanews/2008-08/23/content_14202468.htm.

25. See www.chinarjw.com [in Chinese], August, 16, 2011, http://www.chinarjw .com/n25/n544/n550/c4529/content.html.

26. "Foxconn Officially Confirms Plan to Build Factory in Henan" [in Chinese], *Economic Observations*, July 4, 2010, http://www.bianews.com/news/ 62/n-240662.html.

27. Zhengzhou Hi-tech Industrial Development Zone, 2004, "The History of Zhengzhou Hi-tech Industrial Development Zone" [in Chinese], August 27 (accessed August 20, 2012), http://www.zzgx.gov.cn/html/40288158157efd2901 15826a04090042/631.html.

28. "Interview with the Deputy Chief of the Henan Provincial Bureau of Commerce" [in Chinese], December 15, 2010, http://news.shangdu.com/101/ 20101215/7_149409.shtml.

29. See "The 11th Five-Year Plan," website of the government of China, http://english .gov.cn/special/115y_index.htm.

30. "The Relocation of State-Owned Enterprises in Zhengzhou" [in Chinese], *Gongren ribao* [Worker's Daily], April 5, 2006 (accessed August 20, 2012), cited at http://finance.sina.com.cn/g/20060405/12042476337.shtml.

31. "The Relocation of State-Owned Enterprises in Zhengzhou" [in Chinese], *Worker's Daily*, April 5, 2006 (accessed August 20, 2012), cited at http://finance .sina.com.cn/g/20060405/12042476337.shtml.

32. See www.chimaacc.com, "Several Opinions of the Henan Provincial Government on Speeding Up the Development of Economic Development Zone" [in Chinese], July 25, 2005, http://www.chinaacc.com/new/63/74/117/2006/7/ zh60043555561027600229865-0.htm.

33. See China Location website, "The Opinion of the Zhengzhou EDZ Administrative Committee on Promoting the Steady and Rapid Economic Growth" [in Chinese], May 18, 2009, http://www.cnlocation.com/Zone/ Content.aspx?newsid=544&id=88&type=11.

34. See www.Baidu.com, "Profile of Yinchuan EDZ" [in Chinese], http://baike .baidu.com/view/440660.htm.

35. See www.business.sohu.com, "Automobile Industrial Policy" [in Chinese], June 2, 2004, http://business.sohu.com/2004/06/02/31/article220353167 .shtml.

36. Long Guoqiang, "A Review of China's Automobile Industrial Policies" [in Chinese], December 1995, http://wenku.baidu.com/view/f5c3c0f5ba0d4a7302763a2b.html.

37. See *Time Weekly* website [in Chinese], January 4, 2010 (accessed August 20, 2012), http://www.p5w.net/news/gncj/201001/t2758263.htm.
38. Zhong Cai Wang [in Chinese], December 31, 2009 (accessed August 20, 2012), http://www.cfi.net.cn/p20091231000412.html.
39. The city of Beijing ranks as a province-level entity in China's system of government administration.

# References

Beijing Municipal Government. 1998. "Beijing Municipal Government's Advice on Reform of the General Company of Agriculture, Industry, and Commerce." [In Chinese.] Beijing Municipal Government, Beijing. http://www.chinalawedu.com/news/1200/22016/22017/22040/2006/3/fe2355213619523600210354-0.htm.

BJStats (Beijing Municipal Bureau of Statistics) and NBS (National Bureau of Statistics of China). 2011. *Beijing Statistics Yearbook 2011*. Beijing: China Statistics Press. http://www.bjstats.gov.cn/nj/main/2011-tjnj/index.htm.

Buyang Group. 2012. "Company Profile." [In Chinese.] http://baike.baidu.com/view/1109701.htm.

China E-Commerce Research Center. 2010. "Yongkang Establishes Conversation between Taxation and Banks to Solve Financial Difficulties of SMEs." [In Chinese.] August 7. http://b2b.toocle.com/detail--5322464.html.

Ding, Ke. 2006. "Distribution System of China's Industrial Clusters: Case Study of Yiwu China Commodity City." IDE Discussion Paper 75 (October), Institute of Developing Economies, Japan External Trade Organization, Chiba, Japan.

Hebei Provincial Bureau of Statistics. 2010. *Hebei Development Zone Yearbook 2010*. [In Chinese.] Hebei, China: Hebei Development Zone Yearbook Editorial.

Henan Provincial Bureau of Commerce. 2007. "An Analysis of Industrial Parks in Henan Province." [In Chinese.] August 24, China Academy of International Trade and Economic Cooperation, Beijing.

NBS (National Bureau of Statistics of China). 1989. *Zhongguo fenxian nongcun jingji tongji gaiyao 1980–87* [China: Outline of village economic statistics by county, 1980–87]. [In Chinese.] Beijing: China Statistics Press.

———. 2011. *China Statistical Yearbook*. Beijing: China Statistics Press.

———. 2012. *China Statistical Yearbook*. Beijing: China Statistics Press.

NDRC (National Development and Reform Commission). 2010. "NDRC to Curb the Automotive Overcapacity: 27 Provinces Can Assemble Whole Vehicles." [In Chinese.] *New Beijing Daily*, September 5. http://news.sohu.com/20100905/n274710004.shtml.

Panagariya, Arvind. 1995. "What Can We Learn from China's Export Strategy?" *Finance and Development* 32 (2): 32–35.

Perkins, Dwight H. 1977. *Rural Small-Scale Industry in the People's Republic of China*. Berkeley, CA: University of California Press.

RIME (Research Institute of Market Economy) and DRC (Development Research Center of the State Council). 2009. "Research Report on the Development of Sichuan Industry Cluster." China Development Press, Beijing.

Sit, Victor F. S., and Weidong Liu. 2000. "Restructuring and Spatial Change of China's Auto Industry under Institutional Reform and Globalization." *Annals of the Association of American Geographers* 90 (4): 653–73.

State Council. 2011. "Directive Opinions in Support of a Faster Construction of Central Plains Economic Region by Henan Province." [In Chinese.] October 7, State Council, Beijing. http://www.gov.cn/zwgk/2011-10/07/content_1963574.htm.

WTO (World Trade Organization). 2011. *World Trade Report 2011; The WTO and Preferential Trade Agreements: From Co-existence to Coherence*. Geneva: WTO.

Part II
# Tales of Other Countries

# 6

# Agribusiness

## Introduction

Looking at the highly productive and formidably competitive light manufacturing sector in China today, policy makers and entrepreneurs in low-income countries may be inclined to doubt whether they are able to compete head-on. However, China's current boom began in the 1980s, a time when Chinese light manufacturers faced a host of difficulties that would make familiar reading to anyone conversant with the obstacles to industrial growth in low-income environments now (see chapter 2). Moreover, rapidly rising wages are eroding the competitiveness of China's low-end, labor-intensive products, thus providing a market opening for low-income countries. Thus, as discussed in the companion volume, *Light Manufacturing in Africa* (Dinh and others 2012), low-income countries in Africa and elsewhere have the potential to be competitive in light manufacturing because of their low wages, the availability of excellent natural resources, their privileged access to high-income markets for exports, and the growing domestic and regional markets.

Policy makers and firms in developing countries can create productive jobs by first identifying and then prioritizing and removing most binding constraints in each sector. There are six major binding constraints to competitiveness in light manufacturing:

- Availability, cost, and quality of inputs
- Access to industrial land
- Access to finance
- Trade logistics
- Entrepreneurial capabilities, both technical and managerial
- Worker skills

Governments can help firms overcome these constraints. Sometimes, this may mean intervening directly to address a market failure by establishing industrial parks and special economic zones to accelerate growth in output, employment, and exports in light manufacturing or by providing access to credit, land, or information. Sometimes, it may mean simply getting out of the way so businesses can grow.

To illustrate these points, the case studies below and in the next chapters draw on detailed analyses of four labor-intensive light manufac- turing sectors: agribusiness, wood products, leather products, and textiles and garments. The lessons presented in these tales, including both the successes and the failures, offer hope and encouragement that low-income countries everywhere can overcome important constraints in adverse business environments. Industrialization need not wait for all obstacles to be removed.

As with the case studies on China, there are three types of case studies on other countries. First is the case studies on individual firms or individual entrepreneurs that focus on the characteristics shared by successful industrial entrepreneurs and on the way individuals adapt to changing circumstances. Examples are flowers in Ethiopia and tomatoes in Senegal.

Second is the case studies on industries, for instance flowers in Kenya and textiles in Lesotho. These cases are most useful in addressing issues revolving around the investment climate—land, finance, and skills— and around spillovers.

Third is the case studies on clusters. Cluster case studies are most interesting from the point of view of trying to understand the nature of agglomeration economies and the dynamics of industrial location.

Some of the cases contain elements of two or all three of these types.

We have selected the cases according to a number of criteria. First, they represent different sectors in light manufacturing. Second, sufficient time (measured in years) must have lapsed so that the cases may be judged accurately. Third, as in the cases on China (part I), we present both successes and failures. Finally, we have tried to include only cases in which we could interview the owners or managers. The main exceptions are the case studies on Morogoro and Bata shoes because these enterprises closed long ago. All interviews were conducted in 2010 and 2012.

This chapter and the next three chapters go into considerable detail about the experiences in four broad light manufacturing sectors. These case studies are presented in a consistent format that facilitates comparisons across cases and across light manufacturing sectors. The number of cases also facilitates a systematic analysis of what works and what does not work.

Because processing agricultural goods is a practical first step toward industrialization in many low-income agrarian economies, the case studies in this chapter show how enterprises in Ethiopia, Kenya, and Senegal have taken advantage of favorable climate, abundant low-skilled and low-cost labor, and access to high-quality land to achieve success in horticulture and tomatoes.

In Ethiopia, exports of cut flowers constituted only 0.6 percent of total manufacturing exports and 0.1 percent of total exports in 1995; 10 years later, these shares had risen to 8.6 and 1.3 percent. By 2010, this sector accounted for 45 percent of all manufacturing exports and more than 6 percent of total exports.[1] In Kenya, too, cut flowers became increasingly important, rising from 2.1 percent of manufacturing exports and 0.6 percent of total exports in 1980 to 16 percent and almost 8 percent, respectively, in 2010. In Senegal, tomato production accounted for more than 50 percent of employment and 40 percent of output in agribusiness in 2010.[2] Production peaked in 1990, accounting for 58 percent of manufacturing employment and 54 percent of manufacturing output. While the export shares are considerably lower at 3.6 percent of employment and 2.0 percent of output, the sector's contributions have been substantial.

## Cut Flowers, Ethiopia

The recent rise of Ethiopia's cut flower industry has been one of East Africa's spectacular successes. Within only 10 years, a single, initial Ethiopian rose farm had triggered the rapid emergence of a competitive rose export industry that now supports around 100 firms, employs more than 50,000 people, and has an export value of more than $200 million. Cut flowers account for an estimated 4 percent of manufacturing output in Ethiopia.

Launched in the early 1990s with only a few workers, the industry has expanded dramatically since 2005 (figure 6.1), aided by government support. While most exports go to the Amsterdam auction, the industry is exploring direct sales to Japan and the Russian Federation, in addition to the current focus on China, the Middle East, and the United States.

Ethiopia exports mainly agricultural products. Coffee is the highest export earner, followed by oilseeds and pulses, cut flowers, and other horticulture products such as green beans. Ethiopia's favorable climate, comparatively abundant land and labor, and reasonably good water resources have created ample opportunities for flower production.

However, the cut flower industry, struggling to carve out a market niche, faces growing challenges. The global financial crisis lowered demand and raised fuel costs. The demand for cut flowers has declined in countries in Western Europe, especially France, Germany, and the United Kingdom,

**Figure 6.1  Growth of Flower Exports, Ethiopia, 2005–12**

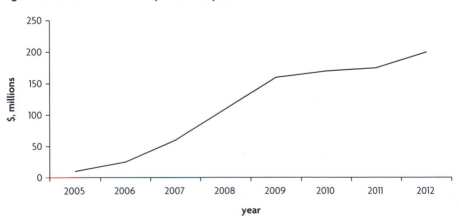

*Source:* Data of the Ethiopian Horticulture Development Agency.

in the wake of the crisis. More developing countries are also entering the market. Cut flowers are becoming important exports for many countries in eastern and southern Africa, such as Kenya, Uganda, Zambia, and Zimbabwe. The exportation of flowers to the Amsterdam auction— less advantageous than supplying distributors directly—is an opportunity available to other new suppliers as well, such as growers in Kenya. The Ethiopian industry is trying to penetrate higher-price markets, but promotional and representational costs are also higher in these markets.

Despite a favorable resource endowment and an abundance of cheap land, Ethiopia is at an early stage in the industry. Of the almost 100 flower producers in the country, more than half are non-Ethiopians; many are Netherlanders. Because of a shortage of skilled personnel, Ethiopian cut flower producers are using more expensive expatriate experts (mostly Indian and Kenyan), reducing their competitiveness. Finally, although it has good air transport capabilities, the Ethiopian industry has been held back by weak domestic infrastructure, including cold storage, transport facilities, and power supplies. Ethiopia currently ranks 121 among 144 countries in the competitiveness ranking of the World Economic Forum (Schwab 2012).

Despite these challenges, the industry continues to show resilience. Like the local climate, the macroeconomic regime has also been generally favorable to the industry. The exchange rate has been competitive, and the growth in gross domestic product (GDP) has been respectable, averaging more than 8 percent a year over the last decade. A series of good harvests and government-led investments to increase food security have accelerated rural growth and catalyzed the flower industry. Inflation has been contained so that it is not impeding growth. Wages have remained relatively low.[3]

## Origin and Course of Development

The idea of starting a rose farm came to Abdul Hamid Shamji—the father of Ryaz, a third-generation Ugandan of Indian origin and the owner of the first flower farm in Ethiopia—after a visit to Ethiopia in 1999 to scope out business opportunities. He considered banking and bottled water at first, but the highly favorable soil and climate conditions (the days are warm, and the nights are cold), the competitive cost of fuel and electricity, and, above all, the competitive airfreight costs—airfreight accounts for more than 50 percent of the export-related production costs of cut flowers—made rose farming an easy choice although Ethiopia had no flower industry to speak of at the time.

The son, Ryaz, launched a floriculture enterprise in Ethiopia and started production in 2000. He made a profit almost immediately. By 2002, after the success of Ryaz's farm had become evident, the prime minister agreed to support the sector, offering tax incentives and facilitating access to land, duty-free imports of inputs, and long-term financing. Investors started to pour in, and the government met its five-year target of developing 800 hectares of rose farms.

By 2008, Ryaz's enterprise was the only fair-trade rose farm in Ethiopia and one of only 19 in Africa. To ensure proximity to markets, Ryaz, like most other subsequent flower farmers, had located his flower farm, Golden Rose, a 22-hectare property in the Oromia region, within 100 kilometers of Addis Ababa Airport. (The flower farms are mainly concentrated in the highlands, at 1,550 to 2,600 meters above sea level.) Currently, a dedicated cargo plane flies out every night, carrying more than 150 tons of Ethiopia's flower production to overseas markets in Europe, the Middle East, and West Africa.

Ryaz's tale illustrates the highs and lows associated with the entry of enterprises into agribusiness or simple light manufacturing in Africa. At the outset, Ryaz's farm faced first-mover risks, but, over time, supportive government measures reduced the risks. The business grew steadily thanks to the government's high level of facilitation, the emergence of a cut flower cluster, and the consistent government policy reform in critical areas.

Ethiopia's cut flower industry is now mature. Most farms are small, at 2–30 hectares, though one company has developed 500 hectares to be leased by flower farms. Some farms have partnered with foreign investors, mainly among the Ethiopian diaspora. Ownership of the other flower companies is fairly evenly split between local and foreign firms.

## Competitiveness and Binding Constraints

Several constraints have impeded the industry's development, but none more than land. Indeed, the first big constraint Ryaz had to overcome was finding land. Because Ethiopia had no privately owned land and no land market, it took him more than a year to obtain 7 usable hectares. Finally, the national authorities intervened, offering Ryaz a 30-year lease (at favorable terms) on land that had been abandoned following a failed bean project by a nongovernmental organization. The success of the rose industry encouraged the private leasing of agricultural land. Traditional farmers traded their land to rose farmers for an initial down payment (with which they could buy livestock) and the promise of jobs for their families on the rose farms. Ryaz estimates that these trades doubled the average annual income of farmers to around $940 (at the current exchange rate). The government was soon earmarking land for investors in high-value agricultural products, offering long-term leases at low cost. Ensuring a reliable water supply was also a big concern (most water comes from underground wells). Ryaz investigated options with the help of an Israeli company specializing in farm irrigation systems.

The second serious constraint was financing. Private banks in Ethiopia were unwilling to lend to a new or otherwise unproven venture. The horticulture industry has little access to investment finance in physical capital and land for start-up or expansion. In the case of Ryaz, the government finally agreed to provide, through the state-owned Development Bank of Ethiopia, a loan of $1 million at 8 percent interest to finance 30 percent of the project, well below the market rate of 10–12 percent charged by commercial banks. Ryaz said that he could not have proceeded with the investment without the loan. The bank allowed the project's fixed assets to be used as collateral. Most firms continue to obtain investment capital from the Development Bank of Ethiopia, though some deal with other banks.

The emergence of a cut flower cluster made Ethiopian rose farming more competitive because the industry was able to negotiate airfreight collectively, lower the cost of chemical inputs through bulk imports, and jointly market products abroad through a trading company owned by the rose farms. The firms selected and imported their own technology. They overcame the lack of specialized managerial capability by bringing in professionals from India, Israel, Kenya, the Netherlands, and other countries. The government has also made some progress in supplying professionals through programs at Jimma University. The Netherlands is helping the Ethiopian Horticulture Producer-Exporters Association train experts locally using expatriate trainers.

Firms are facing challenges on the business and the marketing fronts. Rose farm owners are struggling to reduce their costs. Because electricity is unreliable, Ryaz has to pay $36,000 a year to run his own generator. Unraveling red tape takes up the time of the equivalent of one and a half qualified staff ($20,000 a year), and delays at customs in importing chemical inputs reduce the number of crops that can be produced each year ($200,000). Together, these extra costs account for more than 20 percent of Ryaz's turnover, the difference between making and losing money.

Like others in the business, Ryaz is now looking to diversify into fruits and vegetables, but he lacks the time and resources to investigate this option. Though floriculturists see great potential for the industry, no one knows which fruits are the smart investments for the region: peaches, apples, or something else. Even the green beans that failed earlier feasibility tests are now coming back. A feasibility report could cost well over $80,000 per fruit, and several may be needed. Despite many eager incumbents and many more potential entrants, even Ethiopia's pioneer rose farmer is unwilling to bear the first-mover risks.

The total cost of worker skills has remained competitive. Unskilled workers cost $35–$50 a month, while semiskilled workers command around $100 a month. Professionals cost much more, about $500–$800. However, as more businesses open near Addis Ababa, it is becoming more difficult to find good-quality workers. This may become a serious challenge going forward if workers have to be brought in from more distant regions.

For now, though, Ethiopia retains its labor cost advantage, and overall costs remain low thanks to the cheap land and capital and thanks to the relative efficiency of trade logistics, including the duty-free import of inputs and other materials. Moreover, unlike farms in other countries, Ethiopian farms have no cooling and heating costs because of the good weather conditions.

Ethiopia has done well in input provision for this industry. To meet the latest global demand for taste, color, and other qualities, local producers have to buy seeds from foreign breeders who follow market trends and charge royalties for the use of their seeds. Farms cannot produce flowers using their own seeds because there is no market for flowers produced from local seeds. To meet logistics and supply services, cut flower firms have established the Horti-Share Company, while packaging materials, such as boxes and wrapping paper, are generally produced locally.

The industry has a well-developed supply chain. There are multiple direct flights to Amsterdam daily. The time between cutting and arrival at the Amsterdam auction is about 20 hours, including 8 hours in the air. Firms send full cargo loads when the orders have been secured. Almost all exports are carried by state-owned Ethiopian Airlines, which has rapidly expanded its cargo capacity: one ad hoc Boeing 777 has been delivered, and more are expected soon, as exports are expected to exceed more than $500 million within a few years.

Individual farms typically have their own cold chain cooling facilities. Bole International Airport—the exit point for all exports—also maintains cold storage facilities, which are open 24 hours a day and are serviced by operators, loaders, palletizer operators, and other personnel. Refrigerated trucks owned by the flower farms and other service providers deliver flowers to the airport. Flowers need to be loaded onto aircraft within a few hours of arriving at the airport. Ethiopia Perishable Logistics provides many of these services, and another logistics company is coming soon. Ethiopian Airlines has its own cooling facility at the airport, and it is expanding this capacity as part of the cargo terminal. Exporters pay the freight costs. The Export Board, chaired by the prime minister, watches these rates closely; no increases are allowed without the board's approval.

The industry has created a level playing field in production, marketing, and transport for firms of all sizes. All local firms are certified by GlobalGAP and other certifying agencies, according to buyer requirements, and are expected to follow the horticulture association's code of conduct, which is based on international best practice. Because of market demand, almost all firms are using hydroponic technology for growing plants without soil. There are still some differences, however, including in the ability to regulate greenhouse temperatures and in the quality of some inputs, such as fertilizers and chemicals.

## The Role of Government

The government has helped the cut flower industry emerge in several ways. It has provided land and eliminated many bureaucratic impediments to starting a flower business. It offered Ryaz a loan to supplement his equity investment. It created a welcoming environment for foreign direct investment (FDI). A foreign investor can invest alone or jointly with domestic investors. To start a business, a sole foreign investor needs to bring to the table a minimum of $100,000 in cash or in kind, while a foreign investor who teams up with a domestic investor needs to invest a minimum of $60,000. The investment law guarantees capital repatriation and the remittance of dividends.

The government has provided institutional support by establishing trade associations, such as the Ethiopian Horticulture Development Agency, which oversees the sector and provides facilitation services to individual firms, including skill development and marketing support. Ethiopia has about 110 horticulture firms, 95 of which are members of the Ethiopian Horticulture Producer-Exporters Association. The industry relies on the association to lobby the government and speak on behalf of members. Small-scale firms have organized to strengthen their position by, for example, financing investments or negotiating with the government. The association conducts two large flower fairs in Addis Ababa every year, inviting buyers and supply chain firms. The association also arranges participation in international trade fairs for its members.

The government has offered a generous incentives package to investors, including access to low-cost land and to credit (up to 70 percent of the total capital needs) at below market rates of 7 percent, with a three-year grace period and 10 years for repayment. A three-year loss carryforward privilege is also offered, though it might not be necessary because most cut flower start-ups turn a profit from the beginning. Inputs, including packaging materials, are imported duty-free. The government also facilitates customs clearance and transport services.

## Summary

Ethiopia's thriving cut flower industry shows how ambitious entrepreneurs, foreign investors, and a responsive government can come together to overcome constraints in land and financing and create a dynamic niche in an industry in which a country has a potential comparative advantage.

## Cut Flowers, Kenya

One of the great recent success stories in Africa has been the dramatic growth of the Kenyan cut flower industry. A rising economic power in Africa, Kenya is strategically located on the eastern coast of the continent, giving it ready access to international trade through the port of Mombasa. Horticulture is now the third-largest foreign exchange earner after tourism and tea and is one of the economy's most rapidly expanding industries, with average annual growth of almost 20 percent over the last two decades. The global flower market is valued at $40 billion and supplied by 80 countries. Kenya's success owes much to its ability to provide high-quality products using a skilled labor force backed by daily airfreight departures to key destinations, particularly in Europe. Moreover, Kenya's climate favors the year-round cultivation and export of high-quality flowers.

Now the world's fifth-largest flower exporter, Kenya exports 30 percent of its flowers to the United Kingdom and supplies 38 percent of all cut flowers sold in the European Union (EU). By 2010, it was exporting $400 million in flowers to European markets. Cut flower exports expanded rapidly, from about 100,000 tons to nearly 1 million tons, in only two decades (figure 6.2).

The Kenyan cut flower industry is a tale of cooperation between foreign and domestic entrepreneurship and the command of input industries and trade logistics. Multinationals supply the capital and facilitate the transport corridors, and local producers provide the labor

**Figure 6.2  Cut Flower Exports, Kenya, 1990–2010**

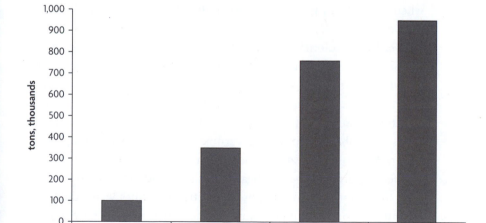

*Source:* Data of the government of Kenya.

and the products. Flowers are shipped from local farm to foreign auction within 72 hours, reflecting the effectiveness of the supply chain.

The Kenyan cut flower industry is large and versatile, though a small number of firms are dominant. There are an estimated 5,000 flower farms. However, about 40 large and medium growers account for 75 percent of the total production on plots of 20–100 hectares, and 4,000–5,000 smaller growers serve 5–13 percent of the market. The three largest growers are Oserian Development Company, Finlay's, and Homegrown, which, together, control 40 percent of the country's flower exports. Most of the large companies are owned by foreigners or Kenyans of foreign descent. While there is considerable geographic dispersion, most of the 5,000 growers are concentrated around Lake Naivasha, northwest of Nairobi. The industry employs some 100,000 people, mainly young women; about 2 million people depend indirectly on the flower industry for their livelihoods.

## Origin and Course of Development

Kenya's economy grew at an average annual rate of 3.7 percent over 2000–10 and has expanded at a 2.7 percent rate since the 1990s. Although inflation averaged in the single digits in 2000–10, Kenya has recently experienced high inflation and strong exchange rate pressures. Following a peak in 1993, the average inflation was moderate until 2011, when it rose to 14 percent and began threatening the country's growth outlook (figure 6.3).

Even in the colonial era, exports of fresh horticultural produce were important for the government budget. After the country's independence in 1963, the industry continued to flourish, and exporters started to target Europe. The industry expanded and experienced considerable structural transformation. Flower production was launched in the 1980s with subsidies from the government of the Netherlands to finance commercial rose cultivation. There is no evidence that the Kenyan government prioritized the sector at that time or provided support. Later, once the sector was thriving, fiscal and trade regimes were adjusted to favor the sector, and support was provided through skills development. Initially, the industry relied on low-value production, but, in the 1990s, production shifted to high-value flowers and greenhouse cultivation, which offered greater export potential (Hornberger and others 2007).

**Figure 6.3 Average Inflation, Kenya, 1995–2011**

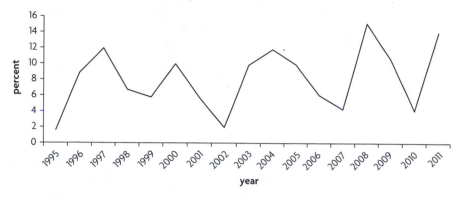

Source: International Financial Statistics (database), International Monetary Fund, Washington, DC, http://elibrary-data
.imf.org/FindDataReports.aspx?d=33061&e=169393.

The door was kept open for foreign investment, a key factor in the sector's success. Benefiting from a surge in foreign investment in the 1990s and the first decade of the 2000s that brought in needed financing and entrepreneurial skills, production increased, supported by private investment from Israel, the Netherlands, and the United Kingdom. The EU and the International Finance Corporation, together with the government of the Netherlands, followed up by supporting infrastructure development and providing additional subsidies to the private sector. This flow of funds helped upgrade skills, technology, and marketing expertise, and the industry emerged as a world-class producer.

## Competitiveness and Binding Constraints

The Kenyan model demonstrates the importance of an effective supply chain. Farmers can breed seeds themselves or purchase them from seed companies, including local firms (Kenya Seed Company, East African Seed Company) and locally based international firms (Pioneer Hi-Bred, Monsanto). The purchasing is normally based on franchise or license agreements to ensure tested, high-quality seeds. It is not clear why the Ethiopians do not procure their own seeds in the same way the Kenyans have done (see the case study on Ethiopia above). Local suppliers provide inputs for the preharvest supply chain, such as breeding seed, greenhouse and shading structures, irrigation and precooling, and herbicides and pesticides. Local suppliers also nourish the postharvest supply chain, including packaging and labeling materials and cooling technology.

Marketing and freight costs are distributed among growers. Most flower growers export through the same distribution channels as fruit and vegetable growers. New flower buyers are emerging in China and Japan, and auction houses have been established in India (Mumbai) and the Middle East (Dubai). Direct flights are also planned for Japan and the United States. All this market expansion ensures that Kenyan exporters will continue to perform well.

The Kenyan flower industry benefits from a variety of sophisticated investments along the supply chain that simplify trade logistics. Large-scale farmers have invested in a sophisticated postharvest cold chain infrastructure. From cutting to market takes about 72 hours. Flowers are delivered to the airport in refrigerated trucks about four hours before departure. Nearly all (90 percent) of Kenya's flowers are handled by airfreight forwarders, three of which are linked to the top flower producers. Because transport costs are important elements of total cost, tight control and efficiency in the supply chain are key for ensuring industry competitiveness.

The economics of the industry have been quite profitable, with low labor costs and sufficient access to finance for the largest firms. The favorable climate along the equator (22°C–30°C during the day and 6°C–12°C at night) allows year-round production. The cost breakdown for a large farm (10 hectares) comes to 45 percent for production, 4 percent for postharvesting, 25 percent for transport and marketing, and 26 percent gross margin. For medium farms, the costs are 25 percent for production, 4 percent for postharvesting, 61 percent for transport and marketing, and 10 percent gross margin (figure 6.4). Labor costs are low for large and medium farms.

Financing is provided by banks and development finance institutions. Kenyan exporters use letter-of-credit services on the domestic finance market, which includes major banks such as Barclays, Citibank, Commercial Bank of Africa, and Standard Chartered Bank. Small-scale growers struggle with finance, however.

Kenyan flowers are sold in auction markets, which allow for speedy marketing and sale. There are four categories of buyers: auction houses, supermarkets, wholesalers, and florists. Most sales are arranged through

**Figure 6.4 Cut Flower Production Costs, by Size of Farm, Kenya, 2010**

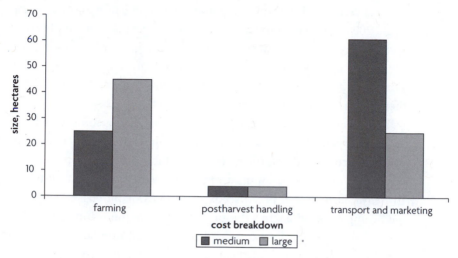

Source: Data of the Kenya Horticulture Crops Development Authority.

auctions in the Netherlands, where Kenyan flowers are lumped with Netherland flowers and labeled as Netherland flowers. Auctions are the cheapest method; however, growers must still pay auction costs. Small-scale growers prefer selling through auctions, where they can sell to wholesalers and retailers. Retailers and supermarkets, such as Marks & Spencer, Omniflora, Sainsbury's, and Tesco, have traditionally preferred to buy through auctions because of the bulk supply. However, supermarkets are shifting to direct sources through vertically integrated suppliers, putting the survival of small-scale growers at risk. The largest growers prefer to brand their flowers and market them directly to supermarkets. Wholesalers purchase flowers for import or export, and other firms reexport after value addition.

Size is a significant determinant of success. Large-scale growers are vertically integrated and take advantage of economies of scale to master trade logistics and become drivers of the industry. The high capital- and knowledge-intensive nature of the flower industry and the strict market regulatory requirements give the larger growers a clear advantage over small-scale growers. The typical capital investment in flower production is about $50,000 per hectare, besides a vigorous marketing network. These requirements confine most small-scale growers to summer flowers that can be grown outdoors and do not require a heavy investment in greenhouses and other sophisticated technologies (Bolo 2006). The larger growers invest in the postharvest supply chain, including refrigerated transport trucks. Most growers use only a few specialized airfreight forwarders and are able to negotiate cargo rates. The small growers also use these freight forwarders by consolidating their flowers with other commercial products.

Kenya's cut flower industry presents an interesting comparison with the industry in Ethiopia. While the two countries are similar in terms of the structure of the industry, there are a few differences. First, Kenya has higher-quality seed inputs and product variety relative to Ethiopia. In Kenya, farmers can breed seeds themselves or purchase them from seed companies, while, in Ethiopia, most of the innovation in seeds is generated by foreign investors, and only a small number of firms sell directly to wholesalers and the supermarket channel. Second, there is better access to capital among small-scale farmers in Kenya relative to Ethiopia. However, an important factor that is starting to favor Ethiopia over Kenya is the latter's higher labor and transport costs. On the whole, both countries have performed well in recent years despite unstable global market conditions.

## The Role of Government

The Kenyan government has sought to facilitate the cut flower industry rather than directly intervene. A supportive trade and fiscal regime has alleviated some of the financing constraints of firms and has eased licensing and other regulatory constraints with the aim of allowing the private sector to flourish. Firms in the export processing zone receive a 10-year tax holiday on domestic taxes and on withholding taxes on repatriated dividends, plus exemption from the value added tax. The government also allows cut flower exporters to import plants, machinery, equipment, and raw materials free of tax. Investors are able to obtain allowances on capital investments, including wear-and-tear allowances on items such as vans, tractors, other motor vehicles, aircraft, computer hardware, copiers, and plant machinery; industrial building allowances cover all industrial buildings; and farm work allowances cover all structures necessary for a farm to function properly. The new Investment Promotion Act requires a minimum foreign investment threshold of $500,000, thus favoring larger companies. Imported packing materials are still subject to protectionist tariffs.

Kenyan exporters have gained from a favorable exchange rate. The beneficial euro-to-shilling exchange rate means that exporters get more money in shillings for their flowers, which are paid in euros, even if the earnings are converted into dollars.

Kenya has received preferential access to the EU market under the Cotonou Partnership Agreement and to the U.S. market under the African Growth and Opportunity Act (AGOA).[4] Kenya's preferential duty-free access under the Cotonou Agreement expired in 2008, after which Kenyan producers were subject to a 5 percent tariff. Floriculture competitors Colombia, Ecuador, Ethiopia, and Zambia are exempt from the tariffs, giving them an advantage for exports to the EU (PwC 2006). In August 2010, the Kenya Flower Council proposed amending the agreement to secure preferential market access. The proposal to include all agricultural products in the list of products exported to the United States free of duties and quotas under AGOA is currently under discussion in the U.S. Congress. Preferential access under AGOA has helped Kenya's flower exports to the United States, which grew from $700,000 before AGOA to $1.7 million as of June 2010.

The Kenyan government has provided strong institutional support for the cut flower industry by helping to foster skills development. The main horticulture regulatory body, the Horticulture Crops Development Authority, a government entity established in 1966 under the Agriculture Act, is responsible for promoting horticultural crops, licensing exporters, enforcing ethical standards, and disseminating information on horticultural marketing. The authority is run by a board of directors drawn from the public and private sectors. Its main revenue comes from levies and fees charged on produce. The Kenya Flower Council, a voluntary association formed in 1996, represents independent Kenyan cut flower and ornamental plant growers and exporters and provides advisory services. It has a membership of 45 independent growers and exporters that account for around 70 percent of Kenya's cut flower exports. The council bestows three levels of certification (silver, gold, and platinum), which are benchmarked to European standards. It is involved in issues such as industry lobbying, worker safety, environmental protection, and industrial regulation and development.

## Summary

The Kenyan cut flower industry emerged through an alliance between FDI and local entrepreneurs and reflects a strong supply chain. As one of the world's biggest horticultural exporters, Kenya has demonstrated that African agribusinesses can penetrate export markets if they are supported by an appropriate policy regime and the appropriate caliber of foreign investment. Challenges remain, however, including high freight costs and high input prices, especially for fertilizer, seed, and pesticides.

## Tomatoes, Senegal

Senegal is in the vanguard of agricultural diversification in West Africa. A country of 12.8 million people on the Atlantic coast, with a good general business environment, it has seen strong economic growth since the mid-1990s. Its economy is based largely on agriculture, fish processing, and mining. Local authorities have tried to reduce the dependence on groundnut exports, long the export mainstay, because output has dropped 60 percent over the past 20 years and, with it, exports and foreign exchange revenue (Hazard, Barry, and Anouan 2006). Meanwhile, exports of fruits and vegetables have grown steadily, with a focus on exports for the European market for cherry tomatoes, green beans, mangos, and melons. Senegal is also the only francophone Sub-Saharan African country that has created a local tomato processing industry. More than 70 percent of Senegal's workers are active in agriculture. The potential employment effects of expanding horticulture are therefore considerable. Senegal has combined foreign investment, which has provided capital, skills, and mastery of trade logistics, with semiskilled local workers, a favorable climate, and good growing conditions.

Tomato cultivation was introduced into Senegal in the 1970s. Originally, tomatoes were sold to state-owned tomato paste factories. Production took off in the 1990s and soon became the most well paying activity among rural households. Production surged even more in the first decade of the 2000s.[5] By 2009, Senegal was exporting more than 9,000 tons of fresh tomatoes to the EU (the tomato imports of which totaled 500,000 tons). A key focus was on the Benelux countries and

France. Senegal is the world's second-largest exporter of cherry tomatoes after Israel, and its good-quality cherry tomato exports are highly sought in Europe. Between 1995 and 2010, the fruit and vegetable exports of Senegal to Europe quintupled, reaching 35,000 tons. The cherry tomato and mango exports to Europe accounted for only 2–3 percent of European domestic production.[6] There is thus ample room for expansion. The Senegal River Valley offers huge potential for growing industrial tomatoes.

Because of its significant growth and good export potential, Senegalese horticulture has attracted vital flows of FDI. Since the devaluation of the CFA franc in 1994, when many traditional sectors were struggling, including groundnuts and fisheries, horticulture has done quite well. Groupe Compagnie Fruitière, a French horticultural import company, for example, invested more than $10 million over 2003–09, and its subsidiary, Grands Domaines du Sénégal (GDS), has been increasing its production and export capacity in cherry tomatoes for the European market.

## Origin and Course of Development

Under a new vision for economic growth in the early 1970s, the government promoted phosphate production, tourism, and horticulture, especially tomato farming and processing. Thanks to collaboration among the government, foreign scientists, and local farmers, Senegal became the world's 23rd-largest tomato processor. Scientific experiments in tomato production and processing that relied on contract farming were conducted throughout the country in the 1970s. Small horticultural growers thus became part of the export value chain.

By welcoming foreign investment, horticultural firms avoided several constraints, including the lack of skilled workers, technical expertise, and finance. By the early years of the first decade of the 2000s, the local industry was attracting the interest of the France-based multinational company GDS, which led efforts to increase exports to Europe (figure 6.5). GDS supplied technical knowledge and managerial skill, thus making up for some of the domestic shortcomings. By around 2010, GDS was handling virtually all (99 percent) tomato exports from Senegal in a seamless system of input provision, downstream trading, transport, and distribution.

**Figure 6.5' Horticulture Exports to the EU, Senegal, 1990–2010**

Source: Data of the Ministry of Economy and Finance, Senegal.

Groupe Compagnie Fruitière's objective is to raise the production of fruit and vegetables for export to European markets during the European off-season. Its projects typically run in four phases: production in GDS greenhouses, on-site refrigeration and packaging, shipping to Europe in refrigerated containers by a subsidiary, and marketing in London or Paris by two subsidiaries. Groupe Compagnie Fruitière chose Senegal as a production site because the country is located on maritime lines that the group manages and because there were similar projects on the other bank of the Senegal River, in Mauritania. Thanks to this partnership with GDS, which has its own freighters, Senegal now enjoys a rapid sea link to the EU that is competitive with air transport. As a result, a sectoral cluster sprang up around GDS.

At the same time, the structure of the industry was changing. GDS and other major operators were investing in a fully independent farming system. There was a shift from small-scale outgrowers because of concerns over the need for product traceability, food safety, and hygiene (which are important in the export value chain) and the legal and market requirements in the countries of the Organisation for Economic Co-operation and Development. The new structure is based on vertical integration across the subsidiaries of multinational companies. Today, seven large-scale private operators account for 75 percent of Senegal's horticulture exports.

GDS has simplified the trade logistics for Senegal's tomato producers through a stable, low-cost marketing and distribution channel. GDS ensures that the in-house handling of all links results in a smooth, strong supply chain. Producing fresh fruits and vegetables from December through March enables Senegal to remain a low-cost producer and compete with Morocco and other exporters. Grown in fertile river deltas in Senegal, the tomatoes are refrigerated on site and then graded, packed, and shipped to Europe in refrigerated containers. The tomatoes are sold in 2.5-kilogram plastic containers. The basic cost structure is low: salaries are about $5 a day; transport costs are $2 per kilogram; and sea transport costs are $0.40 per kilogram. The transport costs are lower and the returns are more than 30 percent higher for cherry tomatoes than for regular tomatoes.

## Competitiveness and Binding Constraints

The key constraint on agroprocessing in Senegal has been in trade logistics, which foreign investment has helped improve. The supply chain for Senegal's tomato exports is based on the vertical integration of GDS, which lowers costs and simplifies the trade logistics (Maertens, Colen, and Swinnen 2009). GDS has invested in irrigation and high-technology production techniques, together with improved seeds, fertilizers, and phytosanitary measures, all imported from the EU. Stringent EU quality and food safety requirements have been important factors motivating the company to set up its own integrated agroindustrial production system. However, this tomato supply chain excludes smallholder producers.

Senegal is an ideal producer of tomatoes because of its access to arable land and large potential for irrigation along the Senegal and Niger rivers. Moreover, Senegal enjoys exceptional sunlight during winter, with temperatures at around 25°C–30°C during the day and 17°C–22°C at night, a good climate for cultivation. Senegal also benefits from proximity to export markets in Europe and the United States by sea and air.

Senegal has a tradition of dynamic farmers who respond well to incentives to innovate and expand production. Through the spread of vertically integrated farms, Senegal has shifted from contract farming based on smallholders to larger-scale production on agroindustrial farms to adapt to EU sanitary and phytosanitary standards. As contract farming has declined (more than 20 percent in the last five years), employment on estate farms has risen. Many Senegalese workers have moved to these industrial farms because of the better wages and working conditions. In 2006, GDS recruited more than 3,000 workers from nearby villages for its fields and its processing centers. About 80 percent are temporary seasonal workers or day laborers. This step boosted employment in the adjacent rural areas in jobs paying more than the national average. Thus, despite the vertical integration of the supply chain and the exclusion of smallholder farms from tomato production for export, tomato exports have had positive employment effects. Wages stagnated among workers who did not join the agroprocessing effort. Producers who exported their output could sometimes earn twice what they would receive in local markets. Given the intensity of land use and the semiskilled labor in this sector, coupled with the longer growing season, Senegal used this production structure to capture a larger share of world trade.

Access to finance has been another benefit of foreign investment. Physical capital was made available through GDS stock because small domestic tomato producers had rarely been able to obtain bank loans. The spread of agroindustrial farming was also facilitated by the government's allocation of previously uncultivated land to small farms. The government assigned GDS an additional 400 hectares of land in the Senegal River Delta region to expand production and exports.

## The Role of Government

Macroeconomic reforms over the last two decades have provided a boost to the horticulture industry. After years of GDP contraction in the late 1980s and early 1990s, the large devaluation of the CFA franc in 1994 stimulated real GDP growth, which averaged 5 percent a year over 1995–2010; inflation dropped to single digits. Reforms were introduced to liberalize the economy, remove trade and investment barriers, attract FDI, and promote regional integration. These all created a more open policy regime for the horticulture industry.

Senegal's macroeconomic stability supported export competitiveness and reduced the costs of trade logistics. The country's political, macroeconomic, and fiscal stability; reasonably good infrastructure; and well-educated elite have created a favorable climate for FDI. The Investment Promotion and Major Projects Agency of Senegal helped address issues ranging from gaining access to more land to reducing red tape. The government established an investment code that guarantees approval of any project, regardless of size, that meets established criteria. As part of a reform agenda to improve the country's business environment, the Ministry of Trade introduced an electronic one-stop trade facilitation system. Launched in 2004, the system has streamlined customs clearance to allow transparent electronic transactions initiated by a single request from an importer or exporter. Although the government has not provided facilities for industrial development zones or parks, it has met the needs of foreign investors in other ways.

As part of a national initiative to raise food production in a country on the southwestern end of Africa's arid Sahel, the policy regime for horticulture firms has been supportive, reducing financing constraints. Multiple incentives make horticultural exports remunerative. For example, agricultural companies that export at least 80 percent of their output are exempted from income taxes on distributed dividends, customs and stamp duties for production and transport equipment, and wage and business license taxes. The corporate tax rate is only 15 percent. Every investor in the agricultural sector is exempted from the value added tax and customs duties. In 2008, the government announced a program to increase agricultural production that included a five-year suspension of foreign exchange controls for agricultural investors, allowing these investors to expatriate their profits freely. Preferential deals have helped Senegal export its products in European markets. AGOA has encouraged Senegal's horticultural sector to break into the U.S. market. To benefit from all these opportunities, Senegal needs to address phytosanitary concerns and improve its packing, distribution, and transportation capabilities.

## Summary

Senegal's experience with horticulture exports shows that a skillful combination of good climate, FDI, a supportive policy regime, semi-skilled workers, and land can foster a sustainable export industry. Senegal has been a pioneer among Sub-Saharan African countries in successfully initiating programs that have diversified agricultural products and reduced the country's dependence on the export of groundnuts. The experience with cherry tomatoes demonstrates that agribusiness is potentially a lucrative industry in Sub-Saharan Africa, provided the conditions in the field are favorable. First, the Investment Promotion and Major Projects Agency, together with a range of other bodies, has provided appropriate investment and fiscal incentives to attract businesses to relocate to Senegal. Second, the supportive policy regime has welcomed foreign investment and helped Senegal overcome important constraints to firm expansion. FDI has brought in skilled workers to provide technical expertise and financing support to alleviate local credit constraints. Third, Senegal has shown that foreign investment can help lower trade logistics costs by building the supply chain and ensuring compliance with international standards. The use of refrigerated containers and freighters by Groupe Compagnie Fruitière has provided Senegalese agribusinesses with quick access to European markets. In sum, Senegal's booming horticulture industry can be a model for other African economies.

## Notes

1. For relevant data on the cases of Ethiopia, Kenya, and Senegal, see Statistical Databases, United Nations Industrial Development Organization, Vienna, http://www.unido.org/resources/statistics/statistical-databases.html.
2. Besides tomatoes, these data include food products and beverages at International Standard Industrial Classification 15.
3. See World Development Indicators (database), World Bank, Washington, DC, http://data.worldbank.org/data-catalog/world-development-indicators.
4. Signed in May 2000, AGOA provides reforming African countries with the most liberal access to the U.S. market available to any country or region with which the United States does not have a free trade agreement.
5. The government estimates that Senegal was producing about 73,000 tons of tomato concentrate by 1990 and was a significant exporter to its African neighbors already in the 1990s.
6. FAOSTAT (FAO Statistical Database), Statistics Division, Food and Agriculture Organization of the United Nations, Rome, http://faostat.fao.org/.

## References

Bolo, Maurice. 2006. "Knowledge, Technology and Growth: The Case Study of Lake Naivasha Cut Flower Cluster in Kenya." WBI Africa Cluster Case Study (April), Knowledge for Development Program, World Bank Institute, Washington, DC.

Dinh, Hinh T., Vincent Palmade, Vandana Chandra, and Frances Cossar. 2012. *Light Manufacturing in Africa: Targeted Policies to Enhance Private Investment and Create Jobs.* Washington, DC: World Bank. http://go.worldbank.org/ASG0J44350.

Hazard, Eric, Mamadou Alimou Barry, and Alexis Aka Anouan. 2006. "Aid for Trade and Agro-Based Private Sector Development in Africa: Senegal

Country Case Study." OECD Development Centre, Organisation for Economic Co-operation and Development, Paris. http://www.oecd.org/trade/aft/37587061.pdf.

Hornberger, Kusi, Nick Ndiritu, Lalo Ponce-Brito, Melesse Tashu, and Tijan Watt. 2007. "Kenya's Cut-Flower Cluster." May 4, Microeconomics of Competitiveness Series, Institute for Strategy and Competitiveness, Harvard Business School, Harvard University, Cambridge, MA.

Maertens, Miet, Liesbeth Colen, and Johan F. M. Swinnen. 2009. "Globalization and Poverty in Senegal: A Worst Case Scenario?" Paper presented at the International Association of Agricultural Economists Conference, Beijing, August 16–22.

PwC (PricewaterhouseCoopers). 2006. "Sustainability Impact Assessment (SIA) of the EU-ACP Economic Partnership Agreements, Phase Three: Horticulture in Eastern and Southern Africa (ESA); Final Report." September 11, PwC, Neuilly-sur-Seine, France.

Schwab, Klaus, ed. 2012. *The Global Competitiveness Report 2012–2013: Full Data Edition.* Insight Report. Geneva: World Economic Forum.

# 7

# Wood Products

## Introduction

The two case studies covered in this chapter—one in Ghana and one in Vietnam—deal with wood products. The furniture sector in Ghana has been struggling, despite the country's comparative advantage in wood production. Meanwhile, the sector in Vietnam has been booming. The main difference appears to arise from three factors. First, Vietnam has been much more successful than Ghana at courting foreign direct investment (FDI). While the policy regimes for furniture exporters in the two countries have not been strikingly different, Vietnam has received substantial amounts of FDI, which has allowed the industry to benefit from the knowledge and managerial expertise of firms, along with finance, which has helped improve the quality of the furniture dramatically. In contrast, Ghana's furniture industry has been operated mostly by domestic producers and has not been supported by foreign knowledge or technology, resulting in mediocre quality.

Second, Vietnam has managed to develop a strong supply chain and procure good-quality wood imports from many countries. Ghanaian companies have secured mostly low-quality wood: most of Ghana's higher-quality wood is exported in raw form.

Third, the financing cost of the Vietnamese furniture industry appears to be lower; commercial banks there are lending to some furniture export companies at interest rates of 12.0–12.5 percent a year (mid-2010), while, in Ghana, the costs of financing are more than 17 percent, and loans are only short term. Thus, the two countries have not had the same track record in furniture exports.

## Bonsu Furniture Works, Accra, Ghana

There are mushrooming workshops and furniture centers springing up on a daily basis. It is like everyone is operating on his own, God for us all.

—*Ghanaian furniture entrepreneur*

Ghana has been one of Africa's best performing economies in recent years, but economic diversification is still elusive. During the 1990s and early in the first decade of the 2000s, real growth in gross domestic product (GDP) averaged more than 5 percent annually, and poverty declined. GDP growth could accelerate to more than 8 percent in coming years if recent oil discoveries pan out. Agriculture still accounts for about a third of GDP, and growth in nontraditional exports has been slow.

The government has singled out furniture and wood processing as a promising route to industrialization and diversification. So far, however, Ghana has been unable to build a dynamic furniture sector, despite its positive performance history. This slow progress is perplexing, given the country's strong comparative advantage in timber production: Ghana's wood industry accounts for 10 percent of export earnings. The economy's growth in recent decades has given impetus to small furniture manufacturers, but this dynamism has not translated into a vibrant furniture industry. The sector is dominated by dozens of small companies that produce well-crafted and well-designed home and office furniture for a growing number of middle-class consumers and small businesses, but these companies have been unable to crack the international export market.

The chief constraints are a weak supply chain, difficult access to financing, and the lack of a government policy vision.

Most of Ghana's timber is exported as unprocessed logs, and the timber available domestically is expensive. Transport and energy costs are high, and local small and medium producers, without the availability of economies of scale, have been undersold by cheaper Asian imports; sales have declined drastically in recent years. Imports account for 78 percent of furniture sales in Ghana (AGI 2012). Most firms are not equipped with the machinery or skilled staff needed to produce furniture of the design and quality demanded by international markets. Lack of capital and the high costs of opening and maintaining a business are additional impediments.

Ghana's exports have grown slowly. The value of exports increased from about $821 million in 1980–84 to about $2.5 billion in 2000–04, reflecting mainly more exports of the same products, rather than diversification (Chandra 2006). Nontraditional exports stagnated at around $850,000 over 1993–2004. Today, nontraditional exports make up less than a third of total exports, and the share of nontraditional industries such as furniture and horticultural products is below 2 percent.

Nonetheless, Ghana has a strong comparative advantage in furniture production. It has ample timber. Some 66 percent of its land is covered by savannahs and savannah woodlands. Its 216 forest reserves cover 17,000 square kilometers; 71 percent are productive forests managed for the sustainable production of wood. Wood is Ghana's third-largest commodity export: totals were at more than $200 million in 2010. Nigeria is the largest market; other large markets are France, Germany, Italy, the United Kingdom, and the United States.

Until recently, a combination of high inflation and high real interest rates hurt the furniture sector, slowing growth by boosting production costs. High inflation in the 1990s gradually subsided in 2000–10, reaching 8.6 percent in 2010. The government competes with the private sector in the financial market, keeping interest rates high and discouraging private sector borrowing. Interest rates peaked at 45 percent in 1996 and then fell steadily to 13.5 percent in 2010, though the rate in the furniture sector was higher, at 13–28 percent.[1] The real effective exchange rate of the Ghanian cedi fluctuated widely from 1990 to 2000 (figure 7.1). Over the years, Ghana has had a history of exchange rate issues, with a chronic overvaluation of the cedi (and a thriving black market), creating significant pressure on labor-intensive manufacturing to maintain competitiveness in the international market. However, in

**Figure 7.1  Index of the Real Effective Exchange Rate, Ghana, 1990–2011**

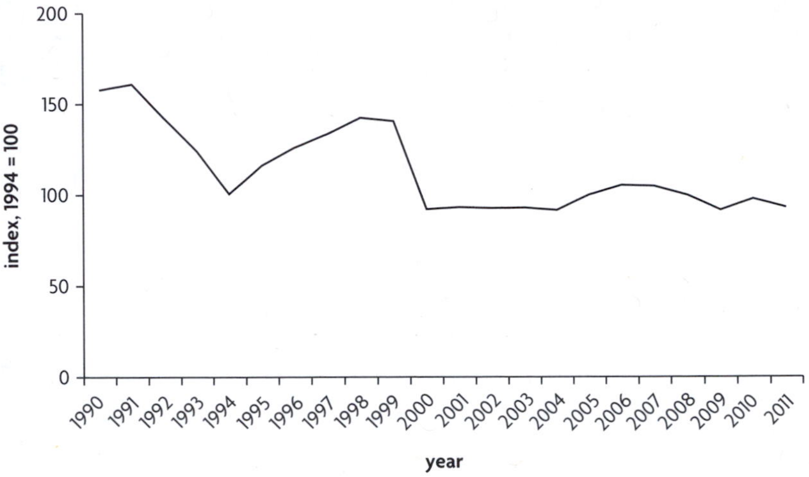

*Source:* Data of International Financial Statistics (database), International Monetary Fund, Washington, DC, http://elibrary-data.imf.org/FindDataReports.aspx?d=33061&e=169393.
*Note:* The rate is based on the consumer price index.

the wake of major macroeconomic reforms in the last decade, the currency has regained some competitiveness.

## Origin and Course of Development

One of the early movers in the furniture industry was Bonsu Furniture Works. Founded in 2004 by an entrepreneur with a high school education, prior experience in the construction industry, and savings of ¢100,000 ($50,000), the company has become Ghana's third-largest furniture maker. Interviews with the owner and managing director in October 2012 confirmed that the company had expanded from 6 employees in 2004 to 68 in 2012, with a capitalization of almost ¢1 million ($500,000). Much of the capital is being used to buy land and build showrooms. Like other top furniture companies in Ghana, Bonsu has had almost no exposure to FDI and little support from the government or industry associations. Most of its output is sold domestically; exports go mainly to regional markets, especially Benin and Côte d'Ivoire.

Ghana is known for its rich supply of durable, top-quality timber used in making furniture, handicrafts, and toys. Companies that have integrated wood processing with logging activities account for about

**Figure 7.2 Inflows of FDI, by Sector, Ghana, 2011**

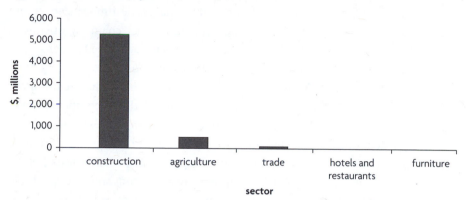

*Source:* Data of UN Comtrade (United Nations Commodity Trade Statistics Database), Statistics Division, Department of Economic and Social Affairs, United Nations, New York, http://comtrade.un.org/db/.
*Note:* FDI = foreign direct investment.

95 percent of the logs harvested in Ghana. Three types of operations make up the local timber industry: logging, the bulk of the country's industry, represents about 250 firms; secondary processing (saw, ply, and veneer milling) accounts for about 130 firms; and tertiary operations (such as furniture parts, moldings, and flooring) take up about 65 firms (10 medium firms and the rest with fewer than 50 workers each).

There is enormous growth potential in the downstream processing of timber, especially for furniture. A succession of government administrations have identified wood processing as an activity in which Ghana has a comparative advantage. Yet, as the wood industry cluster has evolved, small and medium firms have not scaled up. The furniture industry has attracted little FDI (figure 7.2). Experience in other countries, such as China, shows that expansion requires access to the financing, technical and managerial knowledge, and the skills that often accompany FDI. In Ghana, the government has done little to help firms overcome the financing constraint. Also unlike the China case, family and personal networks have apparently not been able to fill the financing gap.

## Competitiveness and Binding Constraints

Ghana's furniture industry is uncompetitive for many reasons, including the high price and uncertain supply of raw materials, antiquated processing equipment, lack of skilled labor, suboptimal production techniques, and structural constraints. Most furniture firms operate in the informal economy, dealing with small-scale timber traders and operators such as millers, carpenters, and illegal chainsaw operators. Low profits prevent them from scaling up. The lack of FDI means there is no external mechanism to help finance local businesses.

The high cost of raw materials and other inputs is the predominant constraint that raises production costs and reduces competitiveness. Local raw materials, especially wood and polish, are expensive. Local production costs are high because transport and energy costs are high and because the government bans logging. The domestic supply is also unpredictable, making it difficult to meet consumer demand and encouraging firms to import their supplies from countries such as China, the Republic of Korea, and the United States.

Access to financing is another major constraint. Bank interest rates are high, often prohibitively so, averaging 25 percent. Starting from a weak financial base, most producers are unable to obtain sufficient capital to grow. None of the leading companies in the industry, including Bonsu, has relied on bank loans because of the high interest rates, short loan terms, and steep collateral requirements.

Although there are labor issues, finding workers is not a serious constraint. Companies have been able to find semiskilled workers with adequate abilities. Most workers have been exposed to the widely inherited tradition of craftsmanship in Ghana, but they are typically unfamiliar with the latest technologies and design techniques.

Ghana lacks a standardized product market for furniture. Indeed, the country has been experiencing a proliferation of furniture marts, showrooms, centers, and workshops. Furniture entrepreneurs do not work closely with the two main associations, the Federated Association of Ghanaian Exporters (the umbrella organization of export trade associations) and the Furniture Association. Because there are almost no networks of entrepreneurs and no trade fairs, there are few channels for disseminating the latest techniques.

## The Role of Government

Unlike in China, the government in Ghana has invested little in the furniture industry. It has influenced the sector, however, through its trade policies, which have lowered the costs of imported inputs.

Ghana's simple tariff structure has three rate categories: a tariff-free category—the tariff on some items has recently been raised to 5 percent—reserved for primary products, capital goods, and some basic consumer goods; a middle rate of 10 percent, primarily for raw materials and intermediate inputs, as well as some consumer goods; and a high rate of 25 percent, mainly for final consumer goods.[2] Furniture companies can thus import inputs subject to tariffs of only 5 or 10 percent and then add value domestically. The industry is also insulated from competition by the 25 percent tariff on imported finished furniture.

The government has also tried to support labor-intensive manufacturing by creating a fiscal regime favorable to investment. Ghana has one of the most attractive investment environments in Sub-Saharan Africa, including long tax holidays, duty-free entitlements, low capital requirements, and unrestricted repatriation of profits, dividends, and related income. To encourage diversification, the government refunds 95 percent of import duties on goods destined for reexport and cancels the sales tax on manufactured goods sold abroad. The government has also devised a scale of tax rebates, ranging from 20 to 50 percent, based on the total amount of production exported.

## Summary

The furniture industry in Ghana in the last decade has been built on strong craftsmanship and entrepreneurial energy. However, high input costs and difficult access to finance have constrained growth.

## Ho Nai Furniture Company, Ho Chi Minh City, Vietnam

In contrast with Ghana, the furniture industry in Vietnam has grown rapidly, showing that transformation can be quick if the conditions are appropriate to growing an industry. At an export value of close to $2.8 billion in 2010, the wood processing and furniture manufacturing sector is Vietnam's fifth-largest hard currency earner, and Vietnam is the world's fifth-largest wood product exporter after China, Malaysia, Indonesia, and Thailand. The United States, Vietnam's largest market for wood products, accounts for more than half the industry's exports. The furniture industry is export-led and employs nearly 200,000 people. Its products have a solid international reputation and are displayed prominently at international exhibitions and trade fairs. Macroeconomic stability until 2008, low labor costs, quality craftsmanship, convenient location, and a highly adaptable workforce make Vietnam a great production center for furniture and a magnet for FDI.

Growth has been spectacular. The output value of the sector soared from $250 million in 2000 to $1.2 billion in 2005 and nearly $4 billion in 2011 (figure 7.3). Since 1990, the industry has grown more than tenfold. Vietnam had about 2,520 wood processing establishments in 2010; 420 were foreign owned.[3] Its roundwood capacity totals more than 2 million cubic meters a year.

The geographical concentration of the furniture industry is the product of a gradual process. The main export manufacturers are located in a dense cluster around Ho Chi Minh City and in a secondary cluster in the Central Highlands Region. The manufacturing cluster around Ho Chi Minh City, the nucleus of the industry, houses nearly 70 percent of Vietnam's 600 largest furniture producers. The typical large furniture factory has at least 1,000 workers. Industry data reveal that more than 50 are foreign-owned or joint venture factories, with a total registered capital of nearly $150 million. More than 65 percent of Vietnamese production is exported to more than 100 countries. Over 70 percent of the exports go to the European Union (EU), Japan, and the United States.[4]

Thanks to a surge in foreign investment and the healthy growth of local companies, the Vietnamese furniture industry has become a major manufacturing and exporting force in less than two decades. The industry is a hybrid of state firms, foreign-funded enterprises and joint

**Figure 7.3 Growth of the Furniture Industry, Vietnam, 1990–2011**

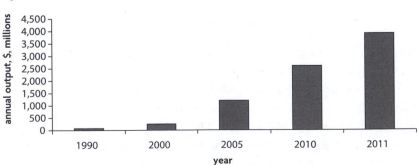

*Source:* Interviews at the Vietnam Furniture Association, Ho Chi Minh City.

ventures, and large and small private enterprises. Roughly 30 percent of the firms are state owned; 60 percent are privately owned; and 10 percent are foreign companies or joint ventures. Some of the bigger local companies, such as Khai Vy, have close to 5,000 workers and export more than 500 containers of wood furniture each month. Binh Dinh Province, a major furniture export hub in central Vietnam, accounts for more than 100 wood processors employing around 40,000 workers. The available capital among small furniture manufacturing enterprises is less than D 1 billion ($50,000) each; among medium plants, D 1 billion–D 50 billion; and among large plants, more than D 50 billion. There are also many unregistered companies. Asian companies from Singapore and from Taiwan, China, as well as Scandinavian companies, including IKEA and Scandia, are well represented. These foreign investors have been accompanied by new technologies that have modernized furniture manufacturing and have contributed to greater access to new markets.

Vietnamese furniture exports have risen in the industry's traditional markets in the Asia and Pacific region and in newer markets in Europe and North America. The United States is a new market for Vietnamese furniture that has high growth potential.[5] However, the domestic wood processing industry is facing challenges in marketing, materials, and logistics that are hurting the quality and marketability of the products.

The success of the Vietnamese furniture industry can be attributed to a combination of domestic entrepreneurship, the transfer of foreign capital and skills, and the provision of land. The industry has benefited from broad access to input industries and from the low outlays associated with trade logistics made possible by decent infrastructure and simplified customs clearance procedures, which have allowed firms to take advantage of the substantial international demand for wooden furniture. The government's commitment to economic growth has been manifested in several ways, including an open-door policy toward FDI and the establishment of industrial development zones to compensate for deficiencies in infrastructure, finance, technology, and skills. Although the government has not intruded on investment decisions, the placement of industrial development zones has influenced the location decisions of some firms in the industry.

## Origin and Course of Development

Vietnam's economy grew at an average annual rate of 7 percent over 1990–2010. Inflation was in single digits over 1996–2007, but rose to 23 percent in 2008 before falling back to 9.2 percent in 2010. Unlike other developing countries, Vietnam has had large and widening trade deficits since it embarked on the *Doi Moi* reforms in 1986.[6] Some of the deficits were generated by importing wood and agricultural raw materials to provide resources for the country's growing industrial and agroprocessing capability. Over 1990–2010, only Thailand and Vietnam among major Asian exporters had trade deficits over more than two or three years, and, since 1998, Thailand has enjoyed a trade surplus (figure 7.4). In contrast, Vietnam's deficits have worsened over the last decade. The dong continues to appreciate relative to the Chinese yuan, as evidenced by the real effective exchange rate (figure 7.5). Unless the yuan appreciates in real terms and bridges this gap, Vietnamese products will have to struggle to compete with Chinese products.

**Figure 7.4  Trade Deficits, Major Wood Product Exporters, Asia, 1990–2010**

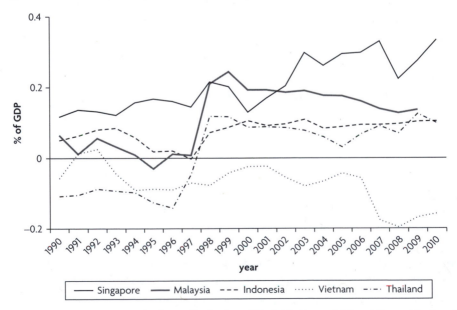

*Source:* Data of World Development Indicators (database), World Bank, Washington, DC, http://data.worldbank.org/data-catalog/world-development-indicators.
*Note:* GDP = gross domestic product.

**Figure 7.5  Changes in the Real Effective Exchange Rate, Chinese Yuan and Vietnamese Dong, 2000–10**

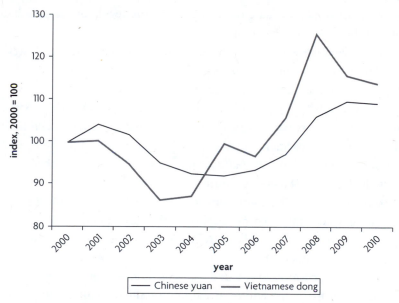

*Source:* Based on data of International Financial Statistics (database), International Monetary Fund, Washington, DC, http://elibrary-data.imf.org/FindDataReports.aspx?d=33061&e=169393.

We interviewed representatives of Ho Nai—one of the large joint ventures—in the suburbs of Ho Chi Minh City in 2010 to learn more about the beginnings of the industry. Mr. Nguyen, the entrepreneur, had been a college graduate in his late 30s when he was working with a state enterprise that produced and marketed logs. However, business was slow, and the company was plagued by inefficiencies. He had substantial savings and friends who were willing to help him in the early stages of a new business; so, he began looking for a fresh opportunity.

In 1991, Nguyen formed a joint venture with Scansia, a Norwegian company long established in Malaysia. Vietnam was changing, and government policies were creating an environment more conducive to FDI and new ideas. Foreign investment offset many of the deficiencies that still beset the economy. The foreign investor was interested in producing bamboo furniture in Vietnam for export to Europe. The furniture would be a labor-intensive, low-skill product that matched Vietnam's comparative advantage. The local entrepreneur, with access to inexpensive skilled labor in a country with a long tradition of craftsmanship, understood his cost advantages. A new law on foreign investment would facilitate the merger, and the regulatory regime had already become more favorable to joint ventures.

The Vietnamese entrepreneur brought labor skills and industrial land to the table, while the Norwegian company brought financing and technical and managerial expertise. At start-up, the company had 50–60 machines, mostly imported, and the average wage was about $30 a month. The Norwegian company provided valuable modern machinery. The Vietnamese partner contributed $200,000 in land, and the foreign company contributed $300,000 in capital. By 2010, wages in the enterprise had risen to $80–$90 a month.

Over the years, the joint venture has benefited from the foreign investment and improved production technologies and become more efficient. Profits are regularly reinvested in the company, fueling expansion. Products have been made according to increasingly sophisticated customer-provided designs and specifications. Under the terms of the joint venture, the domestic manufacturers supply the craftsmanship and finishing, but do not participate in product development.[7] Most of the machinery is imported from China, Germany, Japan, or Taiwan, China. Most of the raw materials and components (80 percent) are imported, and the furniture is exported mainly to the EU and the United States.

The directors of the joint venture decided to relocate to the Hanoi industrial zone in 1991.[8] The joint venture benefited from a two-year tax holiday, plus another two years at a 50 percent tax discount and preferential corporate income tax rates of 10–15 percent (instead of 21–25 percent) for foreign investment in priority areas. It also enjoyed duty-free access to machinery, equipment, and raw materials and a one-stop mechanism that reduced trade logistics costs for registration and for import and export dealings. Water and electricity were provided at subsidized rates. Although the industrial park had many benefits, it lacked others, such as housing for workers. After 2003, the fiscal regime became more difficult as Vietnam was preparing to join the World Trade Organization (WTO), which does not allow subsidies, and the company faced a corporate tax rate of about 20 percent. Over time, its costs rose to market rates.

## Competitiveness and Binding Constraints

Several factors explain the success of the Vietnamese furniture industry: its macroeconomic stability (prior to 2008), skilled craftsmanship, cheap labor, reliable infrastructure, easy access to global shipping, and practical sourcing of raw materials. The industry has compensated for the lack of technical expertise and investment capital with a steady flow of FDI. Vietnam's WTO membership has helped the industry gain access to global markets. The industry's good transportation network and supply chain have facilitated exports. Access to sea transport and to export markets through nine ports and harbors on the Gulf of Tonkin and the South China Sea is another advantage. (The Vietnamese garment and shoe industries share these advantages.)

Vietnamese firms have overcome a key binding constraint by obtaining good access to input markets and by importing most raw materials. Vietnam's forest resources are scarce, and most wood must be imported from Australia, Canada, New Zealand, South America, Sweden, or the United States. Machinery and equipment are also imported. Despite the recently rising prices for inputs, the industry remains strong and competitive, with relatively cheap, semiskilled labor as the foundation. The low-wage structure makes Vietnam one of the world's lowest cost producers. The average wage in the industry is about $40 a month, though wages vary widely according to firm size.

The firms have found innovative ways to improve their access to finance. While many smaller producers rely on savings, larger ones obtain bank loans. As of mid-2010, commercial banks have been lending local capital to some furniture export companies at interest rates of 12.0–12.5 percent a year as long as the exporters agree to sell back the foreign exchange they earn. Many smaller exporters, which lack strong credit relations with banks, complained that loans are out of reach.[9] Land is not a constraint for most large firms, which are located in industrial parks that provide subsidized land and utilities. Smaller firms, lacking access to land and capital, produce for the limited domestic market and rarely grow.

Furniture producers have taken advantage of WTO agreements to penetrate the lucrative U.S. market. They also benefit from the import duties imposed on Chinese furniture in the U.S. market. Vietnamese exports face favorable duties in Japanese markets as well. Vietnam has long exported furniture to the EU, where it tries to comply with all EU regulations on material origin and EU environmental standards to strengthen the relationship.

## The Role of Government

While the government's macroeconomic, trade, and industrial policies under the Doi Moi initiative have benefited business overall, the government has not directly targeted the furniture sector. The critical investment has come from foreign-owned manufacturers. The Vietnamese furniture industry has benefited from a favorable tariff regime, which has reduced input costs. Most intermediate goods and raw materials are taxed at low rates, if at all. There is no import duty on wood, except a 10 percent value added tax that is excused if the final product is reexported. Shipping costs can add as much as 60 percent to the costs of wood, however. The duty exemption and refunds became a central part of the policy regime beginning in the early 1990s.[10] Import tariffs are high for processed agricultural products and for consumer goods such as finished furniture, garments, footwear, ceramic products, leather, and cosmetics.

The industry has been helped through the steady support of the government. Both the central and local governments have courted foreign investors and trade partners in the key regions where the furniture industry is active. The Vietnam Ministry of Industry and Trade and the Ho Chi Minh City government have sponsored trade exhibitions and fairs, thus matching furniture exporters with foreign buyers. The Handicraft and Wood Industry Association of Ho Chi Minh City, the leading trade association for the wood industry in Vietnam, represents more than 330 companies, mainly in wood processing and furniture manufacturing. A focal point for industry expansion, it promotes the development of handicraft fine art and wood processing and provides consulting and business services to its members. In recent years, Ho Chi Minh City has held the International Furniture and Handicraft Fair and Exhibition to publicize the nation's thriving furniture industry and help build contacts and cement deals.

## Summary

Furniture has been one of the Vietnam's dynamic growth sectors, benefiting from a combination of FDI and strong local entrepreneurs. The Vietnamese experience with the industry contrasts with the Ghanaian tale. Vietnam has established itself as a large furniture producer exporting to the EU and North America, while Ghana has continued to struggle with a nascent sector.

## Notes

1. International Financial Statistics (database), International Monetary Fund, Washington, DC, http://elibrary-data.imf.org/FindDataReports.aspx?d=33061 &e=169393.
2. Manufacturers facing high import tariffs (25 percent) on key raw materials are allowed to apply for concessionary rates (10 percent) so that they may acquire these goods at lower cost. The application must be made on a consignment basis and can be processed only after the goods arrive in Ghana.
3. Interviews with the Vietnam Furniture Association, Ho Chi Minh City, November 2010.
4. Vietnam has 9.5 million hectares of natural forest, with a reserve of 720.9 million cubic meters. The government allows harvesting of 300,000 cubic meters of timber a year to satisfy domestic needs (construction and furniture) and the demand for wooden handicrafts for export (Government of Vietnam 2005).
5. Vietnamese furniture has benefited from the imposition of antidumping duties on U.S. imports of Chinese wood furniture. There is evidence that Chinese manufacturers are shifting some production to Vietnam because of these duties.
6. The Doi Moi (renovation) reforms were aimed at changing the planned economy to a market-oriented economy.
7. According to the entrepreneur, a few domestic firms produce furniture directly for large foreign furniture suppliers such as IKEA.
8. Vietnamese industrial parks (zones) have become important tools of government industrial policy since the launch of the Doi Moi reforms in the mid-1980s. The parks were set up as havens for foreign investors and large private investors. In 2010, there were about 223 industrial parks throughout the country, accounting for 40 percent of the registered FDI. They employed about 1.5 million workers.
9. During the recent global financial crisis, the government began providing a 4 percent interest subsidy on loans to companies that export, import, or produce essential goods and offered interest subsidies for short-term loans.
10. Vietnam's duty drawback system has also helped the industry. Exporters are exempt from the value added tax and the special sales tax, and firms

exporting 50–80 percent of their production are taxed at 20 percent for 12 years, while those exporting more than 80 percent are taxed at only 15 percent for 15 years.

# References

AGI (Association of Ghana Industries). 2012. "Q1 Business Climate Survey." AGI, Accra.

Chandra, Vandana, ed. 2006. *Technology, Adaptation, and Exports: How Some Developing Countries Got It Right.* Washington, DC: World Bank.

Government of Vietnam. 2005. "National Report to the Fifth Session of the United Nations Forum on Forests." January, United Nations, New York.

# 8

# Leather Products

## Introduction

Several Sub-Saharan African countries have attempted to develop shoe production. The two cases presented here, in Kenya and Tanzania, both failed. These countries have a comparative advantage in the production of leather products because they have a rich supply of hides, are favorably located near potential export markets through their ports on the Indian Ocean, and have reasonably skilled labor.

The sector's main constraints have been trade logistics and the rising cost of labor and raw materials. Local officials have responded by providing training and incentives for employers and employees.

## Bata Shoes, Kenya

You can become very poor making shoes, or you can become very rich making shoes.

—*Michael E. Porter, talk at Strathmore University, Nairobi, June 25, 2007*

Kenya is East Africa's largest economy, and the people have always had a strong, resilient entrepreneurial spirit. The country is more private sector–oriented than most African economies, with few state enterprises. As a principal hub in Africa, Kenya has performed reasonably well economically, based in large part on a favorable policy regime, a fairly liberal foreign trade regime, an educated elite, and a solid infrastructure base. Annual growth in real gross domestic product (GDP) averaged more than 5 percent in 2000–10 in the face of the global economic crisis and national governance challenges.

Despite these advantages, the development of the manufacturing sector and economic diversification have been a struggle. Horticulture exports have done well, but that has been the exception. The leather industry, with a long history based on Kenya's strong comparative advantage, has shown promise. The livestock sector contributes about 10 percent to GDP and employs more than half the labor force.

The Kenyan shoe industry has not fulfilled this potential. Multiple factors, both endogenous and exogenous, have hurt the industry.

In the last two decades, gross revenue in footwear and leather has fallen almost 70 percent, and the shoe industry has shed more than 30,000 jobs. The industry has faced growing competition from cheaper imported shoes, especially from East Asia. Allegations of dumping abound, as do claims that other countries unfairly subsidize their own industries. In Kenya, the tendency has been to export hides and skins rather than processed leather. In 2000–10, more than 85 percent of the raw hides and skins were exported to countries in Asia and Europe, where prices are higher than in Kenya. Other constraints include high electricity prices, frequent power outages, and high transport costs because of inadequate infrastructure and high fuel costs.

The industry has never had control over its inputs, especially leather and hides, and has faced a prohibitive cost structure, making it tough to compete with Asian producers. Problematic access to finance and the low domestic savings rate have impeded the entry of new firms, despite the widely available industry knowledge and skills. The inability to acquire good industrial land has deprived shoe manufacturers of the opportunity to scale up production. Complex trade logistics and an unfavorable economic environment have made the lives of entrepreneurs difficult.

Though a leader in East Africa, Kenya has not been able to benefit from foreign ideas and managerial skills. High administrative costs have deterred many foreign firms from setting up shop. The foreign investment flowing in has been directed mainly to horticultural products and has been more focused on trade logistics than on manufacturing. *World Investment Report 2008* identifies Kenya as East Africa's least effective suitor in attracting foreign direct investment (FDI) (UNCTAD 2008). To improve its export prospects and take advantage of the managerial expertise, capital, and technology that have accompanied FDI, Kenya needs to improve its attractiveness to foreign investors.

## Origin and Course of Development

Kenya's footwear industry has roots that go back several decades. Bata, a shoe manufacturer and retailer originally located in an area now in the Czech Republic, was a pioneer in this high-volume, low-margin business. Bata was one of the first non-British European companies to open manufacturing in Kenya, attracted by the cheaper inputs and less expensive labor. At the time, there was no evidence of strong government endorsement of economic growth as a top national priority. Bata's investment was thus an independent decision made by a foreign company rather than an element in a national development plan.

During World War II, Bata established a small tannery in Limeru, north of Nairobi, to process leather for the manufacture of footwear for the British army. Because the labor costs in Africa were low, the company decided to relocate production there. By the late 1940s and early 1950s, the East African Bata Shoe Company, a subsidiary of Bata (which had become a Canadian multinational in the meantime), was an important shoe producer in Africa.

Bata's goal was to become East Africa's largest shoe producer and serve the region's growing market. Bata's shoe production fluctuated between 6 and 14 percent of Kenya's exports during the 1950s and reached 30 percent in the 1960s and 1970s (Swainson 1980). Its focus was on low-cost synthetic leather shoes made of textiles and rubber, which accounted for 6 million of the 8 million shoes produced in 1975; the remaining 2 million were leather. Bata imported rubber from plantations in West Africa. In response to demand for shoe production, the leather industry grew considerably, and, within three decades, more than 30 medium to large registered tanneries were supporting the shoe industry.

As a first mover and a large foreign company with modern technology and good financial resources, Bata commanded a substantial presence in the market. Its early domination was built on vertical integration. Most of its inputs were imported through the company's supply chain and subsidiaries. Local entrepreneurs could enter the industry at the production and distribution stages, but Bata controlled its own 30-plus retail outlets. Traders made large profits under this foreign distribution system. Through this strong supply chain, Bata had the economies of scale needed to survive in the industry. Subcontracting lowered its costs even more. Because the barriers to entry were prohibitively high, especially capital costs, competition was weak.

This changed in the 1960s and 1970s as the economic landscape was altered in Kenya and globally. Although the company tried to keep its supply system under strict control, the system had weakened, and growing competition at home and abroad undermined Bata's dominance. Many of the new domestic firms failed because of difficult access to financing and because of substandard technology. In the 1980s and 1990s, shoe manufacturing migrated from Africa and Europe to the countries along the Pacific Rim, known for its vibrant entrepreneurs and lower labor costs. Bata managed to survive the onslaught, though its Kenyan production fell to well below the peak.

## Competitiveness and Binding Constraints

The key constraint on Bata has been the input industry. The supply chain was initially competitive, but it weakened over time. Bata worked to gain control of the supply chain, including the most difficult segment, the procurement of hides. East African hides are among the lowest quality in the world, and only a company as large as Bata could find a way around the problem. Yet, in the long run, even Bata was weakened by a difficult global economy and suboptimal input provision.

Over the years, Bata invested heavily in better machinery and labor productivity. In the 1950s, the 500 workers in its leather shoe plant made 1,000 shoes a day (2.0 per worker), and the 200 workers in its rubber shoes plant made 1,500 shoes a day (about 7.5 per worker) (Swainson 1980). By 1974, Bata had more than 1,000 workers, and they made close to 8 million shoes in that year, suggesting significant productivity gains.

As shoe production became more competitive, new firms emerged, and the industry segmented. Large firms such as Bata had reasonably good technology, adequate access to capital, and well-developed supply chains. The smaller, more labor-intensive firms lacked the necessary financing and supply chains to compete with Bata. As a result, despite the emergence of new domestic firms, Bata continued to strengthen the level of its control over production.

Then, in the 1990s and the first decade of the 2000s, external competition from Asia began to undercut Bata's position. Bata's already small export market share shrank, and the business became unprofitable. Soon, the other local companies were struggling, too, as their productivity stagnated because of a lack of investment in machinery and the escalating cost of raw materials.

The industry obtains its raw materials mainly from domestic tanneries, and the quality is poor; the best leather is generally exported because prices are higher in foreign markets. Surveys of shoe manufacturers find that an unpredictable supply chain makes responding to orders on time difficult. The technology needed to process leather to the final stage is too expensive for small enterprises. Import duties are too high to make imports of raw materials profitable.

Financing has been another persistent problem. Capital is scarce in Kenya, and interest rates are high. The lack of financing has crippled new entrants. The Industrial and Commercial Development Corporation, established by the colonial authorities in 1954 to provide credit to new and expanding firms, did not help provide loans for the nascent manufacturing sector. Capital went instead to entrepreneurs in the trading and service sectors to purchase equipment and expand stocks.

To discourage exports of hides and skins, the government increased the tax on such exports to 40 percent in 2006 and 2007. Exports of raw hides and skins declined sixfold from 2003 to 2007, and finished leather production increased more than fourfold (Curtis 2010). The policy has given the industry a lift. Exports of leather rose 54 percent in 2008, though they are still lower than they were in the 1970s and 1980s.

Many consumers buy imported shoes at the high end of the market. Bata has been more successful in the middle and lower segments of the market, though these segments are also becoming increasingly saturated with imports. Local shoe production caters to lower-income consumers.

However, competition from imports affects all segments of the market. The Kenyan government has not done much to market the Bata brand overseas, and small retail stores across the country account for the bulk of sales. Also, the uneven quality of the shoes and the lack of quality control diminish the ability to compete in foreign markets. In 2000–10, Bata produced fewer than 2 million pairs of shoes in Kenya each year.

## The Role of Government

One of the main problems faced by Kenya's footwear industry has been the punitive macroeconomic regime. Macroeconomic stability was difficult to achieve in the two decades following Kenya's independence. Growth was slow, and fiscal deficits mounted. Kenya followed an import-substitution strategy of industrialization, imposing a mix of tariffs, licensing, and import quotas, along with the overvalued exchange rate. Intended to protect the domestic economy, the strategy penalized manufacturing by making exports expensive, while failing to make the industries more competitive. As a result, the share of manufacturing in GDP has stalled at 14 percent since independence. Abrupt changes in laws and regulations have added administrative costs.

Many of the policies the government adopted to shield the sector backfired. High import duties on chemicals, machinery, spare parts, and other accessories meant that manufacturers had difficulty obtaining the equipment they needed to expand, while duties of 21–29 percent on imported leather—to protect Kenyan tanneries from cheaper imports—raised the cost of inputs. Manufacturers have been prohibited from owning and operating their own retail outlets, which has prevented many shoe companies from expanding.

The government has also placed additional barriers in the way of manufacturing firms. Estimates put the total tax burden of Kenyan firms at close to 50 percent, a combination of the uniform 30 percent East African Community corporate income tax and national levies. Moreover, industries trying to become established are required to apply for numerous licenses, sometimes running into the hundreds. In recent years, the government has undertaken macroeconomic and structural reforms to provide a more robust footing for Kenyan manufacturing. Some of the reforms have been generic, but a few have been specific to sectors. The government has tried to make the sourcing of domestic and imported raw materials easier for companies. The liberalization of the foreign exchange market has helped companies overcome some of the liquidity constraints and reduce the time necessary to import vital raw materials. The revamping of export duties on tanners, coupled with some liberalization of the tariff regime and licensing procedures, has helped the industry, though the sector needs deeper transformation if it is to compete internationally.

## Summary

Bata has a long history in Kenya, but its weak control of input industries, coupled with growing competition from Asia, has led to the near collapse of the shoe industry.

## Morogoro Shoe Factory, Tanzania

Morogoro is a small town about 200 kilometers west of Dar es Salaam. It is not an obvious strategic location, but the government selected it for a shoe factory because of the tannery nearby and the proximity of the area to Tanzania's agricultural hinterland. Although the site selection may seem logical, it was made by the government, not the market. Its distance from the coast proved detrimental.

Following World War II, the government introduced an ambitious industrial strategy and undertook a search for appropriate export products. In the late 1960s, it crafted an industrial development and policy framework to advance self-reliance, economic growth, and structural transformation. The hope was to develop a strong, indigenous manufacturing capability. The Morogoro shoe factory, established in the 1980s, was envisioned as part of this strategy, an attempt by the government to develop and strengthen the local leather industry.

In many respects, Tanzania was in a prime position to launch a successful footwear industry. Its closeness to eight countries was expected to provide a good market. The large population, skilled labor force, adequate government capacity, and many heads of cattle all seemed to be favorable. However, despite the advantages, Morogoro failed, and the cost to the government was substantial.

Morogoro's is the tale of a state-owned shoe company that never produced a single high-quality shoe for export and of an industry beset by poor planning and worse implementation. As a state enterprise with monopoly power, the Morogoro shoe factory started big, with expensive and advanced equipment. Its focus was on a fairly simple final good and a proven path to development success. Morogoro was one of Africa's first light industry experiments. Receiving World Bank loans in the 1980s, the factory was built in 1984 at a total cost of $23 million. It was equipped with imported machines. The factory never really started production and was shut down in the 1990s. By the late 1990s, Tanzania's leather industry had collapsed, and the country's six main tanneries had shut down. Over its brief life, Morogoro operated at less than 5 percent capacity and was unable to produce acceptable shoes for export or to meet local demand. The Morogoro shoe factory became a textbook case of what not to do in seeking to build a local industry.

Morogoro's fatal flaw was its negative value added: its inputs cost more than the value of its output. At its maximum level of output, Morogoro produced at less than 10 percent of capacity; average production was much less (figure 8.1). Estimates suggest that, to keep the firm in business in the mid-1980s, it cost $500,000 each year (close to T Sh 800 billion) (World Bank 1990). On top of this was the interest and principal on the World Bank loan used to support the factory.

**Figure 8.1 Production Indicators, Morogoro Shoe Factory, Tanzania, 1980–90**

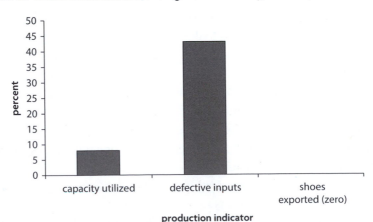

*Sources:* Data of the government of Tanzania; World Bank 1990.

## Origin and Course of Development

Tanzania's economic environment during the 1980s did not support private sector growth or exports. During the 1970s and 1980s, the government followed a state-led interventionist approach to the economy that involved price controls and import-substitution industrialization to catalyze growth. Weak internal macroeconomic management and external terms-of-trade shocks generated fiscal and balance of payments crises in the 1980s (see below). Reforms were undertaken, and greater macroeconomic stability was achieved by the 1990s.

In the early 1970s, the National Development Corporation, which is responsible for industrial development in the country, established several tanneries. At the time, based on the concept of self-reliance, Tanzania was striving to become one of Africa's leading industrial powers. With the help of Italmacchine, an Italian consulting firm, an ambitious plan was hatched to build the biggest shoe factory in Africa. The plan was to establish an industrial park with a canvas mill, a tannery, and a leather goods factory. The plan called for building two large shoe factories: Tanzania Shoe Bora, with an annual production capacity of 6 million pairs of shoes, and the Morogoro shoe factory, with a capacity of 4 million pairs. These factories would operate as state enterprises coordinated by Tanzania Leather Associated Industries, while the trade in raw hides and skins would be controlled by Tanzania Hides and Skins, also a state enterprise. The resources were to be obtained from both inside and outside the country.

The first phase of the project envisioned an industrial estate, with the necessary infrastructure and facilities for small and medium firms, and focused on a shoe factory that would produce 2 million pairs of leather shoes and 2 million pairs of canvas shoes a year. The plant was to supply the entire Tanzania shoe market, and 85 percent of the output was to be exported to Europe. A leather goods factory to fabricate handbags, suitcases, jackets, and other items was subsequently added to the plan.

An internal World Bank review team concluded that the project had failed because of flawed design and implementation. The output numbers were based on wishful thinking rather than on a careful market analysis or plant capacity. The design of the shoe factory was far too ambitious, and the plan had overestimated capacity and the demand for products that were low in quality and high in price.

From the concept stage, the project was plagued by poor-quality inputs and equipment, unskilled entrepreneurs, top-down management, and defective products. The project never took off because both management and workers lacked the requisite skills to follow through with such an enormous undertaking. The overdependence on expensive imported inputs and foreign experts resulted in suboptimal products because work was frequently interrupted by shortages of parts and of foreign currency. The industry was designed from the top rather than through entrepreneurial initiative. The technology transfer required to produce high-quality products never occurred.

### Competitiveness and Binding Constraints

In addition to the problem of the overestimation of market demand, the Morogoro project failed to address the binding constraints properly, particularly the problems in inputs and in labor skills. More than 1,700 machines were installed, and the plan was to employ more than 2,000 workers and staff members. By 1986, only about 450 workers and 196 staff members had been employed. Output was less than one pair of shoes per person per shift, while capacity was 10–15 pairs. No one tried to understand the supply chain for raw materials. Inputs were poor in quality. In Tanzania, cattle hides, goatskins, and sheepskins are produced on farm homesteads and rural butcheries; there were no modern slaughtering facilities. The standard of the hides has been described as among the worst in the world by a range of industry experts. The hides were transported to the three state-owned tanneries for processing. Half the hides were rejected because of defects. Another 30 percent of the hide value was lost to indiscriminate branding (animals are sold many times and receive a fresh brand each time). The trade in skins and hides was controlled by state-owned Tanzania Hides and Skins. No effort was made to build abattoirs or to improve the quality of the tanneries.

In the early 1980s, the industry still had potential, though raw materials were a serious challenge. The leather industry performed well, employing 5,200 workers and supplying the Morogoro shoe factory. Thereafter, it faltered because most of the skins and hides were exported as raw or as semifinished (wet blue) after processing by the tanneries.[1] These exports, mainly to Kenya and Uganda, flourished because prices were higher abroad. As a result, the Morogoro shoe factory had no reliable supply of good-quality finished leather, and it went bankrupt in the late 1980s. With a high fixed overhead cost, production levels were far below the break-even point. Economies of scale could not be realized because the absence of a stable and cheap source of raw materials meant that production was at 10–15 percent of capacity even in the best years.

Most of the design problems can be attributed to the fact that the public sector was making the decisions for the private sector. The projected scale of production was wrong. With a capacity of 4 million pairs of shoes, Morogoro was many times the size of typical plants, where annual output averaged 0.5 million–1.5 million pairs. Machinery was poorly maintained. Little attention was paid to the availability of spare parts, and breakdowns and power outages were frequent. There were separate production lines for exports, with special machines for selected processes to ensure export quality, but, in practice, these production lines relied on poor, inadequate machines. Much of the machinery and equipment were imported, and there was no local technical expertise in running and maintaining the machines. Italmacchine, the Italian consulting company, offered to sell at least 85 percent of the total production outside Tanzania at the best prevailing price through its subsidiaries. This never materialized. If Morogoro had been owned by a private entity, these problems might still have arisen, but, in that case, they would have occurred on a much smaller scale and would not have cost the country so much.

Workers received no training in maintaining the machines. The effluent treatment plants were inadequate; so, tannery runoff flowed into Lake Victoria, with adverse environmental impacts. While the project had a $40 million line of credit, local capital was scarce, and the investment needed to upgrade technology to meet higher quality requirements was frequently not available.

Morogoro's demise was predictable within only a few years of the onset of operations. The industrial park set up by the government did not have factory shells or its own utility supply. Within a year of the commissioning of the factory, structural cracks appeared in the walls and floors, and water seeped in, damaging the machine platforms. The roof also leaked, and there were problems with drainage and sewage disposal. Morogoro never had a profitable year. The lack of profits meant that the firm lacked the foreign exchange to expand business and pay for critical spare parts. The Italian machines either sat idle or were misused by workers who were not trained in operating them. The lack of profits meant that workers and suppliers were not paid regularly. Failures to pay utility bills resulted in power shortages. Instead of cutting losses and liquidating the firm, the government kept it limping along through subsidies.

The absence of entrepreneurial skills, especially marketing and management knowledge, was another grave shortcoming. The Italian company that was supposed to train two groups of managers for six months in Italy failed to establish a good training plan, and the trainees failed to acquire the necessary skills. World Bank reviews found that the management of the shoe company made no serious effort to capture a share of the domestic market or even to develop a practical plan for running the facility. Finally, imports of secondhand shoes and new footwear from China were unregulated in the country, and consumers preferred these shoes because they were cheaper and higher in quality. This flood of inexpensive imports undermined the Morogoro shoe factory additionally.

To encourage the growth of the shoe industry and reduce the influence of the inefficient state-owned enterprises, the government decided to open the industry to private investment. Private companies sprang up to trade in raw hides and skins. The three tanneries were also privatized in 1993–95, ensuring a reliable supply of good-quality leather at reasonable cost. The two shoe factories were also privatized. After years of ineffective policies, the government had finally created a more favorable environment for small and medium enterprises (SMEs).

Another challenge for the Morogoro shoe factory was the difficult macroeconomic environment. The period from the 1970s to the mid-1980s was one of stagflation (slow growth, high unemployment, and high inflation), an overvalued currency that raised the price of exports, and unsustainable fiscal deficits financed through bad fiscal policies. All these factors cut into the competitiveness of Tanzanian industry. In the mid-1980s, the government began the transition toward a market-based economy by liberalizing prices, trade, and, eventually, the exchange rate. However, inflation remained high, at 30 percent, throughout the 1980s, and the macroeconomic environment continued to be hostile to firms such as Morogoro. Finally, by the late 1990s, some macroeconomic stability was achieved as the economy grew, inflation eased, and the budget deficit shrank by half, to 9.3 percent, during 1990–97 compared with 1985–90. By then, however, the Morogoro experiment had failed entirely, and the Tanzanian shoe industry was in shambles.

## The Role of Government

The multiplicity of policies prevented the Morogoro shoe factory from succeeding. First, while the Export Processing Zones Act of 1970 provided special incentives to exporting firms, the Morogoro shoe factory was not included in the export processing zones. Second, the failure to provide reliable infrastructure and utility services in the industrial park also hurt the shoe industry. Third, the company never received assistance with marketing and export development and, as a result, was never able to identify the appropriate products for its markets. The lack of a strong private sector partner was a major shortcoming.

The bad sequencing of trade liberalization policies weakened Morogoro. The government reduced tariff barriers in 1986 and allowed foreign manufactured products, including Chinese shoes, to penetrate the market before the reduction in input tariffs could exert any impact on domestic producers. Thus, at the time of Morogoro's expansion, the country was being flooded by cheap imported shoes. The restructuring and privatization of state enterprises in the early 1990s occurred too late. Between 1990 and 2000, installed private industrial capacity rose from an average of 20 percent to approximately 50 percent, and some privatized industries improved their capital structure, production technologies, and management and marketing systems. But all this happened after the Morogoro shoe factory had gone out of business.

## Summary

Morogoro was one of the first failed economic growth policy experiments in the developing world. It failed because it was conceived from the top down and was not driven by the private sector. The lack of entrepreneurial skills and of supportive government policies prevented adequate control of the input market and hurt profitability.

## Sialkot Sporting Goods Cluster, Punjab Province, Pakistan

The best thing the local government did was to let us grow and not interfere.

—*Interview with the chairman, Sialkot Chamber of Commerce*

The sporting goods cluster in the city of Sialkot and adjoining rural areas is a tale of success in the development of light manufacturing in Pakistan. Sialkot is 130 kilometers northwest of Lahore, the provincial capital, and has about 800,000 people. The city produces sporting goods, surgical instruments, and leather goods of high quality and world renown and has the highest export earnings per capita of any Pakistani city. After Karachi, it is Pakistan's largest export center, annually shipping goods worth more than $500 million, mostly to North America and Western Europe (figure 8.2).

Sialkot is one of the light industrial hubs in Pakistan, producing about 99 percent of all exported sporting goods. On average, more than 40 million soccer balls, worth $210 million, are produced annually by some 60,000 highly skilled workers. The city produces as many as 60 million hand-stitched soccer balls in a World Cup year.[2] By some estimates, Sialkot produced close to 90 percent of the world's soccer balls in 1990–2010. Among the city's nonleather products, stainless steel surgical instruments account for 20 percent of total trade. Foreign producers have formed collaborative production arrangements with Pakistani

**Figure 8.2 Exports of Sialkot, Pakistan, 1990–2010**

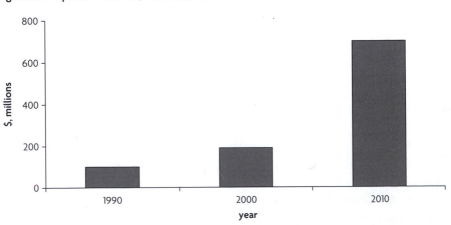

*Source:* Interviews at the Sialkot Chamber of Commerce, 2010.

manufacturers in the city. The city's annual growth rate towers above the national average, and its mean income is double the national average.

An outlier in Pakistan's feudal structure, Sialkot is predominantly middle class. The city has a web of industries that has helped it address employment problems.[3] In 2007, Sialkot opened a modern private sector–financed airport with the longest runway in Pakistan to allow foreign companies to fly into the city and unload urgently needed supplies. Sialkot has benefited from a strong tradition of local entrepreneurship and easy access to inputs. Because of its numerous small firms, Sialkot has developed one of the most advanced forms of industrial clustering in Pakistan. Many international firms, including Adidas, Puma, and Slazenger, have collaborated with firms in the cluster. A particularly positive feature of Sialkot's industrial development has been the large spillover benefits to the adjoining rural communities.

## Origin and Course of Development

Despite some macroeconomic instability during the formative years of the Sialkot cluster in the 1970s and 1980s, economic growth, which was driven by agriculture, was respectable. In the 1990s, economic reforms helped create a favorable regime for investment, and Pakistan's economy grew at an annual average of 4.4 percent over 1990–2010. The real effective exchange rate was 103.4 at the end of 2010, down from 125.4 in 1990, and has remained relatively steady since 2000 (figure 8.3).

**Figure 8.3  Index of the Real Effective Exchange Rate, Pakistan Rupee versus Chinese Yuan, 1990–2011**

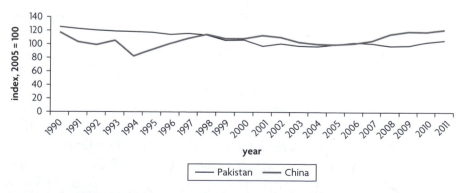

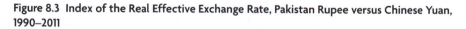

*Source:* Data of International Financial Statistics (database), International Monetary Fund, Washington, DC, http://elibrary-data.imf.org/FindDataReports.aspx?d=33061&e=169393.

*Note:* The rate is based on the consumer price index.

The real effective exchange rate of the rupee has depreciated relative to the yuan, contributing to the competitiveness of Sialkot industry. The government has been progressively dismantling its legacy of import-substitution industrialization and liberalizing the policy framework for FDI. It has faced chronic fiscal and balance of payments pressures, partly financed by remittances and strong aid inflows. Despite the economic reforms, the policy regime for manufacturing has not been consistent or favorable, and the government has mostly ignored the sector.

A sporting goods cluster, Sialkot has a strong concentration of industry within a compact area. It has a century-old industrial base and a long history of cluster development and skills upgrading. It developed through the response of its traditional craftspeople to the growing demands of the British Empire. In 1895, Sialkot was famous for tennis racquets, and, by 1903, it was producing cricket bats with imported British willow. In 1922, a local manufacturer received an award from the British Empire for supplying soccer balls to the British army. By the time of the partition of the Indian subcontinent, middle-class craftsmen had become entrepreneurs, filling the vacuum created by the departure of the primarily non-Muslim trading and industrial class to India.

Most firms in Sialkot are family owned and are managed by craftsmen who learned the trade through apprenticeship. The cluster developed organically in response to demand from the British government. The local legend is that Sialkot emerged as the world capital of soccer ball production after a local man repaired a leather ball for British colonial military officers about a century ago and then began to make soccer balls. The cluster's ascendency and location were unrelated to government decisions or priorities.

Most entrepreneurs in the soccer industry are in their 30s and 40s, and most lack strong education qualifications or management degrees, but come from local families with a tradition of craftsmanship. They all started small and simple, developing skills on the job and building their enterprises from simpler workshops. Most have had some international exposure through trade fairs and buyer networks. These entrepreneurs started without strong formal financial backing, which impeded their expansion, but they are part of strong family and personal networks that can be tapped for financial assistance, trusted employees, and partnerships.

## Competitiveness and Binding Constraints

The main constraints on the expansion of Sialkot's sporting goods cluster are weak trade logistics, input supply, and access to finance.

The sporting goods industry has more than 3,000 small and medium industrial units and some 50 well-established companies in and around Sialkot. Sialkot has developed an industrial structure that boosts its efficiency by facilitating access to inputs and improved trade logistics. Producers have a dense network of vertical ties with buyers, suppliers, and subcontractors and horizontal links among themselves.

In many ways, Sialkot's success defies the theory of development economics. It is distant from ports and rivers. Credit inflows to the area have been minimal. No special industrial parks have been established. Large-scale enterprises are conspicuously absent. Infrastructure in the area is shoddy and characterized by dilapidated roads and weak power generation capability. The government has largely ignored Sialkot.

The Sialkot cluster has used smart initiatives to improve trade logistics. Though the city is landlocked and far from ports and has poor surrounding infrastructure, the cluster has managed to facilitate the movement of merchandise and exports to international markets. One of the outstanding successes of local initiative has been the formation of the Sialkot Dry Port Trust, the first-ever dry port in Asia. An initiative by leading exporters, the self-financing public trust was set up in 1985 to provide collective services to the export-oriented cluster. The trust leased land from the Punjab government; its working capital was generated by loans from banks and leading local producers. The trust brought all necessary customs formalities to the producer's doorstep and introduced cheap and reliable warehousing and services for the transportation of bonded goods to and from ports. This arrangement spared entrepreneurs in landlocked Sialkot from the administrative complexities of traveling to Karachi and Lahore to satisfy customs formalities. The first privately owned public airport in Pakistan and South Asia, Sialkot International Airport, went into operation in 2007 and has been quite successful.

The Sialkot industrial cluster benefits from an unusual web of relationships and a supply network that guarantees good inputs at reasonable prices. In the soccer ball industry, subcontractors, called makers, operate out of geographical clusters where they have forged arrangements with individuals and households skilled in assembling the balls. The subcontractors negotiate a rate with the manufacturers, take the components to the rural cottage industries, and return with the finished balls; they are paid only for the balls that pass quality control. A network of marketing agents, raw materials suppliers, and ancillary units makes this all possible. Almost all the firms are family owned and managed. The exporting companies have built close ties with the subcontractors, who have long worked with the manufacturers, thus forming a dense triangular network of relationships connecting village-based artisans specializing in particular product lines with dynamic exporters operating in niche markets. The city has cultivated good links with international buyers, who have built long-term business relationships with local exporters.

The cluster has been resourceful in overcoming the lack of access to formal finance. Most enterprises are financed through family savings because the city has no venture capitalists and does not fund start-ups. These enterprises remain lean, with low overhead, by subcontracting 20–90 percent of their manufacturing to piece-rate workers. The low capital overhead leads to higher profit margins and quicker returns on investments. In-house production focuses on material cutting, testing, and packaging. The firms obtain the leather inputs from adjoining rural areas at market rates and then subcontract to local family workshops. This system requires only a modest investment in advance payments to subcontractors and thus allows for more efficient cash flows and fewer liabilities as manufacturers begin filling orders.

The Sialkot Chamber of Commerce, a large association of exporters established in 1982, has helped firms overcome the skill shortages. The chamber had some 6,500 members in 2010, most of them active in sporting goods, leather, and surgical goods. The chamber also provides trade assistance by disseminating export information, arranging trade fairs, and marketing.

Allegations of exploitative child labor practices within Sialkot's network of skilled workers have led to a restructuring of the industry. Firms typically prefer to subcontract rather than make the investments in equipment and staff needed for in-house manufacturing. For years, there were some concerns that children under the age of 12 were stitching soccer balls, leading to an international outcry and a potential public relations disaster for sporting goods companies.[4] In 1997, Pakistani suppliers and representatives of the United Nations Children's Fund and the International Labour Organization signed the Atlanta Agreement, which obligated the industry to stop using child labor. Subcontracting makes it more difficult to monitor the use of child labor, but all evidence suggests that the practice has been greatly reduced. The sporting goods industry in Sialkot funds the Independent Monitoring Association for Child Labor, which regularly visits factories and checks worker identification papers.

Another concern is the level of pay. A recent survey of more than 200 workers in Sialkot companies that export balls and other products to sports retailers, including Adidas and Nike, found that more than half of Sialkot's soccer ball stitchers reported that their pay in 2009 was below the monthly minimum wage in Pakistan of PRs 6,000 ($70) (UNIDO 2009).

Low labor costs in and around Sialkot have helped keep firms competitive. Even after adjusting for transaction costs, exporters in the soccer ball industry can pay wages in the surrounding rural areas that are much lower than they would pay in the city. On average, workers in Sialkot earned more than PRs 100,000 ($1,114) a year in 2010, twice the national average, while people in the surrounding rural areas earned roughly half of this amount. The wages among stitchers in the surrounding rural areas may even be only half the minimum wage because rural stitchers are paid by the piece (ball) and work fewer hours relative to factory workers. The wages of rural artisans are sometimes a quarter or a third the wages in Sialkot city, although, in the wake of the child labor allegations, a growing number of rural workers are migrating to centers closer to the city and receiving higher wages. Subcontracting in rural and periurban areas also benefits from the concentration of skilled artisan workers.

Sialkot has faced strong challenges in recent years that threaten its success. First is the growing competition from lower-cost producers in China and India, which have dramatically increased their share of soccer ball production. Second, there have been changes in the industry, including a rise in machine-produced balls and a consequent decline in the market share of hand-stitched balls. Third, power and gas shortages have kept industries from meeting their deadlines and caused

**Figure 8.4  Cost Structure of Soccer Balls, Sialkot, Pakistan, 2010**

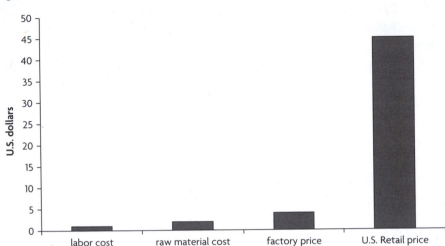

*Source:* Interviews with personnel of SAGA Sports, 2010.

production costs to go up. Fourth, rising labor costs have threatened to erode some of the cost competitiveness of Pakistani soccer balls, though retail margins remain high (figure 8.4).

### The Role of Government

The government has largely ignored Sialkot. Because the government has not subsidized capital for large industries, the business environment in Sialkot remains competitive. Though it has also ignored the area's credit and infrastructure needs, the government has not stifled private initiative and has helped enforce quality standards in the industry. Tax rates are less than 1 percent of income. Export-oriented industries in Pakistan have been granted customs duty and sales tax exemptions on the import and purchase of raw materials, and the duty-free import of machinery and equipment for industries is also allowed. None of the inputs required by the sporting goods industry is on a restricted import list. The government instituted a new textile development policy in 2000 that affects the silk industry, with various directives covering productivity, quality, quantity, product diversification, and competitive pricing.

## Summary

The Sialkot cluster developed organically with little government involvement, overcoming difficult constraints in financing and trade logistics to become a world-class exporter of sporting goods. Its success shows that a subcontracting system can flourish in a competitive business environment with strong traditions of entrepreneurship, specialization in niche industries, a core of skilled artisanal workers, effective local initiatives, and the absence of excessive government regulation.

## Notes

1. The United Nations Industrial Development Organization sponsored the $18 million All Africa Hides and Skins Improvement Project from 1987 to 1994. It tried to improve the standards of fleshing, flay, and preservation by training veterinary assistants, butchers, and farmers in hide improvement techniques, by offering practical demonstrations, and by supplying vital equipment.
2. The city became well known internationally when it produced the Tango soccer ball for the 1984 Summer Olympics in Los Angeles.
3. Our interviews among several firms in the cluster revealed that the industrial web is well linked. All the exporters have networking equipment, as well as experience in trade fairs and interaction with foreign buyers.
4. The International Labour Organization found that, in Sialkot District in 2000, more than 7,000 children aged 7–14 years were stitching soccer balls 10–11 hours a day and earning PRs 20–22 ($0.35–$0.38) per ball (Dogar 2000).

## References

Curtis, Mark. 2010. "Developing the Leather Sector in Kenya through Export Taxes: The Benefits of Defying the EU." Traidcraft Exchange; Oxfam Germany; World Economy, Ecology, and Development; Association Internationale de Techniciens, Experts et Chercheurs; and Comhlámh, Nairobi. http://www2 .weed-online.org/uploads/case_study_leather_sector_in_kenya.pdf.

Dogar, Nasir. 2000. "Workplace Monitoring as a Tool for Combating Child Labour: Experience in Pakistan." ILO Technical Paper 2, presented at the International Labour Organization–Japan Asian Regional Meeting, "Monitoring Child Labor at the Workplace," Dhaka, Bangladesh, October 24–26. http://www.ilo.org/ public/english/region/asro/bangkok/paper/dhaka/tpaper2.pdf.

Swainson, Nicola. 1980. *The Development of Corporate Capitalism in Kenya 1918–1977*. Berkeley, CA: University of California Press.

UNCTAD (United Nations Conference on Trade and Development). 2008. *World Investment Report 2008: Transnational Corporations and the Infrastructure Challenge*. Geneva: United Nations.

UNIDO (United Nations Industrial Development Organization). 2009. "Global Value Chains, Local Clusters, and Corporate Social Responsibility: A Comparative Assessment of the Sports Goods Clusters in Sialkot, Pakistan, and Jalandhar, India." Technical Paper 17, UNIDO, Vienna.

World Bank. 1990. "Tanzania: Morogoro Textile Project Report." Project Performance Assessment Report 8696, Operations Evaluation Department, World Bank, Washington, DC.

# 9

# Textiles and Apparel

## Introduction

This chapter presents five case studies: three successful ventures, and two that are struggling. The studies illustrate how policies may shape the outcomes of industrialization.

Bangladesh's successful garment sector began not as a government initiative, but as a joint venture combining Bangladesh's low-cost labor with the expertise, technology, marketing, and training of the Korean firm Daewoo to launch a productive and competitive industry that now employs about half the industrial workers in Bangladesh. This partnership was possible because the government had liberalized policies to encourage foreign direct investment (FDI). An export processing zone eased constraints and enabled the sector to expand. Ready-made garment production flourished in the zone, which furnished firms with land, factory buildings, reliable access to utilities, quick permitting procedures, and a host of other incentives, including tax holidays and duty-free imports of raw materials and machinery. The sector's employment share in manufacturing rose from 1.5 percent in 1970 to 49 percent in 1998, while its output share increased from 3.3 percent to 35 percent. The export figures are even more impressive. Textiles, which made up less than 1 percent of manufacturing and less than 1 percent of total exports in the 1980s, climbed to 79 percent and 72 percent, respectively.

The case study of sari production in India illustrates how an industry must upgrade and innovate to remain competitive. Sari production started small, using simple tools. Skills were transferred across generations in this traditional craft. Low labor costs and an abundance of raw materials point to a strong comparative advantage. The industry did well until new technology arrived. Handmade saris have largely been replaced by saris produced by power looms. Rising input prices, low labor productivity, skilled-labor shortages, and poor infrastructure have further burdened the industry. Rising production costs, coupled with a lack of credit, are making investment in modern machinery and equipment difficult.

Lesotho is a landlocked country that has succeeded at garment production. The small, young industry originated in South African textile firms, which moved to Lesotho to evade the sanctions imposed on South Africa during the 1980s. South African investors alleviated many constraints that Lesotho entrepreneurs faced by providing financing, improving trade logistics, and easing access to input industries. These investors were followed by others from China and from Taiwan, China, demonstrating the importance of FDI for the sector's growth and development. Additionally, fiscal incentives provided by the Lesotho government and low labor costs contributed to the garment sector's success.

When the sector evolved and showed signs of success, the government introduced policies to facilitate the sector's expansion by building and installing factory shells, reducing import duties to zero, lowering taxes, and making credit guarantees available to exporters. A business association was also established to look after the interests of textile firms.

The excellent performance of Mauritius's textile and apparel sector can be attributed to the launch of an export processing zone in 1970. The export processing zone ensured smooth access to inputs and land in a favorable location between producers of raw cotton and end users. Incentives such as the suspension of import duties on raw materials and equipment and a well-managed exchange rate kept input costs low, a boon to export companies early in development. Moreover, underemployed women were trained, thereby providing a steady source of labor for production. Openness to foreign investment was a key to success, and the investments helped alleviate domestic financing constraints.

Zambia's apparel industry was adversely affected by the government's macro and industrial policies. Currently, the three main constraints on Zambia's competitiveness in apparel are poor trade logistics, low labor efficiency, and high input costs. In addition to Zambia's great distance from ports, other cost-inflating factors include delays at intermediate borders, high fuel prices, and poor-quality roads.

An absence of competitive input industries in Zambia raises the input costs for apparel producers. While the country produces high-quality cotton, this does not translate into lower input costs for local producers because Zambia exports all its cotton, the price of cotton is high, and the spinning and textile industries are weak.

## Apparel Production, Bangladesh

The garment industry has been a source of economic growth in Bangladesh. From modest beginnings, it is now world renowned, accounting for 5 percent of the country's gross domestic product (GDP) and close to 50 percent of industrial employment. Over 2007–11, the industry doubled its export volume to $17.5 billion, close to 80 percent of the total exports of the country. Its output has remained strong despite myriad obstacles. Ready-made garments and knitwear have accounted for more than 70 percent of manufacturing investments over the last two decades. The industry began with the production of final goods before advancing to more complex production, including intermediate goods.

The industry has grown dramatically under the guidance of the Bangladesh Garment Manufacturers and Exporters Association, from about 30 factories in the early 1980s to an estimated 5,100 in 2011. The sector employs 3.6 million people, 80 percent of them women. As wages in China rise, there will be pressures on Chinese factories to move to Bangladesh to take advantage of the combination of price competitiveness and quality.

The garment industry has put Bangladesh on the international industrial map. The country is the fourth-largest garment exporter among developing countries, after China, Turkey, and India (GDS 2011). Its wage rates remain among the lowest in the world and are currently around half those in China. Companies such as Walmart and H&M increasingly see Bangladesh as a lowest cost producer. Recently, with an investment of $200 million, Multiline Limited, a top trading firm, started building a textile factory, one of the world's largest, 50 kilometers north of Dhaka. Investors from Taiwan, China, have also set up more than two dozen footwear, textile, and furniture factories in Bangladesh. About 18 percent of Bangladesh's exports are produced in the country's export processing zones. Bangladesh is now second only to the Republic of Korea in the number of firms in such zones. However, the literacy rate is only 55 percent, well below China's more than 92 percent, and workers in Bangladesh are only a quarter as productive in making woven clothes relative to workers in China (Bajaj 2010).

The industry consists of a low technology base and a semiskilled workforce. Most exports go to the European Union (EU) and the United States. The industry has been in transition because of the expiration of the Multi-Fiber Arrangement, which governed world textiles. It employs directly nearly 3.6 million people, mainly illiterate rural women, and several estimates suggest that there are links and ancillary channels to another 15 million. The presence of large amounts of surplus labor has helped the industry because the industry builds on low technology and is labor intensive.

## Origin and Course of Development

Bangladesh has experienced renewed macroeconomic stability and robust growth over the past three decades. Annual real GDP growth averaged 3.2 percent in the 1980s, 4.8 percent in the 1990s, and 5.9 percent in 2000–10 (World Bank 2012). Though still volatile, inflation has been in single digits since 1996 (figure 9.1). Interest rates peaked at 11.3 percent in 1985 and gradually dropped to 5.0 percent in 2010, tracking inflation.

The industry has benefited from government reforms that have improved the business and investment climate. Since the mid-1980s, tariff and nontariff barriers have fallen substantially, making Bangladesh one of South Asia's most open economies. Exchange rate adjustments during the 1990s and 2000s caused garment exports to become more competitive, while strong monetary reform to reduce inflation

**Figure 9.1 Inflation Rate, Bangladesh, 1980–2010**

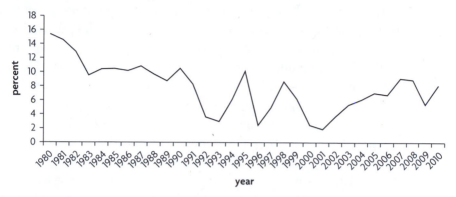

*Source:* International Financial Statistics (database), International Monetary Fund, Washington, DC, http://elibrary-data
.imf.org/FindDataReports.aspx?d=33061&e=169393.
*Note:* The rate is based on the consumer price index.

has lowered input costs. Other measures have improved the business environment, making Bangladesh more attractive to FDI.

**Development of the garment industry.** The tale of the Bangladeshi garment industry begins in 1979. Korean textile producers were searching for new markets (Rhee 1990). Daewoo, a leading Korean garment exporter, and Desh Company, a local private garment start-up established by a former civil servant, signed a five-year agreement to collaborate on technical training, machinery and fabric purchases, plant start-ups, and marketing. The Desh-Daewoo alliance allowed Daewoo to bring capital and expertise into Bangladesh. Desh would provide the labor and the land, while Daewoo would train managers and workers, install and supervise the use of new machinery it sold to Desh, advise on production, procure raw materials, and market the company's products internationally.

Under the terms of this collaborative venture, Desh would pay Daewoo royalties for technical training and supervision that would be equal to 3 percent of sales, as well as a sales commission for marketing services equal to 5 percent of the sales value during the contract period. The agreement did not include any investment or financing other than for fabric and other intermediate inputs bought using short-term credit. Under the agreement, 130 Bangladeshi workers were sent to the Pusan Garment Factory in Korea for intensive on-the-job skills training and hands-on experience in running a factory. When the training ended, they returned to Bangladesh, along with three Daewoo engineers assigned to install the machinery, and helped start up production. Three production lines were set up within five months, with 450 machines and a total of 500 workers. An additional three production lines were formed to educate new recruits. Desh exported its first products in 1980: 43,000 shirts at an export value of $56,000.[1]

Desh's experience and reputation grew. It cancelled its collaborative agreement with Daewoo in 1981, about 18 months after factory operations started. Over a short six years, Desh grew at an average annual rate of 90 percent; its workforce nearly tripled from 500 to 1,400; and the number of machines jumped from 450 to 750. Desh's successes motivated large numbers of local entrepreneurs to start their own businesses, including some of the 130 workers trained by Daewoo in Korea. Foreign buyers retained majority control in the marketing operations of the local mills. This provided a solid foundation for successful expansion, and, in subsequent years, the industry proliferated because of the initial investment in training. Some former Desh employees joined new garment factories established by affluent businesspeople, while others founded trading houses, which helped the sector grow by providing a variety of services, including international procurement and marketing and design reengineering.

So successful was Desh's collaboration with Daewoo that, in 1985, the United States imposed quotas on imports of Bangladeshi garments under the Multi-Fiber Arrangement: the country's apparel exports had captured 1 percent of the U.S. market. The Multi-Fiber Arrangement ended in 1994, and, by 2000–01, Bangladesh had captured 3.3 percent of the U.S. market. Exports were 43 percent higher in Europe, where Bangladesh enjoyed better trade access, particularly under the Everything but Arms Generalized System of Preferences scheme introduced in 2001. Although formal collaboration with Daewoo had ended, guidance and consultation continued through other means. Other East Asian and Korean companies followed Daewoo's lead, providing garment-related import and export trade intermediation and production line expertise for product upgrading and diversification.

**How the garment industry flourished.** The innovative back-to-back letter-of-credit system helped achieve the phenomenal growth in Bangladeshi garment exports. The founder of Desh and the father of the 100 percent export-oriented garment industry, M. Noorul Quader, developed and formally launched the system in the mid-1980s. Operating in stages, the system minimizes the need for working capital or foreign exchange, resulting in substantial reductions in the cost of producing garments.

The system works as follows: A foreign buyer places an order with a garment exporter, and a master letter of credit covering all risk is issued guaranteeing payment to the exporter. The letter is transmitted to a bank in Bangladesh. The exporter then opens an import letter of credit with the same bank to cover imports of raw materials and other inputs, with a term of about 180 days. The purchase price of raw materials may not exceed 70 percent of the export earnings. After the exporter has produced and shipped the garments, and the buyer has confirmed receipt, the buyer's bank makes a cash transfer to the exporter's bank in Bangladesh.

The system gives entrepreneurs the opportunity to set up factories with a low capital investment and enables the industry to grow rapidly. For firms that have acquired sufficient scale, export credit may be available in the local currency from commercial banks at concessional interest rates.

The Bangladeshi garment industry mastered the supply chain early on. The industry depends largely on imported yarns and fabrics; only about 10 percent of the export-quality cloth used by the garment industry is produced domestically. A large share of Bangladeshi machinery and fabric is imported from China, the industry's biggest supplier.

The labor cost structure of the industry has guaranteed its competitiveness, making the cost of Bangladeshi textiles among the lowest in the world. As of October 2010, garment labor rates in Bangladesh ($46) were roughly a third those in China ($117–$147) and less than two-thirds those in Cambodia and Vietnam, thereby ensuring competitive production costs (figure 9.2). The low wages reflect, in part, widespread noncompliance with labor laws. Since 2006, workers have gone on strike demanding better wages and working conditions. Following

**Figure 9.2  Monthly Labor Rates, Selected Asian Countries, 2010**

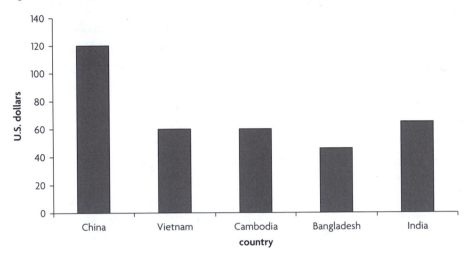

*Source:* Interviews with authorities at the Dacca export processing zone, 2012, and with directors at textile companies, Guangzhou, China, 2012.

protests in textile factories over wages in 2010, a government oversight board nearly doubled the minimum wage in the garment industry.

Meanwhile, garment prices have been rising. Together with the higher minimum wages, the cost of doing business has risen because of erratic gas and power supplies, higher freight charges, rising yarn prices, and the higher costs of transport and capital machinery. Production costs rose 25 percent in 2009, an increase reflected in high output prices as well.

## Competitiveness and Binding Constraints

The garment industry's key constraints—lack of entrepreneurial skills, land, and reliable power—were relaxed through the creation of export processing zones and joint ventures with foreign firms. The government helped determine the location of the zones and helped build factory shells, solving many problems for garment firms. Nearly 20 percent of garment exports come from the zones. Many Bangladeshi textile firms relocated to the zones to produce garments for export. Firms in the zones may produce only for export; they are forbidden from selling their products on the domestic market. Land and factory buildings are available for lease, and the zones provide stable sources of power, water, and electricity. Import and export permits are issued within 24 hours, and work permits are issued by the Bangladeshi zone agency. Workers are forbidden by law to form labor unions. Tax holidays for 10 years, income tax exemptions on the interest on borrowed capital, and no restrictions on the repatriation of capital have helped attract foreign investment. Machinery, equipment, and raw materials can be imported duty-free, and exports are also duty-free.

## The Role of Government

The policy regime in Bangladesh has evolved, and protection levels have gradually been reduced. Following independence in December 1971, Bangladesh nationalized large-scale industries, including jute, sugar, and textiles. However, the government has since encouraged the development of private sector manufacturing companies. Import licensing was liberalized in 1980 and abolished in the 1990s. Progressive liberalization and an easing of the restrictions on private FDI have helped the industry grow.

Policies in the export processing zones have fostered industry expansion. The fiscal regime is favorable to small and medium firms. The government allows companies to import machinery duty-free. To encourage the use of local fabrics in the export-oriented garment industry, the government provides incentives for the spinning and weaving industries, including a 15 percent cash subsidy for the cost of fabric to exporters sourcing fabric locally.

Bonded warehouse facilities have reduced capital costs and trade logistics costs. The facilities, introduced in the 1980s, enable firms that produce only for export to import fabrics and other inputs duty-free. Tight controls by customs authorities prevent the imported inputs from being used to produce for the domestic market. The bonded warehouse facilities have lowered administrative costs for exporters by exempting them from import duties and taxes immediately rather than requiring them to apply for refunds.

The Bangladesh Textile Mills Corporation is the industry's regulatory body. The Bangladesh Garment Manufacturers and Exporters Association is a trade facilitation body for the industry. It works to promote corporate social responsibility and offers courses in design, merchandising, and related topics. It negotiates with foreign buyers, businesses, trade associations, chambers of commerce, and research organizations to strengthen the export base. It also protects worker rights and lobbied successfully to raise the minimum wage by 80 percent, from Tk 1,660 ($24) in 2006 to Tk 3,000 ($43) in 2010.

The association has strongly supported skills upgrading. This support helps make up for the lack of formal education, technical knowledge, and managerial skills among entrepreneurs and workers.

Bangladesh has the lowest garment wages in the world. Worker unrest led to an 80 percent increase in the minimum wage in July 2010. The sector also suffers from worker safety issues, high input costs, gas shortages, energy blackouts, perceptions of poor product quality, inefficiencies in trade facilitation, and long lead times. The collapse of a garment factory in April 2013 has prompted a debate about safety standards and led to greater awareness and protests to enforce building regulations. The country has begun to partner with the International Labour Organization to improve working standards.

## Summary

The Bangladeshi garment industry took off as a result of the local entrepreneurial spirit, which was advanced by FDI and supported by good government policies. An innovative first mover created a strong emulation effect, creating one of the world's leading textile production centers. The development of an export processing zone with a supportive policy regime, coupled with novel financing arrangements under the back-to-back letter-of-credit system, has led to the mushrooming of the sector. As wages in China rise, the Bangladeshi textile industry will grow and become a central player in the global garment industry.

## Sari Production, India

As an emerging major economy in the world, with more than a billion people, India has registered average GDP growth of more than 6 percent a year since it began to implement a series of liberalizing reforms in the 1990s. Now the global call center capital, it has one of the world's most rapidly growing service sectors. Despite these successes, manufacturing lags. The textile industry has had some achievements, with a 12 percent share of the country's export earnings, 14 percent of the country's industrial production, and 4 percent of GDP in 2011, according to India's Ministry of Textiles. Yet, global competition, especially from East Asia, has been threatening the industry. The handloom sector, which makes saris, faces strong competition from imports and from mechanized power looms in the modern Indian textile sector. For the moment, it remains India's second-largest employer. The handloom sector represents a microcosm of the small-scale sector, which contributes 40 percent of industrial value added in India, but faces significant challenges.

More than 60 percent of the handloom industry has collapsed in Varanasi in north India since 2003. In Kanjeevaram, weavers produced output valued at $10 million in 2011, barely a quarter of the $40 million in 2004. Similar dynamics afflict the entire industry, a collection of small-scale establishments throughout the country: 10 million weavers and 3.8 million handlooms produced more than 5 billion meters of fabric in 2005. The modern textile industry and the power loom have cut sharply into traditional handloom production. The industry began small and simple, by using inexpensive equipment to produce a low-end final product for well-defined markets, but the industry has suffered in the step toward more mechanized production. What was once a promising process of industrialization, with high labor intensity and low skill requirements, appears to have become too complex so that saris are internationally uncompetitive. The government has provided some support, but not enough to turn the industry around.

The once vibrant sari industry faces major cost difficulties. In recent years, the emergence of power looms has led to the decline of sari weaving on handlooms. Computer-aided units imprint the design onto power-loomed cloth, a process that is cheaper and more rapid than handlooming. This technology reduces design and processing time from an average 5–15 days per sari on a handloom to four saris a day on a power loom.

High silk prices have also hurt the handloom industry. India is the largest consumer of silk and silk products and the second-largest producer of silk. During 2009–10, India imported raw silk worth $200 million from Brazil, China, and the Islamic Republic of Iran. After China joined the World Trade Organization (WTO), the Chinese silk industry rose quickly to prominence. Silk exports from India fell 23 percent, from $251 million during April–September 2000 to $193 million during April–September 2001 and have slightly increased to $260 million during April-September 2010. Many traditional firms have been unable to compete because of a lack of technological inputs for modernization and the lack of skill development. The difficulty of acquiring land for factory expansion has impeded growth. The industry is stagnating in a changing world.

## Origin and Course of Development

The Indian sari industry has a long history. Large, but fragmented into thousands of small-scale shops throughout the country, the industry has a major cluster centered around Varanasi, where 700,000 of India's 10 million weavers work. Traditionally, most weavers have been Dalits and Muslims who passed down their skills over generations. Working conditions are poor, with little opportunity to improve skills. Many weavers work in bonded conditions, taking cash advances from a master weaver and repaying in installments when the saris are sold. In Kanjeevaran, in southern India, where more than 50,000 people are producing saris, a local union estimates that one in five weavers is bonded. Lack of education, lack of market information, weak technical knowledge, and inadequate access to finance all prevent the small companies from growing.

Competition is mounting at all levels of the industry. In 2010, the most prized saris were from Kanjeevaram and Varanasi. These sumptuous saris are worn at weddings and other formal functions, can take up to a month to weave, and sell for $70–$1,500. The silken gold-brocaded saris woven in Varanasi are especially prized for their workmanship. Kanjeevaram saris are made by cooperative societies of weavers. The high prices have attracted counterfeiting: fake Varanasi saris are usually made on power looms. Sometimes, counterfeiters of the Kanjeevaram silk sari use artificial silk and pass the saris off as genuine.

## Competitiveness and Binding Constraints

The cost structure for saris has been favorable to some in the industry, including the weavers, but the economics has changed. Handloom weaving relies on simple, low-cost machinery, but the machinery prevents scale production. Sari weaving is labor intensive, paying only Rs 2,400 ($53) per month (Rs 350–Rs 1,000 per sari) in the mid-1990s to Rs 1,440 ($32) per month in 2010. The input costs for sari weavers have dropped because of imports of Chinese silk. Despite a 10 percent

**Figure 9.3  Cost of Indian- and Chinese-Made Saris, 2007**

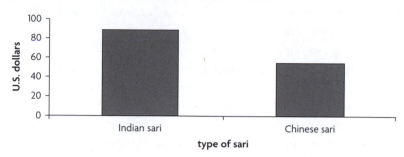

*Source:* Gupta and Alley 2012.

duty, Chinese silk, at $1.00–$1.25 per meter, is less than half the cost of Indian silk ($2.50–$4.00) resulting in a large difference in the production cost of Indian versus Chinese saris (figure 9.3). In 2012, Chinese saris cost Rs 2,500 ($30), while standard Indian saris cost slightly less than Rs 3,000 ($50), and the more luxurious Kanjeevaram and Varanasi silk saris cost from about Rs 4,000 and up ($75) at the retail level (Gupta and Alley 2012). So, there is some profit at the higher niche.

Difficult access to financing has prevented expansion and employment growth in the sari industry. Most of the industry's capital comes from the generally well-off master weavers. Access to credit is difficult for those on the lower end of production who lack sufficient collateral.

A serious challenge is the shortage of skilled workers. The average daily wage for a sari weaver is about Rs 250 (close to $4.60), significantly below wages in service sector jobs in India. In many clusters, workers are leaving to find jobs at higher pay in the country's growing service economy, especially in telecommunications and information technology. Many of the unskilled workers in the sari sector are women and are unable to transition to the service sector. Some companies have responded to the labor exodus by raising wages. Low labor productivity has also constrained industry expansion. Production in the handloom sector is generally at less than half capacity because of the obsolete machines and frequent power shortages, which have prevented firms from upgrading. Sari producers routinely complain that inadequate machinery is hurting industry expansion.

The cost structure varies with the type of weaver. Self-employed weavers have their own looms and buy silk on credit from suppliers. They weave the sari and sell it to traders through master weavers, who oversee weaving and marketing. Contract weavers obtain silk from master weavers and weave saris on a piece-rate basis. Wages depend on the design and bargaining power of the weaver, but are generally about 80 percent of what they would get working alone. Finally, most weavers work on handlooms owned by master weavers, who supply the silk and pay the wages.

In some sari-producing areas, cooperatives have been set up to help the industry grow. The cooperatives are controlled mainly by traders who have their own registered businesses. The government provides concessional loans to the master weavers and cooperatives to improve the access to financing, as these two groups account for the bulk of retail sales. In a cooperative, members contribute the share capital. The government provides financial assistance in the form of share capital contributions; loans for the construction of premises and for the purchase of handlooms and silk at subsidized rates; and subsidies to meet managerial expenses, to allow rebates on the sari sale, to cover the cost of insurance and pensions, and to modernize cooperative retail outlets.

Only one in five weavers belongs to a cooperative; so, most do not benefit from the related advantages. For this group, the lack of access to finance makes the expansion of production and improvement in skills difficult. The sector's low productivity arises because of the marginalization and lack of capital of most weavers, which prevents them from benefiting from closer relationships with bigger players.

A key weakness in the marketing of saris has been the lack of support for the enhancement of design skills in small and medium enterprises (SMEs). There is considerable versatility at the higher end of the industry, but little adaptability to consumer demand at the lower end, where there are no industry associations to provide this kind of feedback. Changing consumer preferences have hurt the industry. Buyer demand has varied with shifting trends in fashion. Younger women prefer shirts and jeans over traditional saris. The good-quality saris that were originally targeted to the mass market are being remarketed to a niche market.

## The Role of Government

The government has tried to attend to the needs of the industry, but without much success. While helping the industry in some ways, India's economic environment has raised input and capital costs.

Despite competitive labor costs and an abundance of raw materials, the handloom industry and India's manufacturing sector generally suffer from multiple constraints. The most obvious constraint is the fragmentation of the industry, which makes the achievement of scale difficult. The lack of capital to expand production is another problem. After years of restrictive policies on foreign capital, the government has simplified the licensing regime and lowered import duties on capital equipment, enabling foreign investors to set up manufacturing facilities in India. Yet, few foreign investors have been attracted to sari production. Years of restrictions have deprived the industry of much-needed foreign capital, expertise, technology, and information, including technical knowledge, market information, managerial skills, and education.

India's labor laws have also impeded the industry from expanding and scaling up. Many companies have remained small and informal to avoid stringent labor regulations.[2] By keeping firms out of the formal sector, such legislation prevents companies from upgrading worker skills and from obtaining sufficient capital to reinvest in the business.

The infrastructure deficit in India has also hurt the sector. Poor transport infrastructure slows the delivery of raw materials, while high, unpredictable electricity costs have impeded machinery upgrading that could boost output and drive costs down. Many spinning mills and small handloom shops have failed because of problems along the supply chain. Greater government commitment to industrial growth and development is needed to enable the industry to expand.

Multiple government measures are designed to shield the industry from competition. For example, the government imposed import duties on raw silk and fabric. Over 1995–98, the government banned imports of Chinese raw silk, but the silk was smuggled in because of its quality. As of January 2011, the duty was 30 percent on raw silk and 14 percent on silk fabrics. However, because the annual demand in India exceeds supply by 8,000 tons, the duty was subsequently reduced by the government to 5 percent to help the big weavers benefit from cheaper Chinese silk; more than 75 percent of the silk in sari weaving areas such as Varanasi comes from China. This measure, while unpopular with Indian silk farmers, has helped reduce costs among weavers. India currently produces only about 22,000 tons of raw silk each year against the demand for 30,000 tons of silk.

The government has instituted a new textile development policy for the silk industry, a five-point directive covering productivity, quality, quantity, product diversification, and competitive pricing. To protect handloom weavers from competition from power loom operators, a 1985 law prohibits sari weaving on power looms. The government has also subsidized power looms to enable industry expansion. In 2009, the government granted a patent to protect silk saris made in Varanasi. All these measures have been fairly ineffective in changing the cost parameters in the industry. To become fully competitive again, the industry needs a broader and more decisive transformation in inputs, financing, and skills.

## Summary

Sari production has a rich tradition in India as a labor-intensive industry. It has recently faced increased competition from other countries that are able to replicate designs more cheaply. Lacking advanced machinery and damaged by cheap imports, the industry is struggling to remain viable.

# The Apparel Industry, Lesotho

Lesotho has built a strong and thriving garment industry thanks in large measure to the U.S. African Growth and Opportunity Act (AGOA), which allows any of 1,600 African products to enter the United States duty-free. The industry has been spurred by hardworking labor, a favorable fiscal regime, and a progressive government, which has endorsed economic growth as a development priority. Lesotho has emerged as a top beneficiary of AGOA and is now the largest Sub-Saharan exporter of apparel to the United States, despite the small economy. The Lesotho apparel industry has been transformed from a marginal industry to a globally integrated industry assembling garments for some of the world's most well known brands.

Lesotho has partnered with the International Labour Organization to improve labor standards and to promote the country as an ethical sourcing location. A large reason for the success of Lesotho textiles has been the open-door policy toward FDI. Foreign ownership has brought in finance, simplified trade logistics, eased the supply of inputs, and provided access to technical knowledge, managerial skills, and market information.

**Figure 9.4  Textile Industry Employment, Lesotho, 1999–2009**

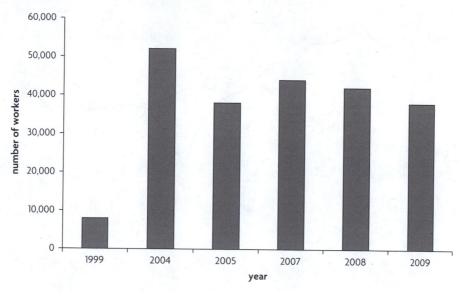

*Source:* Mthente 2009.

Lesotho's clothing exports to the United States totaled more than $500 million in mid-2002, five times the $100 million in 2001. Lesotho produces more than a quarter of Sub-Saharan Africa's exports of ready-made garments to the United States. Total production is estimated at 90 million knitted garments at 25 factories, with sales of $340 million in 2008. Lesotho has been dubbed the jeans capital of Africa, producing 26 million pairs of denim jeans a year at eight factories. Textile employment increased from fewer than 10,000 workers in 1999 to close to 55,000 in 2004 and 39,000 in 2009 (figure 9.4). After losing migrant worker jobs in the 1990s to South Africa's gold and coal mines, the Lesotho economy has recovered.

## Origin and Course of Development

Lesotho has grown robustly during the past decade. Real GDP growth averaged 3.4 percent annually over 2000–10. Interest rates declined from a peak of 19.5 percent in 1996 to 9.5 percent in 2010. Inflation has been in single digits since 2002 (except in 2008). The loti has remained fairly competitive with the yuan (figure 9.5).

The textile industry in Lesotho originated in the 1970s when members of an agricultural mission from Taiwan, China, visited Lesotho to discuss

**Figure 9.5 Real Effective Exchange Rate, Lesotho Loti and Chinese Yuan, 1990–2011**

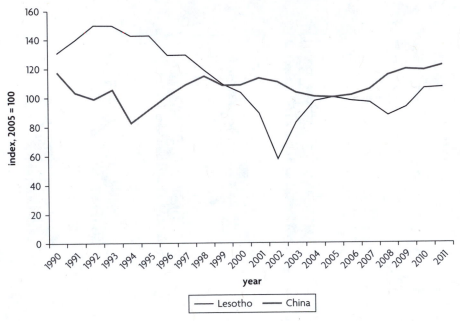

Source: Data of International Financial Statistics (database), International Monetary Fund, Washington, DC, http://elibrary-data.imf.org/FindDataReports.aspx?d=33061&e=169393.
Note: The rate is based on the consumer price index.

potential areas of collaboration and decided to stay on and set up a retail shop. Lesotho, a mountainous kingdom, has no industry other than textiles. Surrounded entirely by South Africa, Lesotho benefits from that country's good logistics. Textile and apparel production facilities in Lesotho have been largely foreign owned and export-oriented. In the early 1980s, South African investors established facilities in Lesotho to evade the sanctions imposed on South African manufactured goods in Lesotho. In the early 1990s, industrialists from Taiwan, China, invested in Lesotho, bringing valuable capital and skills. Many of the investors faced growing competition at home, where their outdated technologies were reducing their efficiency. Under apartheid, the South African government had offered incentives for firms to locate in the Bantustan industrial zones, and many of them moved to Lesotho in the mid-1990s when Lesotho was liberalizing its investment regime to attract FDI to the textile sector.

The government of Lesotho offered several attractive incentives to foreign investors. Visa requirements were waived, and investors were offered cheap rents for preconstructed factory shells, streamlined administrative procedures, and a five-year tax holiday. Investors also had access to government ministers. Encouraged by these measures, subsidiaries of large international garment manufacturers gradually set up operations locally. Entrepreneurs from China and from Taiwan, China, provided most of the capital. For example, the vertically integrated Formosa Denim Mill, with investments of $120 million in 2004, produces 6,300 tons of denim jeans (1.3 million yards of denim fabric) and 900 tons of cotton yarn a year.[3] Using 16,000 tons of cotton imported from Benin, Malawi, Mozambique, Tanzania, and Zambia, Formosa Denim Mill includes spinning, weaving and knitting, dyeing, and garment making. It also sells denim fabric and yarn to other garment manufacturers. Most of its 40 main manufacturers are from Taiwan, China.

The cluster emerged in the late 1990s in response to new international trade preferences and rules of origin. After the early expansion because of AGOA, the industry suffered, shedding 13,000 workers in 2004–05 and shutting down factories. Strong appreciation of the exchange rate, as the value of the U.S. dollar fell from M 11.4 in 2002 to M 6.9 in 2006, made exports to the United States more expensive and imports cheaper. The loti is linked to the South African rand; so, volatility in the rand leads to volatility in the loti. Expiration of the Multi-Fiber Arrangement eliminated the quota system and preferential treatment. In 2002, Lesotho's garment factories had to sell roughly $55 in clothing in the United States to cover a factory worker's monthly wage. By early 2005, the figure had risen to $109–$115. The industry suffered another downturn in 2008–09, when 8,000 workers were laid off because of falling demand in the United States associated with the financial crisis. In the face of these setbacks, the industry has demonstrated good resilience.

## Competitiveness and Binding Constraints

The Lesotho supply chain is competitive on price and has demonstrated a strong mastery of inputs and trade logistics. The parameters of the industry are high-volume, low-margin final products, with a clear, efficient cost structure. In recent years, there have been some challenges of the underlying model, but the advantages remain.

The input industries are managed efficiently and serve the textile industry. Cotton and yarn are imported from other African countries and from China. Some inputs are sourced from China; Hong Kong, China; and Taiwan, China. Because Lesotho has only one textile mill, fabrics are imported for local processing. Many major textile companies also use third-country denim fabric to supplement their own production and to respond flexibly to their end customers. Economies of scale exist for vertically integrated firms such as the CGM Group, which is engaged in spinning, weaving, dyeing, and garment making.[4] Vertical integration has increased the quality and reliability of inputs and minimized supply disruptions. Buyers gain economies of scale and quality control because the fabric sourcing is concentrated in a few factories, and this lowers costs.

Ideally, vertical integration also reduces trade logistics costs. Sourcing fabrics locally reduces lead times, mainly in shipping. However, the local industry does not have sufficient economies of scale to produce the raw material inputs and must import them from Asia. It costs $3,000 to ship a 40-foot container from China to Port Elizabeth or Durban, South Africa (21 days), and $2,500 for road transport through South Africa to Maseru, the capital of Lesotho (2–5 days). Road transport costs from Arusha to Dar es Salaam and Port Elizabeth to Maseru are almost as much as shipping costs (FIAS 2006). Customs clearance and loading and unloading at ports are a source of frequent delays. The U.S. Agency for International Development finds that the land component of the total transport and logistics costs is greater than the sea component (Mpata, Giersing, and Kaombwe 2005).[5] Nonetheless, importing from Asia remains the optimal choice for obtaining the highest quality inputs efficiently.

Several factors constrain the expansion of Lesotho's exports despite the strong market presence. Poor infrastructure, particularly the shortage of factory shells and industrial infrastructure, discourages new investment. Establishing additional industrial parks could ease these constraints. The distribution network is excellent, but Lesotho's landlocked status lengthens the shipping times to export markets. Industry sources repeatedly cite water and wastewater treatment infrastructure as key areas for improvement. Other constraints are poor road networks, frequent power outages, and inadequate water supplies. In recent years, an increase of more than 10 percent in the cost of water and electricity for the industry has eroded some of the cost advantages.

Skilled and semiskilled workers have been plentiful in Lesotho, and textile factories have had a positive effect on local employment. The textile industry employs more than 40,000 semiskilled workers and is the largest employer after the government. Industry estimates suggest that about 36,400 workers are employed full time, while about 3,600 are employed on a temporary or casual basis. Workers engaged in Lesotho's textile and garment industry earned about M 306 million ($48 million) in 2005 (Bennett 2008). Workers are semiskilled, predominantly women, and well educated. With wages averaging $125 per month, labor costs are relatively low.

According to several experts, Lesotho's labor laws meet International Labour Organization standards, which include a ban on child labor and a maximum 55-hour work week. Workers sometimes log 11-hour days and receive no health or pension benefits. Lesotho's textile and apparel manufacturers must comply with the same labor laws as the country's other private sector firms.

Garment firms have begun to invest in staff training, sometimes with spectacular results. There are ancillary effects in related industries such as packaging (which uses paperboard imported from South Africa), freight transport, courier services, shipping and forwarding agents, security, taxis, and street traders who sell food to factory workers. All these links make the industry a strong employment generator.

The Lesotho textile cluster consists of a variety of firms selling a diverse array of products, with considerable specialization. Intermediate products (textiles) make up the largest share of industry output. In 2007, the textile industry consisted of woven garment producers (19,045 workers in 11 firms), knit garment producers (26,218 workers in 30 firms), and denim fabric and cotton yarn producers (1,255 workers in 1 firm), for a total industry employment of about 47,000, which is 80 percent of all manufacturing jobs. In 47 of the firms, women constituted the largest group of workers. Productivity differentials abound within the industry, which needs to move beyond low-margin, mass-produced products by offering more sophisticated finishes on products such as T-shirts and jeans and by producing more sophisticated final goods.

## The Role of Government

The Lesotho textile industry has benefited from a range of government incentives to reduce trade logistics and fiscal costs. A key contribution has been the building and installation of factory shells to help companies get started. Government incentives are intended to enable manufacturers to import fabric duty-free as long as they export the garments they make from these fabrics outside the South African Customs Union. Exports are eligible for duty-credit certificates, which are tradable instruments that can be used to offset the duties on fabric and garment imports. Certificates earned in Lesotho could be sold in South Africa until 2010, but firms earning the certificates must spend 3 percent of their payroll on training.[6] (Lesotho has no other training taxes or levies.) Finally, the Lesotho National Development Corporation can finance projects through loans or take equity investments. An interministerial body monitors issues of investment promotion and tax concessions. The Central Bank of Lesotho provides credit guarantee assistance to exporters.

Exporters have a more favorable domestic tax regime than do manufacturers providing for the domestic market. The export sector's tax regime has improved the access to finance. The government has reduced the corporate tax rate from 15 percent to 0 percent for firms that export products outside the South African Customs Union and to 10 percent for firms that sell products within it. The regime has been liberal, with a permanent maximum tax rate of 15 percent on profits. There is no withholding tax on dividends distributed by manufacturing firms to local or foreign shareholders, and companies pay no advanced corporation taxes on the distribution of manufacturing profits. Finally, the value added tax is 14 percent (ensuring harmonization with South Africa).

Trade incentives have complemented these preferences. AGOA provides preferential access to the U.S. market, and liberal rules of origin allow duty-free and quota-free export to the United States. Until August 2012, as a least developed country, Lesotho could source fabrics anywhere (single transformation rules of origin), but there were some concerns that the provision would expire. However, in August 2012, the U.S. Senate renewed the AGOA third-country fabric provision through September 30, 2015, allowing Lesotho continued liberal rules of origin for three more years. As the preference regime evolves, the resilience of

Lesotho textiles will be monitored closely. It costs as much as 30 percent less to make goods in China than in Lesotho, and, with the erosion of preferences, there is the added concern of even greater costs for Lesotho textile production.

## Summary

Lesotho's textile industry has risen to prominence in recent years, carving out an international niche and generating 20 percent of the country's GDP. Lesotho textiles demonstrate how input constraints and difficult trade logistics can be overcome to create a strong supply chain and a viable industry, which has become Africa's number one garment exporter to the United States and the biggest source of local employment. As in Mauritius (see below), the industry has benefited because the government has attracted FDI through favorable fiscal regimes and industrial zones, together with the successful use of preferential trade deals. However, unlike Mauritius and others, the Lesotho apparel industry has been mostly a phenomenon associated with FDI; there are few strictly local firms and few technological spillovers to the domestic economy. Nonetheless, the industry has prospered and helped Lesotho become a global exporter.

## The Textile and Apparel Industry, Mauritius

We are very adaptable and we have a strong network of suppliers and buyers, which we cultivate.

—*CEO, interview, Mauritius textile firm, June 2010*

One of the most successful industrial policy experiences in the developing world revolves around the production of textiles and apparel in Mauritius. A small island in the Indian Ocean far from markets and with only major resource, sugar, Mauritius has achieved middle-income status through visionary leadership and strong economic management (Zafar 2011). Export processing zones have played a prominent role in the Mauritian achievement. The country's experience building an industry from scratch offers several lessons for other developing countries. The ingenuity of Mauritians has been evident in their ability to capitalize on the country's location between producers of raw cotton and end users. By combining good-quality industrial land, good entrepreneurship, and a well-developed input industry, Mauritius has built a strong and vibrant textile and apparel sector.

The success of Mauritius's industrial policies has been dramatic. Starting with almost nothing in the 1970s, the industry has risen to international prominence. By the 1980s, thanks to export processing zones and other smart industrial policy interventions, textiles had become the leading industrial sector in the country, accounting for more than 60 percent of gross export earnings and a third of employment. The share of the textile sector in GDP tripled from 4 percent in 1980 to more than 14 percent by 1988 (figure 9.6), and the sector grew at close to 30 percent a year over 1983–88. Unemployment in Mauritius fell from 12 percent in 1980 to less than 5 percent in 1990. By the mid-1980s, the textile zones were so successful they had surpassed sugar as the principal export earner and employed more workers than the sugar industry and the public sector combined. Nearly three-fourths of exports went to the EU under a preferential arrangement, helping Mauritian firms expand.[7]

Mauritius followed an industrialization strategy that involved an initial focus on a specific sector, the concentration of resources on a single area of reform (the textile and garment industry), a full commitment to economic growth, and the implementation of the relevant policies at all levels. Moreover, Mauritius has managed to create strong backward links with other sectors of the economy, thereby spreading the beneficial effects of growth in the textile and apparel industry.

### Origin and Course of Development

Mauritius's economy grew at an average annual rate of 4.7 percent over 1980–2010. Inflation has been in single digits since 1994, reaching a decade high of 9.7 percent in 2010. The exchange rate and fiscal regimes have helped keep input costs low. To maintain a competitive exchange rate, the government devalued the rupee by 30 percent in 1979 and another 20 percent in 1981. The real effective exchange rate has since been maintained below equilibrium to guarantee that Mauritian exports remain competitive internationally. That exchange rate competitiveness stands in stark contrast to the situation in Kenya and Tanzania, which had long periods of exchange rate overvaluation.

**Figure 9.6  GDP, by Main Economic Sector, Mauritius, 1976–2009**

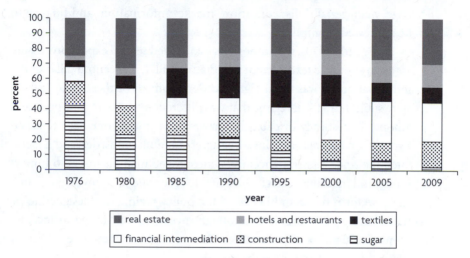

Source: World Bank 2009.

The emergence of the textile industry in Mauritius reflects visionary public policy. In the 1970s, leading policy makers grew concerned about the country's overdependence on sugar. Even though the Sugar Protocol with the EU guaranteed high prices for the country's sugar exports, policy makers wanted to diversify the economy to reduce the risk of economic shocks. A team of policy makers visited export processing zones in Hong Kong SAR, China; Singapore; and Taiwan, China. Cognizant of Mauritius's distance from markets and the high freight and shipping costs, the team identified textiles as an appropriate product for specialization. Their plans benefited from a network of local entrepreneurs who were well connected to Hong Kong SAR, China, and who had sufficient savings to start small, simple production activities.

According to our interviews with senior government officials in 2010, the decision to build the initial export processing zone was based on comparative advantage, an analysis of the low costs of textile transport compared with heavier products, and the growing demand in the EU and the United States for industrial goods. Moreover, Mauritius's many underemployed women were perceived as an asset for the new industry. In fact, women became the prime force in the growth and expansion of the country's export processing zones. In addition, many investors from Hong Kong SAR, China, were ready to take advantage of preferential deals.[8] The open-door policy to FDI enabled deficits in technical knowledge, managerial skills, education, market information, and finance to be addressed promptly.

In the early 1970s, the authorities established several export processing zones to stimulate textile exports and attract FDI. The central pillar of the industrial policy was the design and development of these zones, which were subject to a fiscal regime that was different from the regime prevalent among domestically oriented industries. The initial zone accomplished two goals: it allowed easy, duty-free access to input industries, and it facilitated the trade logistics. Incentives encouraged manufacturers to import inputs and machinery. Start-up capital for the zone was provided through sugar sector revenue and FDI, and the policy regime was designed to be friendly to both domestic and foreign investors. Established to increase domestic financing and attract foreign capital, the zones were extremely successful in accomplishing these goals.

## Competitiveness and Binding Constraints

The growth of the textile and apparel industry in Mauritius is a tale of the triumph of both the macroeconomic environment and the firm-level cost structure, which benefited from good input markets and favorable quotas in the markets of the EU. The pool of relatively cheap labor available because of the significant number of underemployed women, the large amounts of domestic capital, and the proximity to local raw materials also helped the industry take off. Mauritius's textile companies have been competitive on many key indicators, including price, product quality, rapid order responsiveness, and market channel strength. Each key constraint was overcome rapidly through public-private cooperation.

**Land and inputs.** The access to land was facilitated by the government provision of subsidized land and plug-and-play factory shells.

Mauritian textile and apparel firms source their raw materials from domestic and foreign suppliers. Although firms in the zones can buy imported raw materials duty-free, most of them source their fabrics from domestic firms because of the trust network, the good quality, and the low prices. Some companies obtain key products overseas, including yarn from India (which takes 12 weeks to arrive) and various items from

Europe. Few raw materials are sourced within the Southern African Development Community because of the dearth of good-quality inputs.

**Labor.** Textile and apparel firms in the zone have benefited from the availability of relatively cheap labor, drawing on unemployed workers across the island. In the early years, wage ceilings were in place, and workers were forbidden to unionize. The preferred labor pool consisted of semiskilled women workers with high school education. Training was provided, but wages were considerably lower at the textile firms than outside the zone, where an import-substitution industrialization regime was still in place. Because unemployment was widespread in the early 1980s, it was not difficult to find workers at low wages.

Companies followed flexible labor policies. More than 70 percent of firms now employ foreign labor. The reasons most often cited for this are lower absentee rates and higher productivity. The lower wages paid to the workers in the export processing zones in the early years allowed the firms to accumulate capital and reinvest the earnings in expansion. In recent years, wages have increased and are now higher than those in many competing countries (figure 9.7). To compete with lower-wage

**Figure 9.7  Labor Compensation in the Textile Industry, Selected Countries, 2002**

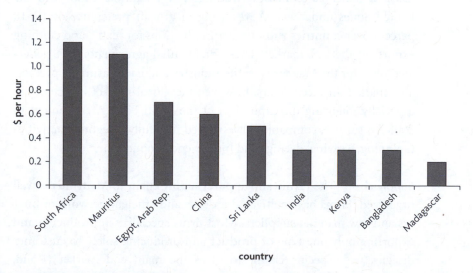

*Source:* Rojid, Sannassee, and Fowdar 2008.

producers, Mauritius has had to improve quality and productivity. Because of higher labor productivity, Mauritian firms do well on labor costs as a percentage of value added.

**Finance.** Ready access to capital has been vital to the success of the industry. Unlike many failed economic zones in much of the developing world, the program in Mauritius has benefited from the inflow of local capital to expand production (Bheenick and Schapiro 1989). Much of the local capital had been accumulated by investors in the sugar industry who benefited from numerous special sugar trade agreements. The large flow of domestic capital ensured a degree of local ownership that was not common in other countries. Many of the companies remain privately run, and, with no dividends to pay, the companies can reinvest their gains.

**Preferential trade arrangements.** Preferential arrangements have helped guarantee a good export market for Mauritian products. Mauritius has benefited from years of preferential arrangements in the EU market. The Cotonou Agreement provided for duty-free access for clothing exports until 2008, giving Mauritian exporters a 12 percent advantage (the most-favored-nation EU tariff rate on clothing). Mauritius has also benefited from duty-free access for clothing exports to the United States under AGOA, resulting in a tariff preference of 17–18 percent over countries without tariff reductions for textile and clothing exports to the U.S. market. These preferential agreements have generated rents for the Mauritius textile industry and have ensured a predictable market. In recent years, however, the global market has changed, especially following the expiration of the Multi-Fiber Arrangement in 2005. To survive, companies have moved into fully integrated activities (spinning, weaving, dyeing) and higher-end production.

**Supply chain.** The textile and apparel supply chain in Mauritius is well organized. Firms have cultivated a dense and efficient network of buyers and raw material suppliers. Most firms specialize in producing and exporting only one type of product and producing solely to customer designs, with specific chain stores as the main end market (Rojid, Sannassee, and Fowdar 2008). Most firms sell directly to their clients, though a few rely on trading companies and other intermediaries. Firms take around 30 days between order confirmation and the delivery of finished garments to the port of embarkation.

## The Role of Government

The government greatly facilitated the industry's expansion through industrial policies that have alleviated constraints on firms. The first step was passage of the Export Processing Zone Act in 1970. The act introduced powerful incentives for manufacturers to export. Key components of the new legislation included protective import duties and quotas for fledgling industries, suspension of import duties on inputs and equipment not locally available, rebates of import duties on other raw materials and components for specified industries, duty drawback schemes, and favorable long-term investment loans. Duty-free imports of inputs for manufactured exports were especially important in maintaining the sector's competitiveness in world markets.

Throughout the rise and growth of the textile and apparel export industry, the exchange rate and fiscal regimes have been favorable, helping keep input costs low. The government has maintained a competitive exchange rate so that Mauritian exports have remained competitive internationally. It has provided numerous incentives to export. Tax incentives in the early years subsidized export firms. These incentives, combined with the availability of relatively cheap semiskilled labor, led to a strong wave of investment in the export sector in the 1980s. Firms in the zone were given a tax holiday of 10 years; no taxes were imposed until 1993.

Strong institutional support has helped deepen market penetration and disseminate skills. The Mauritius Export Development and Investment Authority, formed in 1985 as a public trade and investment promotion agency (with some private sector membership), has been a pivotal institution behind the country's export growth and industrial upgrading. Providing overseas marketing support for exports and arranging buyer-seller meetings, it has helped explore niches for Mauritian garments in European and U.S. markets. Textile companies articulate their concerns through the private sector–funded Joint Economic Council, the primary private institution for business relations in Mauritius. The Chamber of Commerce, in operation for more than

100 years, has also played a central role in economic growth as a forum for the private sector.

## Summary

Strong government leadership and creative entrepreneurs in Mauritius have offset the country's disadvantage of distance from international markets and created a strong textile and apparel industry. The government created a conducive environment for investment, especially with the establishment of the export processing zone program in 1970. Preferential trade agreements under the Lomé Convention helped Mauritian textiles and apparel reach markets overseas. Exchange rate adjustment and strong institutional support through banks and the Mauritius Export Development and Investment Authority have helped the textile cluster grow and meet international standards. The country has also benefited from positive exogenous factors, including the relocation of Asian exporters who faced Multi-Fiber Arrangement restrictions in their own markets. Many of these foreign entrants view Mauritius as a safe haven.

## The Textile and Apparel Industry, Zambia[9]

You can walk for miles at a time here and not see anyone wearing anything remotely resembling African clothing.

—*Howard Gatchell, chairman, Chamber of Commerce, Ndola, Zambia*

Zambia has tried unsuccessfully to build a robust indigenous manufacturing sector. In the 1980s, its vibrant textile and garment sector consisted of more than 140 companies employing more than 25,000 people (Chikoti and Mutonga 2002). This success was made possible by substantial tariff protection and government subsidies. In the 1990s and the first decade of the 2000s, when the government could no longer afford these subsidies and had to liberalize the trade regime following severe macroeconomic shocks, garment factories closed across the country. A volatile macroeconomic environment, including an overvalued exchange rate and a flood of cheap used and charity clothes, dealt the industry new blows. Contributing to the industry's woes were the lack of a competitive input industry, obsolescent machinery, and a dearth of skilled managers familiar with the global industry. Difficult access to working capital also played a role.

The Zambian textile and garment industry was unable to survive the strong international competition, especially in the new post–Multi-Fiber Arrangement environment. As of mid-2012, the industry consisted of an estimated 12 medium and large companies producing primarily niche products for domestic and regional markets, such as school and work uniforms, protective clothing for the mining industry, and local ethnic garments. Total employment is a paltry 1,500, three-quarters of which are men. According to the Central Statistical Office, annual apparel production totaled less than 8,700 metric tons in 2009, down 39 percent from 2007. Fabric and finished products (including a large volume of secondhand clothing), mostly imports, are valued at around $18.7 million.

The history of Zambia's textile and garment industry demonstrates the importance of government policy in successful industrial transformation. Zambia's government swung from complete state control of the industry in the 1980s to complete abandonment in the 1990s. These drastic changes, coupled with unstable macroeconomic policies, an appreciating real effective exchange rate, and significant wage inflation doomed the industry.

## Origin and Course of Development

From independence in 1964 to the early 1990s, Zambia followed an economic policy of state intervention in factor and product markets and large-scale state ownership of productive assets (World Bank 2000). The devastating effects of these policies were not immediately evident because of the windfall revenues generated by copper production and copper exports. However, when world copper prices fell, the economy's inefficiencies stood out as domestic incomes and output came under increasing downward pressure. The government attempted to offset the decline in copper earnings by borrowing heavily from abroad, but the economic decline continued. GDP and incomes fell rapidly in the 1980s, and the country became heavily indebted.

The government that took office in 1991 launched a program of economic stabilization and liberalization designed to reverse the economic decline and put the country on the path to sustainable growth. Prices were decontrolled and subsidies eliminated; inflation was lowered; market forces were allowed to determine the exchange and interest rates; quantitative restrictions on imports were lifted; and the tariff structure was compressed and simplified. State monopolies were ended; crop marketing was liberalized; and a far-reaching privatization program made good progress.

The development of the textile and garment sector needs to be viewed in this context. The government intervened in the early years to shelter large state enterprises from external competition and help the industry grow, but state ownership did not guarantee adequate levels of managerial and worker skills, logistics, or access to market information. After liberalization, the cotton industry grew from one company, the Lint Company of Zambia, to six ginning companies. The Lint Company of Zambia was privatized in the mid-1990s. As a result, the cotton-producing sector grew rapidly with the emergence of Dunavant Limited, Clark Cotton Limited, and Zambia-China Mulungushi Textiles. The cotton spinning industry included Sakiza Spinning Limited (acquired in 2002 by a Kenyan-Indian owner with investments in machinery) and Swarp Spinning Mills (privatized in 2004). Swarp invested in state-of-the-art machinery, provided a high level of operator training, installed good management controls, and paid steady attention to quality control and customer service.

The key vertically integrated textile mills were Kafue Textiles and Zambia-China Mulungushi Textiles Joint Venture Ltd., a joint collaboration of the Zambian government (34 percent) and the Chinese government (66 percent) in 1997. The latter was the largest textile company in Zambia, employing 2,000 workers and producing 100,000 garments a year. Over time, the company set up its own cotton ginneries, but it then failed in 2008 because of high production costs, inadequate funds to run and upgrade the mill's obsolete equipment, and the inability to take advantage of favorable policies. To resuscitate the industry, the government has recently revived the Mulungushi Textile Mill as a joint venture and is installing new machines and state-of-the-art technology to make the company competitive.

Yarn and fabric are cheaper to import than produce locally. Because of the high production costs, most of the large garment enterprises have closed or are for sale, including Swarp Spinning Mills. As of 2010, there were only eight garment enterprises left in the country. The Zambian textile and garment industry is now struggling to survive. Imports of secondhand clothes have contributed to the industry's decline. Most of the surviving companies now spin yarn from locally grown cotton for export, while others are producing woven and knitted fabrics for the domestic market, but at far below capacity.

## Competitiveness and Binding Constraints

The seemingly vibrant textile and garment sector of the 1980s, which employed many Zambians at high wages, was kept alive by government subsidies and the high tariffs that sheltered state-owned firms from external competition. Once these supports were removed, the cost structure of many enterprises was exposed as uncompetitive.

The government's failure to control the imports of donated second-hand garments proved disastrous for the Zambian garment industry. Secondhand garments from the West flooded the Zambian market.[10] This market grew a remarkable 600 percent over 15 years, as charitable clothing donations (Goodwill Industries, Oxfam, the Salvation Army) were sold by for-profit brokers, exporters, and used clothing resellers, all of whom charged a markup. Although the quality of locally made clothes is better, consumers opt for the cheaper imported products. Instead of relying only on market forces, the Zambian government could have petitioned the WTO or introduced safeguard legislation to allow temporary duties to be levied on the imports that were flooding the market.

Besides the secondhand clothes and the volatile macroeconomic environment, poor trade logistics, low labor efficiency, and high input costs have been the key binding constraints on Zambia's textile industry (Dinh 2013).

**Poor trade logistics.** Zambia is landlocked; so, imported inputs and all exports have to be transported through the ports at Dar es Salaam or Durban (more than 1,900 and 2,100 kilometers from Lusaka, respectively). The country's ranking on the trading-across-borders component of the World Bank's doing business index illustrates the challenges.[11] In 2012, because of the significant time and cost requirements to import or export goods, Zambia ranked 153rd among 183 countries in trading across borders, compared with its much better ranking overall of 84th among 153 countries. The cost differences between China and Zambia are large. It costs $3,315 to import a 20-foot, 10-ton container in Zambia, but only $545 in China; for exports, the cost is $2,678 for Zambia and $500 for China. More than 85 percent of the cost difference derives from the higher costs for inland transportation and handling in Zambia (around 20 times greater than in China). Similarly, the time required to export or import a container in the case of Zambia is more than twice the corresponding time in the case of China. Half the difference arises because of the extra time needed for document preparation, and a third arises because of the extra time needed for inland transportation given the great distances to ports, the delays at intermediate borders, the high fuel prices, and the poor-quality roads. The poor trade logistics are particularly disadvantageous for large firms, though all firms are affected to some extent because they must import inputs. The one bright spot is Zambia's competitive trucking industry, which offers lower costs per ton-kilometer relative to other African countries (Raballand and Whitworth 2011).

**Low worker efficiency.** Labor efficiency in Zambia is low because of a combination of lower worker skills and motivation, outdated equipment, the small scale of operations, and the captive customers that allow firms to sit far below the optimal productivity level.[12] In our interviews, managers of apparel firms expressed concern about rising labor costs and declining motivation among workers because of laws and regulations that complicate efforts to compensate workers based on performance, to lay off workers, to hire skilled foreign workers to train Zambian workers, and to employ women. Wages in the informal sector—where workers are not subject to the same regulations—are much lower, and motivation and productivity are reportedly higher. Yet, labor regulations are not the only problem: China seems to be more competitive despite the more stringent labor regulations there.[13]

Aside from their impact on productivity, many of these factors also contribute to low product quality. Thus, for example, employers have few tools to encourage workers to put in the extra effort to produce export-quality products.

**High input costs.** Input costs are high largely because of the absence of competitive input industries. In the case of polo shirts, for example, raw materials such as fabric, collars, thread, and buttons account for more than 70 percent of production costs. Although Zambia produces high-quality cotton, this does not translate into lower input costs for Zambian producers of textiles and apparel. The domestic price of cotton is high; the spinning and textile industries are weak; and all of Zambia's cotton is exported as lint.[14] There are significant inefficiencies in the cotton-to-apparel value chain, and Zambian apparel producers are forced to import most of their inputs from Asia at high cost. They pay well above world market prices due to cash constraints, and they have to pay premiums to cover the storage costs and the holding risk of the ginners (World Bank 2003). A quantitative survey of small and medium firms found that few manufacturers import inputs directly; the vast majority of imported inputs are provided through local importers (Fafchamps and Quinn 2012). The poor trade logistics thus reinforce the disadvantage of high input costs.

## The Role of Government

The dependence of the Zambian economy on copper has led to frequent external shocks. As a resource-based economy, Zambia is at risk of both currency volatility (which makes investment and operational decisions by businesses more difficult) and long-term currency appreciation (the Dutch Disease, which hinders the competitiveness of non–resource-based export sectors).[15]

In this environment, government economic policies swung from complete control over the economy through protectionist policies in the 1970s and 1980s to complete liberalization in the 1990s. Neither extreme helped the country diversify the export base away from copper to agriculture and manufacturing goods, and the economic context remains volatile. In recent years, the macroeconomic situation has improved considerably in response to the government's more prudent fiscal and monetary policies. Over time, this more stable macroeconomic framework, if accompanied by structural measures resulting in a more viable cost structure, can enhance the conditions for the textile and garment sector.

The competitiveness of Zambia's apparel sector could be improved by reducing production costs and increasing productivity. Among the measures that could be considered are the following (Dinh 2013): (1) improve trade logistics by reducing the time required to prepare import-export documents and the waiting time at borders; (2) provide workers and managers with the training, incentives, and equipment necessary to improve productivity and product quality; (3) reform the labor market; (4) facilitate the development of competitive input industries such as spinning and textiles; (5) establish a plug-and-play industrial park; and (6) establish partnerships between the government and the private sector to address the key constraints, including dealing with the problem of secondhand clothes through a WTO petition or the introduction of safeguard legislation.

## Summary

Zambia once had a promising textile sector, but the sector has been greatly weakened by a combination of macroeconomic shocks, severe constraints in trade logistics, low worker skills, high input costs, and market flooding by secondhand clothing.

Neither too much government interference with the market (as in the 1970s and 1980s) nor complete reliance on the market (as in the 1990s) helped Zambia grow and diversify. Creating viable employment in light manufacturing requires that the government alleviate the constraints facing industry. To do this effectively, the government must work closely with the private sector. The government greatly reduced its involvement in the economy through the liberalization reforms of the early 1990s, but it never established a true partnership with the private sector. Transforming the dynamic informal sector into a base for economic growth and employment requires that the government become a visible stakeholder in private sector development.

## Notes

1. The trainees had no previous garment manufacturing experience, but were required to know English and to have completed the equivalent of a junior college education. The training was intended to develop the group as fully qualified workers and supervisors who would train future Desh employees.

2. Indian labor laws require companies with more than 100 workers to obtain government permission before letting employees go for any cause other than criminal misconduct. The laws also impose strict rules on hiring.

3. The company indicated that it was investing in Lesotho with the understanding that the third-country fabric provision would expire at the end of 2004, as stipulated in the original AGOA legislation.

4. The CGM Group undertakes spinning, weaving, and dyeing in South Africa and produces jeans in Lesotho. It is located on 23,400 square meters of land and employs 4,200 workers. It sells to K-Mart, Levi Strauss, and Walmart, among others. South African customers are Edgars, Mr. Price, and Woolworths. There are also a number of manufacturers of woven garments. Lesotho has two embroidery firms doing contract work for other manufacturers, as well as one company providing screen printing.

5. Local shipping times are longer and local shipping costs are higher in Lesotho than in Asia: $4,620 for the export of a 40-foot seafreight container in Lesotho compared with $2,600 in Vietnam, $2,800 in Cambodia, and $3,100 in Bangladesh. Land-freight costs are higher still: $2,250 compared with $400, $800, and $1,350, respectively. High cargo handling fees at Durban of $632 for imports and $341 for exports are part of the problem. Bangladesh, Cambodia, and Vietnam have no such charges. See Doing Business (database), World Bank and International Finance Corporation, Washington, DC, http://www.doingbusiness.org/.

6. The sale of these certificates to South African importers was abolished in March 2010, and this had an adverse impact on the garment industry.

7. Subramanian and Roy (2003) find that rents in Mauritius from preferential access in sugar and clothing together amounted to about 7.0 percent of GDP in the 1980s and about 4.5 percent in the 1990s.

8. In more recent years, the entry of Mauritius into the U.S. market received a boost from investors looking to move capital out of Hong Kong SAR, China, in anticipation of the end of British rule in 1997.

9. For more information, see Dinh (2013).

10. While many goods are donated by charities, the market is dominated by small traders who make millions of dollars in aggregate by selling these clothes for less than a dollar each. The used clothing shipped to Sub-Saharan Africa by the United States accounts for nearly $60 million in sales annually. Wholesalers mark prices up as much as 400 percent.

11. Doing Business (database), World Bank and International Finance Corporation, Washington, DC, http://www.doingbusiness.org/.

12. "Zambia's obsolete industrial base of spinning and weaving machinery precludes any significant production of globally competitive finished apparel articles" (USITC 2009, 70). For example, most of the installed capacity in Zambia still consists of shuttle looms, which generally weave fabric at lower speeds, with more defects, in narrower widths, and at higher costs than shuttleless looms. They also require more power, space, and labor.

13. Doing Business (database), World Bank and International Finance Corporation, Washington, DC, http://www.doingbusiness.org/.

14. Producers of cotton products claim that a cartel of ginneries refuses to sell cotton on the domestic market at less than the Liverpool price, some 25 percent higher than the price would be without transport costs. At this price, they claim, Zambian cotton costs twice as much as Chinese cotton.

15. The Behre Dolbear index ranks Zambia in the bottom 3 of 25 mining countries in currency stability (Behre Dolbear 2011).

# References

Bajaj, Vikas. 2010. "Bangladesh, with Low Pay, Moves In on China." *New York Times*, July 16. http://www.nytimes.com/2010/07/17/business/global/17textile .html?pagewanted=all&_r=0.

Behre Dolbear. 2011. "2011 Ranking of Countries for Mining Investment: Where 'Not to Invest.'" Behre Dolbear, London. http://www.dolbear.com/news-resources/documents.

Bennett, Mark. 2008. "Spotlight on Lesotho." iFashion, August 13. http://www.ifashion .co.za/index.php?option=com_content&task=view&id=1013&Itemid=113.

Bheenick, Rundheersing, and Morton O. Schapiro. 1989. "Mauritius: A Case Study of the Export Processing Zone." EDI Development Policy Case Studies 1, Economic Development Institute, World Bank, Washington, DC.

Chikoti, S., and C. Q. Mutonga. 2002. "Textiles and Clothing in Zambia." Ministry of Commerce, Trade, and Industry, Lusaka, Zambia.

Dinh, Hinh T. 2013. *Light Manufacturing in Zambia: Job Creation and Prosperity in a Resource-Based Economy*. With contributions by Praveen Kumar, Anna Morris, Fahrettin Yagci, and Kathleen Fitzgerald. Washington, DC: World Bank.

Fafchamps, Marcel, and Simon Quinn. 2012. "Manufacturing Firms in Africa." In *Performance of Manufacturing Firms in Africa: An Empirical Analysis*, edited by Hinh T. Dinh and George R. G. Clarke, 139–211. Washington, DC: World Bank.

FIAS (Foreign Investment Advisory Service). 2006. "Lesotho: The Competitiveness of Regional and Vertical Integration of Lesotho's Garment Industry." April, International Finance Corporation and World Bank, Washington, DC.

GDS (Global Development Solutions). 2011. *The Value Chain and Feasibility Analysis; Domestic Resource Cost Analysis*. Vol. 2 of *Light Manufacturing in Africa: Targeted Policies to Enhance Private Investment and Create Jobs*. Washington, DC: World Bank. http://go.worldbank.org/6G2A3TFI20.

Gupta, Alok, and Emily F. Alley. 2012. "Reimagining the Varanasi Sari: Condoms Lubricate the Wheels of the Varanasi Sari Industry." *Little India*, March 16. http://www.littleindia.com/life/12388-reimagining-the-varanasi-sari.html.

Mpata, Stallard B., Bo Giersing, and S. M. A. K. Kaombwe. 2005. "Improving Land Transportation Logistics for International Trade Competitiveness of Lesotho: Final Report." September, Southern Africa Global Competitiveness Hub, Regional Center for Southern Africa, U.S. Agency for International Development, Gaborone, Botswana. http://pdf.usaid.gov/pdf_docs/PNADT369.pdf.

Mthente. 2009. "ComMark Textile and Apparel Sector Program Impact Assessment (Final Report)." Mthente Research and Consulting Services, Cape Town.

Raballand, Gaël, and Alan Whitworth. 2011. "Should the Zambian Government Invest in Railways?" ZIPAR Working Paper 4 (December), Zambia Institute for Policy Analysis and Research, Lusaka.

Rhee, Yung Whee. 1990. "The Catalyst Model of Development: Lessons from Bangladesh's Success with Garment Exports." *World Development* 18 (2): 333–46.

Rojid, Sawkut Ally, R. Vinesh Sannassee, and Sooraj Fowdar. 2008. "The Net Contribution of the Mauritian Export Processing Zone Using Benefit-Cost Analysis." *Journal of International Development* 21 (3): 379–92.

Subramanian, Arvind, and Devesh Roy. 2003. "Who Can Explain the Mauritian Miracle: Meade, Romer, Sachs, or Rodrik?" In *In Search of Prosperity: Analytic Narratives on Economic Growth*, edited by Dani Rodrik, 205–43. Princeton, NJ: Princeton University Press.

USITC (U.S. International Trade Commission). 2009. *Sub-Saharan Africa: Effects of Infrastructure Conditions on Export Competitiveness, Third Annual Report.* Investigation 332–477, Publication 4071 (April). Washington, DC: USITC. http://www.usitc.gov/publications/332/pub4071.pdf.

World Bank. 2000. "Report and Recommendation of the President of the International Development Association to the Executive Directors on a Proposed Fiscal Sustainability Credit of SDR 105.5 Million (US $140 Million Equivalent) to the Republic of Zambia." Report P-7379-ZA (May 31), World Bank, Washington, DC.

———. 2003. "Zambia: The Challenge of Competitiveness and Diversification." Report 25388-ZA (January 2003), World Bank, Washington, DC.

———. 2009. "Mauritius: Investment Climate Assessment." Report 52794 (December 22), World Bank, Washington, DC.

———. 2012. "World Development Indicators." World Bank, Washington, DC.

Zafar, Ali. 2011. "Mauritius: An Economic Success Story." In *Yes Africa Can: Success Stories from a Dynamic Continent*, edited by Punam Chuhan-Pole and Manka Angwafo, 91–106. Washington, DC: World Bank.

Part III

# Policy Lessons

# 10

# The Chinese Policy Experience

## Introduction

This chapter draws on our analysis, including extensive interviews at Chinese enterprises, to distill policy lessons from China's experience. Chapters 1 and 2 show that the conditions facing China in the early years of industrialization were not so different from those facing low-income countries today. Based on our findings and on our discussion of the policy tools that China, following other East Asian countries, implemented to support the growth of light manufacturing (chapter 3), we now summarize the key factors that contributed to the speed and extent of industrialization in China and explain how Chinese enterprises have managed to overcome the six key constraints to accelerate the growth of light manufacturing. In chapter 11, we assess the extent to which the Chinese experience may guide policy reforms in other developing countries based on our team's collective experience and the case studies presented in chapters 4–9.

# Policy Ingredients of Success

## Policy Experimentation

Policy experimentation is a fundamental building block of China's development efforts that remains highly visible even today.[1] Efforts to jump-start light manufacturing to capitalize on its potential to support the growth of output, employment, exports, and technical capacity need not await economy-wide improvements in roads, power supply, education, openness, and so on. China's massive spurt in the development of light manufactures was launched from a foundation of poor infrastructure, little protection of private business assets and property, no contract enforcement, limited scope for markets, and denial of export rights to private producers. The policy matrix has gradually improved thanks to a combination of top-down initiatives (for example, a shift toward market pricing of most commodities and services, new legislation supporting private property rights, the assignment of export rights to private firms) and greater official responsiveness to the needs of both large and small business operators.

Despite immense progress, Chinese policy and institutional structures still display substantial defects. China's new leaders have repeatedly denounced the pervasive corruption that surrounds official agencies at every level. Chinese commentators continue to lament the inability of most small and medium enterprises (SMEs) to tap organized credit markets.

China's success in driving growth despite incomplete reforms and periodic backsliding demonstrates the potential for development to progress in difficult environments. For China, what has mattered has been the resolution of a series of big issues such as the close alignment of official and private incentives favoring rapid growth in output, productivity, and incomes; allowing price signals to influence large and growing segments of economic decision making; and abandoning the socialist suspicion of international markets; encouraging rather than condemning individual economic success.

## Strong Public Endorsement of Private Sector Development

Manufacturing enterprises in developing countries face an extremely high-risk environment that makes risk-adjusted rates of return appear low in the eyes of would-be entrepreneurs. The high risk stems from, among other factors, uncertainties concerning the government's motives and commitment with regard to private business. Government commitment to industrial development, including strong public endorsement of economic growth and private sector development as a national priority, followed by action at both the local and national levels, helps reduce perceived risks. In 1992, following short-term setbacks to China's reform program, Deng Xiaoping rekindled the momentum for growth, marketization, and economic opening with a widely publicized tour of south China. During his travels, Deng attacked reform skeptics, emphasized the necessity of rapid economic development, and insisted that market allocation was fully consistent with China's socialist orientation. Deng's strong, unambiguous stance heartened reformers and sparked renewed experimentation with market-linked arrangements, including a major expansion in the number of development zones and industrial parks. By the end of 1992, more than 2,700 development zones had sprung up across the country, 23 times the number in 1991. Confidence in industry and open pledges of high-level support are crucial to encouraging the private sector to take on risk and invest in new activities. The decision by Jiang Zemin, Deng's successor, to welcome entrepreneurs into the Communist Party and to appoint prominent entrepreneurs to highly visible political bodies provided an equally clear endorsement of the continued expansion of China's private sector.

## Tailoring Government Support to the Business Life Cycle and Backing Winners

In China, government support for manufacturing enterprises varies according to phases of the business life cycle. The support ranges from doing nothing to financing and facilitating enterprise growth, creating business incubators, and providing technology advisers. While government support has been wide-ranging, including fiscal incentives, infrastructure development, and advisory support on upgrading, assistance has not always involved heavy spending. The government has advised firms on global market niches, cluster development, and business services such as customs and taxation. Our findings on the advantages of this flexible government support confirm Lin's (2012) analysis of China's development strategy.

**Start-up phase.** In light manufacturing, government support for domestic start-ups is typically limited and may amount to little more than providing infrastructure in the same way other countries have done. In some cases, for example, in Guangdong Province, some seed or start-up funding has been supplied to local entrepreneurs. Among joint enterprises receiving foreign direct investment (FDI), official support takes the form of across-the-board policy measures such as rebates on customs duties, undervalued exchange rates, income tax exemptions, and so on. In this respect, government support in China hardly differs from that of many other developing countries. What seems unusual is the way in which China's policy structures provide central government officials and, especially, local officials with strong pro-growth incentives that make them eager to see businesses succeed because private sector success may elevate their own financial prospects and career trajectories. In many other developing countries, government officials consider the private sector an opportunity to share the wealth of the community, while the private sector looks at government officials as robbers.

**Growth phase.** In the growth phase and the maturity phase (see below), the government support in China is substantial and provides clear evidence that the government's industrial strategy is designed not so much to pick winners as to back winners. This is a crucial difference with the strategy typically adopted in other countries.

*Government preferential policies.* The support in China includes policies across all levels of government, and policies may vary from region to region and from locality to locality.

An example is the government policy vis-à-vis the Qinye Industrial Company in Ganzhou, Jiangxi Province (chapter 5). To attract investors from the coastal regions, Ganzhou has implemented business-friendly policies affecting land supply, infrastructure, utilities, financing, taxation, and freedom from administrative surcharges. The government support for Qinye takes place at three levels: the central government, the provincial government, and local governments.

The central government's preferential policies under China's Great Western Development Strategy include lower corporate income tax rates, customs duty exemptions on imported equipment, and favorable terms on land use, mining ventures, and foreign investment.[2]

Under provincial policies, key export firms and high-technology firms enjoy preferential tax treatment, and firms undertaking qualified technological upgrading projects are exempt from import tariffs on imported equipment.

City and county governments are required to subsidize the cost of land for companies moving into the local industrial park.[3] They are also required to invest at least 20 percent of their land revenues in improving park infrastructure. Relocated enterprises enjoy priority access to land. The government offers land discounts, exemptions from administrative fees, and tax refunds to encourage private investors to construct warehouses in the park.

The municipal government provides 10 percent of an initial fund, up to Y 5 million ($0.74 million), to a financial guarantee company, which offers services to enterprises within the industrial cluster. The government also provides subsidies up to Y 2 million ($0.3 million) in the form of equity for leading enterprises that invest in business expansion. Subsidies are likewise offered on loan interest rates. The municipal government has worked to improve the transparency and efficiency of its administrative approval mechanisms.

The municipal government financed these and other extensive interventions through land deals. Through the intervention of the municipal government, state enterprises located in the city's central district sold their downtown land parcels and moved their operations to suburban industrial parks. The municipal government then resold these valuable plots to commercial developers. The relocated companies used the proceeds from the land sales to repay debt and upgrade technology.

*Other areas of intervention during the growth phase.* Other areas of intervention include the following: (1) creating knowledge spillovers through the establishment of enterprise associations and chambers of commerce to strengthen local communication among enterprises and identify shortcomings in zone administration, (2) improving managerial and worker skills, (3) reducing the bureaucratic burden, (4) expediting payments, (5) reinforcing market signals, and (6) providing services such as quality control.

**Maturity phase.** Government support during the maturity phase tends to be geared toward research and development (R&D), networking, marketing, assistance through trading companies, and completing the value chain through investment in upstream and downstream activities. Chinese officials, acting as matchmakers, connect firms with research agencies and consultants, reducing the costs of access to information.

In matching producers with research facilities, the government creates cooperative relationships that strengthen both sides. Bringing actors together reduces transaction costs, resolves key constraints, and saves firms time and money. Researchers thus gain inside access to information on how firms operate. In another kind of matchmaking, industrial park authorities in the Dieshiqiao home textile cluster in Jiangsu Province tried to link firms with banks to improve the access of firms to finance (chapter 5).

Along with instances of successful official intervention, we find episodes of failure. The automobile project in the Yinchuan economic development zone in Ningxia Province failed mainly because of premature government-led efforts to build an industrial cluster from scratch for a sophisticated manufacturing product (chapter 5). The result demonstrates that a viable cluster cannot be built from above, but must rest on private initiatives that can stand up to market discipline. This reinforces our recommendation that government industrial policy should not aim at picking winners, but rather at backing winners, a lesson that also emerges from the failure of the Morogoro shoe factory in Tanzania (chapter 8). Policies that provide preferential treatment for certain investors without taking account of comparative advantage may encourage moral hazard and damage the local economy. This illustrates the downside of policies linking the advancement of local administrators to growth in local gross domestic product (GDP) and inflows of investment: if there is no regard for the market or for local comparative advantage, such a policy may not represent an incentive to succeed, but a temptation to take risks.

The case of the home textile industrial cluster that sprang up in Dieshiqiao, an area where private trading had been forbidden before the onset of the reforms, offers an example of backing a winner. In this unlikely place, farmers covertly sold vegetables and handicrafts, and commodity exchanges thrived and evolved outside of government oversight. When the reforms came, the embroidery business took off spontaneously from a foundation that had already become established. The local government did not intervene for the first four years, but, once the industry was turning a profit, the government facilitated expansion. Public services now include copyright protection, quality testing, information technology infrastructure, and information exchanges.

FDI in China has also taken different forms depending on the stage of development of an enterprise or economic development zone. In the initial stage, with little knowledge of management and overseas markets, zone authorities would typically reach compensation trade agreements with foreign investors and undertake intermediate processing. Compensation trade refers to the arrangement whereby the foreign investor receives a share of finished goods in return for providing equipment, technology, parts, and components. The foreign partner is responsible for marketing the finished products outside China. However, this kind of cooperation arrangement generates only a small share of the profits for the local partner, and the transfer of technology is quite limited. Compensation trade and intermediate processing arrangements were thus discouraged after the mid-1980s (Wong 1987). As local industrial capacity improved, firms entered equity joint ventures and cooperative production arrangements with foreign investors. Under these forms of investment, the firms are permitted to sell part of their production in the domestic market. Sole proprietorship, equity joint ventures, and cooperative production have become China's main forms of foreign investment.

## Competition

Competition is a key chapter in the tale of China's economic success. Manufacturers in Jiangxi Province and in Zhejiang Province report two sources of competition: fellow producers within the province and producers in neighboring coastal areas. Inland provinces such as Jiangxi tend to be more competitive in terms of labor costs, while the cost of raw materials is often higher, supply chains are less mature, and technological and productive and managerial capacities are weaker. In general, the internal provinces compete at the low end, and producers closer to the coast compete at the more-sophisticated higher end of the product spectrum.

The central government has fostered nationwide competition by establishing awards and certifications that carry substantial monetary and reputational benefits. This is the positive role that competition plays in enhancing group identification (Stiglitz 1992). Japan and the Republic of Korea have followed a similar path, but China's steep reduction in the barriers to both overseas imports and FDI has elevated the intensity of competition in domestic product markets far beyond what we may observe in these neighboring economies. China's local governments help firms develop competitive strength and pursue official awards and certifications, which can enlarge local budgets and enhance the career paths of local officials. For example, to qualify for preferential tax rebates, high-technology firms must have a certificate confirming their status. Qipai Motorcycle in the Jiangmen development zone in Guangdong Province received local government assistance to obtain its certificate (chapter 3):

> Before 2009, national economic development zones had the right to issue the certificate to high-tech firms. However, in 2009, the [national] Ministry of Science and Technology created a Torch Center. ... So local government helped firms, like Qipai, to prepare materials for the application. (July 2012 interview)

Other awards are bestowed if enterprises or zones meet enhanced environmental standards, allowing the winning firms and zones to boast of their environmental reputations, compete for regional and national awards, and attract investment.

## Industrial Parks, Industrial Clusters, and Trading Companies

The Chinese system of SME-oriented plug-and-play industrial zones, industrial clusters, and trading companies is one of the most important and least publicized factors behind the country's extraordinary competitiveness in light manufacturing. It has been a key tool in government industrial policy over the last two decades. As shown in chapter 3 and confirmed during our missions, the government at all levels has come to understand the benefits of providing support for the development of clusters and trading companies. This contrasts with Africa, where the experience with industrial parks has been less than spectacular because of problems in strategic planning, location decisions, infrastructure, implementation capacity, and high-level support and where clusters and trading companies have not been developed (Farole 2011).

As China's industrial parks have increased in number and size, their output has contributed substantially to the growth of aggregate GDP, exports, and industrial production. Industrial parks have helped SMEs mature and increase in scale. Our interviews confirm that government agencies and park managers—while often focusing their efforts on particular industries, for example, leather and textiles in Nanchang, furniture in Ji'an, or electronics in Ganzhou—do not see their role as picking winners.

Both private and public sector respondents describe the government role as facilitation rather than direction. The general consensus is that industrial parks are based on cluster development and do not occur in a vacuum. The authorities have built parks in areas where there is already a concentration of firms, and the parks are centered around specific industries. They are, in many respects, smaller versions of special economic zones.

All the industrial parks we visited were located in suburban areas of major cities and occupied a defined geographical space. There is an assortment of types of parks. For example, around Nanchang, the capital of Jiangxi Province, there are two national-level economic zones and seven provincial-level economic zones. Parks vary from province to province, but they are essentially under the authority of local or provincial governments. Industrial parks are frequently run by administrative committees that oversee park management on behalf of local administrations. In many cases, private developers have helped finance and build the parks.

China's success with industrial parks has relied on intense competition among producers for domestic and export markets; decentralized implementation, which has resulted in competition among local governments; and the involvement of banks and private sector developers. The parks, including the standard factory shells and housing units, are financed by local governments and the private sector, such as private zone developers who charge capped rents to companies. The local government share is often financed through bank loans with the zone's real estate as collateral; the loans are repaid using the additional taxes generated by the increased economic activity.

Preferential policies are a key tool in attracting firms to parks (see above). Our interviewees at companies located in industrial parks stressed that the myriad benefits in terms of infrastructure, cheaper land, the stable supply of utilities, and lower tax rates were key motivating factors in the decision to relocate. There was variation in the degree to which governments allocated cheap land that depended on the zone and the industry. Initial tax holidays, subsidized credit, and a range of other incentives attracted some enterprises to the parks. Others noted the advantages of gaining access to the centralized and efficient provision of business registration, licensing, and customs clearance services. Entrepreneurs in some clusters remarked that park managers help investors address the problems encountered in launching a business, including obtaining the permits needed to operate.

There is some variation in the responses of our interviewees regarding the degree of government assistance. Based on our discussions with personnel both at the firms and with the government, we found that the more advanced industrial parks offer market analysis, accounting services, import-export information, and management advice and help firms recruit and train workers. Parks located in the Yangzi River Delta region focus on helping firms acquire business licenses and recruit workers. Parks may also have integrated facilities to address environmental difficulties. The government has focused on the provision of public goods and on regulatory policies. In the early stages of park development, the strong local government investment in infrastructure, especially in the provision of stable water, electricity, gas, telecommunications, and sewerage services, was noted by many entrepreneurs.

The parks typically provide low-cost standardized factory shells allowing entrepreneurs to plug and play, thereby significantly reducing the initial investment costs and risks. Parks have their own legislation in conformity with national laws. Companies within parks have discretion over labor contracts provided they meet certain standards.

Firm managers highlighted the availability of free dormitory facilities for workers, many of whom are migrants from distant localities. Firms located in industrial parks offer extensive services to their workers, often including housing, meals, and security for valuables, typically at little or no cost. Such arrangements enable workers to save a substantial proportion of their cash incomes. In contrast, in Africa, much of a worker's wage goes for housing, food, and transportation. Many Chinese factory workers can enhance their incomes through extra hours and productivity bonuses. Such arrangements allow migrant workers from poor rural areas to save enough within a few years to change the lifestyle of their families. These circumstances contribute to the motivation and productivity of Chinese workers and to China's high rate of household savings.

The toothbrush industrial cluster in the town of Hangji, Yangzhou, Jiangsu Province, shows how industrial parks can help foster agglomeration, which in turn supports the completion of the value chain. Concentrating the entire production process, from the purchase of raw materials to the distribution of final products, within the cluster lowers the cost threshold for new firms to enter the industry. For example, in the past, companies had to source the titanium powder for dyeing toothbrushes from Chongqing, 1,500 kilometers away, but, with only Y 300 ($44), a local housewife opened a business producing powder for toothbrush firms in the cluster, an innovation that has benefited the entire cluster.

"The supply, production, and sale of toothbrushes, from raw materials to packaging and transportation, have long become an integrated process within Hangji," noted the secretary-general of the Hangji Toothbrush Association.

China's experience shows that trading intermediaries can facilitate exports and directly or indirectly help overcome the constraints that manufacturers often face in the initial stages of industrialization. Trading companies play a key role in helping both small and large manufacturers explore new markets and enhance their competitiveness through constant product and technology upgrading. The spectrum of trading options available to Chinese manufacturers, including independent export or import, along with fierce competition, helps support light manufacturing ventures ranging from small start-ups to large, sophisticated producers. The collaboration of producers with trading companies has yielded multiple advantages, such as lower transaction costs, more market information, and financial benefits. Perhaps more important, the trading companies are helping small enterprises integrate with larger companies and gain access to foreign markets, expertise, technology, and ideas. Chinese manufacturers have profited from these services and increased their exports dramatically over the past 20 years. Such growth would not have been possible without the liberalization of foreign trade and the contributions of trading companies.

## The Binding Constraints on Light Manufacturing

The first volume of our project, *Light Manufacturing in Africa: Targeted Policies to Enhance Private Investment and Create Jobs*, shows that, to grow the light manufacturing sector, policy makers in developing countries need first to identify, prioritize, and remove the most binding constraints in each sector (Dinh and others 2012). These constraints vary by country, sector, and firm size. Six binding constraints on African competitiveness in light manufacturing are identified:

- Entrepreneurial skills, both technical and managerial
- Worker skills
- Availability, cost, and quality of inputs
- Access to finance
- Trade logistics
- Access to industrial land

Among small firms, entrepreneurial skills, land, inputs, and finance are the most important constraints, while trade logistics, land, and inputs create the most difficulties for larger enterprises. Annex tables 10A.1 and 10A.2 illustrate how the enterprises described in each of the 29 case studies discussed in chapters 4–9 have addressed these six constraints.

### Entrepreneurial Capabilities

The first generation of Chinese entrepreneurs in the postreform era generally established new businesses without the benefit of formal training in business management. They acquired entrepreneurial skills through imitation and by learning from failures. Influenced by a deep-rooted regional commercial culture, local entrepreneurs are not cowed by failure, but continue pursuing success. Many successful business owners and managers we interviewed had failed repeatedly either in the same field or in a different field. That they are able to survive in business is a tribute to their determination and persistence, as well as the informal support network of families and friends.

Entrepreneurs in the light manufacturing sector in Jiangxi and Zhejiang provinces do not choose their industries and products randomly. Entrepreneurs learn their business from three sources.

First, about half of the entrepreneurs we interviewed acquired product-specific knowledge and tacit skills through prior work experiences in the production of these items, as well as through interactions with friends and relatives involved in this production. Learning how to shop for good-quality raw materials and machines and how to transform them into products helped to sharpen the entrepreneurial capabilities of these producers. For most of them, savings from prior work and from family networks have been the main source of the required initial investment capital. The owner of a large furniture business grew up with an uncle who was a carpenter. Apparently, he knew carpentry when he was 13 and had ambitions to start his own business. The owner of a seamless underwear company with 1,200 employees learned the trade from friends in the same business. It seems that he could turn to them whenever he needed assistance.

Second, about 40 percent of the entrepreneurs we interviewed gained knowledge and experience by trading in the products that they eventually began to manufacture. In buying or selling inputs and final products, these entrepreneurs gained useful industry-specific market information and imbibed a knowledge of industry standards, trends, and practices, as well as information about suppliers and manufacturing processes. Sutton and Kellow (2010) find similar patterns among African entrepreneurs.

Trading helps develop acute business skills and generate the savings necessary to invest in manufacturing. The owner of a 500-employee garment business started out in a government export trade department before he moved into the private sector to work as a manager in a garment trading company in Shanghai. It was there that he learned about the garment industry before he decided to invest his savings in his own business.

The third source of learning among entrepreneurs in China has been networks and contacts established through former jobs in state-owned enterprises in the same light manufacturing sector. Regardless of whether it is a large enterprise with over 500 workers located inside an industrial zone or a smaller one inside or outside the zone, networks or simply contacts with traders play a central role in shaping an entrepreneur's ability to organize and manage a business.

Clearly, light manufacturing can flourish even where entrepreneurs lack formal education. Many successful manufacturers began by capitalizing on a particular skill or experience that was then developed further through learning by doing. Ambitious people with specific skills and personal networks can often become successful entrepreneurs, illustrating that formal education is not essential to start a successful business.

In Guangdong Province, our study team encountered a metalworking entrepreneur and a shoe firm co-owner who began their business careers by acquiring experience in trading and later moved into manufacturing with technical help from friends and relatives who had manufacturing expertise. An entrepreneur with a third-grade education in Nanhai, Guangdong Province, explained how her business got started:

> We were peasants, doing farm work. Later, we wanted to increase our income. My uncle was working in state-owned enterprises in the metalworking business. He suggested that I try the metalworking industry. Then he retired and came to help me as the "master" on technical issues. So we started our business in 1990. (July 2012 interview)

There are also many instances of workers and managers leaving large industrial firms to start their own companies. For example, the Haining warp knitting industrial park in Zhejiang Province developed because employees in a local pioneering firm branched off and created new firms:

> There were four or five warp knitting firms at the beginning. One of them, JinDa Warp Knitting Company, is now a large firm. This early starter trained a pool of talent for the cluster, including technicians, front-line workers, and middle managers. Later, many talented people left their employers and started their own businesses. (July 2012 interview)

In Wenzhou villages, even though "the techniques and skills of industrial production are unfamiliar and even mysterious," inexperienced operatives learned to "master the necessary skills and techniques after only a short period of training," repeating earlier patterns observed in Japan (July 2012 interview; see also Patrick and Rohlen 1987). The Julong High-Technology Company in Maodian Town, Jiangxi Province, was built by Xie Ruihong, a man with no formal education. His ingenuity, drive, and skills learned in the army and in his own trading company helped him succeed as a manufacturer of a globally marketed sweetener.

Another entrepreneur, Wu Youjia, began professional life as a farmer; after failing his college entrance exam, Wu worked in several state and private enterprises, where he gained business experience and developed networks of business contacts. As a result of Wu's careful preparation, research, and good timing, his Jiangxi Youjia Food Manufacturing Company took off.

The Huaqiang Oil and Chemical Equipment Company Ltd., in Foshan, Guangdong Province, makes oil storage tanks. A woman farmer with three years of formal education established this petrochemical equipment company in 1990 as a joint venture, using Y 30,000 she had saved from her husband's income as a bricklayer. Her uncle's experience as a technician, combined with her training in welding in a state enterprise and expert advice from a hired engineer, helped her launch her business.

Learning requires persistence in the face of repeated failures. The tale of Zhang Hanping (chapter 4) demonstrates the importance of resilience and determination. Zhang had no training in business management, but picked up entrepreneurial skills by imitating other businesspeople and by learning from his failures. He kept on trying until he became the head of Aihao Writing Instruments Co. Ltd., which has developed into the world's largest producer of roller ball pens (using water-based ink). This is quite an achievement for someone who never finished elementary school and could not even write his name well because, as a child, he dropped out of school to help support his family. Zhang was among the first to start a business in the early days of the economic reforms and failed several times in the 1970s and the first half of the 1980s. Only in the mid-1980s, when Zhang switched from other businesses to pens, did he succeed.

## Worker Skills

Virtually all entrepreneurs we interviewed have difficulty finding front-line workers, the relatively unskilled workers responsible for production lines. Without exception, most of the less well skilled employees in Chinese firms have migrated from rural areas, often from distant provinces. The availability of surplus labor has thus far enabled migrants to find jobs quickly at a standard entry-level monthly wage of about Y 1,800–Y 2,000 ($266–$295) (in 2010), including bonuses and overtime, as well as free housing and subsidized food. Jobs in the manufacture of products that require slightly more sophisticated skills pay Y 2,500 ($369) a month. The training of a new worker takes one to six months. In recent years, however, wages have been rising rapidly, and a shortage of workers is emerging. These trends are posing a new challenge for the sustainability of light manufacturing in China.

The ability to acquire and run machinery represents the most important investment of Chinese light manufacturing firms. (Firms typically do not make the largest investments in factories because many plants are leased from the government entities that built them.) At the beginning of China's opening-up in the early 1980s, machinery was often supplied from abroad, including shipments of used machines from Hong Kong SAR, China, or from Taiwan, China. Now, much of the machinery comes from China-based manufacturers.

Many of the sophisticated high-end machines continue to be delivered from developed-country manufacturers (for example, Germany, Italy, Japan, and Korea). Our interviews revealed no complaints about the availability of parts or maintenance services because most foreign machine manufacturers have established local offices, and some now even produce machinery directly in local plants. The ready availability of high-quality machinery is a key advantage of manufacturing in clusters and of the existence of economies of scale.

In one case, a Chinese company created a leading-edge sugar processing technique and, in cooperation with Chinese manufacturers, designed and developed the required machinery. In another case, an entrepreneur (previously a hydropower engineer) developed the machinery for a new, highly energy-efficient process to produce snacks.

The government facilitates technological upgrading through one-off financial grants. The cost of machine replacement depends on whether the technology is local or foreign. Nearly all producers use some domestically made machinery, but about half of our interviewees also used machines manufactured by foreign companies, often in Chinese plants. For instance, brand-name Italian and Japanese machines for the production of seamless underwear are now manufactured locally; similarly, machinery for the production of synthetic polyurethane leather is produced in China by a manufacturer from Taiwan, China. Both these examples attest to the ongoing process of upgrading within China's manufacturing sector.

Chinese garment entrepreneurs tap multiple sources of information to keep abreast of global fashion trends. In recent years, many Chinese firms have invested heavily in in-house design capabilities even if they do so only to apply the latest patterns and designs from elsewhere. While all firms make products with design specifications provided by their customers, at least half of the entrepreneurs we interviewed have in-house design capabilities. Many firms have introduced their own brand names. As an entrepreneur in high-end garments pointed out, this is a costly undertaking because it places the burden of promoting the brand name onto the producer. Investment in the development of a design capability is financed by the firms and is often carried out in collaboration with foreign designers.

We see similar trends in other sectors. A producer of furniture made with medium-density fiberboard, for example, spends nearly 1 percent of his total production outlays on design.

Access to machinery does not automatically enable entrepreneurs or their technical staff to master its use. In almost all firms, equipment suppliers are the most common and effective channel of technological capability building. Typically, the suppliers come on-site to train the clients' technical staff, who then train workers to run the new machines. Other channels of technological skill upgrading noted by firms are study tours, government-financed training, and on-the-job training.

## Availability, Cost, and Quality of Inputs

The ability to acquire raw materials and other inputs quickly, smoothly, and at competitive prices was considered critical by most entrepreneurs we interviewed. Many entrepreneurs considered the existence of a supply chain a key determinant of investment location decisions (often ranked among key determinants as number two after political stability). Efficient input supply is crucial because materials typically account for more than 70 percent of the final product cost in light manufacturing (Dinh and others 2012). For example, the production of padlocks requires 12 parts, all of which are being manufactured in Yiwu; the case of zippers is similar whether they are made of nylon, plastic, or metal.

None of the entrepreneurs we interviewed complained about shortages in the supply of raw materials, most of which are sourced domestically, often from the same region or cluster. Interviewees said that the prices in China are the lowest, that the choice is immense, and that quality has improved markedly. Some clusters have been built around the availability of raw materials (for example, the wood cluster in Nankang and the sugar cluster outside Ganzhou, both in Jiangxi Province). Even fabrics and other materials requiring capital-intensive processing are manufactured within China. Materials that are still being imported include rubber from Vietnam (for shoes), high-end textiles from Japan and Korea, high-end sheep and goat leather from Australia, and high-end wood from countries in Africa and from the Republic of the Union of Myanmar and from Thailand. In the garment industry, for most materials procured in China, the time required for delivery once an order is placed is 30 days.

The expansion of processing activities is having a major positive impact on suppliers, especially in agroprocessing. Thus, a sugar processor has improved the livelihoods of 100,000 farmers in Jiangxi Province, and a large meat processor in Yiwu has helped pig farmers through farm cooperatives in northeast China. Large-scale demand from processing operations has contributed to official efforts to encourage the consolidation of farmland into efficient scale operations.

## Access to Finance

The initial start-up investment among our entrepreneurs has been mainly sourced using personal savings or through financing supplied by informal networks of family, business colleagues, and friends. The savings are typically accumulated through migrant or other factory work, trading, or family workshops. In the button and zipper case studies, the initial capital was supplied by friends and family or personal savings (chapter 5). In Jiangxi Province, local entrepreneurs built up savings through migrant work in nearby Guangdong and other coastal provinces during the 1990s, then returned home to set up garment, leather, and shoemaking enterprises. We found few instances of bank credit or of FDI in the start-up phase.

Some Chinese start-ups have deviated from this standard model. In Yiwu, Zhejiang Province, township and village enterprises (TVEs) that had been developed during the planned economy era managed to take over part of a failing state-owned garment manufacturer. Elsewhere in Zhejiang Province, start-up capital came from entrepreneurs in Guangdong Province or other coastal areas who were seeking to establish secondary production facilities.

To succeed, start-ups must effectively combine initial savings with market knowledge, effective networking, and technological expertise. Networks and personal connections have sometimes enabled entrepreneurs to import the first machines from Taiwan, China. Later, arrangements with companies in Hong Kong SAR, China, and in Taiwan, China, allowed the firms to upgrade technology and gain access to managerial skills, technical knowledge, and market information.

**Low start-up investment.** In only 2 of the 11 garment firms where we conducted interviews in 2010 had the initial investment been greater than Y 4 million (approximately $600,000). The two outlier firms have moved into more high-technology synthetic fabric and home textile manufacturing. In agroprocessing, the start-up costs have been greater in a few firms because of the sophisticated nature of the technology for producing a sugar substitute. For smaller firms making snack foods or starting meat processing, the original investment was less than Y 20,000 (around $3,000).

The financing for expansion into new factories and for new technology has more often come from a combination of bank loans and reinvested profits. Several firms have never paid dividends, but have saved the majority of their profits. In two cases, firms brought in foreign investors. The manufacturer of a sugar substitute is owned by a Malaysian company that bought the failing state-owned predecessor, upgraded the technology, and now operates the factory as part of its global production chain. A meat processing firm in Yiwu started with an initial investment of Y 2,000 and subsequently sold a 50 percent share of the business to a firm in Taiwan, China, for Y 1.4 million.

**Financial institutions are central in the growth from small to medium firms.** In China, financial institutions have played an important role in manufacturing development, but not at the genesis stage. Once they have achieved considerable success, start-ups may obtain bank loans to expand production facilities, build new factories, buy machinery or land, or acquire the working capital needed to execute large orders. Many interviewees pinpointed access to capital as a serious obstacle to scaling up successful start-ups. In recent years, larger, more well established firms in Zhejiang Province have found banks more than willing to lend.

The case of the Fudebao Furniture Company shows how bank financing can help businesses expand and how the government can help acquire technology and expertise, making it possible for small companies to grow into medium and large companies (chapter 4).

The most common reason firms fail to gain access to bank loans at an earlier stage of their growth is the lack of collateral. If firms are able to take out loans, factory premises or land can be used as collateral, sometimes combined with a loan guarantee from a friend or from special companies created for this explicit purpose. In 2007, the government established public guarantee companies, but these do not seem to have played a key role in the growth of light manufacturing firms. There is strong evidence, however, that firms rely on informal networks involving friends who own factories and who can provide guarantees for part or all the loan collateral. One entrepreneur reported that he had, in turn, provided guarantees for others after he had benefited from such an arrangement.

**Local governments facilitate private finance mechanisms.** We have found no evidence of the government directly financing firms except during the 2008 economic crisis, but the government has played a facilitating role in matching up investors with enterprises. Thus, in Jiangxi

Province, the Small and Medium Enterprise Association, a government agency, is active in matching up entrepreneurs with financial institutions and investors. The association holds an annual meeting of representatives of firms, government agencies, and financial institutions that, in 2009, resulted in new contracts worth Y 860 million (about $130 million).

Officials of municipal governments in Zhejiang Province explained that, in some cases, the government subsidizes interest payments on bank loans for firms that are upgrading technology or expanding production facilities. The subsidy is equivalent to 7.8 percent of the commercial interest rate on the bank loans.

The clear implication of China's light manufacturing experience for other developing countries is that help from a financial intermediary is not a necessary precondition to start an enterprise. Entry into formal credit markets can make a big difference for businesses that have achieved initial success and aim to enlarge the scale of operations, upgrade equipment and production processes, or both.

The case of the metalware cluster in Yongkang in Zhejiang Province illustrates the role of government financing (chapter 5). It also illustrates how donors and aid agencies might help improve the access of developing countries to financing and information on bankable projects available as a public good.

Most metalware firms in Yongkang are SMEs that face difficulties obtaining financing. Limited access to credit can slow efforts to pursue technological innovation and expansion. In 2008, the local Yongkang government launched a program to promote collaboration among the government, banks, and enterprises. Under the program, the local government recommends promising projects and firms for loans from financial institutions. In 2009, the local tax authority joined with local bank branches to establish a platform for information exchange and resource sharing. The city recommended to local banks SMEs with good credit histories, annual tax payments of more than Y 200,000 ($29,277), and tax revenue growth rates of more than 10 percent. In the first half of 2010, 921 SMEs were on the list, of which 735 obtained loans totaling Y 1.59 billion ($235 million) (China E-Commerce Research Center 2010). This contrasts with the more typical pattern in China whereby banks hesitate to make loans to small private firms.

## Trade Logistics

Reliable transport services and streamlined customs clearance are critical for the Qinye Industrial Company Ltd., an original equipment manufacturing firm in Ganzhou, Jiangxi Province (chapter 5). Although located in a landlocked area, Ganzhou has developed an administrative system for dealing with overseas trade, including customs and inspection, foreign exchange, trade facilitation, and port clearance. Goods can be exported directly to foreign markets through integrated railway-sea and truck-sea transport services.

"For export enterprises, timely fulfillment of orders is critical," said Wu Yukun, chief of the Longnan customs office, in our interview. "What we can do is improve the efficiency and speed of the customs clearance process. By doing so, we can also attract more business volume."

The Longnan customs office collaborates with peers in Guangdong Province to expedite the commodity transfer and customs clearance services between Guangdong; Hong Kong SAR, China; Jiangxi; and Macao SAR, China. An agreement with Guangdong customs officials allows enterprises in Ganzhou, located across the provincial border in Jiangxi, to submit customs declarations at the local office, while containers are inspected at coastal customs checkpoints. This means an exporter needs to go through only one declaration and inspection process instead of two (in the place of origin and at the departure port), thereby reducing customs clearance for a cargo vehicle from Ganzhou from 10 hours to 4 hours. Customs clearance costs also plunged from Y 300 yuan ($44) per vehicle to about Y 2 ($0.30). Qinye's management estimates that expedited customs clearance delivers annual savings of Y 200,000 ($29,544).

Several government policy decisions have had a strong impact on the development of Weihai Zipper Company Ltd., in Yiwu, Zhejiang Province, and helped lower logistics and input costs. In 1982, the local government created the *sige xuke* (four permissions) policy, which allowed Yiwu residents, including Weihai's founders, to engage in local and long-distance commerce, enter businesses formerly reserved for state-owned enterprises, and establish local commodity markets. This provided the first catalyst for the Weihai founders. In 1985, the local government helped develop the Yiwu commodity market.[4]

In 1994, a market-managing company, Zhejiang China Commodity City Group, helped develop the Yiwu market. The market is managed by a group of small producers, small buyers, and a public sector management committee. The Yiwu commodity market now helps catalyze information and the inputs of cluster members, and, because the value chain is important for zipper production, the creation of the commodity city group has promoted a natural clustering of similar companies and eased transport costs.

## Access to Industrial Land

Land is particularly important for manufacturing enterprises. In 2002, local governments in Jiangxi Province allocated 33 hectares inside an industrial park to allow Aihao Writing Instruments Co. Ltd. to develop a pen manufacturing cluster that is now known as China's Pen Capital (chapter 4). The government invested Y 600 million ($72 million) to build 480,000 square meters of workshops and office buildings and sold or leased them to 45 pen manufacturing companies at the market rate. Aihao obtained about 20,000 square meters of space. This effort created the world's biggest pen manufacturer.

In China, governments, particularly at the local level, have provided access to industrial facilities through industrial parks. This important policy is a driver of China's industrialization. All the Chinese case studies show that industrial parks supply access to land. Thus, the Weihai Zipper Company Ltd., in Yiwu, Zhejiang Province, acquired industrial land that allowed it to scale up and to house workers. The company expanded from 400 workers to more than 2,000 within 10 years, and its production skyrocketed. The government made abundant industrial land available at preferential rates starting in the 1990s, offering Weihai an incentive to move into the industrial zone.

## Summary

The tale of China's success is complex. We have found evidence that could support multiple theories, but our main conclusions are that the government's contribution varies according to the business life cycle of firms, increasing with the scale, sophistication, and maturity of manufacturing enterprises, and that public sector involvement in light manufacturing has provided considerable benefit by backing winners rather than picking winners.[5] It has also become clear that China has been able to combine and leverage the country's factor endowments, particularly human capital and the huge domestic market, while establishing stable macroeconomic policies and promoting domestic competition for entry into the global market. It has thus leapfrogged to its current dominant position in the global production of consumer manufactures.

Several ingredients have been key to China's success.

First, intense domestic competition among firms and regions has boosted the country's products to their current favorable position. The competition has emerged among producers for both domestic and export markets. Some enterprises started by forming joint ventures supported by FDI—in the Pearl River Delta, for example—and producing high-quality goods for export. Only when domestic employment had increased and consumers were earning higher incomes did domestic demand rise sufficiently so that these firms turned to the domestic market. Now, the domestic demand for high-quality goods has expanded, and all firms are trying to gain larger market share. Meanwhile, other firms started small and catered only to the domestic market (for example, in Jiangxi and Zhejiang provinces). Only after they had reached a certain scale did these firms expand into export markets. The Yangzi River Delta has myriad examples of SMEs that followed one path or the other.

Second, China has benefited from policies on the exchange rate and on import tariffs as well as from macrostability in terms of domestic fiscal and monetary policies. This macrostability has been supported by political stability, which many other developing countries lack, including countries in Africa.

Third, industrial policy has not been a singular prescriptive policy applied in all districts and provinces. Instead, various policy approaches have been adopted depending on the local context and the particular stage of development. For example, the government does not promote SMEs at the expense of large enterprises. The SMEs provide jobs, while the large enterprises provide subcontracting work for the SMEs. Similarly, the government does not support new firms except through the provision of land and factory shells, but, once a firm is established and is doing well, the government is available to offer many services. These services might include streamlined administrative procedures, support for technological upgrading, and access to market information through networking. The goal is to guide the firm and the industry to become nationally competitive. The government has thus played a critical role in facilitating the creation of the input and output markets around which industrial value chains and clusters have evolved.

Fourth, in the last decade, because of the rapid development of clusters and industrial parks and because of reliance on a combination of skilled labor and a large domestic market to integrate value chains, China has become a world-class competitor in light manufacturing across an enormous range of products. The Dieshiqiao and the Haining economic zones illustrate how China has moved from assembly industries to upstream and downstream activities covering the whole supply chain, and the huge size of the domestic market has certainly helped China attain this position by facilitating competition.

While rising wages remain an issue in China, the constant upgrading of technology, combined with the supply of labor from the interior regions, will continue to keep most mid-level and high-end Chinese industries at home, while low-end manufacturing may begin moving to neighboring low-income countries and to countries in Africa.

There is an excellent opportunity for these countries to begin the industrialization process (chapter 11). In a way, the recent success of Chinese industry has completely redefined the production standard of developing countries and, in view of globalization, has raised the entry barriers facing many mid-level and high-end industries in Africa, at least relative to a decade ago, before China's success.

Developing countries should therefore not seek simply to duplicate what China has done. Instead, they should learn the lessons of China's light industry in the context of today's production landscape, which is also being shaped by China's presence. These countries will have to focus their scarce resources on selected areas, discover the binding constraints in each area, apply policies to remove these constraints, and proactively develop competitive value chains and clusters in the industries where they have a comparative advantage in resource-based, labor-intensive light manufacturing.

# Annex 10A: Case Study Matrix

**Table 10A.1 Case Study Matrix: China**

| Case study | Start-up year | Access to industrial land | Input industries | Access to finance | Entrepreneur skills | Worker skills | Trade logistics |
|---|---|---|---|---|---|---|---|
| Yiwu Huatong Meat Products Company Ltd. | 1986 | Starting in early 1980s, local governments allowed farmers to start family workshops on allocated land or collectively owned land; local government offered low-priced land in the industrial park once business reached sufficient scale | Started with animal feed production and expanded business along the value chain in which the suppliers are also the consumers of the first business | Started with self-raised funds and a small loan from a local rural credit cooperative guaranteed by a friend; investment from Taiwan, China, played a seminal role in company expansion and upgrading | Accumulated skills from early forays into business; partner from Taiwan, China, provided management skills and production expertise | Region famous for traditional meat product; imported technology and equipment accompanied by trainers; local authorities support upstream work with farmworkers by offering training in agricultural best practices | Trade logistics not constraint because of good infrastructure and proximity to ports |

| Jiangxi Youjia Food Manufacturing Company Ltd. | 1996 | Company rents standard workshops developed by government in industrial park | Made from agricultural products cultivated in the region | Started with own savings, plus money borrowed from relatives; upon business expansion, firm received bank loans with the support of government-backed credit guarantee agency for SMEs | Entrepreneur learned and practiced skills through employment in state-owned enterprise, companies in coastal areas, and his own failed business; he also took university courses | Proximity to major city enables firm to recruit workers with skills in making local specialty foods | Not a major constraint because of the well-developed infrastructure, coupled with wholesale and retail system |
|---|---|---|---|---|---|---|---|
| Fudebao Furniture Company | 1988 | Rights of use for industrial land can be purchased and traded on market; local industrial park offered cheap land to attract firms | Proximity to wood trade market in Zhejiang and nearby areas | Started with money borrowed from individuals, sometimes, with the informal guarantee of friends; after the company grew and the owner acquired land assets, he was able to apply for bank loans | The entrepreneur received no systematic training, but managed to acquire skills in the process of operating business, sometimes by copying peer companies | Wenzhou is home to a major furniture cluster, with many migrant workers; firm offers free meals and housing subsidies for new workers and trains with rigid procedures; suppliers of machinery are responsible for training workers | Infrastructure network well developed; good port facilities allow rapid movement of merchandise |

(continued next page)

**Table 10A.1 (continued)**

| Case study | Start-up year | Access to industrial land | Input industries | Access to finance | Entrepreneur skills | Worker skills | Trade logistics |
|---|---|---|---|---|---|---|---|
| Julong High-Tech Company Ltd. (Stevia) | 2002 | A star firm in the region, the company was allocated 180 mu (12 hectares) of land in a local industrial park for the construction of warehouses | Firm signed supply contract with local farmers to ensure the adequate supply of stevia leaves | Use of personal savings and bank loans secured with land and equipment; FDI and subsidized credit available | Skills accumulated through work experiences in state-owned enterprise and self-started trade business | Reliance on experts and staff workers from the acquired bankrupted state-owned enterprise | Good infrastructure network in landlocked province that is a destination for FDI |
| Aihao Writing Instruments Company Ltd. | 1992 | Started as backyard workshop; land is not a major constraint | Complete supply chain serving the pen manufacturing cluster in Zhejiang, supplying parts, molds for pens, packing and printing materials; technical support obtained from former workers at state-owned enterprises | Started with private savings and money borrowed from relatives and friends; expansion investment mainly from company savings | Influenced by a deep-rooted merchant culture in the region, local entrepreneurs are not afraid of failures and keep trying until they succeed; owner also obtained skills by watching other businesspeople | Large group of hardworking migrant workers in Wenzhou provides good labor pool, however, there are issues about the wages and skills of workers; these issues are being addressed | Good transportation network and port facilities |

| | Year | | | | | | |
|---|---|---|---|---|---|---|---|
| Women's Shoes, Wuhou Industrial Park | 2002 | Good access to industrial land and park facilities; in 6 km², the park and its surrounding facilities host more than 1,500 manufacturers | Proximity to quality leather inputs from neighboring cities in Sichuan | Entrepreneurs financed through savings; some savings were obtained from years of working in state-owned firms | State-owned companies helped transfer skills to entrepreneurs; some entrepreneurs relocated from coastal areas and brought skills | Chengdu has major shoe cluster with pool of labor of more than 100,000 skilled and semiskilled workers | Strong infrastructure; complete supply chain that spans backward and forward links; although inland, connection to ports is relatively smooth |
| Dieshiqiao International Home Textiles Market | 2006 | Provincial-level development zone with strong industrial park | Cheap, abundant local supplies of cloth and booming processing trade | Entrepreneurs relied on own savings; low capital requirements of industry; local government financing platforms | Entrepreneurs relied on sophisticated networks to upgrade embroidery techniques and use commodity markets | Close to 500,000 semiskilled and skilled workers (migrants from all over China) provide ready pool of labor | Complete industrial value chain in southeast China; good roads and proximity to ports |
| Warp Knitting Science and Technology Industrial Zone | 1999 | Warp knitting industrial park established to provide better infrastructure and services for enterprises | Proximity to inputs; integrated industrial supply chain from raw materials and knitting to processing | Own savings; company profits reinvested in business expansion and technology upgrading | Skilled entrepreneurs with good networks; professional platforms provide support for research and development, business consulting, and trading | Pool of 20,000 workers, mostly unskilled migrants from inland provinces, with some skilled workers | Proximity to Shanghai; dense network of road, railway, and air links |

(continued next page)

**Table 10A.1 (continued)**

| Case study | Start-up year | Access to industrial land | Input industries | Access to finance | Entrepreneur skills | Worker skills | Trade logistics |
|---|---|---|---|---|---|---|---|
| Button City, Qiaotou | 1980 | Only when industry achieved a certain scale did government help build industrial parks and the commodity city | Careful mastery of input industries, especially plastic via the bicycle peddler network; rise of apparel industry nearby helped | Self-financed; SME and family workshops | Used strong entrepreneurial skills and Wenzhou trading instincts to discover niche product in obscure town; connection to Taiwan, China | Low skills of workers in early years; only recently have skills improved | Bicycle peddlers navigated system in early years; rapid truck access to the port now |
| Weihai Zipper Company Ltd. | 1982 | Peasant entrepreneurs used government-subsidized land to upgrade size | Easy access to factor inputs allowed Weihai Zipper Company to grow and specialize | Self-financed; SME family workshops; reinvested profits allowed expansion | Technology and information on zippers were obtained through the first mover's network via an entrepreneurial network of Taiwan, China | Recruiting quality workers from inland areas, mostly women between ages 18 and 25 | Easy access to the Yiwu commodity city; proximity to ports; low transaction costs for exports |
| Toothbrush Cluster, Yangzhou | 2001 | Industrial park facilitates enterprise conglomeration and expansion | Proximity to inputs; cluster located near local suppliers | Dependence on family savings and money borrowed from friends and relatives; important role of FDI | Skilled entrepreneurs use local government and FDI to upgrade constantly | More than 20,000 semiskilled migrant workers | Solid infrastructure; cargo trucks travel around the clock shipping products to the nearby port |

| | Year | | | | | | |
|---|---|---|---|---|---|---|---|
| Metalware Industrial Cluster, Yongkang | 1999 | Established as industrial park; one of largest in the province | Supply chain with fixed local suppliers using recycled metal | Local savings; profits reinvested for expansion | Metalworking skills learned from networks | Pool of 300,000 skilled and semiskilled workers | Great roads; proximity to Shanghai |
| Qinye Industrial Company Ltd. | 2005 | Firm relocated from Guangdong to inland province to take advantage of more abundant, cheaper supply of land | Most supplies are acquired from nearby regions through long-term supplier networks | Investment from Hong Kong SAR, China, and from local capital vital in early stages | Entrepreneurs developed skills through diaspora networks | Labor supply is abundant and cheaper than in coastal areas; local government helps with skills training | Well-connected transportation network and supportive customs service (local government support) enable export firms to deliver orders |
| Zhengzhou Economic Development Zone | 1993 | Industrial park was established in early 1990s; development zone helped attract local investment and FDI | Many inputs procured provincially; large companies tap into a larger supply chain | Entrepreneurs used own savings and networks; state finance supports investment projects in zone | Zone administration helps link enterprises and research institutes to ensure good entrepreneurial skills | Abundant supply of skilled and unskilled labor; low labor costs in inland province | Networks of railways, highways, air routes, and telecommunications compensate for lack of proximity to ports |
| Auto Industry, Yinchuan | 1992 | Provincial-level high-technology industrial development zone of 7.5 km² | Distant from supply networks and auto parts manufacturers | Entrepreneurs used own savings and loans and credits from local government | Weak educational system makes it difficult to have good local engineers and managers | Skilled workers from neighboring provinces | Far from main suppliers of auto parts, who are concentrated in coastal regions and northern China |
| Yongle Economic Development Zone | 1992 | Economic development zone established, but small size and high cost | Regional and local supply of inputs | Failure to engage the private investors in developing the zone | Lack of strong local entrepreneurs; top-down initiative | High labor costs have been obstacle to zone growth | Proximity to Beijing, but too far from city center and small size |

*Source:* World Bank interviews, 2010, 2012.
*Note:* FDI = foreign direct investment; SME = small and medium enterprise.

**Table 10A.2  Case Study Matrix: Other Countries**

| Case study | Start-up year | Access to industrial land | Input industries | Access to finance | Entrepreneur skills | Worker skills | Trade logistics |
|---|---|---|---|---|---|---|---|
| Cut Flowers, Ethiopia | 1980 | Private leasing of agricultural land from government (30-year leases) | Good input provision; local farmers buy quality seeds from foreign breeders; duty-free import of inputs and other materials | Own savings, together with concessional financing from the state-owned Development Bank of Ethiopia | Dynamic entrepreneur with global knowledge and access to latest research | Pool of semiskilled workers and farmers in horticulture industry | Good trade logistics; competitive fuel and airfreight charges, but delays at customs in importing chemical inputs constitute an extra cost |
| Cut Flowers, Kenya | 1990 | Alliance between FDI and medium-scale growers | Relationship of horticultural exporters and contract farmers constitutes the nucleus of system; seeds are provided by local and locally based international firms; purchasing is based on franchise or license agreements to ensure that cut flower exporters can import plant, machinery, equipment, and raw materials free of taxes | Financing by banks and development finance institutions; Kenya's exporters get letters of credit from the domestic finance market in which major banks such as Barclays and Citibank are present; small-scale growers struggle with finance | Strong entrepreneur skills developed via industrial association | Work is low skilled; pool of agricultural laborers with low levels of schooling | Advanced trade logistics with strong supply using refrigerated trucks, freight forwarders, and aviation links |

| | | | | | | | |
|---|---|---|---|---|---|---|---|
| Tomatoes, Senegal | 2005 | Land allocations by government to multinationals near river delta; investment in unallocated land | Direct control of tomato processing through vertically integrated supply chain | Capital from French multinational physical stock | Joint venture between French multinational and local companies allows for knowledge spillovers | Work is low skilled; temporary and seasonal workers are hired from nearby villages | FDI company controls entire supply chain (production, refrigeration, shipping, and marketing); manages maritime lines located close to the production site and uses planes for agroindustrial product |
| Bonsu Furniture Works, Ghana | 2006 | Serious lack of export processing zone or industrial land for entrepreneurs | Poor quality of the wood used for furniture; local raw materials, especially wood and polish, are expensive; furniture companies can import inputs at tariffs of only 5 or 10 percent and add value domestically; tax rebates have been introduced; the scale of these varies with the total production exported | Entrepreneurs lack working capital to scale up business; banks lend short term at high interest rates and high collateral requirements; governments have done little to attract FDI | Entrepreneurs have some skills, but cannot tap into network or association for upgrading | Companies have been able to find semiskilled workers with adequate abilities; most workers are part of an inherited tradition of craftsmanship, but are unfamiliar with the latest technologies and design techniques | No major trade logistics challenge |

*(continued next page)*

**Table 10A.2** (continued)

| Case study | Start-up year | Access to industrial land | Input industries | Access to finance | Entrepreneur skills | Worker skills | Trade logistics |
|---|---|---|---|---|---|---|---|
| Ho Nai Furniture Company, Vietnam | 1991 | Industrial parks and joint ventures with FDI formed base of industry; tax holidays | Mastery of wood imports from neighboring Asian countries; local wood not of good quality | Capital provided by entrepreneur savings and capital from Scandinavian FDI | Knowledge comes from foreign FDI | Tradition of craftsmanship; easy access to workers | Good transportation network and supply chain make trade logistics easy |
| Bata Shoes, Kenya | 1980 | No access to industrial land and unfavorable FDI regime (least effective in East Africa) | Poor-quality skins and hides and little processing; highest quality leather is exported | Lack of financing is notable; even companies with good skills find obtaining working capital difficult | Good historical skills inherited from Bata, but limited adaptability to new realities | Workers were trained in basic shoemaking, but there has been no skills upgrading | High transport costs and congestion in Mombasa make trade logistics difficult |

| | | | | | | | |
|---|---|---|---|---|---|---|---|
| Morogoro Shoe Factory, Tanzania | 1984 | Factory site has an area of 35,000 m² of which 22,700 m² are covered by buildings; site chosen by the government for a collaborative project with the World Bank; project envisioned the construction of an industrial estate with the necessary infrastructure and facilities for SMEs; however, the project failed | Poor command of inputs, with defective hides and leather | Various credit sources, for $40 million | No private entrepreneurs selected; top-down approach | Poorly trained workers; no training on shoe production or on repairing machines | Lack of mastery of supply chain; large infrastructure deficit and no consideration for export channels; factory located far from the coast |
| Sialkot Sporting Goods Cluster, Pakistan | 1980 | No industrial parks, but small and medium shops operating in a cluster | High-quality leather is procured locally | Some degree of savings from entrepreneurs; financing problem solved through web of subcontracting arrangements | Over decades, industrial cluster has fostered entrepreneurial tradition and information sharing | Network of skilled workers because of history of craftsmanship | Bad infrastructure compensated by building of dry port and airport financed by private sector |

(continued next page)

| Case study | Start-up year | Access to industrial land | Input industries | Access to finance | Entrepreneur skills | Worker skills | Trade logistics |
|---|---|---|---|---|---|---|---|
| Apparel Production, Bangladesh | 1982 | Favorable regimes for export processing zones, with tax holidays and exemptions; strong relocation of firms to export processing zones | The Bangladesh ready-made garments industry largely depends on imported yarns and fabrics, mostly from China | Innovative financing arrangements using letter-of-credit system | Classic story of joint venture between native private garment industry (Desh Company) with a Korean business group, Daewoo; Korean firm provided in-house training to 130 workers | Tradition of local craftsmanship dating back several decades | Good management of export processing zones has reduced problems in trade logistics in a country with bad infrastructure |
| Sari Production, India | 1980 | No industrial land allocations | Fabric is not a key constraint because inputs are of good quality, although expensive | Larger weavers obtain credit, but smaller weavers may obtain government concessional loans to cooperatives | Entrepreneurs have rich historical tradition of craftsmanship | Varied worker skills; labor laws prevent formalization and skills upgrading | Poor transport and logistics make it difficult to keep industry internationally competitive |
| Apparel Industry, Lesotho | 2000 | Lack of export processing zones, although government built factory shells | Good mastery of inputs; most inputs are sourced from China; Hong Kong SAR, China; and Taiwan, China | Foreign capital, plus Central Bank of Lesotho credit guarantee assistance to exporters and for Southern African Customs Union certification scheme | Asian entrepreneurs with considerable experience | Workers are semiskilled, predominantly women, well educated, and paid about $100 a month | Good control of supply chain with exports to niche markets in European Union (EU), although high logistics costs persist because of landlocked status |

| Textile and Apparel Industry, Mauritius | 1970 | Development of export processing zones; government built the factory shells | Asian network ensured access to good-quality fabric | Self-financed; some use of local capital from sugar plantations | Asian connections provided transfer of skills and knowledge to indigenous entrepreneurs | Pool of underemployed younger women became backbone of industry; use of foreign labor later | Good control of access to ports in small open economy, with shipping and aviation |
|---|---|---|---|---|---|---|---|
| Textile and Apparel Industry, Zambia | 1980 | No access to industrial land or export processing zone regime (exists only in legislation) | Poor control of inputs; mills generally pay import parity prices, plus premiums to cover storage costs and the risks of the ginners leading to the procurement of cotton lint at prices above world market prices | Lack of savings and working capital prevented firm expansion; high domestic costs of borrowing | Joint collaboration with Asian firms has led to some knowledge spillovers and entrepreneurial skills | No outstanding issues with worker quality | Poor supply chain and trade logistics; significant time to move goods from factory to export markets |

*Source:* World Bank interviews, 2010, 2012.

*Note:* FDI = foreign direct investment; SME = small and medium enterprise.

457

# Notes

1. Thus, in 2011, Beijing addressed the growing problem of the indebtedness of local governments. Although forbidden from issuing debt, local governments have circumvented this restriction by guaranteeing loans made to government-controlled entities the operations of which fall outside official budgets. In response to this mounting debt problem, Beijing allowed a handful of jurisdictions to issue their own bonds. See "China Allows Four Local Governments to Issue Bonds to Curb Debt Risks," Xinhua English News, October 20, 2011, http://news.xinhuanet.com/english2010/china/2011-10/20/c_131202777.htm. Heilmann and Perry (2011) offer a broader treatment of Chinese policy experimentation.
2. See http://wenku.baidu.com/view/b1441920192e45361066f563.html [in Chinese].
3. The text here draws on www.chinarjw.com [in Chinese], August 16, 2011, http://www.chinarjw.com/n25/n544/n550/c4529/content.html.
4. Ding (2006) finds a substantial transformation of the market over 1992–97 because a large number of merchants from other regions began operating in the Yiwu market, the number of comparatively well-educated and young merchants in the Yiwu market increased, and the booth keepers in the Yiwu market gradually built up sturdy business relationships with producers.
5. This conclusion applies only to light manufacturing and is likely not true in other areas deemed strategic for national development plans such as steel, coal, and aerospace.

# References

China E-Commerce Research Center. 2010. "Yongkang Establishes Conversation between Taxation and Banks to Solve Financial Difficulties of SMEs." [In Chinese.] August 7. http://b2b.toocle.com/detail--5322464.html.

Ding, Ke. 2006. "Distribution System of China's Industrial Clusters: Case Study of Yiwu China Commodity City." IDE Discussion Paper 75 (October), Institute of Developing Economies, Japan External Trade Organization, Chiba, Japan.

Dinh, Hinh T., Vincent Palmade, Vandana Chandra, and Frances Cossar. 2012. *Light Manufacturing in Africa: Targeted Policies to Enhance Private Investment and Create Jobs*. Washington, DC: World Bank. http://go.worldbank.org/ASG0J44350.

Farole, Thomas. 2011. *Special Economic Zones in Africa: Comparing Performances and Learning from Global Experiences*. Washington, DC: World Bank.

Heilmann, Sebastian, and Elizabeth J. Perry, eds. 2011. *Mao's Invisible Hand: The Political Foundations of Adaptive Governance in China*. Harvard Contemporary China Studies 17. Cambridge, MA: Harvard University Press.

Lin, Justin Yifu. 2012. *New Structural Economics: A Framework for Rethinking Development and Policy*. Washington, DC: World Bank.

Patrick, Hugh T., and Thomas P. Rohlen. 1987. "Small-Scale Family Enterprises." In *The Domestic Transformation*, edited by Kozo Yamamura and Yasukichi Yasuba, 331–84. Vol. 1 of *The Political Economy of Japan*. Stanford, CA: Stanford University Press.

Stiglitz, Joseph E. 1992. "The Meanings of Competition in Economic Analysis." *Rivista Internazionale di Scienze Sociali* 100 (2): 191–212.

Sutton, John, and Nebil Kellow. 2010. *An Enterprise Map of Ethiopia*. London: International Growth Center. http://eprints.lse.ac.uk/36390/.

Wong, Kwan-Yiu. 1987. "China's Special Economic Zone Experiment: An Appraisal." *Geografiska Annaler, Series B, Human Geography* 69 (1): 27–40. http://www.jstor.org/stable/490409.

# 11

# Policy Lessons for Developing Countries

## Introduction

In this chapter, we review the extent to which the policy lessons of China and other countries can be applied elsewhere in the developing world, especially in the context of manufacturing in the current global landscape. Based on the previous chapters, particularly the case studies in chapters 4–9, we highlight five factors of success for the development of light manufacturing in today's world: creating a supportive environment for manufacturing, filling knowledge and financial gaps through foreign direct investment (FDI) and networks, using substitution policies and sequencing, starting small and building up or cutting back, and establishing islands of success by keeping targeted policies selective and within a country's limited resources.

## The Uniqueness of China's Experience

While other developing countries can learn much from China's achievements in light manufacturing, no one should lose sight of China's exceptionalism. No other country has a domestic market of 1.4 billion people, which allows for huge economies of scale and fierce competition and facilitates the swift completion of supply chains.

Much of China's recent industrial success is attributable to the facilitating role of local and provincial governments that financed their efforts through coercive large-scale land sales and leases. Few other countries can pursue such policies. Moreover, China began with a labor force that was not only large, but also literate. Although the quality of the work force was initially low, this was not a problem for the initial "imitation" stage. The value and respect traditionally accorded to education proved timely in the later stages of light manufacturing in China. This was also true earlier in the case of the Republic of Korea; Singapore; and Taiwan, China, but contrasts with the situation in many low-income countries.

China's large diaspora was an indispensable source of knowledge about commerce, technology, and trade. The strong ties and allegiance demonstrated by overseas Chinese promoted rapid transfers of expertise and financial resources, benefits not available on such a scale to most other countries. China has also benefited from the unusual depth of entrepreneurial resources among the domestic citizenry and overseas migrants.

Measurements of social trust reinforce the impression of Chinese exceptionalism. Estrin and Mickiewicz (2010, 26) argue that the decades of Communism in the countries of the former Soviet Union and the transition economies of Eastern Europe have undercut trust and other informal arrangements that support entrepreneurship and private business. They report that "generalized trust was severely damaged during the command economy period and is only recovering slowly." They see the malign social consequences of Communism continuing to limit entrepreneurship two decades after the collapse of Communism.

In contrast, China, though still ruled by a communist party, consistently ranks among the highest scoring countries on generalized trust. This probably explains the prevalence of cooperative behavior among producers and between producers and government officials even in the absence of well-developed systems of property rights, commercial law, and corporate governance (see chapter 9).

At the early stages, China's progress in light manufacturing derived enormous benefit from pioneer postwar developing areas, notably, Hong Kong SAR, China, and Taiwan, China. As the rising cost of land

and labor eroded the profitability of garments, toys, and other light manufactures built around the use of low-skill workers during the 1970s, Chinese-speaking entrepreneurs from these neighboring economies jumped at the fresh chance to relocate operations to south China. The combination of the business experience and market knowledge of these entrepreneurs and the new availability of low-cost Chinese land and labor generated streams of light manufacturing products, first from a small number of special economic zones and eventually from a wide array of Chinese production sites. Goods originating in China's rapidly expanding special economic zones filled the void created by the withdrawal of producers in more well developed areas of East Asia from the bottom rungs of the international price-quality ladder. Thereafter, China-based producers, including domestic firms and enterprises linked to outside investors, expanded the quantity, quality, and variety of light manufactured exports far beyond the niches initially occupied by goods from erstwhile producers in Hong Kong SAR, China, and in Taiwan, China.

Now, the process is repeating itself. The current phase of China's industrial development represents an open door for other countries to achieve fast-track growth. Peaking productivity and rising wages among China's labor force, creeping inflation, steeply increasing land prices, and the upward drift in the international value of the yuan are gradually eroding the comparative advantage of Chinese light manufactures. These pressures are particularly evident at the low end of the price-quality spectrum. In 2012, for example, Chinese exports of apparel declined, and overseas footwear sales recorded only tiny increases, while exports of electrical machinery, optical equipment, and vehicle parts achieved substantial gains (Frangos 2013). The gradual retreat of Chinese goods from global markets for labor-intensive products is creating significant and growing opportunities for new entrants.

Although prospective new entrants face the task of overcoming their own domestic constraints, today's newcomers, like the Chinese start-ups of the late 1970s and early 1980s, can benefit from the knowledge, experience, and resources accumulated by successful overseas entrepreneurs. This process is accelerated through Chinese FDI in low-income countries, including Sub-Saharan Africa.

## Elements of Success for Developing Countries

Our study shows that low-income countries face a vicious circle of pervasive poverty and low industrialization so that the economy-wide policies recommended by the Washington Consensus are unlikely to overcome the inertia that is impeding progress. Furthermore, because the binding constraints vary by sector and by firm size, economy-wide policies are not even effective in addressing the constraints. What these economies need is a focused initiative to inject new elements of prosperity and growth even as large segments of the economies remain unaffected. Without such a breakthrough, poor countries are unlikely to eliminate the persistent low equilibrium of poverty and limited industrialization. The targeted development of light manufacturing—specifically, consumer goods manufactured using modest inputs of fixed capital and technology and the extensive application of unskilled or semiskilled labor—is a promising entry point for accelerating industrialization and prosperity in low-income countries.

Our companion volume, *Light Manufacturing in Africa* (Dinh and others 2012), proposes a framework for applying targeted policies to enhance private investment and create jobs in low-income countries. The case studies in our volume here illustrate important dimensions of this framework: creating a supportive environment for manufacturing, filling knowledge and financial gaps, starting small and building up or cutting back, and establishing islands of success by keeping targeted policies selective.

### Creating a Conducive Environment for Manufacturing

**Government support.** Constant governmental support is central to the sustainable development of light manufacturing. This support need not take the form of subsidies or active government intervention, which could introduce unwelcome distortions to the economy. Government's key contribution is to create a landscape favorable to enterprise development by identifying and then acting to roll back the most serious constraints. Some of these constraints may be caused by government policy; if so, removing constraints may mean that the government should change or terminate earlier interventions.

Foremost among possible official actions is for national leaders to issue forceful public endorsements of economic growth and private sector development as a key government priority. Clear signals of support from the top levels of government increase the chance that would-be entrepreneurs will take the risk of creating and expanding small business ventures. China's experience shows that some entrepreneurs will step forward even without active official support. The more visible and consistent such support is, however, the greater the likelihood of committed entrepreneurial effort. The widespread and positive response to Deng Xiaoping's tour of southern China in 1992 when he repeatedly proclaimed his support for market-leaning reform illustrates the importance of consistent support from the top.

**Macroeconomic stability.** Macroeconomic stability is an essential ingredient for successful development initiatives. In our successful case studies, entrepreneurs benefited from policy stability, while, in most unsuccessful cases, they suffered from an unstable macroeconomic environment. Policy reversals and a lack of fiscal discipline were much more frequent in Kenya and Tanzania, for example, than in China (chapter 8). In Zambia, too, industrial growth suffered from macroeconomic shocks and from policies that encouraged the wrong sequencing of import liberalization, resulting in imports flooding the market (chapter 9).

The case of Bonsu Furniture Works in Ghana shows how the absence of government support—in terms of macrostability (inflation and interest rates were high), the capacity to attract FDI (see below), and the provision of public goods such as showrooms, centers, and workshops (chapter 7)—can undermine ventures designed to build on comparative advantage. Without macrostability, supportive trade and fiscal policies (low, simplified tariff rates, plus a favorable fiscal regime) did not seem to matter for the Bonsu venture. A more active government approach to attracting FDI and to disseminating knowledge might have changed the outcome.

Maintaining a competitive exchange rate and avoiding inflation are especially important. In nearly all the successes, governments kept the real exchange rate competitive and maintained fiscal and monetary discipline; in nearly all the failures, an overvalued exchange rate hurt exports. In four of the five cases of failure outside China (India is the only exception), an overvalued or appreciating exchange rate hurt exports. Strong appreciation in Lesotho caused factories to shut down in 2004–05, and thousands of workers lost their jobs (chapter 9). This challenge was exacerbated by the U.S. financial crisis in 2008. In Zambia, exchange rate appreciation led to a 30 percent decline in cotton prices, driving tens of thousands of farmers to abandon cotton production. The importance of a competitive exchange rate poses a dilemma for resource-based developing countries such as Ghana, Tanzania, and Zambia where foreign exchange earnings from minerals exert pressure on the real exchange rate (Dutch Disease) and discourage labor-intensive growth.

**Trade policies.** Trade policies also helped Chinese industries in the initial stages. China entered the post-1978 reform era with high tariffs on many imports, including many light manufacturing products. During the early 1980s, China sheltered buttons under tariffs averaging 80 percent; by the first decade of the 2000s, the tariffs had been gradually reduced to slightly more than 10 percent (figure 11.1). Thus, the button industry did not face a flood of cheap imports in its nascent years. The Yinchuan auto industry shows clearly that the Chinese have used tariffs as a way to develop local industry (chapter 5). Beginning in 1986, China imposed a protective tariff on automobiles: 180–220 percent for assembled vehicles and 20–50 percent for auto parts.[1] These high

**Figure 11.1 Import Tariffs on Buttons, China, 1992–2009**

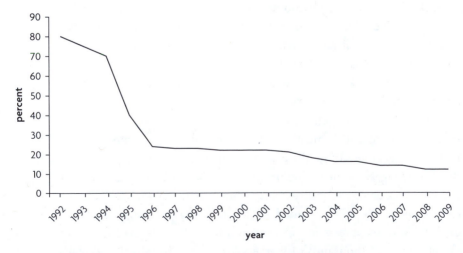

Sources: Data of the World Trade Organization; interviews in Qiaotou, Zhejiang Province, October 2010.

tariffs blocked most imports, and rising domestic demand spurred local governments to build their own automobile plants.

This situation stands in contrast to many African countries that simultaneously liberalize imports of finished goods, raw materials, and intermediate goods. The case of Zambia's garment industry shows how sudden trade liberalization unleashed a flood of imports that left domestic producers no opportunity to adjust before cheap imports wiped out the entire industry. This case also illustrates the importance of close cooperation between the public and private sectors, without which there is little chance for private manufacturers to achieve sustained growth.

China introduced trade reforms in the 1980s that improved the input industry and trade logistics. A duty drawback system refunded the duties paid on the imports used in producing exports. Raw material imports and allocations, controlled under the prereform plan system, were gradually liberalized, allowing firms to obtain what they needed through the market and reducing costs along the supply chain. A foreign exchange retention system was introduced at the provincial level, allowing exporters to keep their foreign exchange earnings. Licensing authority was decentralized, allowing entrepreneurs to deal directly with local authorities on licensing matters. Customs procedures were simplified. All these reforms made it easier to start and run private businesses, and most of them took place before imports of final goods were liberalized.

Most developing countries today do not have the same opportunity as China with regard to exchange rate policy and tariffs. In part, this is because of the changing rules of the World Trade Organization (WTO) and, in part, because of China's unique size. Another problem is that many countries have weak governance structures so that trade policies may be captured by vested interests. However, by paying close attention to the constraints that hinder the potential growth of manufacturing, cooperative efforts by governments and private firms in any setting can relieve particular bottlenecks and ease the cost of adjusting to changes in the external environment or in domestic policies.

An important element in China's economic success has been its prudent macroeconomic policies and the high level of private domestic savings, which helped the country maintain a competitive exchange rate and low inflation. The low exchange rate catalyzed exports and growth. The previously overvalued yuan lost about 70 percent of its value against the U.S. dollar over 1980–95 as measured by the trade-weighted real effective exchange rate index, making exports cheaper relative to the exports of some competitors. If developing countries today cannot, for the most part, manage the exchange rates to their advantage, this means they have to maintain wage restraint, which in turn, requires government policies to ensure labor market flexibility, including the proper role of trade unions in wage formation. [2]

**Public-private cooperation.** In China, unlike in other countries, the line between the public and private sectors seems blurred: it is difficult to tell where one ends and the other begins. Partly because of the historical development of the country, the interests, incentives, objectives, and instruments of the two sectors are all intertwined (chapter 1). Nonetheless, when reform began during the late 1970s, there was as much suspicion, doubt, and contempt between the two sectors as we encounter elsewhere. Only later, when the incentives of officials and the profit motive in the private sector became aligned, did a partnership emerge.

Button City in Qiaotou, Zhejiang Province, illustrates this gradual convergence of interests (chapter 5). Initially, the button cluster was a private initiative. The friction between the public and private sectors that existed at the early stages of cluster development gradually gave way to cooperation, not least because of the vested interests of local authorities (their careers, salaries, and future all depended on the success of the local economy). Once firms had settled in, the government introduced industrial policies to facilitate expansion and provide financial support, land, and an industrial park.

China's fiscal reform of 1994 and the political performance evaluation system based on growth in gross domestic product (GDP) gave local governments strong incentives to promote local industries. These incentives encouraged local governments to become more involved in the development of clusters. Thus, while all levels of government now benefit from the growth of clusters, no single level of government totally controls cluster development. The Chinese style of federalism has created a political basis for the success of cluster-based economic development (Montinola, Qian, and Weingast 1995).

China's experience also illustrates the potential of local governments to support and contribute actively to industrial development. In some countries, the central government plans and develops strategic industries by mobilizing and allocating resources. These efforts to pick winners often fail. Local governments have fewer options. They cannot change the macroeconomic environment or build national monopolies, and they lack many of the resources for building industries that are available to the central administration. As a result, local governments have generally supported profitable firms that are already in business in local communities.

China's experience in the development of clusters offers rich evidence of what public-private cooperation can accomplish. This experience substantiates the argument that the government's role is to nurture and support existing cluster firms rather than trying to create clusters from scratch.

Unlike the strategy of building national champions that exists in other industrial areas, cluster-based industrialization in light manufacturing emphasizes locally grown entrepreneurship. Entrepreneurs, rather than governments, create clusters. In China, at the initial stages of cluster formation, when production was concentrated in home workshops, governments typically paid little attention, adopting a hands-off policy. Chinese start-ups, especially in coastal provinces such as Guangdong and Zhejiang, benefited from a key official response: tolerance. Easing up on stifling tax policies, removing obstacles to the transportation of goods, or reducing barriers to entry allows entrepreneurs more space to explore and take risks.

Once clusters expand, the public sector can initiate a more active involvement to develop general infrastructure (roads, utilities, land) and target facilities to meet the specific requirements of emerging clusters (market structures, financial institutions, training programs, quality control mechanisms, and so on). The case of Dieshiqiao illustrates the benefit of allowing emergent clusters to develop on their own, without governmental interference (chapter 5). Jiangsu Province, where Dieshiqiao is located, and the nearby provincial-level municipality of Shanghai have long histories of organically developed textile and garment clusters. Their legacy of expertise in all aspects of cotton production, textiles, embroidery, distribution, and marketing provided a natural breeding ground for the formation of new clusters in these industries; once the government abandoned the antieconomic policy of suppressing business development, entrepreneurs stepped forward to promote start-up ventures, some of which eventually blossomed into prosperous multinational giants.

The success of cluster-based industrialization in China builds on one feature that may limit the applicability of this model to other countries. The success of Chinese industrialization has come in part at the expense of farmers whose land was forcibly purchased with paltry compensation and then transferred to industrial users or real estate developers at vastly higher prices. The system whereby all land belongs to the state and can be taken readily only exists in a few countries. So, all lessons on cluster practice in China need to be interpreted cautiously.

The Sialkot sporting goods cluster in Punjab, Pakistan, shows that, at times, the best government policy is government absence (chapter 8). The cluster was established through private initiative, and the industry was able to find the resources necessary to build infrastructure, even an airport, without government assistance.

In the same vein, the Morogoro shoe factory in Tanzania illustrates that (1) no matter how capable a government is, the choice of the location, size, and all other features of a factory are best left to the private sector; (2) large-scale start-ups can easily founder because scale tends to limit flexibility in business decision making; and (3) the role of government should be to provide macrostability, determine the constraints facing the industry, and help resolve the constraints. If the government had adopted this approach, the Bata (Kenya) and Morogoro shoe factories would not have faced such a critical problem with inputs of poor quality and availability (chapter 8). Efforts should have been devoted to diagnosing this problem, including, if necessary, facilitating the appropriate imports.

One clear example of failure in China is the attempt to create an automotive cluster in Ningxia (chapter 5). Officials at Ningxia Auto pushed ahead to create the cluster despite the refusal of well-known vehicle firms to participate even after they were offered subsidies. Meanwhile, local officials sought to develop the cluster in the face of a lack of local suppliers of components and raw materials (steel, glass, rubber). They focused on their belief in the existence of a local market for vehicles, but failed to consider how local production would be able to compete with vehicles from well-established producers in other regions. Inevitably, the industry failed.

But even when the absence of government intervention is good for the private sector, the role of the government in ensuring that the rights of workers are protected is crucial. The disastrous fire that killed more than 1,000 Bangladeshi garment workers in April 2013 points to the need for effective public and private cooperation to make worker safety the first priority.

**Incentive-compatible industrial policies.** Developing countries often initiate cluster-based industrial policies, but achieve little success because of conflicting interests among the levels and departments of government involved in policy implementation. In some instances, the government views the private sector with suspicion, adopting a naive zero-sum perspective that views private profit as a consequence of the exploitation or victimization of workers or customers and concludes that the state should capture and redistribute business profits. Such views encourage the private sector to regard government as a grabbing hand that aims to steal hard-won earnings from successful entrepreneurs. These views cannot be changed in a short time. Often, the best one can hope for is a gradual shift toward a realistic system of incentives that promotes the achievement of the common goal of economic prosperity.

### Filling Knowledge and Financial Gaps through FDI and Networks

The economics literature usually emphasizes the benefits of FDI in supplementing domestic savings. A lack of financial resources is only part of the problem, however. The lack of expertise, technology, and ideas is equally limiting, and both FDI and networks play a fundamental role in providing this knowledge. Romer (1993) noted that FDI is not only a source of financing, but is also accompanied by the knowledge needed for production, marketing, and so on.

**FDI and the role of foreign expertise, technology, and ideas.** From the start of China's opening-up policy, which reduced barriers to international trade and private foreign investment, the domestic economy benefited from an influx of knowledge, capital, and market information. Chinese investors from Hong Kong SAR, China; Singapore; and Taiwan, China, whose linguistic and cultural affinity facilitated easy communication, were particularly influential. These emigrants had remained fiercely loyal to their ancestral homelands and were thus willing to contribute to homeland projects even after decades abroad.

> Local leaders ... throughout the [south China] region have encouraged the involvement of émigrés in local economic development ... since the reform initiatives began. [These] overtures ... have met with substantial success. (Johnson 1994, 77)

Bateman and Mody, quoted in Romer (1993, 563), "observe that the best one-variable explanation for development in China, even if one restricts attention to the special economic zones, is geographic distance from Hong Kong."

Education migrants have also contributed to the success of Chinese businesses; consider the many Chinese students enrolled in schools abroad. Precisely as in the case of Korea and of Taiwan, China, few of these students returned at first, leading to concerns about a loss of human capital. However, growing prosperity at home eventually induced many overseas graduates to come back. Even the graduates who remained abroad influenced the success of Chinese businesses through networks that created links between international groups of entrepreneurs and researchers in China (Saxenian 2006).

FDI may compensate for deficits in education, managerial and entrepreneurial skills, technical expertise, commercial knowledge, and market information, allowing entrepreneurs to succeed without a formal education.

In virtually all successful Chinese cases, FDI plays a fundamental role not so much among domestic start-ups, but in the expansion of these firms to acquire technology, management expertise, marketing support, and finance. Thus, the button and zipper case studies show that domestic industries can benefit greatly from FDI, especially through joint ventures, which can increase access to finance and technology (chapter 5). A key to Weihai's success in the zipper industry was its connections, starting in the late 1970s, with an entrepreneurial network in Taiwan, China, that introduced invaluable professional expertise, efficient management methods, and industrial technology, including advanced machinery, thereby helping Weihai to develop, scale up, and, eventually, innovate. Weihai has had an original equipment manufacturer (OEM) contract with firms in Taiwan, China, since the mid-1990s. Foreign investment has freed Weihai from the long-standing constraints of its deficiencies in finance, technical knowledge, managerial skill, and market information.

One might expect the link between domestic producers in Africa and the large African diaspora to match what we observe in China. However, this is not the case. Among the entrepreneurs we interviewed in Africa, few reported substantive contacts with Africans living abroad (Dinh and others 2012). More research might be useful in clarifying the role of trust in this phenomenon or whether the phenomenon may be related to Africa's heterogeneous mélange of ethnic and cultural groups.

FDI plays a critical part in China as well as in our other developing-country cases. The case of the garment industry in Bangladesh (chapter 9) illustrates clearly how FDI can combine with the domestic resources of a country to provide productive employment. The local Desh Company provided land and labor, while Daewoo, the foreign company, trained managers and workers and installed machinery, thus addressing at least five of the binding constraints in the sector (chapter 10, annex table 10A.2). What is striking in the Bangladesh case is the spillover: of 130 Bangladeshi sent to Korea for training, 115 had set up their own shops back in Bangladesh within seven years and thus began to contribute to the growth of their country's garment sector (Crook 1992).

Over and over again, the role of FDI has been crucial. In Lesotho, South African investors, followed by Chinese investors, have played a key role in raising output, exports, and employment in the textile industry (chapter 9). In the early 1980s, South African investors set up shop in Lesotho to evade sanctions imposed on South African manufactured goods because of apartheid. In the early 1990s, industrialists from Taiwan, China, invested in Lesotho, bringing valuable capital and skills. Many of the investors faced growing competition at home, where outdated technologies were reducing efficiency. Many more South African firms moved to Lesotho in the mid-1990s when Lesotho liberalized the investment regime to attract FDI to the textile sector.

The case of the Mauritian textile and apparel industry illustrates the importance of entrepreneurship (chapter 9). The industry benefited from early waves of FDI, but, over time, it was the transfer of skills that led to renewed energy among domestic entrepreneurs. In Bangladesh and Vietnam, the inflow of foreign investment brought new ideas and techniques. The case of the Ho Nai Furniture Company in Vietnam illustrates the important role of FDI in addressing the binding constraints in the industry, including shortages in knowledge, technology, entrepreneurial skills, and finance (chapter 7).

The role of FDI is evident in the case of cut flowers in Ethiopia and tomatoes in Senegal, where international investors contributed technical knowledge, managerial skills, and expertise in transport (chapter 6). In Kenya, domestic industry and international entrepreneurship joined together to create jobs, increase exports, and generate millions of dollars in revenue (chapter 6). The combination of modern financial and transport capabilities with cheap labor and rich soil has resulted in flower production supported by a strong supply chain. In Ethiopia, government assistance helped provide the land, and FDI added knowledge, expertise, and an export network that brought the cut flower industry to fruition.

The case study on sari production in India illustrates how the absence of FDI can damage a well-established traditional industry confronted by advances in science and technology (chapter 9). Thus, FDI is important not only for start-ups, but also for growth industries and mature sectors, where it can help meet the need for constant upgrades and quality improvements, while the government assists in training workers and helping them find jobs.

FDI and economic growth can also be linked through a virtuous circle. Thus, FDI flow helps promote imitation activities and raise wages in these activities; this acts as a signal for workers to invest in skills, which raises the proportion of qualified workers and further promotes FDI. Borensztein, De Gregorio, and Lee (1998) show that FDI plays a key role in economic growth through the transfer of technology and that this role is enhanced if the host country has a minimum threshold stock of human capital. Wu and Hsu (2008) also show that FDI has a positive and significant impact on growth when host countries have better levels of initial GDP and human capital.

**The critical role of networks.** Many of our cases demonstrate the importance of networks in resolving binding constraints. With a deep understanding of the economies of China and Japan, the economist Shigeru Ishikawa argued that social networks can act as market institutions where these are inadequate. As market institutions become stronger, Ishikawa suggested, the government may shift from direct intervention to indirect support (Sato 2003).

Wenzhou's specialization in cigarette lighters illustrates this advantage of personal networks and shows how an effective partnership between government and private initiative can boost quality and prevent piracy in design (chapter 3, box 3.4). Beginning in the 1990s, emigrants from Wenzhou returned to their native region and "introduced their compatriots to foreign-manufactured lighters ... a product requiring little investment and technical knowledge" (Shi and Ganne 2009, 250). In 1993, some 3,500 companies, largely family operations run out of peoples' homes with four to five workers, spontaneously entered this niche in Wenzhou. Responding to the inevitable problems of quality control that arise under such conditions, the Wenzhou government established an office to inspect each factory. Factories that failed to meet standards were denied the now-required operating licenses. This process thinned the number of lighter and lighter-parts factories to around 300.

The Wenzhou Lighter Industry Association was established at the end of 1992. This association helped improve quality, and Wenzhou soon began to develop its own lighter designs. To protect the industry from unfair competition, each association member signed an affidavit agreeing to defer to association rulings in applying for rights to product designs. The designs were evaluated and published in local newspapers for comment. If no one opposed the new design within five days, the design was granted a de facto patent. The association handles any allegations of design infringement. This practice for maintaining quality and preventing design theft is now an increasingly common feature of industry associations (Mertha 2010).

At the start-up phase, many employees have family connections to the initial entrepreneurs. In Wenzhou, "about 90 percent of hired workers were directly related to their employers" at the early stages (Dong 1990, 79–80). As enterprises evolve, so do their workers.

In general, networks of family and friends allow start-ups to begin production without funding from the formal financial sector. In our July 2012 interviews, Chinese entrepreneurs repeatedly emphasized that bank loans were not essential during the start-up phase, when the key obstacles to success were not money, but the capacity of fledgling entrepreneurs to design, produce, and market their initial products. An entrepreneur of a furniture firm in Chengdu, Sichuan Province, explained how he was able to produce furniture and grow his business even while paying usurious interest rates:

> My wife and I started our business in 1997 from a family workshop. At that time we borrowed 40,000 yuan [about $4,825] at the usurious rate of 4 percent a month, or 48 percent a year. I paid off the debt within a year. Now we have 150 workers and have transformed from a gun to a cannon. (July 2012 interview)

At the beginning, companies such as Aihao Writing Instruments Co. Ltd., in Jiangxi Province, relied on domestic networks for technical assistance, but copied the design of Western pens, particularly German and Italian models, and produced low-quality versions for the domestic market (chapter 4). As Zhang, the founder, recalls,

> My pen-making business started from a household workshop. At that time, almost all households in the village produced something related to pens. If we had any technical difficulties, we went to Shanghai to talk to an expert. (July 2012 interview)

Product quality improved over time, and so did the degree of specialization as the company moved up the learning curve. As quality improved, production for the export market increased. This move up the quality spectrum occurred at Aihao and at thousands of other Chinese companies within two decades.

Other studies make the same point. In rural Yunnan Province, for example,

> banks and RCCs [rural credit cooperatives] are willing to finance collective-owned [township and village enterprises (TVEs)] and large private enterprises, but are reluctant to finance peasant households and small family businesses. Consequently, a large proportion of family businesses rely on the unorganized financial market, . . . [which] mainly consists of money loans among blood relatives. (Sato 2003, 46)

As enterprises grow, they need more access to finance from personal savings, loans from friends, and capital from joint venture partners. Vietnam allows local entrepreneurs to put up land as their contribution in joint venture companies, while foreign partners provide capital, expertise, technology, and ideas.

How much do these networks affect the performance of manufacturing firms in developing countries? Little is known about how developing-country firms use business networks. As part of our Light Manufacturing in Africa Project, Marcel Fafchamps and Simon Quinn

(2012) designed a novel randomized field experiment to measure peer effects among manufacturing firms in Africa. They found only limited evidence of diffusion.

## Using Substitution Policies and Sequencing

Successful development often occurs despite structural or institutional weaknesses. People can use or invent tools to help cope with specific binding constraints they face. As the economists Alexander Gerschenkron (1962) and Albert Hirschman (1984) long emphasized, human ingenuity can devise workable substitutes for missing "key prerequisites" to rapid growth. Thus, Japan invented trading companies to economize on the scarce domestic knowledge of foreign languages and foreign expertise. After rigorously excluding them for several decades, China allowed the revival of individual entrepreneurship and welcomed foreign investors to help bridge the gaps in domestic knowledge about advanced technologies, international market conditions, and the commercial requirements of overseas buyers. China established special economic zones as a shortcut to the introduction of new activities and new business procedures, thereby avoiding a direct confrontation with the entrenched interests associated with central planning and state-owned enterprises.

The case studies on countries other than China also show that there are various ways to address the binding constraints in light manufacturing through policy innovations that provide at least partial substitutes for elements missing from the local environment (chapter 10, annex table 10A.2). Bonded warehouses, for example, can offset difficulties surrounding the availability of inputs and logistics, while business associations can fulfill some of the functions of trading companies. Similarly, the innovative back-to-back letter-of-credit system used by garment exporters in Bangladesh (chapter 9) was developed to ease the constraints in foreign exchange and access to finance, while the Sialkot sporting goods cluster in Pakistan formed the Sialkot Dry Port Trust (chapter 8) to overcome the constraint in trade logistics.

Most successful case studies throughout this book have two common features: FDI and industrial zones. Together, these two policies resolve the six binding constraints on the growth of manufacturing firms that we have identified through this project. Industrial zones resolve the issues of inputs, access to industrial land, access to finance (in Chinese cases), trade logistics, and worker skills, while FDI resolves the problems of access to finance and entrepreneurial skills. But FDI and industrial zones need to be supplemented by other policies discussed in this chapter to make an initially successful project become long-lasting for job creation and prosperity. Note that the substitution policy tools used by China, including industrial parks, industrial clusters, and trading companies, are not new (chapter 3). They were used earlier by Hong Kong SAR, China; Japan; Korea; Singapore; Taiwan, China; and other East Asian economies. The difference is only the scale and the extent to which China's huge domestic market facilitates competition and value chain integration.

Yet, these tools are not part of the standard policy advice for launching industrialization in low-income countries that is promoted by Western countries. One reason is that economists focus on static Pareto efficiency. They seek outcomes that optimize resource allocation on the basis that no reshuffling of resources can increase the output of one product without reducing the output of another, nor increase one person's satisfaction without reducing someone else's satisfaction. Unemployment, excess capacity, entry or exit barriers, and tariff or quota restrictions represent typical deviations from Pareto efficiency. While these market imperfections are recognized in the economic literature, they are usually ignored when it comes to policy making.

Economists use the term *second best* to describe deviations from Pareto efficiency that cannot deliver optimal outcomes. The measures we consider here are all second-best responses to pervasive development problems and to market failures. Industrial parks, for example, provide electricity and transport to specific locations and nowhere else. This is a second-best outcome because the availability of electricity (or cheaper, more reliable power flows) at some locations, but not at others represents a deviation from Pareto efficiency. Still, these second-best measures can have a powerful impact on industrialization in low-income settings. Industrial parks can help countries accumulate the capital and skills needed to advance industrialization throughout an economy. In a theoretical framework, the argument for such second-best measures follows Joseph Schumpeter's (1943) insights on the profound distinction between dynamic and static efficiency. More recently, the influential work of Rodrik (2004) has shown that first order economic principles can be applied in a flexible way to take account of local opportunities and constraints.

Another reason the standard toolkit overlooks the tools discussed in this book is that, since the heyday of cross-country regressions, development practitioners have shown a preference for economy-wide solutions (investment climate, governance, and so on). The more clearly microeconomic approach proposed here can be justified on social cost-benefit grounds (and should be subject to cost-benefit analysis). It makes practitioners uneasy because it involves more conceptual difficulties than does reliance on first principles and pure theory.

A third reason that these tools are not popular is that they deal more with institutions than with the prices and quantities that dominate mainstream economic thinking and policy analysis. The objective of the policy tools discussed in this book is to facilitate the organic growth of small-scale manufacturing initiatives through institutional arrangements that reduce the market transaction costs and magnify opportunities to establish and develop new industrial clusters.

A fourth possible reason is that standard analysis typically neglects the coordination or knowledge spillovers that differentiate static from dynamic comparative advantage. Alice Amsden (2007) points out that, in the early 1950s, if Korea had left its textile industry exposed to market forces alone, without adopting policies to facilitate learning and to protect the industry, wages in the industry would have had to be negative to compete with Japan, even though Korea had an underlying comparative advantage in textile production. Similar reasoning applies to early developmental measures that, in effect, succeeded in benefiting from Japan's comparative advantage in steel, autos, and consumer electronics; the comparative advantage of Taiwan, China, in electronics; and China's comparative advantage in a wide array of light manufactures.

The cost of government's failure to act can be high. In Ghana, a country with skilled labor and a comparative advantage in wood, the furniture industry has been unable to grow and export (chapter 7). Government inaction, which can, at times, stunt private sector development, is widely viewed as the reason Ghana's furniture industry remains so small. Productivity is low; raw materials are increasingly difficult to procure; and equipment is outdated. Both the government and the relevant industrial zone association have failed to regulate or guide the industry.

The tale is similar in Zambia, where the government has failed to help the garment industry obtain low-cost inputs (mainly cotton), train workers, or acquire modern technology and managerial skills. As a result, clothing has become more expensive to produce than to import, and customers prefer the cheaper, if lower-quality imported goods (such as secondhand clothing, which has flooded the market), making the higher-quality, more-expensive, domestically produced clothing doubly unattractive. Policy intervention in this case is needed to help the private sector, especially in addressing the problem of secondhand clothing.

**The domestic market versus the export market.** China's large domestic market allows enterprises to start by focusing on the domestic market or on the export market; our case studies include examples of both (chapter 10). Most developing countries, particularly in Africa, do not have this choice because the domestic market is too small. This has led many economists to recommend that these countries should focus production on the export market. However, in light manufacturing, it is best to start small and simple, and a jump to the export market may not be feasible before the binding constraints are resolved. Hence, efforts to encourage the domestic production of simple manufactured goods that are now being imported and for which the demand has therefore already been established might be a good way to launch the process. At the same time, it would be valuable to enlist FDI to initiate the production of new products or penetrate new markets.

Manufacturing is a powerful source of learning by doing, and only with experience can workers learn. Governments can support the private sector in this process especially by easing the binding constraints. Our companion volume provides a detailed account of how governments can diagnose and combat these constraints (Dinh and others 2012). One key lesson from our volume here: effective cooperation between private business and government agencies can contribute mightily to the process of identifying constraints, prioritizing policy responses, and eventually rolling back the obstacles to the development of light manufacturing clusters.

**Final goods versus intermediate goods.** In most poor developing countries, industrialization begins with the production of final goods in the light manufacturing sector because of the labor-intensity and low-skill requirements. Later, after firms have established themselves in the markets for final goods, the focus can shift from final goods to the intermediate goods (which require more capital and greater skills) linked to the production of these final goods, thus extending the supply chain. Rising productivity and technological capability can then open the door to the production of more sophisticated intermediate goods and components. In China, the transformation of Hailead, a large public firm in Haining's warp knitting industrial park, illustrates this process:

> In 1997, we started by making lamphouse cloth. In 2002, we entered the industrial fiber business when [the] market condition was very good. At first, it was because industrial fibers are used for producing lamphouse cloth. Since then, we adopted a differentiation strategy by focusing our industrial fiber business on a niche market for automobiles. ... In 2009, we further made an effort to develop in the upstream sectors of industrial fibers by producing polyester chips, a material for our products. (July 2012 interview)

Starting with the production of final goods allows large numbers of unskilled or low-skilled workers to find jobs. Investments upstream or downstream that tend to be both capital intensive and skill intensive could be taken up later, or they could be taken up concurrently using FDI.

Another example is garment production in Bangladesh. The sector employs nearly half the country's industrial workers and focuses on final goods (ready-made garments). Though the industry depends on imported inputs, its wage cost advantage places Bangladesh among the world's cheapest locations for garment production and enables an abundant supply of unskilled workers to find jobs.

Beginning with final-stage assembly trains workers at one end of the supply chain and affords entrepreneurs the opportunity to gain the knowledge and expertise necessary to move into higher-value activities, such as input production and design. The case studies on Bangladesh and Mauritius offer good examples of how other countries can overcome some of the disadvantages and constraints we have highlighted (chapter 9). The approaches enterprises in these countries have adopted to develop skills and establish supply chains appear successful though they are quite different from each other.

## Starting Small and Building Up or Cutting Back

Many of the successful case studies reveal that starting small and simple works well in low-income environments. The development of China's light manufacturing clusters illustrates the feasibility of a trajectory that begins with the assembly of simple final products in home workshops and, through the gradual accumulation of knowledge, experience, and capital, results in the emergence of large, sophisticated enterprises capable of competing in global markets. In Wenzhou, for example, plastic shoes were initially made by hand (chapter 3). Then, in a burst of upgrading during the first nine months of 1985, "more than 1.22 million yuan was invested in … [purchasing] 22 sets of plastic injection machinery, … [which] not only raised labor productivity but … improved product quality … and … enabled … rural household industry to become more competitive" (Dong 1990, 94).

Ethiopia's cut flower industry began on 7 hectares in 2000 (chapter 6). The business turned an immediate profit, and, within two years, the government was seeking to aid expansion. Access to additional land and finance, tax incentives, and duty-free imports led to the development of 800 hectares by 2007, an enormous increase. Starting small revealed the potential of cut flower production and sparked government interest. Not long after the government announced its support, dozens of firms entered the market, employing more than 50,000 people and earning more than $200 million a year.

The Chinese zipper industry is another example of starting small and succeeding big (chapter 5). Wang Yue and other entrepreneurs pinpointed zippers as easy to transport and highly profitable, with strong demand for the foreseeable future. The industry started by trial and error in a series of home-based family workshops financed through personal savings. Once the private sector had become established, the government encouraged further growth by providing infrastructure and building an industrial park. The low investment cost, simple manufacturing process, and large profits all contributed to China's status as the world's largest zipper manufacturer. Now, more than 2,000 companies export some $3 billion in zippers globally, but the local government continues to promote a good product reputation by carrying out quality control and exercising a regulatory function.

In contrast, in Morogoro, Tanzania, government officials tried to build Africa's biggest shoe factory instead of waiting for signs of private sector success (chapter 8). Flawed design and implementation, lack of proper training, and limited access to inputs doomed this initiative despite millions of dollars in investment in large factories and machinery. Morogoro never produced an acceptable shoe for export and continued to lose money. The factory's large size made it difficult to introduce incremental improvements or to shut down as losses mounted. Starting small and simple would have allowed workers to learn and adapt production processes; closer attention to electricity supply and proximity to ports for inputs and exports would have suggested a much different strategy and location.

The Morogoro case also illustrates a key policy lesson: if the policy experiment does not work, the project should be stopped right away to cut the losses instead of lingering on and draining national resources further. Mistakes are a natural part of the learning-by-doing process.

Starting small and growing into a large business in less than a decade is not uncommon in the Chinese provinces we visited in 2010. Approximately 45 percent of the entrepreneurs we interviewed had each started a business with fewer than 40 employees that, in one or two decades, had grown into a larger firm with several hundred or, in some cases, thousands of employees. A producer who began making T-shirts in 1992 started with 10 employees and 8 machines; by 2010, he had a workforce of 2,200 and manufactured a range of garments from T-shirts to complex shirts and jackets. Similarly, the Buyang Group in the Metalware Industrial Cluster in Yongkang City, Zhejiang Province, started out supplying cast components such as oven burners and then expanded into binoculars, security doors, auto parts, and, finally, scooters, all for export (chapter 5). The gradual increase in the scope of production activities confirms that China is expanding across what Hidalgo and others (2007) call the product space, whereby enterprises or countries develop new products that share features with products they have already produced; an enterprise is more likely to progress from bicycles to motorcycles, for example, than from bicycles to airplanes.

Chinese light manufacturing firms display an impressive ability to diversify into products that are new to China, but not to the world. All the firms at which we conducted interviews initially manufactured one or two simple products, but rapidly innovated and diversified into multiple product lines at higher levels of product quality. Garment firms have diversified from simple T-shirts into complex garments. A firm that began by producing sweaters has diversified into knitted dresses and jerseys with embroidery, trim, and fur for leading U.S. department stores. An entrepreneur who once made simple beds and tables now manufactures furniture sets for living rooms, bedrooms, dining rooms, and children's rooms. Even a producer of traditional noodles has diversified into fortified wheat and rice foods.

In addition to introducing new products, entrepreneurs have also innovated by expanding the variety of their products through new designs, colors, shapes, and patterns. For example, a producer of furniture made of medium-density fiberboard manufactures 1,200 products. A firm that makes zippers uses a variety of materials to produce several thousand types.

Product diversification has been engineered by Chinese producers through investment in the adaptation of new technologies and in in-house capabilities. Contrary to the widely accepted perception of Chinese as masters of imitation, such investments require substantial doses of time, effort, and money. In some cases, the access to new technologies has also spurred innovations in processing that have reduced the time from order to delivery and improved quality control. In garments and other low-margin industries, turnaround times are critical in obtaining large repeat orders and in maintaining profitability.

**The diffusion of practices.** The experience with the special economic zones that were created in the late 1970s reassured China's central government that its reform policies were effective. Beginning in 1984–85, China established 14 national economic and technological development zones and opened 14 coastal cities, Hainan Island, the Yangzi River Delta, the Pearl River Delta, and the south Fujian triangle area to FDI. The 14 new zones occupied small pieces of land inside the open coastal cities and were meant to serve as regional windows for the development of high-technology businesses and to spur economic growth, thereby improving the hard and soft investment environment more generally. The policy priority was to entice foreign investment and help build an export-oriented economy.

Japanese colonial policy in Korea and in Taiwan, China, during the early decades of the 20th century expanded on measures adopted in the late 19th century to promote Japan's own agricultural development. Government agencies identified master farmers who had achieved particularly good results in implementing new techniques, increasing yields, and other advances. They organized local farmers into agricultural associations that met to hear their successful neighbors explain how to achieve better results.

Similarly, today, the beneficial circulation of information and the exchange of experience are possible among small-scale manufacturing entrepreneurs confronted with similar technical issues, design problems, and so on. Industry associations benefiting from official initiative and encouragement could contribute to such a process.

**The constant need to upgrade and improve.** The sari case study in India clearly shows how an entire industry can be wiped out if no effort is made to upgrade, modernize, and improve the quality and unit cost of the product (chapter 9). In this instance, the failure might have been averted if FDI were available to upgrade the technology. Thus, it appears that the best course would have involved opening the sector to foreign investment.

Yet, the case study on Bata shoes in Kenya shows that FDI alone is insufficient (chapter 8). As pointed out by Lin (2012, 92), "modern economic development is a process of continuous structural change ... beset with market failures" that governments could help address. A country's comparative advantage today may change tomorrow. Thus, China's coastal areas are gradually losing their long-standing cost advantage in light manufactures, especially at the low end of the price-quality spectrum: "as labor costs keep rising, more factories flee to Vietnam and India" (Chu 2013). Companies and industries therefore need to be constantly upgraded through research and development (R&D) to meet shifting demand and foster sustainability. Constant upgrading has enabled apparel accessory industries to overcome the challenges of rising labor costs, shortages of some skilled labor, antidumping legislation, and misaligned or overvalued exchange rates (chapter 5).

The Qinye Industrial Company, in Jiangxi Province, illustrates a successful strategy (chapter 5). Early in 2009, shortly after the global financial and economic crisis had begun depressing global demand,

Qinye surprised many people by expanding employment. The company diversified its international market, shifting from Europe and the United States to new markets such as Australia, Canada, and the Middle East. The company also expanded product varieties to appeal to domestic consumers. In addition to toys, the company produces plastics, electronics, and housewares. With its strong quality control and competitive production costs, the company was able to wrest customers from firms along the coast, and Qinye's business grew during the financial crisis, while many competitors along the coast went bankrupt.

## Creating Islands of Success

Other studies that have reviewed the constraints on the expansion of light manufacturing in developing countries have produced long lists of difficulties and implied that no feasible set of policy adjustments could cause these countries to become attractive to investors. Most frustrating about these lists is the suggestion that, unless all the shortcomings are fixed, light manufacturing cannot be successful.

Our analysis in this report and our case studies document the opposite reality: the successful expansion of production and export in light manufactures can occur without first resolving all the constraints. This reality is evident in the experience of a succession of East Asian economies; China provides the largest and most recent example.

**Economy-wide versus selective policy experiments.** Instead of implementing economy-wide measures, reform policy in China has focused on enabling reform. This has opened the door to new approaches—for example, allowing localities to shift from collective farming to the allocation of plots to individual households—and experimental initiatives, of which the establishment of four small special economic zones around 1980 provides a good instance (chapters 1 and 2). These approaches and initiatives seek to ignite self-propelling developmental sequences that need not await economy-wide breakthroughs, which, in China and elsewhere, are likely to attract opposition from entrenched interests, such as state enterprises and planning bureaucracies. Reliance on developmental imbalances and spontaneous developmental surges aims to generate significant progress without the allocation of substantial funds or management talent, both typically in short supply in a low-income environment. The objective is to create multiplier effects supported by the selective application of private sector initiative.

This sort of policy thinking echoes concepts promoted by Joseph Schumpeter (1950), who emphasized the primacy of dynamism over static efficiency, and Albert Hirschman (1988), who advised policy makers to seek out imbalances that would automatically generate productive responses.

**Growth begins somewhere, not everywhere.** Golden Roses, Ethiopia's first rose farm, was started in 2000 on 7 hectares. Within a decade, it had led to an industry of close to 100 firms that exported flowers worth over $200 million a year.

China's reformers created four small special economic zones. The zones benefited from favorable policies that bypassed, without attempting to dismantle a wide array of restrictions and controls, which continued to apply to activities located outside the new zones. These measures allowed new types of enterprises to develop apart from the planned economy. When the success of the pioneering zones and firms prompted government agencies, enterprise managers, and individuals to seek opportunities to participate in the newly dynamic sectors, the range and intensity of financial incentives, price signals, and market forces gradually expanded. By allowing innovative mechanisms to flourish beyond the boundaries of the state-dominated planned economy, China avoided the need for a life-and-death struggle between planners and marketers. The success of the new economy began to attract unlikely participants, including state enterprise leaders and government officials involved in the planned economy. Thus, people and organizations that might seem like the natural antagonists of reform and marketization gradually joined the new wave without the pitched battle that early efforts to implement sweeping reform measures would surely have incited.

These are only two of the many examples of starting somewhere, but not everywhere.

**A narrow focus on specific constraints.** Given that the trust inherent in fruitful public-private partnerships takes time to build and given the scarcity of financial and human resources in most developing countries, relevant binding constraints should be identified and resolved through targeted policy reforms along the lines proposed in our companion volume, *Light Manufacturing in Africa* (Dinh and others 2012). By devoting limited, sharply focused policies on sectors with the greatest potential, governments can create an environment in which young firms can rapidly develop the capacity to supply domestic and overseas buyers with low-cost, unbranded goods of acceptable quality. Starting small with pilot projects allows successful initiatives to be scaled up, while others are terminated in time to keep the losses low.

This resembles the approach that China adopted in the beginning of its current modernization effort. The Chinese set up small industrial zones. Even so, the initial infrastructure investment in places such as Shenzhen far exceeded the capacity of private resources and could never have occurred without government support. The effort paid off by creating a showcase for overseas investors and domestic enterprises of the government's openness and willingness to reform. The investments required to build smaller economic zones, such as those run by township authorities, are much lower and can be met through the processing fees charged to foreign investors.

The World Bank's Light Manufacturing in Africa Project has applied this targeted approach to Ethiopia, Tanzania, Vietnam, and Zambia (Dinh and others 2012; Dinh and Monga 2013; Dinh 2013a, 2013b). All these cases show that leveraging value chain analyses and other analytical devices to take a microscopic stock of the constraints in each subsector can allow policy makers to trim the inevitably long list of economy-wide constraints to a few vital items. This approach allows governments to assemble concrete packages of specific, feasible, and inexpensive policy initiatives that can create maximum opportunity to jump-start the growth of production, employment, and manufacturing exports in specific light manufacturing industries. Our detailed studies across sectors and products demonstrate that the constraints vary by country, sector, and firm size. Economy-wide reforms have generally been unable to relieve the distinct bottlenecks that exist in each sector, in part because scarce resources are spread too thin to have any desired impact and in part because the political economy of such reforms tends to generate much wider resistance from vested interest groups, leading them to sabotage reforms.

Identifying the most promising sectors, as we have learned in the Chinese case studies on light manufacturing, does not involve picking winners. Instead, it entails backing winners, meaning that the government should follow the lead of the private sector in picking industries and products to support, work closely with the private sector to find the most critical constraints affecting the growth of the industries and products that have been picked, and design policies to remove these constraints.

## Summary

It is interesting to note that the five policy groups discussed in this chapter cannot be initiated by the private sector alone. They require serious government policy actions. This explains why policies that rely on market forces alone have failed to help developing countries duplicate the industrialization success that Singapore, Korea, and other East Asian countries have achieved.

Steadfast government support is central to the sustainable development of light manufacturing. The appropriate kind of government support can help foster a turnaround to a development growth path. In many cases, subsidies or other government interventions can be counterproductive, creating economic distortions. More helpful is an effort to note the economic chokepoints and remove or ease the most serious constraints.

The reward for the adoption of such actions can be substantial. The transformation can be quick. China's development during the early reform years shows that rapid growth can emerge from unlikely beginnings. The Chinese economy suffered from many of the problems that beset today's poor countries, including weak infrastructure, a financial system that bypassed small business, endemic corruption, and high transaction costs, as well as unique problems arising from China's long isolation from international markets. China's astonishing achievements may thus encourage hope that today's low-income countries can find their own paths to better lives for their citizens and that development can accelerate despite long odds.

Sensible, systematic reform can deliver beneficial results in as little as 5–10 years. For example, in Wenzhou, China, over 1980–85, reforms more than doubled the average per capita income of rural households, from Y 165 to Y 417, while prices rose by only 5.6 percent (Li 1990; NBS 1990). Each of the successful case studies examined in this book illustrates the possibility of rapid transformation. Whether it is buttons in Qiaotou or cut flowers in Ethiopia, positive changes can occur quickly if all the pieces are allowed to fall into place.

Throughout this study, the critical role of learning-by-doing cannot be stressed enough. Both the Chinese and non-Chinese cases amply demonstrate this role. In light manufacturing, nothing can substitute for experience, which can only be gained through doing the work. Entrepreneurs from China to Ghana and Senegal have learned on the job and from relatives and friends. Success requires repeated attempts, often in the same line of business, but, in many cases, after repeated tries in other fields as well. Zhang Hanping, the founder of Aihao Writing Instruments Co. Ltd., one of the largest pen manufacturers in the world (chapter 4), failed miserably many times until he found the pen business. The policy implication of learning by doing is that, in countries in which manufacturing offers the prospect of sustainable job creation and economic growth, the sector should be encouraged and facilitated without delay.

## Notes

1. Long Guoqiang, "A Review of China's Automobile Industrial Policies" [in Chinese], December 1995, http://wenku.baidu.com/view/f5c3c0f5ba0d4a73027 63a2b.html.
2. International Financial Statistics (database), International Monetary Fund, Washington, DC, http://elibrary-data.imf.org/FindDataReports.aspx?d =33061&e=169393.

## References

Amsden, Alice H. 2007. *Escape from Empire: The Developing World's Journey through Heaven and Hell.* Cambridge, MA: MIT Press.

Borensztein, Eduardo, Jose De Gregorio, and Jong-Wha Lee. 1998. "How Does Foreign Direct Investment Affect Economic Growth?" *Journal of International Economics* 45 (1):115-35.

Chu, Kathy. 2013. "*Not* Made in China." *Wall Street Journal* May 1: B1.

Crook, Clive. 1992. "Third World Economic Development." Online Library of Economics and Liberty. http://www.econlib.org/library/Enc1/ThirdWorld EconomicDevelopment.html.

Dinh, Hinh T. 2013a. *Light Manufacturing in Zambia: Job Creation and Prosperity in a Resource-Based Economy.* With contributions by Praveen Kumar, Anna Morris, Fahrettin Yagci, and Kathleen Fitzgerald. Washington, DC: World Bank.

———. 2013b. *Light Manufacturing in Vietnam: Job Creation and Prosperity in a Growing Economy.* With contributions by Deepak Mishan, Le Duy Binh, and Pham Minh Duc. Washington, DC: World Bank.

Dinh, Hinh T., and Célestin Monga. 2013. *Light Manufacturing in Tanzania: A Reform Agenda for Job Creation and Prosperity.* With contributions by Jacques Morisset, Josaphat Kweka, Fahrettin Yagci, and Yutaka Yoshino. Washington, DC: World Bank.

Dinh, Hinh T., Vincent Palmade, Vandana Chandra, and Frances Cossar. 2012. *Light Manufacturing in Africa: Targeted Policies to Enhance Private Investment and Create Jobs.* Washington, DC: World Bank. http://go.worldbank.org/ASG0J44350.

Dong, Fureng. 1990. "The Wenzhou Model for Developing the Rural Commodity Economy." In *Market Forces in China, Competition and Small Business: The Wenzhou Debate,* edited by Peter Nolan and Fureng Dong, 77–96. London: Zed Books.

Estrin, Saul, and Tomasz Mickiewicz. 2010. "Entrepreneurship in Transition Economies: The Role of Institutions and Generational Change." IZA Discussion Paper 4805, Institute for the Study of Labor, Bonn.

Fafchamps, Marcel, and Simon Quinn. 2012. "Networks and Manufacturing Firms in Africa: Initial Results from a Randomised Experiment." Centre for the Study of African Economies, University of Oxford, Oxford. http://www.dartmouth.edu/~neudc2012/docs/paper_241.pdf.

Frangos, Alex. 2013. "Behind China's Switch to High-End Exports." *Wall Street Journal,* March 24. http://online.wsj.com/article/SB10001424127887324034804578345551411900878.html?mod=WSJ_business_whatsNews.

Gerschenkron, Alexander. 1962. "Reflections on the Concept of 'Prerequisites' in Modern Industrialization." In *Economic Backwardness in Historical Perspective,* edited by Alexander Gerschenkron, 31–51. New York: Praeger.

Hidalgo, César A., Bailey Klinger, Albert-László Barabási, and Ricardo Hausmann. 2007. "The Product Space Conditions the Development of Nations." *Science* 317 (5837): 482–87.

Hirschman, Albert O. 1984. "A Dissenter's Confession: 'The Strategy of Economic Development' Revisited." In *Pioneers in Development,* edited by Gerald M. Meier and Dudley Seers, 87–111. Washington, DC: World Bank; New York: Oxford University Press.

———. 1988. *The Strategy of Economic Development.* Boulder, CO: Westview Press.

Johnson, Graham E. 1994. "Open for Business, Open to the World: Consequences of Global Incorporation in Guangdong and the Pearl River Delta." In *The Economic Transformation of South China: Reform and Development in the Post-Mao Era,* edited by Thomas P. Lyons and Victor G. Nee, 55–88. Cornell East Asia Series 70. Ithaca, NY: Cornell University Press.

Li Shi. 1990. "The Growth of Household Industry in Rural Wenzhou." In *Market Forces in China, Competition and Small Business: The Wenzhou Debate*, edited by Peter Nolan and Fureng Dong, 108–25. London: Zed Books.

Lin, Justin Yifu. 2012. *The Quest for Prosperity: How Developing Economies Can Take Off*. Princeton, NJ: Princeton University Press.

Mertha, Andrew. 2010. "Society in the State: China's Nondemocratic Political Pluralization." In *Chinese Politics: State, Society, and the Market*, edited by Peter Hays Gries and Stanley Rosen, 69–84. New York: Routledge.

Montinola, Gabriella, Yingyi Qian, and Barry R. Weingast. 1995. "Federalism, Chinese Style: The Political Basis for Economic Success in China." *World Politics* 48 (1): 50–81.

NBS (National Bureau of Statistics of China). 1990. *Quanguo gesheng zizhiqu zhixiashi lishi tongji ziliao huibian* [Compilation of statistical materials for China and for its provinces, autonomous regions, and municipalities]. [In Chinese.] Beijing: China Statistics Press.

Rodrik, Dani. 2004. "Growth Strategies." Working paper (August), John F. Kennedy School of Government, Harvard University, Cambridge, MA.

Romer, Paul. 1993. "Idea Gaps and Object Gaps in Economic Development." *Journal of Monetary Economics* 32 (3): 543–73.

Sato, Hiroshi. 2003. *The Growth of Market Relations in Post-Reform Rural China: A Micro-Analysis of Peasants, Migrants, and Peasant Entrepreneurs*. Vol. 1 of RoutledgeCurzon Studies on the Chinese Economy. London: Routledge.

Saxenian, AnnaLee. 2006. *The New Argonauts: Regional Advantage in a Global Economy*. Cambridge, MA: Harvard University Press.

Schumpeter, Joseph. 1943. *Capitalism, Socialism, and Democracy*. New York: Harper Collins.

———. 1950. *Capitalism, Socialism, and Democracy*. 3rd ed. New York: Harper and Row.

Shi, Lu, and Bernard Ganne. 2009. "Understanding the Zhejiang Industrial Clusters: Questions and Re-evaluations." In *Asian Industrial Clusters, Global Competitiveness and New Policy Initiatives*, edited by Bernard Ganne and Yveline Lecler, 239–66. Singapore: World Scientific.

Wu, Jyun-Yi, and Chih-Chiang Hsu. 2008. "Does Foreign Direct Investment Promote Economic Growth? Evidence from a Threshold Regression Analysis." *Economics Bulletin* 15 (12): 1–10.

# Appendix:
# Interview Questionnaire

The study team interviewed firms based on the questionnaire designed by Professor John Sutton of the London School of Economics. The objective was to learn about each firm's business, its owner/manager, and factors affecting business. The questions go beyond the traditional investment climate surveys to probe the origin and capabilities of the firm's owner/manager and other issues pertinent to the firm's operations and growth.

For the origins and development of capabilities to manage the firm, questions were asked about when and how the firm was set up, the original sources of capital, and where the idea for the business, as well as the know-how or technological knowledge, came from. Questions were also asked about how and why the firm's owner moved from one product to another and the role of family, relatives, or friends in the decision to make a product. For finance, we asked about the initial and later sources of financing to expand the business, reasons for not using bank financing, and the cost of financing. We also asked about staffing, including how hiring decisions were made. On inputs, we asked about sources of raw materials or inputs to produce the final product and the tariff/duty on imported inputs. On market demand, we asked about the customers, the competition, and the government policies that affect the firm's competitiveness. We also asked about domestic competition and imports and about other types of other constraints such as utilities and infrastructure.

## Section A: Private Sector Initiative: Questions for and about Private Firms

### Topic 1: Origins and Development of Capabilities

1. When and how the firm was set up, and what the sources of capital were for the initial investment. We want to know where the idea for the business came from and whether the government had any role in it. For example, many firms are set up in the manufacturing area by pre-existing firms that have decades of experience as traders, and whose deep knowledge of the market acquired during their activities as traders have allowed them to spot a gap in the market for a manufacturing activity.

2. Where does the firm buy its equipment? Where did the firm buy its original equipment? Domestic or imported equipment? What are the key criteria in choosing suppliers? Are there big differences in equipment quality? Are training, installation, after-sales service important factors in choosing suppliers? Any use of secondhand machines now or in the past?

3. Where the know-how or technological knowledge came from. [For example, sometimes technological knowledge comes from (i) equipment suppliers who provide capital equipment and know-how and sometimes training in its use; (ii) hiring someone from another firm; (iii) Chinese research institutes or universities; (iv) from customers, etc.] For small private firms in China, many of them just learn from their neighbors. When one person earned money by making something, the whole village would do the same business. So, we get a socks village, a ties village, a shoes village, and so on. This is most typical in Zhejiang Province. We can ask the interviewees from the government or association about the first mover who started the business and his present status, and, if he/she failed, why.

**Topic 2: Current Circumstances of the Firm**

1. Could you provide a brief summary of the firm's current operations: sales value, share of output that is exported, number of workers in 2010 and how this has changed in recent years?
2. How long has your firm been in its current location? Has your firm relocated in the past 10 years? If so, why did you choose to relocate?
3. Newspaper reports indicate that many firms in labor-intensive industries are considering relocation either to China's interior provinces or even overseas. Has your firm considered such a move? If so, where would you like to go?
4. What is the main product? Has the main product changed during the past decade? If so, what prompted the shift to a new product line? Owner or managers spotted new market demand? Owner or managers used skill and experience from earlier product to move into a more demanding and profitable area?
5. What is your firm's main market? Who are your leading customers? Who are your strongest competitors?
6. Does your firm operate independently or do you cooperate extensively with firms that are operated by relatives or close associates of this firm's owners or are this firm's long-term suppliers or customers? In making decisions about what to produce and when and where to produce, did anyone in your family, relatives, or circle of close business associates play a role?
7. Does your firm belong to a business association? If so, does this association make a major contribution to the success of your operations? Exactly how does the association help your firm?
8. How do you expect your firm and your industry to change in the next 3-5 years?
9. What is the biggest problem facing your firm and others in the same industry in 2012?

## Section B: Cooperation between the Government and the Private Sector

1. What is the role of government in the development of your industry/cluster? Does the government reinforce efforts initiated by the private sector that are already under way (for example, by enlisting the

help of local universities and technical schools to conduct research and development or to assist with stabilizing or improving product quality)? Or, do local officials contribute to or even determine critical choices such as what product lines to pursue?

2. Does the appointment of new officials to key local government or party posts have a big effect on your business? We can also ask in an indirect way: Did you get any help from the government for your business? Do you think this help is the same for everyone or only for firms selected by the government?

3. Are you aware of instances in which you or other entrepreneurs in your industry find that official decisions or initiatives have a substantial negative impact on business operations, planned investments, or the commercial atmosphere in the local economy? What happens under such circumstances?

4. How would the firm owner rate the level of collaboration between the public and private sector?

5. What are his suggestions/needs for a more effective collaboration?

## Section C: Targeted Policies from the Government

We hope to use China's success in developing labor-intensive industries, industry clusters, and industrial parks so that we can help low-income countries in Africa and elsewhere expand these sectors to accelerate the growth of their own economies.

After studying the experience of China and other countries, we have identified key issues that can hold back the development of labor-intensive industries.

Our questions for you:

- In which of these areas has your firm and other firms producing similar products encountered serious difficulty during the past decade?

- When serious problems arise, did government policy help to resolve major issues, or were firms mostly left to respond on their own? If government policy made a big contribution, which government agencies initiated the beneficial policies and at which level of government?

Here is our list of key issues that have the potential to hold back development in industries like yours:

1. **Input industries:** Sources of raw materials or inputs used to produce the final product. Where does the firm buy the main inputs? Are local inputs better than imported ones? Is there a tariff/duty on imported inputs? Are issues such as electricity and water serious and how did the government help resolve them?

2. **Industrial land:** Did the industrial park address the land issues? What was the criteria under which land was distributed and were the criteria fair? How much help did the government provide in the beginning? In the expansion?

3. **Access to finance:** We would like to learn about the initial and later sources of financing that were used to expand the business. If bank financing was not used, why was it not used? Was it available and on roughly what terms? Was it considered or were there adequate in-house funds available, and so on.

4. **Trade logistics:** Do trade parks help resolve the logistics issues? What would happen if there were no industrial parks? In many countries, clusters were formed (either by the government or by private firms) to reduce transaction costs and facilitate industrial development. Has the firm been part of an industrial cluster? If yes, how did this cluster evolve? Who were the main actors? What are the focused policies toward their specific group of activities/firms/subsector to remove binding constraints? Who initiated these policies? Were these policies successful in pushing aside constraints to expansion? If not, why not?

5. **Worker skills:** Discuss how the owner makes hiring decisions when he wants to expand the business. Does he hire outsiders who bring new expertise, or mostly hire individuals who know little about the business and train them on the job, etc.? What kind of education do the workers have? Do any of them come with engineering or management skills such as accounting? Who does the accounting and training related with machinery use and repair? In general, are there any problems with the workforce, i.e., do the workers come to work on time? Are they organized or unionized and is that a problem?

6. **Managerial skills:** see the above questions on origins and development of capability.

In addition, competition plays an important role. Trade liberalization may have led to a large increase in imports, which would signal weak competitiveness. Discuss whether the products that the firm produces are competitive with imports. If not, who is the firm competing with? Is it competing on price, design, or quality or all three? Are there any obvious reasons why imports are more competitive?

## Interview Questionnaire for Zone Administrators

1. Request overview of conditions in this zone: when established, area, number of firms in the zone, number of workers, total output value for firms in the zone, share of output that is exported, pace of expansion in recent years.
2. What are the main industries represented in this zone? Has this changed over the past 5–10 years?
3. What determined the main industries?
   a. Zone set up to serve specific industries (as in Zhongguancun, Beijing)?
   b. Market outcomes (build and open the zone; then see what firms are attracted)?
   c. Combination of plan/market: see what sort of firms the zone can attract; then shape services to fit the needs of client firms (as in Langfang, Hebei)?
4. We hope to use China's success in developing labor-intensive industries, industry clusters, and industrial parks so that we can help low-income countries in Africa and elsewhere expand these sectors to accelerate the growth of their own economies. We would like to study the cooperation between government and business.

   From this perspective, could you please help us by explaining how your administration interacts with firms located in this zone in making important decisions?

   Please explain any specific measures the zone has implemented to help firms to reduce costs and overcome difficulties in the following areas:
   - Quality control
   - Labor training
   - Research and development
   - Access to key materials and components

5. As a close observer of firms, could you explain what you see as the key characteristics of successful firms in this zone? When firms do badly, what is the main cause? We'd appreciate specific examples to help us understand what makes the difference between success and failure.

6. Have some firms left the zone in response to cost increases? If so, where did they go?

7. Are some firms in this zone considering shifting their location to inland provinces or overseas? If so, what locations are they looking at?

## Interview Questionnaire for Foreign Trade Companies

1. Request overview of your company's operations: when established, area of specialization, scale of business, number of firms using your service, recent trends.

2. We hope to use China's success in developing labor-intensive industries, industry clusters, and industrial parks so that we can help low-income countries in Africa and elsewhere expand these sectors to accelerate the growth of their own economies. We see close cooperation between government and business as key to success.

   From this perspective, could you please help us by explaining how your firm interacts with government agencies and with client firms in implementing official policies?

3. Please explain any specific measures you have implemented to help firms to reduce costs and overcome difficulties in the following areas:
   - Quality control
   - Labor training
   - Research and development
   - Access to key materials and components
   - Expediting shipment of materials, components, and final products
   - Access to loans

4. As a close observer of firms, could you explain what you see as the key characteristics of successful firms? When firms do badly, what is the main cause? We'd appreciate specific examples to help us understand what makes the difference between success and failure.

5.  Have some of your client firms moved some or all of their operations to inland provinces or to foreign countries in response to rising costs? If so, where did they go?

6.  Are some of your client firms considering relocating to inland provinces or overseas? If so, what locations are they looking at?

# Index

Boxes, figures, maps, notes, and tables are indicated by *b, f, m, n,* and *t,* respectively.